WITHDRAWN
NDSU

Rewriting History in Soviet Russia

Also by Roger D. Markwick

RUSSIA'S STILLBORN DEMOCRACY? From Gorbachev to Yeltsin
(*with Graeme Gill*)

Rewriting History in Soviet Russia

The Politics of Revisionist Historiography, 1956–1974

Roger D. Markwick
Lecturer in Modern European History
University of Newcastle
Australia

Foreword by

Donald J. Raleigh
Pardue Professor of History
University of North Carolina, Chapel Hill

© Roger D. Markwick 2001
Foreword © Donald J. Raleigh 2001

All rights reserved. No reproduction, copy or transmission of this publication may be made without written permission.

No paragraph of this publication may be reproduced, copied or transmitted save with written permission or in accordance with the provisions of the Copyright, Designs and Patents Act 1988, or under the terms of any licence permitting limited copying issued by the Copyright Licensing Agency, 90 Tottenham Court Road, London W1P 0LP.

Any person who does any unauthorised act in relation to this publication may be liable to criminal prosecution and civil claims for damages.

The author has asserted his right to be identified as the author of this work in accordance with the Copyright, Designs and Patents Act 1988.

First published 2001 by
PALGRAVE
Houndmills, Basingstoke, Hampshire RG21 6XS and
175 Fifth Avenue, New York, N. Y. 10010
Companies and representatives throughout the world

PALGRAVE is the new global academic imprint of
St. Martin's Press LLC Scholarly and Reference Division and
Palgrave Publishers Ltd (formerly Macmillan Press Ltd).

ISBN 0-333-79209-2

This book is printed on paper suitable for recycling and made from fully managed and sustained forest sources.

A catalogue record for this book is available from the British Library.

Library of Congress Cataloging-in-Publication Data
Markwick, Roger D.
  Rewriting Soviet history : the politics of revisionist historiography, 1956–1974 / Roger D. Markwick ; foreword by Donald J. Raleigh.
    p. cm.
  Includes bibliographical references and index.
  ISBN 0-333-79209-2
  1. Soviet Union—Historiography. I. Title.
  DK38 .M2725 2000
  947′.0072—dc21
                                                                        00-048337

10 9 8 7 6 5 4 3 2 1
10 09 08 07 06 05 04 03 02 01

Printed and bound in Great Britain by
Antony Rowe Ltd, Chippenham, Wiltshire

*To **Therese** and our children, **Caitlin** and **Eleanor** –
for all those days and nights far away*

'The history of the Soviet Union is in one sense no more than the history of the attempt to teach the intellectuals their new place in a cosmos of socialist modernity.'

> J. P. Nettl, 'Ideas, Intellectuals, and Structures of Dissent', in Philip Rieff (ed.), *On Intellectuals: Theoretical Studies, Case Studies* (Garden City, New York, 1970), p. 103

'In olden times maps lacked a consistent scale; together with the more or less correct reproduction of a locality they contained fantastic pictures and simply blank spots. Nowadays, some historical narrative is similar to such maps: fabrication coexists with truth, perspective is distorted, while much that is important is reduced to patter or simply passed over in silence.'

> A. V. Gulyga, in *Istoriya i sotsiologiya* (Moscow, 1964), p. 85

Contents

Foreword	ix
Preface	xiii
Acknowledgements	xvi
List of Abbreviations and Russian Terms	xviii

PART I THE CONTEXT OF THE DISCUSSIONS

1 A Resurgent Intelligentsia — 3
  Totalitarian theory — 5
  A civil society in embryo — 8
  Paradigm shift — 11
  Historians as intellectuals — 13
  The conscience of society — 20
  Intellectuals, the state and civil society — 31

2 The Twentieth Party Congress and History — 38
  The *Short Course* paradigm — 42
  Unmasking the 'cult of the personality' — 47
  The Burdzhalov affair — 51
  The production of historical science — 62

PART II SOME MAJOR DISCUSSIONS

3 The New Direction Historians — 75
  Russian imperialism under the tsars — 76
  Rural Russia: capitalist or feudal? — 84
  Russia's 'multistructuredness' — 89
  Towards a paradigm shift — 97
  Crypto-Trotskyism? — 102
  Russian absolutism — 105

4 Writing and Rewriting the History of Collectivization — 111
  Rural Russia in the 1920s — 115
  Archival sources — 119
  An unpublished manuscript — 124
  Censorship at work — 134

	The famine	145
	Revisionism on the retreat	149
5	**The 'Hour of Methodology'**	**155**
	History and sociology	156
	The Sector of Methodology	164
	Precapitalist societies	173
	A paradigm in crisis	179
	History and the present	183

PART III THE POLITICAL CONSEQUENCES

6	**Collision Course**	**199**
	The Trapeznikov offensive	200
	The 'democratic' *partkom*	201
	The Nekrich affair	209
	Volobuev appointed director	219
	Coup de grâce: Volobuev dismissed	229
7	**From *Zastoi* to *Perestroika***	**234**

Notes	248
Bibliography	301
Index	315

Foreword

In the early years of *perestroika* associated with the M. S. Gorbachev era, millions of Soviet citizens participated in a national dialogue on the past and future of their society. This passionate debate, which involved writers, publicists, politicians and historians, not only forced a rethinking of the principles of Soviet-style socialism, but also brought about what R. W. Davies has so appropriately called a 'mental revolution'. The reaction of professional historians to the challenges posed by the public discussion eventually swept away decades of Stalinist dogma, creating conditions that enabled Russian historians to rejoin the world community of historical scholarship. Roger Markwick's articulate and penetrating study of the politics of revisionist historiography in the Soviet Union offers a prehistory of the crisis that befell Soviet historical scholarship in the Gorbachev era, and then some.

Drawing on Kuhn's concept of a paradigm shift, Markwick zooms in on the relationship between the appearance of revisionist currents within Soviet historical writing in the shadow of N. S. Khrushchev's denunciation of Stalin at the Twentieth Party Congress in 1956, and the rise of a new generation of so-called *intelligenty* during the 1960s. In revealing the socio-political implications of the emergence of a revisionist historical scholarship, Markwick shows that the maverick historians carried on not only the Russian historiographical tradition but also that of the *intelligent*. The self-proclaimed conscience of society, the **intelligentsia** had arisen in the nineteenth century. Dedicated to the Russian people or *narod*, the **intelligentsia** espoused a critical world outlook and sought to close the gulf that separated the elite from the Russian masses.

In locating the emergence of revisionist historians within the specific tradition of the Russian *intelligent*, Markwick explains how revisionism represented a form of legal dissent that ultimately threatened the very legitimacy of the party elite. He likewise places his renegade historians within the larger context of the *shestidesyatniki*, the key generation of men and women of the Soviet Sixties Generation, persuasively arguing that they represented a manifestation of an embryonic civil society. The bureaucratic political elite's stifling of the ferment caused by this unique cohort contributed to the onset of stagnation in the Brezhnev years, paving the way for the upheaval in historical writing associated with the Gorbachev revolution.

Building on an earlier generation of writing on the emergence of a dissident historical trend in the Soviet Union, Markwick taps newly-opened archival material and revealing disclosures that saw the light of day under Gorbachev. Markwick also enriches his study with oral testimonies of many of the most prominent players in the events of the 1960s and 1970s. This unique source provides a trenchant commentary on, as well as an element of authenticity to, the more traditional sources. His treatment of the so-called Burdzhalov affair in the aftermath of the Twentieth Party Congress presents the most complete assessment yet of this opening salvo fired by the revisionists. The author then interrogates the major discussions and debates triggered by the 'New Direction Historians' that rocked the historical profession at the time. Particularly revealing is his fascinating case study of the writing and rewriting of the history of collectivization, carried out by Viktor Danilov and his associates. Markwick breaks new ground in chronicling the rise and fall of the Institute of History's Sector of Methodology, which he depicts as 'the institutionalized expression of the self-conscious transition of the post-Stalinist intellectual elite towards a new generation of *intelligenty*, reminiscent of the traditional Russian **intelligentsia'**.

Markwick throws light on the revisionist historians' collision course with the Brezhnev leadership and the imposition of bureaucratic controls over the activities of the nonconformist historians, taking the story to 1974 with P. V. Volobuev's dismissal as Director of the prestigious Institute of the History of the USSR. In his concluding chapter, the author presents his convincing thoughts on the significance of the *zastoi* or stagnation associated with the Brezhnev years. During the period the party could stifle, but not stop, the evolution of critical views on the Russian and Soviet past that first got a hearing during the turbulent time between 1956 and 1974. In peering beyond the veneer of conformity, one sees that the canonical interpretations embodied in the *Short Course*, the catechism of Stalinism, remained nothing more than a 'hollow shell'.

Might the defeat of the *shestidesyatniki*, Markwick queries, have doomed *perestroika*? After all, the 'best and the brightest of those who really believed in the ideals of the October Revolution' lost confidence and faith in the party-state as a result of the political, intellectual, and emotional retrenchment of the period of stagnation. This is a provocative way to end Roger Markwick's thoughtful and original book. It is essential reading for anyone who wants to understand the evolution of historical writing in the Soviet Union, the emergence of civil society in Russia, the role intellectuals play in one-party states, and how subterranean currents during the much-maligned period of stagnation both enabled and constrained the future course of *perestroika*.

Pardue Professor of History
University of North Carolina at Chapel Hill   DONALD J. RALEIGH

Preface

Intellectual production is shaped as much by the present as by the past. This study of the construction and reconstruction of the past by Soviet revisionist historians in the 1960s is a conscious response to the tumultuous developments that preceded the demise of the Soviet Union. It is no accident that this book begins and ends with the upheaval around Soviet history fomented by *perestroika*. Underlying this entire book is the question of where did this ferment originate? – given the stultifying weight of 18 years of the Brezhnev incumbency – not to mention the iron-heel of Stalinism. Despite the totalitarian aspirations of the Soviet state it never quite succeeded in capturing the minds of all the historians, although they were among the most persecuted members of the intelligentsia.

The development of Soviet historical writing in the 1950s and 1960s had a life and logic of its own that made it more than a mere creature of communist party policy. The basic structure of the book reflects that fact. In the first place it pursues the development of the discussions among the historians themselves rather than moving from party political resolution to political resolution, so to speak. The broader political developments are present, of course, but mainly as essential background to the discussions themselves. This endeavour to bring the movement of Soviet historiography into high relief against the political background explains the attention given early in the book to the culture of the production of Soviet history. Hence, too, the endeavour to situate the emergence of historical revisionism in the mid-1950s in the broader sweep of Russian historiographical and intellectual traditions.

Formally, the chronological limits of the book are 1956, the year Stalin was denounced by Khrushchev, and 1974, the year the revisionist historian P. V. Volobuev was dismissed as Director of the Institute of the History of the USSR. However, it was impossible to constrain the book strictly within these limits. In the first place, because this project was precipitated by the *perestroika* upheaval in Soviet historiography; in the second, because it is impossible to understand either the recent upheaval or its precursor during the 'thaw' without at least going back to the 1930s, the period of extreme Stalinism. Further, although the book is organized chronologically, at times it has been necessary either to anticipate later developments or backtrack somewhat.

Some terminological clarification is appropriate. Firstly, throughout I refer to 'history', 'historical writing', 'historical science' and 'historiography'. Historiography is an ambiguous word. It may mean scientific analysis of the process of the writing of history (strictly speaking this is 'historiology'), but it literally means describing historical writing. I have used historiography both as a synonym for the methodology of historical writing and for the writing of history itself. I am taking a cue here from Peter Novick; I rely on the context to clarify in which sense I am using the word 'historiography' and its derivatives (see Novick, 1988, p. 8, n. 6).

The second point relates to 'revisionism' and its derivatives. In Marxist parlance, especially in the former Soviet Union, 'revisionism' has been a term of abuse, meaning an unprincipled abandonment of the fundamentals of Marxism. In Western political science and history, however, this term has fairly positive connotations, meaning a challenge to intellectual orthodoxy. When I refer to 'revisionism' and so forth, I mean it in the second sense.

The research methodology of the book directly reflects the time in which it was researched and written. From the outset it seemed necessary, if I was to make sense of the plethora of discussions among Soviet historians during the 1950s and 1960s, to get 'behind the scenes' of the published record of the discussions, in order to draw out the self-perceptions of the historians who were in the vanguard of historical revisionism. When I first began my fieldwork in Moscow, in February 1992, *perestroika, glasnost'* and the subsequent demise of the Communist Party of the Soviet Union (CPSU) had opened up unprecedented opportunities for access to hitherto inaccessible sources. Not just access to academic and party archives, but more importantly to the personal papers and, above all, the opinions of some of the major players. What began then as an inquiry based primarily on published, written sources – long the staple fare of sovietology – rapidly turned into an exercise in oral history. This unique source base is one of the distinguishing features of this book.

The book is divided into three parts. Part I establishes the context both of the book and of the writing of history in the USSR, exploring in particular the Russian tradition of the intelligentsia in relation to the renaissance in intellectual life after the Twentieth Congress of the CPSU. This undertaking reflects a major objective of the book: to go beyond a mere history of historical revisionism in order to utilize these developments as indices of shifts in the socio-philosophical outlook and self-perception of the historians themselves as intellectuals. This book is therefore an investigation of the politics of knowledge.

Part II is the most historiographical. It details some of the paths by which historical revisionism moved forward, despite the attempts to contain it by the academic administrators and party *apparatchiki*. These quests increasingly encroached on the fundamental postulates of the officially endorsed historiographical paradigm, and, *ipso facto*, put historical revisionism on a collision course with an increasingly conservative academic and political elite.

Part III deals directly with the political repercussions of a sustained challenge to historical orthodoxy by a group of elite historians, homing in on the confrontation between the revisionists and their overseers that developed in the mid-1960s. The final chapter is as much an epilogue as a conclusion. It not only draws out the nexus between the defeat of the revisionists and the onset of the so-called period of stagnation; it also establishes the nexus between the revisionism of the 1960s and the furore around history that erupted soon after the advent of *perestroika*. The book has thus come full-circle, but it leaves open the question of the ramifications of Soviet historical revisionism for the post-Soviet future.

ROGER D. MARKWICK

Acknowledgements

This book has had a long gestation. It began as a PhD thesis in the Department of Government and Public Administration, University of Sydney, research for which commenced in early 1990, including a major research trip to Russia in 1992. The degree was awarded in March 1995. Since that time I have returned twice to Russia, in late 1995 and again in early 1998, to secure additional materials that have enabled me to augment and substantially revise the original thesis.

No scholarship is produced in isolation. My principal debt is to my former supervisor Graeme Gill, Professor of Government and Public Administration, University of Sydney, who guided the original thesis to a successful conclusion. In the years since, Graeme's unstinting encouragement and support have enabled me not only to produce this book but also our own joint study of contemporary Russian politics.

I am pleased that Donald Raleigh, Pardue Professor of History, University of North Carolina at Chapel Hill, has written a foreword to my book. From the very start he has been a passionate supporter of this project. As an examiner of the original thesis it was he who encouraged me to seek additional materials that would enable me to publish a major study of Soviet historical revisionism in the 1960s. R. W. Davies, Emeritus Professor, Centre for Russian and East European Studies, University of Birmingham, who also examined the thesis, recommended publication of the revised work. I am particularly grateful for his critical comments on the historiography of collectivization.

Of course, particular thanks must be given to those scholars in the former Soviet Union, unfortunately many now deceased, who, in straitened times, have generously allowed me extensive interviews and/or access to their papers: A. M. Anfimov, V. S. Bibler, V. I. Bovykin, A. Kh. Burganov, V. P. Danilov, L. V. Danilova, Ya. S. Drabkin, M. Ya. Gefter, Ye. N. Gorodetsky, A. Ya. Gurevich, N. A. Ivnitsky, Boris Kagarlitsky, Yu. A. Moshkov, S. S. Neretina, N. I. Pavlenko, K. N. Shatsillo, P. V. Volobuev, M. A. Vyltsan and I. E. Zelenin. At Moscow State University in 1992 I had the good fortune to have as my supervisor Professor Moshkov, who himself had made a significant contribution to Soviet historical revisionism. An invitation from the late Academician Volobuev to present the findings of my research to the Institute of Russian History, Russian Academy of Sciences, in October 1995 gave me the opportunity to express my gratitude to these scholars. Gul'nara Davletshchina and, more recently, Aleksei Popyrin laboriously transcribed my interviews.

Renfrey Clarke has been a generous host on several occasions in Moscow. Elena Osokina, of the Institute of Russian History, was especially helpful when I first went to Moscow in 1992 and in the years since. Joachim Hösler, formerly of Phillips-Universität Marburg, who generously sent me several documents on the Burdzhalov affair, has since become a friend and colleague. Ron Hoskinson was an indefatigable proof-reader.

A Post-doctoral Fellowship at the University of Sydney provided the opportunity to write the book. Visiting fellowships at the St Petersburg University of the Means of Communication and the Moscow School of Social and Economic Sciences enabled me to pursue the follow-up research for the book. In this regard, an Australian Academy of the Humanities Travel Fellowship provided particular assistance in 1998. I am grateful to Taylor & Francis Ltd, 11 New Fetter Lane, London, for permission to reproduce material from an article of mine originally published in *Europe–Asia Studies*, vol. 46, no. 4, 1994. I am also grateful to Professor Victoria Bonnell for permission to reproduce on the cover a poster from her book *Iconography of Power: Soviet Political Posters under Lenin and Stalin* (California: University of California Press, 1997), Fig. 6.4, from an original image courtesy of the Hoover Institution Archives, Stanford University.

Finally, this book could never have been written had it not been for the encouragement, endurance and unselfish moral and material support of my partner and wife, Therese Doyle, to whom this book is dedicated, together with our children. Therese not only helped me to comprehend Thomas Kuhn but, when the going got tough, offered the most sensible advice: 'write your way out of it'.

ROGER D. MARKWICK

List of Abbreviations and Russian Terms

AIRI	Arkhiv Instituta Rossiiskoi Istorii (Archive of the Institute of Russian History, Russian Academy of Sciences)
aktual'nost'	having relevence to the contemporary world
AN SSSR	Akademiya Nauk SSSR (Academy of Sciences of the USSR)
apparatchik(i)	party-state bureaucrat(s)
ARAN	Arkhiv Rossiiskoi Akademii Nauk (Archive of the Russian Academy of Sciences)
artel'	type of collective farm
aspirant(y)	graduate student(s)
cc	columns
CC	Central Committee
CPSU	Communist Party of the Soviet Union
d.	delo (file)
f.	fond (record group)
frontoviki	front-line soldiers
Glavlit	Glavnoe upravlenie po delam literatury i pechati (Main administration for literature and the press [the censor])
gorkom	gorodsky komitet (city party committee)
IMEMO	Institut Mezhdunarodnoi Ekonomiki i Mezhdunarodnikh Otnoshenii (Institute of World Economy and International Relations)
intellektual(y)	professionally-trained [politically loyal] specialist(s)
intelligent(y)	member(s) of the intelligentsia
intelligentnost'	characteristics of a member of the intelligentsia
I SSSR	*Istoriya SSSR (USSR History)*
IZ	*Istoricheskie zapiski (Historical Transactions)*
Kandidat nauk	Candidate of Science [first post-graduate degree]
KGB	Komitet gosudarstvennoi bezopasnosti (Committee of State Security [political police])
KK	*Istoriya vsesoyuznoi kommunisticheskoi partii (bol'shevikov): kratky kurs,* pod redaktsiei komissii TsK VKP (b), odobren TsK VKP (b) 1938 god (Moscow,

List of Abbreviations and Russian Terms xix

	1952) (*History of the Communist Party of the Soviet Union (Bolsheviks): Short Course*)
kolkhoz	kollektivnoe khozyaistvo (collective farm)
Kolkhoztsentr	Vsesoyuznyi Soyuz Sel'skokhozyaistvennykh Kollektivov (All-Union Union of Agricultural Collectives)
kombedy	Komitety bednoty (Committees of the Poor Peasantry)
kommuna	type of collective farm
Komsomol	Kommunistichesky Soyuz Molodezhi (Communist Youth League)
Kst	*Kommunist* (*The Communist*)
kulak	rich peasant
l.	list (page)
MGU	Moskovsky Gosudarstvennyi Universitet (Moscow State University)
mnogoukladnost'	multistructuredness
MTS	Mashinno-traktornaya stantsiya (Machine Tractor Station)
MVD	Ministerstvo vnutrennikh del (Ministry of Internal Affairs)
Narkomzem	Narodnyi Komissariat Zemledeliya (People's Commissariat of Agriculture)
NEP	*Novaya ekonomicheskaya politika* (New Economic Policy)
NKVD	Narodnyi Komissariat Vnutrennykh Del (People's Commissariat of Internal Affairs)
nomenklatura	list of key posts approved by the party [= elite]
obkom	oblastnyi komitet (regional party committee)
obshchina	traditional village commune [also *mir*]
OGPU	Ob"edinennoe Gosudarsvennoe Politicheskoe Upravlenie (Unified State Political Administration [political police])
OI	*Otechestvennaya istoriya* (*National History*)
op.	opis' (inventory)
partiinost'	commitment to the party line
PD	papers of V. P. Danilov
PN	papers held by S. S. Neretina
RSFSR	Rossiiskaya Sovetskaya Federativnaya Sotsialisticheskaya Respublika (Russian Soviet Federative Socialist Republic)

raikom	raionnyi komitet (district party committee)
shestidesyatniki	the people of the 1960s
stroi	[social] system
TOZ	Tovarishchestvo po sovmestnoi obrabotke zemli (Association for the joint cultivation of land)
TsGANKh	Tsentral'nyi gosudarstvennyi arkhiv narodnogo khozyaistvo (Central State Archive of the National Economy)
TsK KPSS	Tsentral'nyi Komitet Kommunisticheskoi Partii Sovetskogo Soyuza (Central Committee of the Communist Party of the Soviet Union)
TsKhSD	Tsentr khraneniya sovremennoi dokumentatsii (Centre for the Preservation of Contemporary Documentation)
TsPA	Tsentral'nyi partiinyi arkhiv (Central Party Archive)
uklad(y)	[socio-economic] structure(s)
USSR	Union of Soviet Socialist Republics
VAK	*Vysokaya atestatsionnaya kommissiya* (Higher Qualifications Commission)
VF	*Voprosy filosofii* (*Problems of Philosophy*)
VI	*Voprosy istorii* (*Problems of History*)
VI KPSS	*Voprosy istorii KPSS* (*Problems of the History of the CPSU*)
VKP (b)	Vsesoyuznaya Kommunisticheskay partiya (bol'shevikov) (Communist Party of the Soviet Union (Bolsheviks))
Vuzy	Vysshie uchebnye zavedeniya (Higher Educational Establishments)
vydvizhentsy	workers promoted to administrative posts
zakonomernosti	lawful regularities
zakony	laws

Part I
The Context of the Discussions

1
A Resurgent Intelligentsia

'Only an affinity with the vital needs and aspirations of the people coupled with a high spiritual culture and a genuine *intelligentnost'* can bring in these times creative success to the artist.'
A. Tvardovsky, 'Po sluchayu yubileya', *Novyi mir*, 1965, 1, p. 18

At the heart of this book lies the question of what the debates among Soviet historians during the 1950s and 1960s tell us about their evolution as intellectuals in relation to the Soviet state and society in that period. The book is thus political science in that it assumes that the production of history in Soviet society, indeed in any society, had a political function over and above the individual historian's quest for historical truth. It is an exploration of the politics of knowledge that assumes there is a link between knowledge, intellectuals as its bearers, and power. Probing the precise nature of that link in the case of Soviet historians is a major objective of this study.

To this end, this book straddles two disciplines: political science and history. There is no contradiction here. Political science, if it is to be worthy of the name, must be, in the first place, historical.[1] The approach pursued here is historical in that it charts the evolution of revisionist Soviet historiography between the mid-1950s and the early-1970s. However, this book is more than a history of historical revisionism; it is primarily an investigation of the intellectual and socio-political implications of the revisionist challenge to the ruling paradigm in Soviet 'historical science'.

It is a commonplace nowadays to assert that the writing of history and the development of politics are closely related,[2] and that nowhere was this connection closer than in the Soviet Union. Even the most casual observer could not help but be struck by the intimate nexus between the *perestroika* (reconstruction) reform process initiated by Mikhail Gorbachev and his campaign for the radical rewriting of Soviet history, encapsulated in his call to fill in the 'blank spots' in Soviet history.

Direct intervention by the General Secretary of the Communist Party of the Soviet Union (CPSU) in historical science was not unprecedented. Three decades earlier Gorbachev's reformist predecessor Nikita Khrushchev drove the first official nail into the coffin of Stalinism with his celebrated 'secret speech' to the Twentieth Congress of the CPSU in March 1956. Khrushchev's speech was anticipated by the then chief editor of *Voprosy istorii* (*Problems of History*) and central committee member Academician Anna Pankratova who, at a *Voprosy istorii* readers' conference two months earlier, had made quite explicit the nexus between politics and historiography: 'The problems of Soviet historiography are the problems of our Communist ideology'.[3] Of course, Khrushchev's intervention into history was only the reverse of that of his predecessor whom he was now debunking. Twenty-five years earlier Stalin had deliberately and systematically sought to bring historical writing directly under the control of the party.

The success of Stalin's enterprise can be seen in the reluctance of the professional historians to respond to the explosion of interest in Soviet history and historiography in the Soviet Union half a century later. In 1987 it fell to the party leadership to initiate discussion and to appeal for a radical reckoning both with the past and its mode of representation – an appeal answered at first only by writers and media historians and then, a great deal more cautiously, by professional historians. This ferment around the question of history and historical writing, which eventually engulfed both public and professional opinion, has been mirrored in the plethora of studies by Western scholars of this process and its political significance.[4]

This book was stimulated both by these events and their analysis in Western scholarship. It arose out of my suspicion that the roots of the *perestroika* ferment among professional historians lay in the veritable revolution in historiography in the wake of the Twentieth Congress and that even the ousting of Khrushchev and the triumph of Brezhnev had not entirely put an end to this process – a suspicion confirmed by this study. Hence the focus on the rise and fall of Soviet historical science between the 'thaw' of the mid-1950s and the onset of so-called '*zastoi*' (stagnation) in the 1970s – a fall which, according to Soviet historians, epitomized the intellectual stagnation that was the hallmark of the Brezhnev era.

Totalitarian theory

At first sight, such an overview tends to confirm the view that Soviet historical science was simply the dependent variable of politics. Closer examination suggests a more complex relationship; but recognizing it was for a long time impeded by one of the shibboleths of Western sovietology: 'totalitarianism'.

Sovietology, lavishly financed especially in the United States and Germany, emerged as an essential part of the West's cold-war armoury in which the totalitarian paradigm, at least until the mid-1960s, was a vital weapon.[5] Nowhere has this been more evident than in Western scholarship on Soviet historical writing. Here the primary argument has long been that Soviet historiography was nothing more than the 'handmaiden' of politics. As one of the earliest practitioners of sovietology, the Soviet émigré scholar Konstantin Shteppa, put it, 'state control' over intellectual life made 'individual initiative ... impossible'. As '"the most political of all the sciences" ... history was forced to take its place in that organized ideology, which along with the apparatus of physical compulsion and terror ... constitutes the main support of state authority.' Accordingly, 'Soviet historiography has no significance in itself, nor has any other branch of learning in the Soviet state. It is the handmaiden of political authority.'[6] Shteppa's conclusions confirm the tautological method that underlay the 'totalitarian' approach: the omnipotent Soviet state smothered all thought with its pervasive 'ideology'; therefore it was pointless to give any serious consideration to opinions voiced within such ideology. *Quod erat demonstrandum.*

The 'handmaiden' approach to Soviet historiography, the verso of totalitarian analysis, dominated a conference devoted to the question held in Geneva in July 1964, when the cold war was still frosty.[7] Such was the dominance of the totalitarian paradigm that while the editors of the conference papers could welcome the post-Twentieth Congress developments in historiography as confirmation that a 'spirit of free inquiry had developed a momentum of its own', they could draw the bizarre conclusion that 'nothing has really changed since Stalin'. Because 'on the Soviet Olympus Clio still sings to the tune of the CPSU', the relative latitude of the party amounted to an attempt to redirect destalinization along politically acceptable paths. The party had insidiously harnessed the historians' 'inner motivations' so that 'in a sense, therefore, the Soviet historian of the 1960s is less free than his predecessor under Stalin'. Accordingly, Soviet historiography as a whole was written off as 'mythology' rather than history.[8]

Of course, there was considerable truth to these accusations. Under the rubric of *partiinost'* (party spirit) the CPSU did deliberately set strict limits to destalinization,[9] and sought to ensure historians remained within them. But unsubstantiated assertions about the myths allegedly woven by Soviet historians in their psychological prison were a major impediment to non-Soviet scholars taking the work of their Soviet counterparts seriously. Moreover, such an approach, viewed from the vantage-point of the post-cold-war era, strikingly confirms Novick's contention that a hallmark of the totalitarian model was the conviction that 'our' research was 'objective' while 'theirs' was 'ideological'.[10] There was not the slightest sense that adherents of the totalitarian model might themselves have been engaged in myth making.

Above all, such an approach impeded any receptivity to the possibility that Soviet historians might have had the capacity to regenerate their own discipline, in good part by drawing on their own resources and within the framework of Marxism – at the expense of official Marxism–Leninism. As Thomas Kuhn pointed out, the research paradigm of 'normal science' can be extremely resilient.[11] An observation no less valid, apparently, in democratic polities than in totalitarian ones. A contributor to an anthology devoted to the *perestroika* ferment in Soviet historiography, labouring under a kind of Western historiographical burden, argued that it was primarily Western influences and Soviet 'hunger' for the 'Western way of life' that were responsible for the ferment.[12]

Nevertheless, with the passage of time, there was some refining of analysis by the totalitarian school. Thus John Keep, principal editor of the 1964 anthology, could concede more than two decades later that despite the fact that Soviet historical science was '"institutionalized mendacity" ... we must recognize that there are many currents of opinion beneath the harsh facade of official militance' and that during the decade 1956–65 there was a vigorous display of intellectual creativity.[13]

There is a malicious irony in all this; with the advent of *perestroika*, many Soviet historians suddenly endorsed the most negative judgements of their old cold-war foes, for example, Yury Afanas'ev, a former scrutineer of the *Annales* school in the Institute of Marxism–Leninism. Assessing the state of Soviet historical writing in the wake of the Brezhnev era, Afanas'ev bitterly concluded that 'there is probably no country in the world with such a falsified history as ours ... It is important to realize that Stalinism needed history only as a handmaiden of propaganda ... The Stalinist regime created its own history'.[14]

It was precisely acknowledgment of the post-Twentieth Congress upheaval in Soviet historiography that was the hallmark of a new approach by Western, primarily US, students of Soviet historiography, who in the mid-1960s began to challenge the totalitarian model. It is no accident that the cracks in sovietology's totalitarian model and those in the Stalinist approach to history were more or less parallel. Destalinization in the Soviet Union and East Central Europe and growing domestic disquiet about the USA's war on Indochina, in the late-1950s and mid-1960s respectively, were mutually reinforcing elements that served to undermine the ideological consensus, East and West.

Whereas for the exponents of the totalitarian model Soviet historians were, like the intelligentsia at large, an undifferentiated social layer that was completely subservient to state and party, a new generation of Western scholars began to challenge this received totalitarian wisdom. In this regard Nancy Heer's 1971 study *Politics and History in the Soviet Union* was pioneering.[15] While arguing that official history and party history in particular were, in the absence of terror, political weapons *par excellence*, Heer recognized that the growing sophistication of such weaponry could be turned against those who wielded it. Heer's recognition of the potential 'dysfunctionalism' of Soviet historical writing even within the most tightly controlled branch of the discipline, party history, was coupled with her rejection of any 'totalitarian' understanding of 'push-button responses to a single authority'. Similarly she rejected 'false', simplified assumptions that '"old apparatchik" equals "Stalinist conservative" and "sophisticated academic" equals "liberal revisionist"'.[16]

Heer, together with Samuel Baron, subsequently drew attention to the 'inspiriting developments' in Soviet historical science in the mid-1960s that are the focus of this book. For Heer and Baron such developments registered the emergence of 'professional norms' among Soviet historians and their increased autonomy from political tutelage.[17] Emerging professionalism was also the explanation adopted for a 1979 study of a question that was vital for the rekindling of Soviet historiography in the 1960s: Russian imperialism in the Tsarist era.[18] Recognition of emerging professionalism was certainly a step forward in achieving a more sympathetic appreciation of the motivations of those Soviet historians who sought to throw off the administrative and intellectual shackles of the past. But the sub-text of the 'professionalism' argument was that Soviet historians were becoming more like 'us', that is, Western academic historians. As we shall see, however, this approach falls far short of grasping the self-conscious striving for intellectual integrity in a society where the tradition and stature of the Russian intelligentsia had survived the harsh vicissitudes of the Soviet experiment.

Baron and Heer were overly optimistic in their conviction that despite the gloomier political atmosphere in the early 1970s 'the progress made since the Twentieth Party Congress seems likely to be irreversible'.[19] In the long run, however, they have proven to be right. The Brezhnev offensive saw the dispersal and defeat of the anti-Stalinist historians, but not the renunciation of their ideas. The explosion of debates among professional historians that eventually accompanied *perestroika* in 1987–88 was ignited in the main by the *shestidesyatniki* – 'the people of the 1960s'. Such has been the intensity of the heat and light generated by the *perestroika* discussions that this subterranean link in historical science, which survived the permafrost between the 'thaw' and *perestroika*, has at best received passing comment.[20] The impression remains that little was going on among historians, compared to writers, in the Khrushchev period. A major objective of this book is to cast light on this hitherto hidden link.

A civil society in embryo

Recognition on the part of at least some students of Soviet society that behind the totalitarian facade there were some signs of intellectual life was gradually given some theoretical shape as the rudiments of 'civil society'. The resuscitation of the state/civil society dyad, in good part fostered by the (post-1968 'Prague spring') demise of 'totalitarianism' in East Central Europe, offered a conceptual device for appreciating the inherently destabilizing effects of any flowering of civil society against the party-state in Soviet-type political systems.[21] One of the first Western scholars to apply the concept was a student of Soviet economic debates. Moshe Lewin, examining debates among Soviet economists in the 1960s, which coincided with those among historians, saw them as 'seismic' indicators of subterranean shifts in political and social life which he conceptualized as a slowly 'recovering civil society'.[22]

By civil society, Lewin later explained, he meant that 'aggregate of networks or institutions that either exist or act independently of the state or are official organizations' capable of becoming independent and exerting influence on the authorities. The strength of Lewin's approach is that in repudiating any simple antithesis between state and society he has drawn attention to the importance of the social context in which the 'political system' (of which the state is but a part) operates. Recognition that the boundaries between Soviet state and society were not at all clearly defined is particularly important in a system that was, as Lewin says, 'statist par excellence'. This means that developments in the arena of the party-state, which the totalitarian model viewed as exclusively political, were necessarily *social*. Viewed in this way, debates and confrontations among historians or economists could be important indicators of the social evolution of these professions and of the intelligentsia as whole. Moreover, of particular importance for our purposes is that Lewin's approach allows for the emergence of the rudiments of a civil society within 'the very fortress of statism', that is, within the institutions of both state and party.[23] Recognition of a certain degree of autonomy on the part of the official intelligentsia, despite the best attempts at control by the party-state, is a necessary prerequisite for assaying the significance of revisionist historiography as a building block of civil society.

We can concur broadly with Lewin's contention that 'totalitarianism' was conceptually 'useless' because it could not explain the driving forces of change in the USSR. However, it has to be acknowledged that as a description of the strivings of Stalinism to terrorize society into submission and of the post-Stalinist state to control every facet of society, not least intellectual life, it has considerable validity. The fact that the Stalinist state apparatus failed to obliterate every trace of civil society (though the negative effects of its attempts to do so are now glaringly obvious since the failings of *perestroika* and the collapse of the Soviet Union) says more about the physical impossibility of doing so than about the theory of totalitarianism as such.[24] Bearing this caveat in mind this book should be seen as a study of some of the first stirrings of civil society in embryo and their implications for the stability of the party-state apparatus.

The rationale for this book is more than just one of filling in the 'blank spots' in the scholarly literature on Soviet historiography. It is also a question of theory and methodology. This book belongs, broadly speaking, to the anti-totalitarian school of thought outlined above. However, whereas the bulk of the scholarship on Soviet historical writing of the 1960s, with the notable exception of Heer, has been concerned with it *qua* historiography, this study is ultimately concerned with the socio-political role of Soviet historiography and of those who produced it: the historians. This book is therefore at once a study of the historiographical and the socio-political implications of the emergence of revisionist historiography in the Soviet Union in the wake of the Twentieth Congress.

In this twin-track approach the historiographical developments are seen as indicators of a shift in the socio-political outlook and self-perception of the elite intelligentsia. To bridge these processes two approaches are employed. The first draws on Kuhn's concept of a 'paradigm shift'. However, Kuhn's focus on the internal dynamics of change in scientific thought tends to neglect the socio-political context underlying such changes. To redress this neglect, Kuhn is buttressed by a sociological approach in the sense that historians are treated as a subset of the intelligentsia. Accordingly, any understanding of the question of the emergence of revisionist historiography automatically becomes a question of the particular function of historiography in Soviet society. This in turn must be posed in terms of a problematic of the relationship between intellectuals, society and the state. In this sense this book is an exercise in the politics of knowledge. However, before amplifying the two approaches adumbrated immediately above it is necessary to say briefly what this book is not.

A number of studies have interpreted discussions among Soviet social scientists as surrogates for a critique of domestic politics and society. Discussions about Mao's China,[25] the Soviet economy,[26] Russian absolutism,[27] and paths of Third World development[28] have been interpreted variously as cryptic critiques of Soviet society, and Stalinism in particular. Whether it has been metaphors for Stalinism, 'political undercurrents' in debates among economists, 'mirrors for socialism' or, more latterly, a reading of the signification of discussions, all have entailed some kind of 'reading between the lines', or even 'behind' them,[29] on the part of sovietologists. While I am mindful of a tradition going back to autocratic Russia where, in the absence of free speech, Aesopian language has been employed as a vehicle for indirect criticism of state and society, exploring this cryptic critique is not my primary objective. Although part of the oral research undertaken for this book sought to draw out the sub-text of the debates amongst historians, their responses confirmed the approach pursued here: such discussions should be treated first and foremost as scholarly discussions in their own right, the political ramifications of which resided in their challenge to officially sanctioned paradigms rather than as deliberately oblique critiques of Soviet society.[30]

It is appropriate here to touch on another methodological consideration: the status of interviews as historical evidence. Human memory is notoriously inaccurate and the participants in the fights around historical revisionism in the 1960s may or may not have good reason to embellish their role, especially as debate about their role was part of the *perestroika* furore about history. Oral evidence can serve merely to alert a researcher to significant phenomena or events that might otherwise be overlooked. It can also be used as a primary source in and of itself. I have chosen to use it in both senses. While this book rests preponderantly on written sources, I have drawn liberally on interviews both in order to obtain information and, above all, to establish the self-perception of the revisionist historians about their objectives. The latter especially is not self-evident from the written record. Given that overwhelmingly the interviewees were the revisionists themselves then there is always the danger that their perspectives must colour this story. I have tried to guard against this, firstly by establishing the consistency of their views with other, established, facts and secondly, and even more importantly, by locating this saga of Soviet intellectual life in the framework of the literature on the production of knowledge and the intellectual.

Paradigm shift

Despite the fact that the majority of Soviet historians were undoubtedly the loyal lieutenants of the party-state elite, and despite the undeniable intrusion of this bureaucratic elite into intellectual life, this did not preclude a significant minority of historians beginning to rethink, challenge, and even reconstruct Soviet doctrinal orthodoxies. Drawing on Kuhn's paradigm theory we can more readily formulate this process of reconstruction as a response to a 'crisis' in scientific thought.[31]

According to Kuhn, such a crisis arises out of the inability of a 'normal' paradigm endorsed by a scholarly community to formulate and resolve repeated 'anomalies' in relation to the object of its study. This crisis can only be resolved by a 'paradigm shift' or 'scientific revolution' that accomplishes the 'reconstruction of prior theory and the re-evaluation of prior fact'. Of course, Kuhn was advancing a hypothesis based on the evolution of the natural sciences. A major lacuna in his theory, as he later acknowledged, was that such 'crises' are indicative of a social and political crisis, not just an intellectual one.[32] Nevertheless, others have applied Kuhn's approach to the social science community, the historians' guild in particular. They have also abstracted from his work a number of external 'paths to crisis' produced when a research community loses confidence in the 'tradition' that underpins and organizes its paradigm. Among these can be exposure to the stimulus of another culture that destabilizes the accepted research tradition or political upheaval that may well lead to 'new criteria' for understanding society.[33] However, Kuhn allows that a 'scientific crisis' may not necessarily result in a 'paradigm shift'. Moreover, the very existence of a crisis that gives rise to competing paradigms also engenders 'pronounced professional insecurity.'[34]

Translated to the Soviet scenario, and anticipating some of my conclusions, we can discern a quest for a new historiographical paradigm engendered by the inability of the conceptual cage of the Stalinist approach to history to deal with a number of 'anomalies' that became apparent in the post-Stalin era. Chief among these for historians were the preconditions that gave rise to the October Revolution, the Stalin phenomenon itself, and their encounter with an erupting Third World that did not fit easily into the one-dimensional categories of the Soviet version of historical materialism. Further, the upheaval that followed the Twentieth Congress had a direct impact on the outlook of the Soviet intelligentsia in general and historians in particular. One significant side effect of the subsequent 'thaw' was the rapid exposure of Soviet historians to the international community of scholars.

An important qualification is required here. Kuhn insisted that it is the 'scientific community' alone that can choose between paradigms:

> if authority alone, and particularly if non-professional authority, were the arbiter of paradigm debates the outcome of those debates might still be a revolution, but it would not be a *scientific* revolution. The very existence of science depends upon vesting the power to choose between paradigms in the members of a special kind of community.[35]

On this basis, Stalin's *'Short Course'* history of the CPSU, strictly speaking, was not a scientific paradigm, since it was administratively imposed in 1938. Does that mean that the *Short Course* was not a real, working paradigm for Soviet historians, rather than a catechism to which they paid mere lip service? All the evidence suggests the *Short Course* was a real, if non-scientific, paradigm. Accordingly, with the emergence of a genuine community of historians in the mid-1950s, what was being put in place was a genuine *scientific* paradigm.

Ironically, despite these qualifications, Kuhn's paradigm theory is in several senses eminently appropriate for viewing the Soviet historical profession. The Soviets, spurning the accepted division in the West between the natural and social sciences or humanities, attempted to replicate the tightly organized, 'mature' natural sciences.[36] While such organization facilitated political control, it also accorded with the CPSU's natural-scientific view of the social world. Kuhn's approach also has the merit of encouraging us to see what appear to be isolated instances of historical revisionism as in fact the building blocks of a new paradigm, which is ultimately 'incommensurable' with its predecessor.[37] Sooner or later the new paradigm must contest the dominant paradigm. For historians in particular this contestation must occur on the plane of methodology. Further, Kuhn draws our attention to the community of scholars,[38] rather than the isolated work of a few outstanding historians, as providing the environment that nurtures the embryonic paradigm.

This perspective has encouraged my endeavour to depict the particular organization and culture of the production of history, what Regis Debray refers to as the 'material conditions of the existence of thought',[39] that shaped Soviet historical writing during the decade after the Twentieth Congress. It is also this perspective that encouraged my quest to divine what both Kuhn and Lewin refer to as 'invisible colleges', the network of informal contacts that shaped and reshaped intellectual life in general, and historical thought in particular, during this decade.[40]

All of this amounts to an endeavour to go beyond a history of Soviet historiography in order to depict what Pierre Bourdieu has designated as the 'intellectual field', understood as 'the system of social relations within which creation takes place as an act of communication', upon which the revisionist historians of the 1960s sought to raise their standard.[41] In what follows the contours of this 'field' are depicted in terms of the meaning of the intellectual and of the place of the Russian *intelligent* tradition in Soviet society in these years.

Historians as intellectuals

In order to grapple in detail with the function of historians in Soviet political and social life, and in order to treat Soviet historical writing as a problem of the social production of a particular kind of knowledge, rather than just as a problem in the 'history of ideas', we need to see historians as a sub-set of a much larger social category – the intelligentsia. To comprehend this contentious category and its meaning in the context of Soviet intellectual life, we must avoid the trap of ahistorical, sociological formalism,[42] characteristic both of the Soviet approach to intellectuals and of Western mainstream sociology.

Nevertheless it is impossible to bypass these approaches, least of all the Soviet one.

If we were to follow the Soviet definition of the intelligentsia then all Soviet historians would have been *intelligenty*. The Soviets defined the intelligentsia on a purportedly objective basis, according to its skills and qualifications, its place in the social division of labour, and its social function, which differed according to the society in which it operated. In capitalist societies, for instance, the intelligentsia was not designated as a class but as a 'social stratum consisting of people professionally engaged in mental work, primarily of a complex and creative kind, and in the development and spread of culture.'[43] The social function of the intelligentsia was critical to the Soviet definition. The intelligentsia articulates not its own interests, but those of other classes. In capitalist society the bulk of the intelligentsia serves and rationalizes the rule of the capitalist class, while a small minority, who identify with the exploited classes, become members of the 'progressive' intelligentsia. Such was the 'progressive democratic' intelligentsia who, under the aegis of the Bolsheviks, allied themselves with the October 1917 Revolution.[44]

Here, according to the Soviet scenario, was the nucleus of the 'qualitatively new' Soviet intelligentsia. With the October Revolution the social nature of the intelligentsia began to change, in the course of which it 'allied' itself with the workers and peasants. With the 'victory of socialism', proclaimed by Stalin in 1936, the 'socio-political unity' of the intelligentsia with the two principal classes in Soviet society, the working class and collective farmers, was secured. The infant Soviet state set about creating a new intelligentsia by educating the mass of the workers and peasants and by reeducating those bourgeois *intelligenty* who were loyal to the new regime.[45] Thus the Soviet intelligentsia, in contrast to its predecessor, allegedly acquired a 'great degree of homogeneity'[46] and harmony with Soviet society, and, by implication, the polity at large.

Soviet claims about the radical social transformation of the intelligentsia had more than a grain of truth to them. More dubious were the assertions about its loyalty and homogeneity, not to mention glossing over the terrible human cost with which this transformation was secured. Of more immediate concern here is the political implication of the Soviet definition of their intelligentsia. Several critics have pointed to the ironic political effect of the Soviets singling out the intelligentsia as a specific stratum, but not a class, of Soviet society. The party-state, by definition differentiating the intelligentsia from the peasantry and the working class, while simultaneously denying its autonomy as a political actor in relation to them, effectively muzzled the intelligentsia's right to assert its specific interests or those of its 'class allies'. The 'stratum' concept thereby enshrined the bureaucracy as the ultimate arbiter of social and intellectual life, while denigrating the creative and scientific intelligentsia.[47] The pronounced 'princely arrogance' of the Soviet bureaucracy, even in comparison with its East Central European counterparts, resulted in a *'spiritual wretchedness'* that brooked no inquiry into the *nomenklatura*'s 'false picture of the world.'[48] Paradoxically, this anti-intellectual disposition was strengthened by the improved educational profile of the Soviet party apparatus, especially during the mid-1950s. The influx in these years of technically educated specialists (engineers, agronomists and so forth) at the expense of those with social science training took an increasing toll on 'qualified ideological cadre' and 'intellectual-educational work'. The ensuing 'tendency towards the technocratization' of the *apparat* consolidated it as a citadel of 'dogmatism and rote-learning'.[49] The imperious *apparatchik* required at most 'instrumental knowledge', couched in an extremely scientistic discourse, for the reproduction of the political system.[50]

This is readily apparent when we look at the place of historians within the intelligentsia. The catch-all Soviet definition embraced a very wide category of persons, roughly equivalent to white-collar workers, without regard to their formal qualifications or occupation. Applied to Soviet society it meant that everybody with more than a basic secondary education, from state and party functionaries to academicians, were all classified as *intelligenty* – mere technicians of knowledge. Within this classificatory swamp the only concession to the usual Western understanding of intellectuals, if not that of the traditional Russian intelligentsia, as 'critical thinkers' was the grudging acknowledgement of the existence of the 'creative intelligentsia' that included writers, artists and 'leading scholars'.[51] There was one notable omission: historians. As the titles of their degrees (candidates and doctors of historical sciences) suggested, they were classified as scientific workers. This is a decisive distinction and says a great deal about the ideological import attached to historians by the CPSU. Given that their discipline was governed by the principle of *partiinost'*, historians were called upon to elaborate the truth, as established by the party, not to create it.

As noted above, the Soviet definition of the intelligentsia not only lumped together heterogeneous social groups, it also pointedly excluded any subjective criteria of classification. On these grounds it refused to acknowledge any particular status for the classical Russian intelligentsia.[52] On this last point the Soviets were not alone. In Western sociology the major trend has been not to make any distinction between the intelligentsia and intellectuals.[53] Yet if we are to understand the significance of the emergence of revisionist historians then we not only have to view this process in terms of the meaning of the intellectual, but locate it within the specific tradition of the Russian *intelligent*.

Unlike the Soviets, in at least one strand of Western literature on intellectuals there has been a tendency to emphasize the elaboration of a world outlook, and usually a *critical* one, as the common denominator of intellectuals. By this criterion, intellectuals are castigators of the 'men of power for the wickedness of their ways'.[54] This is a continental European, especially French, tradition rather than an Anglo-Saxon one. Indeed the word *intellectuel*, coined by Clemenceau in the midst of the Dreyfus affair, immediately became synonymous with 'unscrupulous, irresponsible disloyalty to the nation'.[55]

Such a subjective definition was largely excluded from the functionalist approach that dominated much Western sociology in the 1960s. For the sociologists, intellectuals were defined primarily by their social function as articulators of cultural symbols.[56] In a rich essay Peter Nettl took both approaches to task, the subjective approach for reducing the problem to little more than anecdotes about 'men of ideas' and the functionalists for putting the institutional cart before the intellectual horse. In contrast to both approaches, Nettl argues the intellectual

> must be defined from inside out, *from* certain types of ideas *toward* certain categories of idea-articulators; only then can the related variable of institutionalization be added. Thus the problem of institutional location and significance depends primarily on *types* of ideas rather than types of people.

For Nettl what is crucial is not so much the production and articulation of ideas as their social acceptability and the 'role-taking of their articulators'. In other words, he argues for a clear distinction, but not a divorce, between 'idea formation' and 'articulating social structure'. Failure to maintain such a distinction has led mainstream sociology to focus almost exclusively on the social role of intellectuals at the expense of the categories of the ideas they articulate. Reversing the usual priority, Nettl makes the former a function of the latter.[57]

Nettl's approach provides us with some very fine instruments for probing the role of the intelligentsia in Soviet society, and ultimately of Soviet historians as a subset of the intelligentsia. His approach also helps us to bridge the gap between the internal dynamics of 'paradigm shifts' in intellectual life and the larger social dynamics of this process. Particularly pertinent here is the crucial distinction he makes between ideas of 'scope', that is, those ideas that merely broaden out knowledge, and those that radically challenge the accepted paradigm, and therefore constitute a 'qualitative dissent'. The former, characteristic of the 'particularistic' physical sciences, seem to arise in a mainly academic environment whereas the latter, characteristic of the 'universalistic' humanities, seem to require a socio-political environment to take root.[58]

Equipped with this typology Nettl proffers a definition of the intellectual that goes further, however, than a mere articulator of qualitatively new ideas. The crucial ingredient is that these ideas must be capable, potentially at least, of being projected into 'socio-structural dissent'. On this basis he advances a three-dimensional definition of the intellectual: '(1) a profession that is culturally validated, (2) a role that is socio-political, and (3) a consciousness that relates to universals.'[59]

Nettl insists on the necessity for dissenters to 'attach' themselves to a 'suitable social structure' if they are 'to fulfill the [potential] role of a social stratum of intellectuals', or ultimately 'crystallize as a self-conscious group'. The mere holding of dissenting ideas is not enough. Given this approach it should not be surprising that the nineteenth-century Russian intelligentsia should provide the archetype of intellectuals who, having forged the strongest nexus between their intellectual dissent and their socio-political role, were a 'self-conscious collectivity *ab ovo*'.[60]

Intellectuals, Nettl observes, are almost by nature an 'occasional' phenomenon; they have not been an indelible feature of the socio-political landscape. Only intermittently, between sustained periods of 'smoothness', have they impinged on that landscape, and then theirs was usually a fleeting presence. On those few occasions when the intellectuals have found themselves closest to the locus of power, most tellingly for our purposes the Soviet Union at the end of the 1920s, they were shunted aside by the 'non-innovating bureaucrats'.[61] Stalin established an 'Arakcheev regime', terminating a short-lived golden age in the arts and sciences, bureaucratizing the writing of history in particular.[62] Nettl's assertion, based on the experience of the October Revolution, that 'non-innovating bureaucrats are always the logical successors of the intellectuals', has more than a little relevance also for the fate of revisionist Soviet historians a half century after the revolution. The Brezhnev offensive against the revisionist historians of the 1960s was definitely a crucial element of the triumph of the *apparatchiki* and their acolyte mandarins over 'qualitative' intellectuals, confirming the dictum that power and intellectuals are mutually exclusive.[63]

In the 1930s Stalin forged an alliance between remnants of the old intelligentsia and the new technocratic intelligentsia promoted from the new working class: the *vydvizhentsy*. This was a *modus vivendi* between culture and power. The *vydvizhentsy* were the major beneficiaries of the Great Purges, the brunt of which was borne by the Marxists of 1917 and their proteges trained in the 1920s. In the new industrial-military order, scientists and technocrats generally received more favourable treatment, at the expense of the 'creative' intelligentsia.[64] In effect, Stalin's academic mandarins had presided over the transformation of erstwhile dissent into orthodoxy, that is, of Bolshevism into Marxism–Leninism, and then proceeded to wield it against renewed dissent. Paradoxically, and definitely unintentionally, they also set in place the subsequent post-Stalin 'institutionalization of dissent'.[65] This latter development, far from being uniquely Soviet, has been characteristic of the situation of intellectuals in general in the modern era; a product of the proliferation of higher education in modern industrial societies, both West and East. The resultant 'reintegration of qualitative or intellectual dissent' into institutions of higher learning, usually the universities, has seen the latter 'self-consciously crystallizing as structures of dissent',[66] despite their intended function as vehicles of social reproduction.[67]

This 'recreation of structured dissent' has not been without its costs. There has been a tendency for traditional intellectuals, such as writers, to be displaced by social scientists and even, in the scientistic culture that is the hallmark of modernity, natural scientists. The advent of mass education and research undermined the 'structural separation of the "optimal" or ideal-typical settings for the production and diffusion of the two types of ideas, [those of scope and of quality]'. In other words, the lectern has increasingly come to occupy the place once almost exclusively the preserve of the pen (although in recent times the lectern seems to have been displaced by the television screen).[68] The net effect has been to destabilize intellectual production in its institutional heartland. As Nettl puts it:

> The combination in one and the same stratum of an institutionally powerful mandarinate and an intellectual *fronde* seems to require a

constant assertion of insecurity, a self-conscious refusal to accept the fact that the political kingdom of the intellectuals is safely established, and above all an incessant appeal to arms against an exaggeratedly menacing right whose aim continues to be the destruction of enlightenment ... But such a combination of academic institutionalization and intellectual leadership of a sociopolitical movement was likely ... to prove unstable. Mandarins and intellectuals live uneasily together and dislike each other intensely ... The evidence suggests that those who claim membership in intellectual professions, who combine a cultural orientation with an appeal to universality, and who have become academically institutionalized, are subject to attacks from new 'outside' groups of intellectuals, often aided by breakaway 'professional' allies from within. This is especially likely to be the case where such a mandarinate successfully exercises political influence.[69]

The Soviet mandarinate established under Stalin conforms particularly neatly to Nettl's model. Outwardly, the Soviet definition of their intelligentsia, as we have seen, was the polar opposite of 'bourgeois' conceptions. In place of an intelligentsia differentiated from the mass of the populace was an intelligentsia that was (allegedly) gradually losing its *differentia specifica* as a stratum, melding as it was with an increasingly educated population; in Nettl's phrase, 'every man his own intellectual'. As a result, Soviet academic discourse precluded any qualitative distinction between science and culture or, in Nettl's terms, between 'scope and quality'. Now that under the aegis of the party, harmony reigned between the intelligentsia, society and the state, 'the problem of dissent' was irrelevant. 'Only the search for scope was left.'[70]

Though the Soviets chose to present themselves as the 'clarion call for a new and revolutionary version of modernity', their approach to their intelligentsia, underpinned by their formal definition, amounted to the very negation of intellectuality. To cite Nettl again,

there was no room here for qualitative dissent. Indeed the very concept of qualitative dissent – and with it the *raison d'être* of intellectuals – had disappeared into the graded limbos of madness, reaction and treachery ... Dissent and therefore intellectuals had become historically unnecessary.[71]

In short, the Soviet intelligentsia was overwhelmingly anti-intellectual.

The institutionalization of intellectual dissent provides a valuable pointer to the objective and technical bases in post-Stalinist Soviet life for the emergence of a latter-day intelligentsia in the Russian tradition within the confines of the academy. To foreshadow my conclusions, the Academy of Sciences provided not only a site for the regeneration of intellectual life but also the institutional basis for the development of a self-conscious collectivity who, in pursuit of their professional activities, in this case historical research and writing, found themselves on a collision course with the academic mandarinate and ultimately, political authority. Their crime was simply to challenge the received historical paradigm. It was not their initial intention to seek an immediate socio-political resonance for their work but clearly it had that potential, or at least was perceived as such by political authority. The revisionist historians who are our concern here began to crystallize as a self-conscious stratum of the intellectual elite, redolent of that powerful, almost unique phenomenon in Russian cultural life, the intelligentsia. Given the importance of this tradition, and the link between it and the emergence of revisionist historiography in the 1960s, it is absolutely necessary to understand this tradition.

The conscience of society

An enormous amount of ink has been spilt defining intellectuals, none more so than on the nature of the Russian intelligentsia. While the original Russian (or Polish) word has been universally accepted into the international lexicon, the precise meaning of the term intelligentsia has not. Whereas in the West it is commonplace to interchange the terms 'intelligentsia' and 'intellectuals' as roughly synonymous with the highly educated, the original term intelligentsia sharply distinguished between them.[72] This term gained currency in Poland and Russia of the 1860s, in concert with the emergence of a gymnasium educated, disaffected, *declassé* layer of the landed nobility. It signified a social stratum differentiated by occupation and social origins but 'united by a shared value system under the motto "serve your nation"'. In Russia this meant a commitment to the abolition of tsarism and destruction of the tsarist state by peaceful or revolutionary means. By definition, *intelligenty* never 'fought for their own group interest and never formulated an ideology of their stratum' and were found 'principally on the left, in the service of social progress, revolution or [in Poland] national independence'.[73] In short, the classical

Russian intelligentsia defined itself, and was seen by others, as the 'voice of conscience against the rulers of society'.[74]

This approach to the classical intelligentsia has played a large part in conceptualizing the modern Soviet dissident movement, particularly, although not exclusively, for adherents of the totalitarian model. At its crudest they tended to treat the official Soviet intelligentsia as if they were little more than the homogenous subjects of an omnipotent state. Even if some intellectual differentiation and autonomy were formally acknowledged, the fact that these 'islands of separateness' remained within the dominant discourse of Marxism–Leninism meant that they were rarely seen as meaningful dissent.[75] The methodological effect has been to treat the intelligentsia as an 'undifferentiated whole'.[76] Ironically, an even more damning indictment of the intellectual suffocation wrought by the totalitarian Soviet state has been advanced in a radical, socialist critique of the dynamics of Soviet-type societies by Ferenc Feher, Agnes Heller and Gyorgy Markus.[77] While recognizing the existence of a Marxist opposition, they argue that such dissent, trapped as it was in a 'language of domination', could at best return to the 'dead-end' of Leninism. Similarly, the dissident movement had so internalized the values of totalitarianism that it lacked the 'social imagination' to even conceive of a democratic alternative.[78]

This relatively undifferentiated approach to the intelligentsia has been buttressed by the view that the dissident movement that emerged in the mid-1960s was the sole legitimate heir to the classical tradition of the intelligentsia.[79] This view rests on a particular conceptualization of the classical intelligentsia. Their self-designation as the conscience of the nation, coupled with their intensely moral, often religious, fervour has been elevated as the *leitmotiv* of this 'class', deemed as finding its ultimate expression in literature.[80] None of these elements is false; what is critical is the weight accorded to certain of them. In particular, the notion of the *intelligent* as the outsider, totally alienated from the state (the '*otshchepenstvo* complex'), who repudiates the entire social system as morally bankrupt, beyond redemption, and therefore needing to be overthrown, has come to the fore. From this it follows that the dissidents, especially, if not exclusively, the outstanding writers such as Aleksandr Solzhenitsyn, who eventually repudiated the Soviet experience in its entirety and sought not its reform but its dissolution, were the logical successors to the classical intelligentsia.

This perspective has had a very important bearing on the way the dynamics of Soviet intellectual life have been perceived in much sovietology. In particular, the focus on the outstanding dissidents such as Roy Medvedev, Andrei Sakharov and, above all, Solzhenitsyn has been at the cost of observing movement *within the mainstream intelligentsia*, which has remained hidden in the penumbra of the dissident phenomenon. The net effects of this blinkered perspective have been twofold. Firstly, an exaggerated focus on the dissident movement has artificially shifted the axis of Soviet intellectual life from its heartland to its periphery. Accordingly, the relationship between intellectual non-conformism and dissidence has been obscured. Though both emerged more or less in tandem in the mid-1960s, in good part it was intellectual non-conformism that fertilized the more vocal dissident movement, rather than vice versa.[81]

Secondly, the implications for the stability of the Soviet political elite of the emergence of anti-orthodox currents within the intellectual mainstream have been overlooked. Indeed, in so far as members of the intellectual elite, working within official institutions, were engaged in a radical reformulation of ideological orthodoxy that went beyond the empirical criticisms of such notable dissidents as Sakharov and Medvedev, the 'legal' dissidents posed, potentially at least, a far more serious challenge to the regime than the 'illegal' dissidents. Nowhere have these processes been more obscured than in the treatment of dissenting historians, which, as we saw above, more often than not have been dismissed as the contemptible 'handmaidens' of the party-state. Even where more discerning scholars recognized the importance of the emergence of historical revisionism in the 1960s, this was generally interpreted in terms of its historiographical significance, rather than as an index of changes in the socio-philosophical outlook and self-perception of the revisionist historians themselves as *intelligenty*.

The emergence of historical revisionism must be located in the broader evolution of Soviet intellectual life after the Twentieth Congress, which detonated a veritable 'revolution' in the existence of the intelligentsia, more than any other social layer. As a result, 'art was transformed into politics and politics was aestheticized'.[82] Even before the Twentieth Congress, with the death of Stalin, literature became the vehicle for the appearance of a genuine 'public opinion' in Soviet life.[83] In the absence of an active working class, it fell to the intelligentsia to take up the cudgels against bureaucratic tyranny and to settle accounts with the past. Writers, nurtured by the latter-day 'thick-journal' *Novyi mir* which 'defined' cultural life in the 1950s and 1960s in terms of the 'great ethical tradition of Russian literature', called for 'Truthfulness in Literature'.[84] Writers, such as Vladimir Dudintsev, Yevgeny Yevtushenko and Solzhenitsyn, were only the most visible signs of this upheaval that engulfed the entire creative and scientific intelligentsia – not least the historians.

It is apparent that in the mid-1950s from within the mass intelligentsia of 'scope' began to crystallize 'intellectuals of quality'. Where the modern dissidents often have been seen as the sole torch bearers of the intelligentsia tradition, following from the hypertrophy of the '*otshchepenstvo* complex', this has neglected the degree to which the *intelligent* could be simultaneously 'insider' and 'outsider' – advocate of both reform and revolution – as were the revolutionary democrats of the 1860s.[85] This 'schizophrenic' situation was very similar to that faced by reform-minded members of the Soviet intelligentsia a century later: on the one hand there was the idea of 'opposing the system as a totality', on the other the 1960s intelligentsia was much more part of that system 'than it admitted'. The parallels are not accidental. In both the 1860s and the 1960s relative stability was afforded by the attempts of the political system, one autocratic the other Stalinist, to reform itself. This provided the intelligentsia in both periods with the space both for lawfully pursuing productive cultural and political work, and for illusions about their chances of success – without becoming dissidents. In this sense the Russian revolutionary movement of the 1870s onwards and the dissident movement a century later were the results of the 'crisis of the liberal concepts' of the intelligentsia born of disappointed expectations of reform from above.[86]

In both cases the intelligentsia were a 'social layer' who sought to genuinely represent the interests of 'the people' (*narod*) against the bureaucrats (*chinovniki*), of the 'oppressed and downtrodden' against tyranny.[87] In this sense the 'new democratic'[88] intelligentsia, which emerged from within the Soviet intellectual establishment in the wake of Stalin's death and especially after the Twentieth Congress, was the scion of the century-old, Russian revolutionary-democratic tradition.[89] However, whereas the Russian pre-revolutionary intelligentsia 'saw as its vocation the education of the masses', whom they 'worshipped' and even felt guilty before, the Soviet *shestidesyatniki* 'regarded as their mission the coaching of Soviet leaders', albeit in the interests of the workers and peasants.[90]

The singular importance and resilience of the intelligentsia tradition in Russian political culture is derived not from some ineffable essence of the Russian soul but in good part from the nature of intellectual activity itself. Ironically, this may be nourished by repression, actually sustaining the stream of the 'great intellectual traditions'.[91] In the case of the Soviet Union the stream did indeed flow onwards. In part this was ensured through the sheer physical survival of representatives of the old intelligentsia who, notwithstanding Stalin's best efforts to ensure their subservience, or their demise,[92] were able to pass down to their students their skills and outlook. Besides the continuity of the prerevolutionary tradition of underground *kruzhki* (discussion circles), such as those of M. M. Bakhtin, there remained a cohort of prominent *intelligenty* who, despite the post-revolutionary flight *en masse* of intellectual capital, threw in their lot with the Soviet state and were eventually rewarded with posts in its educational apparatus. The non-party historian Yevgeny Tarle is a prime example of this process.[93] The most robust conduit for the intelligentsia tradition, however, effectively its 'objective bearer',[94] was the classical Russian literature of the nineteenth century. Published *en masse*, it was not only profoundly subversive of the Soviet polity in terms of its values and ideas but also provided a model for the newly emerging Soviet intelligentsia. As such this officially fostered cultural legacy was 'the greatest humanizing force in Soviet Russia.'[95]

Having recognized this continuity, however, it is equally important to bear in mind the profound sociological transformation that the intelligentsia had undergone in the course of Soviet industrialization. The 'new' intelligentsia of the 1960s was formed in the 1930s and 1940s from a socially heterogeneous amalgam of remnants of the old intelligentsia and the newly educated offspring of the workers and petty-bourgeoisie. Often as not Jewish, they were 'very democratic' in their temper.[96] Further, the new 'democratic' intelligentsia had access to and was exposed to the Marxist classics, particularly Lenin. As we shall see, in the hands of revisionist historians in particular, the classics proved to be the most iconoclastic and, ultimately, subversive of texts.

The long-standing focus on the dissidents of the 1960s and 1970s also neglects to take into account other factors at work, both objective and subjective, which necessarily generated opposition from within the official intelligentsia.[97] The Soviet intelligentsia reflected the inherent contradictoriness of Soviet social development. A growing elite, that was disproportionately educated compared to social needs and political constraints, it was trapped in a 'funnel' that constricted untapped intellectual potential.[98] The resulting vocational frustration was translated into censure of the systemic constrictions on intellectual production, even in the most favoured intellectual sphere, the physical sciences. The famous physicist P. L. Kapitsa expressed succinctly this frustration in his letters to Khrushchev written in the mid-1950s:

Science that is really at the cutting-edge is that which, in studying the specific regularities of our natural environment, seeks and creates fundamentally new directions in the development of the material and spiritual culture of the society ... and in the process changes the make-up of our way of life.

The timid and indifferent attitude of the [scientist] to new, fundamental problems is not accidental. It is related to the fact that ... he has been intimidated, very often 'punished' for nothing, and has come to be increasingly valued as a 'servant rather than a thinker'. This situation has arisen because *the work of the scientist has been evaluated by bureaucratic methods and not the scientific community*.[99]

Kapitsa's complaints conform precisely to what Rudolf Bahro conceptualizes as the 'underutilization of the subjective productive forces' under 'proto socialism'. The state, Bahro writes, 'hierarchically organized as "knowledge-power"', institutionalizes 'absorbed consciousness' while atomizing 'surplus consciousness'.[100] This underutilization of intellectual potential in the late 1950s and the 1960s was symptomatic of a profound structural crisis based on the inability of the 'administrative-command system' to make the leap from extensive to intensive development. This crisis was manifested by the inability of the economic system to translate scientific innovation into industrial development; to realize the potential of the 'scientific-technical revolution'. By the early 1960s the administrative-command system had 'exhausted its possibilities'.[101]

This systemic crisis was compounded by the refusal of the apparatus to incorporate reconsideration of the principles of Marxism–Leninism, actually encouraged by the party leadership itself, into a broader reconceptualization of the model of socialist development inherited from the 1930s and 1940s. This, too, was symptomatic of the *apparat*'s authoritarian contempt for intellectual life. For the *apparat* in the early 1960s, brimming with utopian enthusiasm for the imminent transition to communism, social scientists were seen, and felt themselves, to be mere 'handmaidens' of politics.[102] They were excluded from any meaningful contribution to national decision-making. Moreover, this resentment against bureaucratic tutelage was exacerbated by the intelligentsia's sense of professional inferiority *vis-à-vis* its Western counterparts, whom it also sought to emulate.[103] This resentment was no doubt increased by the contact with Western intellectuals that was encouraged during the Khrushchev era.

That dissent amongst physical scientists might be encouraged by tensions between their social status and bureaucratic impingement on their day-to-day work should come as no surprise; and nor therefore that an outstanding atomic physicist such as Sakharov should emerge as a leading dissident.[104] Given the nature of their education in the principles of Marxist philosophy, no matter how vulgarized, there was always the danger that physical scientists might draw larger sociopolitical conclusions from the restrictions placed on their work. This potential was even more pronounced in the case of social scientists: for them socio-political generalizations were an immanent component of their work. Indeed, it could be argued that given the imposed framework of Marxism–Leninism Soviet social scientists were more likely to embark on the road to critical thinking, if the political space for this developed, than their Western colleagues for whom in the main grand social theories were anathema. Wariness on the part of CPSU *apparatchiki* of this latent danger of the social sciences, the historical sciences in particular, undoubtedly goes a long way to explaining the particularly tight rein kept on social scientists.

The very attempt of the CPSU to turn the natural and social sciences into instruments of ideological subordination necessarily generated its own *oppozitsionist'*. In part there was a moral factor at work here. An *intelligent* must be at ease with his or her conscience. There cannot be any divorce between professional activity and private beliefs. The curbing of the latter in favour of the former transforms the *intelligent* into a *chinovnik* – a bureaucrat. This tension was constantly present for the Soviet creative and scientific intelligentsia. Both 'art and science demand integrity'; accordingly their practitioners constantly chafed against the bit of bureaucratic subjugation, which was by definition hostile to the liberating potential and the 'internal logic' of their production.[105] As the Lysenko phenomenon demonstrated, the scientistic discourse of *partiinost'* could reduce even the physical sciences to a mere buttress of political authority.[106] It is hardly surprising then, given the 'intense historicism of Soviet politics',[107] that historical science fared worst of all at the hands of the Central Committee departments which policed it.

More than a few observers have made the point that in any 'totalitarian' society, culture, in the sense of creative activity, becomes both a refuge from official politics and a functional surrogate for political resistance. In the face of bureaucratic repression those intellectual interests that are most distant from the official ideology, such as art and philosophy, can become a safe haven for opposition, and, because they assume political significance that they might not otherwise have, a danger for the regime.[108] This presented Soviet-type regimes with an inescapable contradiction. Every attempt to restrict the scope of legitimate discussion, that is, to enlarge the number of taboos, only intensified the political sensitivity of the subject matter at hand. In the long run such a policy was necessarily counter-productive because it only politicized domains that, left to their own devices, might well have remained politically marginal. As Stephen Cohen has succinctly put it:

> Imposing a ban on historical controversies caused them to fester and intensify; making the past forbidden made it doubly alluring; monopolizing historical legitimacy for the political leadership diminished it; politicizing history historicized politics.[109]

Given its sensitivity, history, especially party history, could never be politically marginal; but within the discipline of historical science, as we shall see, seemingly tangential fields could be very subversive.

Growing intellectual non-conformism had its roots in more than the vague disenchantment of the highly educated. It was a function of the proletarianization of intellectual labour; itself a function of knowledge becoming a crucial productive force in advanced industrial society.[110] Soviet authorities themselves boasted about the realities of intellectual proletarianization as the basis of a latter-day *smychka* (alliance) between the intelligentsia and the workers and peasants. Proletarianization of the intelligentsia saw a general improvement in the living standards of the mass of the intelligentsia during the 1950s and 1960s. However, it was accompanied by increased 'exploitation' and a relative decline of its living standards, particularly of its elite, in comparison to the industrial working class.[111] Moreover, this relative income decline of the most highly qualified (candidates and doctors of sciences) strengthened the tendency towards the bureaucratization of intellectual life, because administrative posts were better rewarded.[112]

This 'social degradation' of the intelligentsia was not homogeneous, geographically or socially. In Moscow privileges, such as travel, were more readily available than in, say, Leningrad.[113] At the same time, however, the Moscow intelligentsia, who lived in the very shadow of political and academic power, were more easily surveilled than their Leningrad colleagues.[114] Further, this degradation was most visited upon the 'new middle strata' that formed an 'aristocracy' of intellectual labour.

Caught between a 'statocracy' to which it owed its allegiance and livelihood and the mass of the intelligentsia, it had its own interests to defend, not least of which was its professional autonomy from its own patrons. According to Kagarlitsky, the

> political ideal of the middle strata is a very moderate reformism ... Consequently the middle strata, as the intermediate link between the statocracy and the [mass] intelligentsia, form that field in society where a bitter struggle is constantly being waged, 'for the souls of men', between the government ideologists and the dissidents.[115]

Viewed in these terms we can begin to see the socio-political basis for the emergence of revisionist historians within the Academy of Sciences. As a component of the middle strata this community of scholars was pushed into an oppositionist stance, if only initially in defence of professional autonomy. With the maturation of a more sophisticated community, which welcomed the Khrushchevite thaw that followed the cruel winter of Stalinism, there was always the danger for the apparatus that such politicization might go beyond the bounds of mere professionalism; the intellectual community might begin to voice publicly their concerns and aspirations. In other words, that the scholars might become *intelligenty*. Indeed, as we shall see, this is precisely what did occur.

The focus of Western sovietology on the dissident phenomenon was based in good part on scepticism about the possibility, and desirability, of reform of communism; that is, scepticism about a loyal opposition developing among the Soviet intelligentsia. In hindsight, this scepticism seems little more than a prejudice of the cold war. A more fundamental methodological question is at stake here, however: what was it about the internal structure and organization of intellectual activity that seemingly necessarily generated dissent within an outwardly conformist official intelligentsia?

We have encountered some of the macro factors immediately above. Two decades ago the dissident Hungarian sociologists Bence and Kis drew attention to the seemingly innate capacity of the intelligentsia in Soviet-type societies to 'create its own ideology and its own culture, and even its own counter-culture and embryonic counter institutions' in the face of the most systematic policing. Paradoxically, it was the extreme institutionalization of intellectual life, the very purpose of which was to impede the intelligentsia's capacity to influence public opinion or generate 'autonomous ideologies',[116] that created a community with a shared science and culture. This community constituted a 'public sphere' that, in the absence of autonomous political organization, served as a 'functional substitute for political discussion' for its participants.[117] Despite, or even because of, the extremely hierarchical, bureaucratically orchestrated world they inhabited, elements of the intelligentsia were 'still capable of forming and maintaining a relatively high-level social group consciousness'.

The 'institutionalization of dissent' was the unintended side-effect of the regime's need to accumulate scientific capital as a whole in its drive for modernization, even if it stunted or distorted particular disciplines along the way. By erecting a barrier between the 'general public sphere' and the 'inner public sphere of the academic community' a 'relatively free flow of information inside the academic community' could be maintained.[118] Such relative academic freedom obtained least of all within the historical profession. Nevertheless, as this study demonstrates, during the 1960s a community of revisionist historians, accentuated by their enforced divorce from public discourse, was created that provided a site for intellectual exchange and, ultimately, growth. In effect, administrative tutelage over academic life cohered the genuine intellectuals in a unique way compared with other social groups. It created the 'functional equivalent' of independent political organizations in which,

> the relatively broad extent of academic communication ... enables ideological and political allusions within the limits of the regime's ideological tolerance to be encoded and decoded regularly. The ideas which emerge from these decoded signals are, for the intelligentsia, the equivalent of a relatively high-level social ideology. Hence the phenomenon – which often seems so bizarre to Western eyes – of the authorities ruthlessly persecuting certain cultural or scientific expressions which seem to be completely innocent, to judge from their direct content, but which nevertheless keep surging up and defying repression.[119]

Thus the microcosms within the mainstream intelligentsia, formed for the discussion of seemingly innocuous, professional questions, provided fertile soil for the flowering of potentially subversive questions. Such questions, even if they were not intentionally political, could not but encroach upon the boundaries of the intellectual discourse in which they were couched. Such was the fragility of bureaucratic rule, for which *'authority'* was the 'principle of its knowledge',[120] that it could brook no challenge to orthodoxy, especially from within that orthodoxy. Nor could it afford to have such heterodoxy spill over into the public sphere.

The internal dynamics of Soviet intellectual life, which were conducive to generating non-conformism in the late-1950s, need to be situated in the post-Stalinist context. In the absence of the coercion that had characterized extreme Stalinism, reform communism looked to the creative and scientific intelligentsia as an ally in its struggle with the hardened Stalinists. During the ensuing consolidation of post-Stalinism, in the Soviet case a process that began with the ousting of Khrushchev, although the boundaries of the taboo topics had been narrowed, boundaries still existed. Those who did not accept the new boundaries were marginalized, either by the academic authorities or by a process of 'internal' marginalization whereby the most ideologically sensitive topics were avoided. Such self-censorship, however, generated pressures for a more public expression of non-conformism *outside* the official sphere.[121]

This contest between orthodoxy and non-conformism was not simply a product of a clash between the genuine scholars and political authority, it also expressed tensions *within* the intellectual establishment. The mandarinate were anxious to lead a quiet life, not giving political authority any excuse to intervene in their sphere of influence. Fearful as they were of any possibility of the reimposition of terror aimed at preventing the crystallization of heterodoxy, the mandarinate themselves 'erect[ed] a screen over non-conformism as a social phenomenon'.[122] However, by policing, and thereby marginalizing, their deviant, often younger, colleagues the guardians of academic orthodoxy succeeded not only in reproducing non-conformism but also in providing the social soil in which ultimately dissidence could take root.

From the mechanics of the relationship outlined, it is clear that the dissident phenomenon that appeared in the late-1960s was in every sense the offspring of the virulent non-conformism that emerged within the mainstream intelligentsia during the previous decade. It was the stifling of the latter by administrative intervention, coupled with the dashed expectations of the reformist intellectuals, that gave rise to the dissidents and their underground culture which was primarily a derivative of the non-conformist counter-culture. It is therefore no exaggeration to say that the 'illegal' culture of the dissidents was a 'prolongation and product of legal culture'.[123]

Of course, this is at most a skeletal representation of the wellsprings of Soviet intellectual dissent; these need to be fleshed out by historical analysis. Above all, such an objective explanation needs to incorporate the subjective, but no less real, strivings of the intellectuals themselves not just for professional autonomy but to attain intellectual integrity – with all the implications that bore for the relationship between the Soviet political elite and the intellectual community as a whole. It is this relationship we now need to explore.

Intellectuals, the state and civil society

In order to capture the precise status and function of the Soviet intelligentsia in relation to political authority, or in Nettl's terms the relationship between the practitioners of the ideas of 'scope' and the bureaucracy, we must go beyond the ahistorical sociology of the mythical 'eternal intellectual'.[124] What is required is an approach that locates intellectual activity and its bearers in the context of the 'social organization of labour, of the technical and technological standards of production and of the class structure of a given socio-economic formation'.[125] Such a sociological approach, despite first impressions, is not at all at odds with Nettl's call to define types of intellectuals by types of ideas. The point is to locate the functionalism, or disfunctionalism, of certain idea types and those who articulate them, in the dynamics of Soviet society.

Antonio Gramsci has provided the most developed analysis of the relationship between intellectuals, the state and society, albeit on the basis of Italian capitalism. According to Gramsci, every new ruling class generates its 'organic' intellectuals. Their function, in concert with the 'traditional' intellectuals of the superseded mode of production, is to rationalize and organize the hegemony of this ruling class. Their task is to give the dominant class 'homogeneity and an awareness of its own function not only in the economic but also in the social and political fields'. The relationship between the intellectuals, the dominant and the dominated classes is not direct; it is ' "mediated" by the whole fabric of society and by the complex of superstructures of which the intellectuals are the "functionaries" '. Accordingly, the intellectuals secure the political dominance of the ruling class in two 'superstructural' spheres: that of 'civil society' and that of the state or 'political society'. In the former sphere they exercise a consensual function; in the latter, a coercive function. Thus the intellectuals are the 'dominant group's hegemonic "deputies" exercising the subaltern functions of social hegemony and political government'.[126]

Despite the singularity of the nature of elite rule in the Soviet Union, Gramsci provides important insights into the role of intellectuals that we can bring to bear on Soviet society in which, even more than its Russian predecessor, 'the state was everything' while 'civil society was primordial and gelatinous.'[127] In fact, Stalin virtually obliterated civil society. The dramatic shift to the fore of the coercive apparatuses of the state in the 1930s was accompanied by the forced integration of the traditional and new intelligentsia into the state, resulting in the most extreme bureaucratization of intellectual life.[128] These 'organic intellectuals' who survived, deprived of any independent livelihood, increasingly carried out their hegemonic functions in the academic and governmental realm. This gave rise to what we might call a 'collective organic *intellektual*' in the guise of the CPSU – the negation of any genuine intellectual. Under Khrushchev, as the coercive functions of the state ceded place to its hegemonic functions, the locus of power shifted from the secret police to the party-state, which became the collective *directoire* of opinion and the practices of everyday life.[129]

Even this enhanced role for the 'hegemonic deputies' of the Soviet bureaucracy, ensconced in the 'ideological apparatuses' of the party-state,[130] did not see the withdrawal of the apparatuses of surveillance and coercion. In the stunted civil society that was the Soviet Union, the 'imaginary and information apparatuses' were underdeveloped. Lacking an 'omnipresent' media for the purveying of knowledge as a commodity, which in an advanced capitalist society makes the power of the 'intellectuals of scope' so discreetly effective, Soviet political authority resorted to the far more primitive weapon of an 'omnipresent party'.[131] As the 'collective organic *intellektual*', the CPSU socialized and legitimized the rule of the bureaucratic elite, while simultaneously denying a public platform to any potential interlocutor.

For Gramsci, the organic intellectuals allied with the ruling elite are the 'organizers of the practices of everyday life'. More than mere symbol-makers or the disseminators of false ideologies to secure the allegiance of the populace, they elaborate and purvey a discourse that makes it extremely difficult for the non-hegemonized to challenge the prevailing form of knowledge. It is the task of the organic intellectuals to banish any counter-hegemonic views that arise to the 'realm of non-knowledge' so that 'only authorized or expert knowledge is heard'. By such means a self-verifying discourse, 'science in the service of ignorance', is set in place.[132] True to this vocation, maintenance of the ideational consensus by the CPSU involved more than the crude falsification of history or just the administrative denial of a dais to the genuine intellectual interlocutor. It also required a particularly rigid discourse, Marxism–Leninism, within which (let alone outside) it was extremely difficult to challenge the ruling ideology. As Debray so elegantly puts it, 'there can be no interlocutor if, for want of an autonomous logos, there is no interpellation'.[133]

Not for nothing has Stalinist Marxism been called a 'secular religion'.[134] This doctrine was in every sense the latter-day counterpart to medieval theology, with its own dogmas and its own inquisitions to defend them. The difference between Soviet doctrine and medieval theology lay in the organization and sites of their respective discourses. Under feudalism the bishopric addressed both prince and populace from the pulpit. In the Soviet case bishop and prince were one, so the pulpit was located within the Kremlin while the Jesuits resided in the Institute of Marxism–Leninism and the Academy of Sciences. There were located the sites of intellectual power that 'structured the intellectual force-field'.[135]

If we are to understand the particular role that historians (as a subset of the official intelligentsia) and their craft had in Soviet society, this can only be done in relation to the defining features of its social structure. Here the analogy just invoked between feudalism and Soviet-style socialism has some utility. Notwithstanding the vast gulf between pre-industrial feudalism and the highly industrialized Soviet Union, in both social systems the political rule of an 'estate', rather than a class, was at stake. It was Leon Trotsky, and following him Isaac Deutscher, who elaborated the view that the *nomenklatura* constituted a privileged bureaucratic 'caste' that had usurped political power over a society in transition from capitalism to socialism.[136] The Soviet bureaucratic elite was akin to the clergy in pre-capitalist Europe. As such, the Soviet bureaucracy lacked the solid social foundations that possession of productive property, the defining feature of all previous ruling classes, provided. What made the political dominance of this 'estate' particularly fragile and vulnerable to upheaval from below (as confirmed by the 'velvet revolutions' of 1989 and 1991) was lack of its own, discrete ideology such as the nationalism in which the capitalist classes of the West have usually cloaked themselves. The peculiar vulnerability of this latter-day clerical caste was registered by 'ideological monolithism, hunting out heresies, excommunications and scholastic dogmatism'.[137] Moreover, this vulnerability of the Soviet bureaucratic elite was compounded by the fact that it drew its ideology not from religion but from the well of Marxism. Even in its highly-contaminated Soviet form, this was an inherently critical outlook that always had the potential to be turned against the Soviet elite themselves.

If the CPSU was the 'collective organic *intellektual'* then Soviet historians could rightly be deemed the 'managers of legitimation' *par excellence*;[138] and it is legitimacy, as Max Weber suggested, that makes the difference between power and authority. In this sense, far from being a species apart from their counterparts in other countries, Soviet historians have played a very similar socio-political role to historians elsewhere, both past and present, albeit working in quite different social environments.

It is worth reminding ourselves that the historical profession, as it emerged in Europe and the United States, has its own history, and a recent one at that – it is barely more than a century old. The pedigree 'historian', however, is considerably older than this, though not necessarily more distinguished. Everywhere historians (whether endowed with that sobriquet or not) have in the main been the 'enhancers of the realm'.[139] That which first passed for written history – dynastic succession, royal genealogies, boasts of divine favour – recorded variously by scribes, poets, mandarins, monastic chroniclers or courtiers, provided 'obvious ways of consolidating rulers' morale and asserting their legitimacy *vis-à-vis* their subjects'. Because historians were so often called upon to be 'flatterers' of the community to which they owed allegiance and livelihood, from the very start the boundaries between history and myth were very narrow indeed.[140]

Even with the establishment of modern historical practice these boundaries are yet to be overcome. On the contrary, the crucial role played by historians in giving shape to the idea of the modern nation-state, has injected even more vitality into 'mythistory'. The institutionalization of historical writing in the universities, which gave comfort to the colonization of the world by a few dominant Western powers in the latter part of the nineteenth century, has its *quid pro quo* in the twentieth: many ex-colonies themselves, in their pursuit of modern nationhood, moved quickly to establish indigenous historical schools.[141] Likewise, the Soviet Stalinist quest for modernity, albeit under the banner of 'communism', necessitated the creation of a loyal cohort of historians, though by draconian methods, who would celebrate the 'national communist' idea.

Eric Hobsbawm has pointed to the singular contribution of historians to the 'invention of tradition' that has underpinned the national phenomenon:

> All invented traditions so far as possible, use history as a legitimator of action and cement of group cohesion ... The history which became part of the fund of knowledge or the ideology of nation, state or movement is not what has actually been preserved in popular memory, but what has been selected, written, pictured, popularized and institutionalized by those whose function it is to do so ... All historians, whatever their objectives, are engaged in this process in as much as they contribute, consciously or not, to the creation, dismantling and restructuring of images of the past which belong *not only to the world of specialist investigation but to the public sphere of man as a political being.*[142]

Historians, then, Soviet or otherwise, are by definition engaged in 'exercises in social engineering' which from the written page ultimately reach into the heart of civil society. Moreover, despite the diffused organization of historical study in the West, in contrast to the visibly policed historiography of the former Soviet Union, in both cases the state has organized and built an image of the past in terms that have been necessarily consonant with the ruling interests, be they class or bureaucratic. In both cases too, notwithstanding their particular mechanisms for organizing the production of written history, we can concur with the proposition that the past is 'an essential factor in the political relationship of forces'.[143]

If, however, orthodox Soviet historiography was not qualitatively different, in terms of its larger socio-political functions, from that produced under other social systems, why was the interface between politics and written history so much more manifest, and explosive, in the Soviet Union than in the West? A useful way to approach this question is to distinguish between ' "history as political ideology" ' and ' "politics as history", that is the practice of politics being in part based on a specific historical view of the past'.[144] The latter formula captures well the peculiar centrality of historical science in Soviet politics (this peculiarity is, of course, an expression of the structural specificities of Soviet society and the draconian, idiosyncratic mechanisms for administering historiography that flowed from it). Without recognizing this distinctive Soviet feature of 'politics as history' and, vice versa, 'history as politics', it is difficult to grasp the political implications represented by the challenge of revisionist historiography to orthodox historiography.

Bearing this distinction in mind, we can broadly endorse the functions that Nancy Heer attributed to Soviet historiography as a 'political sub-system', even if she veered towards the view that Soviet historiography played a unique political role. Heer, differentiating between the formally articulated objectives of Soviet historiography and its informal, unstated functions, identified its formal functions as twofold: first, as a repository of tradition and legend and, second, as an exhorter and agitator. Its informal functions she identified as legitimation, as a rationalization of policies, as a 'barometer' of the political climate and elite relationships, as a site of ideological and theoretical discussion and as a 'political weapon' in the hands of a dominant faction or individual.[145]

Heer quite rightly singled out the written history of the CPSU as having a special function due to the 'semimystical status' of the party as the 'chosen instrument of history' and its direct relationship with politics. Hence the catechism status of official histories of the CPSU, viz., the *Short Course* and its successors.[146] To this we could add that precisely because of the centrality of *party* historiography to the political process it is necessary to explore the terrain of Soviet historiography that lay beyond the bounds of party history. When the Soviet historiographical stream came up against the dam of party history then it found other channels within which to move forward.

Of all those functions that Heer attributed to Soviet historiography the most crucial for this book is its unstated legitimating function for the Soviet bureaucratic elite, although from time to time the other functions she identified are brought to bear. Given that we are dealing with historical writing at an elite, rather than a mass level, we are examining legitimation – and conversely, delegitimation – in terms of the relationship between the ruling caste and its own intellectual elite, rather than in terms of the relationship between the bureaucratic elite and the populace as a whole.[147]

Sooner or later, however, the question of legitimation within the elite had to become a question of popular legitimacy. In part this was because the symbols and rituals popularly employed by the CPSU were derivative of the officially sanctioned historiography, which was the immediate concern of a narrow layer of professional historians. In the first place, however, elite legitimacy, and accordingly elite stability, was an outcome of the necessary relationship between the Soviet political elite and its official intelligentsia, that is, the *intellektualy*. That relationship has been eloquently formulated by George Schöpflin as one in which the official intelligentsia acted as a 'mirror' in which the rulers sought a positive reflection of themselves. When, however, that mirror began to project a less flattering image of the rulers into the 'public sphere', which was controlled by the intelligentsia 'through their hegemonial control of language', it began to confuse the rulers. 'This confusion was then transmitted through the hierarchy, upwards and downwards, until the ruling party lost its cohesion and became prey to self-doubt.'[148]

Such a scenario existed only *in posse* in the Soviet Union of the 1960s but, in so far as orthodox historians were the brightest part of the intellectual mirror of legitimacy, the emergence of revisionists within their ranks constituted the first tarnish of delegitimation. It is in this sense that we can see the rapid formation of a small, but important community of genuine intellectuals, spurred on by the Twentieth Congress, striving to caste off their old doctrinal fetters, as indicators of a gathering crisis of ideological hegemony for the bureaucratic elite.

2
The Twentieth Party Congress and History

> 'The Twentieth Congress was a dizzying gasp of freedom. Initially, strictly speaking, it was a settling of accounts with Stalin by the method of Stalinist historiography itself.'
>
> M. Ya. Gefter, Moscow, March 1992

Khrushchev's denunciation of Stalin in his 'secret' speech at the February 1956 Twentieth Congress of the CPSU sent shock waves through Soviet society and the international communist movement. The dethronement of Stalin could hardly leave Soviet historiography untouched; but even before the main shock there were several tremors among politicians and historians alike. At the congress itself A. I. Mikoyan, while bemoaning the theoretical poverty of Soviet social science as a whole, singled out party and Soviet history as its 'most backward' branch.[1] The principal editor of *Voprosy istorii*, Academician Anna Pankratova, attributed the oversimplification, embellishing and modernization of the past by historians to the 'cult of the personality', without mentioning Stalin by name.[2] This was an understatement. The triumph of Stalinism had been a tragedy for history – the 'most political of all the sciences' as M. N. Pokrovsky, the leading Marxist historian in the 1920s, had rightly deemed it. The General Secretary's menacing admonition to the editorial board of *Proletarskaya revolyutsiya* back in 1931 that scholarship, history especially, should be nothing less than 'party scholarship' had taken a terrible toll.[3]

Partiinost' (party spirit) as advocated by Stalin meant far more than Lenin's injunction that a class perspective was the necessary basis of objective knowledge.[4] *Partiinost'* meant that the leadership of the communist party should be the sole arbiter of historical truth; 'deeds', not documents unearthed by 'archive rats', should be the only test for party history; certain principles, such as Lenin's Bolshevism, should be axiomatic, not problems open to further interrogation.[5] Nor was it sufficient to pursue a Marxist approach; it had to be a *party* approach to knowledge.[6] Moreover, doctrinal orthodoxy was determined by the views of the party leadership at any given time. Even recourse to the Marxist classics, without the imprimatur of the party, was regarded as potentially subversive.[7] Indeed, given the increasing merger between party and state, dissent from the party line was tantamount to disloyalty to the state. *Partiinost'* reigned then, whether you were a party intellectual or not.[8] Wrong theory, Stalin's henchman Lazar Kaganovich maintained, threatened wrong practice.[9] Henceforth scholarship had a purely instrumental function: it had to reinforce the prevailing party line. Any other reason for scholarship, especially that which challenged received truths, was simply 'rotten liberalism'. Historians, in the militarist argot of Soviet social science, were reduced to mere conscripts on the 'historical front', required to maintain 'class vigilance' against 'Trotskyites and all other falsifiers of the history of our Party'.[10] Thus Stalin's personal intervention into party historical scholarship unleashed a sea-change in Soviet intellectual life as a whole,[11] the repercussions of which would be felt for more than half a century.

The relatively pluralist, autonomous, academic life that had generated a veritable golden age of Soviet Marxism in the 1920s,[12] was abruptly displaced by a draconian tutelage over scholarship and culture in general and historical writing in particular that stunted, distorted and scarred intellectual life. Stalin's war on the historians destroyed the great traditions of Russian historical writing, represented above all by S. M. Solovev (1820–79) and V. O. Klyuchevsky (1841–1911). Instead of the wide-ranging, prodigiously researched, multi-volume histories that were works of literature as much as scholarship, Soviet historians, cramped by their narrow specializations, relied on collective works that were conceptually homogenous and devoid of any literary merit.[13]

Despite all the vicious rhetoric directed at the alleged vilifiers of Bolshevism, the chief victims of Stalin's campaign in the late-1930s were not so much the older generation of historians but younger Marxist neophytes.[14] Just as the old Bolsheviks were to find themselves condemned as traitors by former Mensheviks and even by opponents of the October Revolution, so the devastating demise of the 'Pokrovsky school' after 1934 was accompanied by the restoration of the once reviled older generation of pre-revolution historians, such as S. V. Bakhrushin, Ye. V. Tarle, D. M. Petreshuvsky and B. D. Grekov, though behind each of them stood a party commissar-historian.[15] The decimation of the historical profession in the 1930s, which was most pronounced among modern, especially party, historians[16] was part and parcel of a broader campaign to finally set in concrete the Stalinist notion of 'socialism in one country' at the expense of internationalism.

Just as Pokrovsky's much maligned 'economic materialism' was displaced by 'political voluntarism', so Slavophilism and Great Russian chauvinism surged to the fore in both politics and scholarship. Encouraged by the Great Patriotic War, Stalin basked in the resurrected glory of Peter the Great. Meanwhile, after October 1946, Ukrainian history was declared a 'bourgeois nationalist' deviation. Henceforth it was subsumed within the framework of Russian history.[17] Great Russian chauvinism reached its dreadful climax with the 'anti-cosmopolitan' campaign of 1948–49.[18] Intended to forestall the emergence of opposition engendered by postwar expectations, 'anti-cosmopolitanism' spilled over into anti-Semitism.[19] Those historians who had survived the killing fields of the 1930s and the war, which cut down some of the most talented, young, male, historians of the Pokrovsky school, now faced a new trauma that brought many prominent, mainly Jewish, historians to their knees – and with them the discipline as a whole. These were, in Mikhail Gefter's stark words,[20] 'terrible years, that witnessed the murder and suicide of historical thought. Stalinism was already in its death agony, which naturally took its toll on history. The atmosphere was sinister.'[21] But underlying what appears to be an academic pogrom was a struggle for positions within the academic apparatus; outsiders using their party membership to dislodge the incumbents in order to secure the social privileges that went with such appointments.[22] The ensconcement of 'servile incompetents' was to take its toll on historical science for the next four decades.[23]

Hard on the heels of the anti-cosmopolitan campaign the 'neo-communist state-juridical school' of history, newly-forged to serve the Great Russian 'national-state idea',[24] reached its logical conclusion with the debates about the periodization of Russian feudalism and capitalism. Ivan the Terrible's *oprichina* (administrative-military elite) was hailed as progressive in so far as it strengthened the Russian centralized state, a position not even the most reactionary tsarist historian had countenanced.[25] This was the progeny of a hybrid Russification of Soviet history. Ultra-chauvinism was crossed with an approach that, notwithstanding the gauche economism of the *Short Course*, elevated the communist party to the *de facto* demi-urge of Soviet history.

By the time of the Twentieth Congress the social status of history and historians had reached a nadir; 25 years of inquisition, intimidation and enforced intellectual autarky had seen to that. In the main, only those students who had failed to get into mathematics or the physical sciences, as a last resort, turned to history.[26] If the profession as a whole was degraded, then those who chose party history were the lowest of the low. Generally the products of the Higher Party School, the least able, and lacking any foreign languages that might expose them to new ideas, they were condemned to be the mouthpieces of the *apparat* and the latest *Kommunist* directives to the footsoldiers on the historical front. Yet even in the sombre landscape of Soviet historiography there were a few bright spots, notably in ancient and medieval history, traditional strengths of Russian, prerevolutionary historiography, and also in archaeology.

Moreover, it was an idiosyncrasy of prerevolutionary historical writing and historical consciousness that they were closely allied with politics – a tradition that was maintained in post-October historiography. Historians had played a major, self-conscious role in shaping Russian historical consciousness.[27] Yet, despite appearances, Soviet historiography always had a rhythm of its own, a 'relative autonomy', an 'asynchrony', that made it more than the plaything of politics.[28] History had been integral to the October Revolution from the very start. As Gefter has put it, an 'expropriation of the expropriators' in the realm of historical consciousness, that entailed reevaluating the past and situating the revolution in world history.[29] In the 1920s, when historical writing and research was at its freest, historiography was an essential component of the political process but certainly not the slave of party resolutions that Stalin later sought to make it. Despite the state's 'totalitarian' strivings to bring the historians to heel, a few glimmers of the former majesty of Russian historical writing survived. An example of this is Academician Militsa Nechkina's study of the Decembrists published in 1954.[30] Enough fragments from these traditions remained among historians for the death of Stalin and the stimulus of the Twentieth Congress to embolden them to begin to reassert their autonomy and their place in the polity – and, if necessary, against it.

The *Short Course* paradigm

A crucial component of the culture of historical writing in the USSR was the hallowed place accorded to officially endorsed textbooks. If anything embodied the subordination of history to politics in the Soviet Union it was the biblical status of the textbook. It established *the* paradigm within which all other historical writing was confined.[31] The most notorious textbook was the *History of the Communist Party of the Soviet Union (Bolsheviks): Short Course*. Published in 1938, the *Short Course* was actually edited by a commission of the CPSU Central Committee, and endorsed by the Central Committee, but its authorship was popularly attributed to Stalin himself. Over the next ten years, 30 million copies of the *Short Course* were published, despite the war and shortages of paper.[32]

Hailed as 'the encyclopaedia of Marxism–Leninism' by Kaganovich,[33] the *Short Course* was the codified culmination of the merciless '*auto-da-fé*' against the historians set in train in 1931 by Stalin's letter to the editors of *Proletarskaya revolyutsiya*.[34] On 14 November 1938 a special resolution of the Central Committee declared the *Short Course* the 'only', 'official' guide to Marxism–Leninism and party history, thereby prohibiting 'any arbitrary interpretations' of these fundamental questions. The resolution proclaimed an 'end to the arbitrariness and confusion' and to the 'superfluity of different opinions' that prevailed in previous textbooks.[35] Stalin himself was lauded by the *Short Course* as the sole successor to Lenin as a Marxist theoretician; everybody else, needless to say, was relegated to the dustbin of history as 'foreign bourgeois agents', 'spies', 'wreckers', 'diversionists' or 'assassins'.[36] Thus was established that party 'monopoly' in historiography, the counterpart of its monopoly of power,[37] that 'fettered' historical and theoretical thinking for the next 50 years.[38] The poverty of Soviet historical writing, laid bare during *perestroika*, was a legacy of the retention during the 1960s and 1970s of the 'false schemas' of the *Short Course*, which, though challenged, were never completely eradicated.[39] At the height of *perestroika*, Yury Afanas'ev could justifiably despair that 'In the past decade conceptually we have barely gone beyond the limits of the *Short Course*.'[40]

Notwithstanding its explicit denials,[41] the *Short Course* itself was the ultimate example of the reduction of Marxism to a political catechism. The *Short Course* effectively reduced Soviet history to party history and it reduced party history to the struggle against 'opportunism' of every stripe.[42] This crude celebration of the triumph of Stalinism resorted to outright falsification of Stalin's role in the October Revolution and the construction of 'socialism'. Former comrades were calumniated as 'counter-revolutionaries' or simply omitted from the script, so that Stalin alone dominated the historical stage. It was this specious exultation of Stalin that was the basis of Khrushchev's attack on the 'cult of the personality' at the Twentieth Congress. Soviet history was, in the words of an anonymous Soviet historian, presented in a 'panegyrical spirit', 'undiluted' by 'difficulties, mistakes, and shortcomings' and 'written in the form of expounding axioms, which required no proof and did not have to be understood but memorized, learned by heart'.[43] In short, the *Short Course* was the Soviet equivalent of the Whig interpretation of history: praising revolutions, 'provided they have been successful', and emphasizing 'certain principles of progress in the past' with the aim of producing 'a story which is the ratification if not the glorification of the present.'[44] The *Short Course*, however, took this genre to an unprecedented low; the definitive codification of what Trotsky, himself literally air-brushed out of the photographic record of Soviet history, justly reviled as the 'Stalin school of falsification'.

But the *Short Course* approach was more than falsification of facts; it was a method, a 'method of omission':

> A very limited and specific selection of facts and events, placed in a standard scheme, in conformity with Party directives ... Anything not specifically declared as 'relevant' was passed over in silence. Historiography was nonexistent outside of the Party directives.[45]

The hollowness of the *Short Course* method derived not only from its false method of representation. Its linear, predetermined approach to Soviet history was but an extension of the *Short Course's* theory and philosophy of history as a whole. Historical materialism, which was deemed to be the application of the principles of dialectical materialism to the history of society,[46] was given the attributes of natural science. The history of society was every bit as knowable as natural history and therefore open to the same objective and precise verification as, for example, biology. The reason for this was simple: the development of society was just as 'lawful' as that of nature.[47]

It was in this spirit of history as a mere manifestation of dialectical materialism in the social realm, subject to the same lawful processes as nature, that Marx's famous 'Preface' to the 'Critique of Political Economy' was invoked as the 'essence of historical materialism'.

Marx's proposition that history is a sequence of socio-economic formations resulting from the contradictions between the forces and relations of production was seized upon by the *Short Course* as a description of reality. A number of methodological implications followed from this approach. Firstly, history was reduced to an 'objective logical system'[48] in which the driving force of social change was the development of the productive forces.[49] As a result the motor of social change, specifically the superseding of one socio-economic formation by another, was located in the *internal* contradictions of any given society rather than in the intrusion of external factors, such as a clash between societies.[50] Secondly, and as many historians lamented at the time of *perestroika*, 'formational reductionism' excluded the 'human factor' as the active subject of history.[51] In its place were 'pseudo-subjects':[52] forces and relations of production, labour, economic development or, at best, an anonymous, faceless *narod* (the people). Thirdly, and as a corollary to the fetishization of the productive forces, a crude, socio-economic monodeterminism was set in place in which the political and ideological superstructure was reduced to a mere epiphenomenon of a determining base. Historical science, if it was to live up to the name, had to be the history of the producers of material wealth.[53]

Above all, the long view of history was reduced to an unfolding succession of socio-economic formations that defined the stages through which each society necessarily had to pass. This was the notorious *pyatichlenka* (five-membered set), consisting consecutively of the primitive-communal, slaveholding, feudal, capitalist and socialist socio-economic formations. The *pyatichlenka* omitted other socio-economic formations alluded to by Marx, such as the Asiatic mode of production or the 'ancient mode of production'.[54] Thus the *Short Course* conception of history was essentially a species of nineteenth-century positivism founded on an objectivist, 'naturalistic-historical' approach.[55]

This deterministic, 'productionist' method and focus prevailed in Soviet historical writing, notwithstanding pronouncements on the significance of superstructural phenomena, such as 'social ideas, theories, political views and institutions', for the 'life of society' in the *Short Course* and especially in Stalin's *Marxism and Problems of Linguistics*, which appeared in 1950.[56] Stalin's blow against 'vulgar sociologism' was countered barely two years later by his reassertion of the lawfulness of social development in his *Economic Problems of Socialism in the USSR*, published in 1952.[57] 'Economic lawfulness',

Arkady Sidorov, then pro-rector of Moscow State University, duly reminded historians that same year, was primary in the historical process.[58]

The tasks set by the *Short Course* for Soviet historians flowed logically from this entire outlook. Like natural scientists they were required to study and disclose the 'laws (*zakony*) of production, the laws of the development of the productive forces and of the relations of production, and the laws of the economic development of society.'[59] Further, as the Soviet historian of medieval culture Aron Gurevich has argued, in so far as the *pyatichlenka* interpretation of socio-economic formations effectively embodied the Soviet philosophy of history, as distinct from the materialist method, in the practice of Soviet historians formational theory became 'not a means of socio-historical analysis but an aim: specific historical knowledge was called upon to confirm the truthfulness of the philisophico-historical system ... Consequently a scientific hypothesis advanced by Marx was converted into an infallible dogma.'[60]

In sum, the *Short Course* embodied a teleology, in which Soviet-style socialism was the lawful culmination of the long march of humankind. As such, Soviet society also embodied the future for other societies embarking on the road to socialism. Such a simplistic, teleological rendering of Marxism admirably fulfilled the role of what Isaac Deutscher once called 'primitive magic'. Replete as it was with the 'transmigration of political souls' from Lenin to Stalin and the demonology of 'Trotskyite-wreckers', Stalin's *Short Course* was, like Stalinism itself, the 'mongrel offspring' of a rural society that in the 1930s was going through the first convulsions of replacing the wooden plough with the tractor.[61]

Two decades later the post-Stalin Soviet Union was a rather different society, well on the road to establishing an urban, industrial, educated social order in which there was much less social space and receptivity for the sorcery of the *Short Course*.[62] The text itself, which had been so discredited at the Twentieth Congress, was replaced in 1959 by another textbook, *The History of the Communist Party of the Soviet Union*, from which the crudest examples of the old demonology were exorcised. Thus, for example, the 'white guard pigmies', 'contemptible lackeys of the fascists' and 'dregs of humankind', who allegedly made up the 'right-trotskyite bloc' that was tried and condemned in 1938, became rather more modestly 'former ideological opponents'.[63]

At the same time, however, the sections on dialectical and historical materialism from the *Short Course* were incorporated into *Fundamentals of Marxism–Leninism*. There were some obvious attempts to refine the materialist conception of history. In particular, in the wake of the repudiation of the 'cult of the personality', there was a new emphasis on the 'masses as the creators of history' as an antidote to suggestions that there was any inevitability of the 'lawfulness' of the historical process. Despite these qualifications, the basic teleological paradigm remained. This was especially so in the new textbook's treatment of the evolution of socio-economic formations which, governed as it was by the development of the productive forces, explained

> why, despite the multiplicity of concrete details and particularities, all peoples pass along a basically common path ... [So that] the people living in the more developed formation show others their future, precisely as the latter show the former their past.[64]

Above all what remained in place was a culture of historical writing in which an official textbook (a 'brick' (*kirpich*) in student slang) formally established the politically, and therefore professionally, acceptable paradigm. In the case of party history it was *The History of the Communist Party of the Soviet Union*, the various editions of which reflected shifts in domestic politics. A discussion of a draft of the third edition of the *History of the CPSU*, commissioned by the Central Committee after the October 1964 plenum dismissed Khrushchev, clearly reveals the process of revising the historical record to take into account the party's repudiation of Khrushchev, and also the more benevolent view of Stalin then emerging. Professor V. L. Ignatiev praised the latest edition for correcting the shortcomings of the second, which had 'ignored' the 30 June 1956 resolution and been too 'indiscriminate' in its criticism of the cult of Stalin. Any political figure should be accorded their positive as well as their negative contribution, he said. 'On this plane, it seems to me, it would be desirable, without padding or getting too carried away, to give a more severe criticism of the subjectivism and voluntarism of Khrushchev'.[65] For historical writing in general there was a series of textbooks published under the generic title of 'Historical Science from Congress to Congress' that set the official paradigm.[66] In this sense, notwithstanding the formal repudiation of the *Short Course* at the Twentieth Congress, and the challenge to which its paradigm was subject in the 1960s, the *Short Course* approach, in every sense of that phrase, prevailed in Soviet historical writing at least until the advent of *perestroika*.[67] Finding a way out of this conceptual cage was not as easy as might appear to outside observers, for what was at stake was not just establishing other ways of understanding, researching and writing history. It was a question of historians sloughing off a ruthlessly imposed straight jacket and generating a new historical consciousness – a process that could not occur overnight.

Unmasking the 'cult of the personality'

When Khrushchev strode to the rostrum at midnight on 24 February 1956 to deliver his ringing denunciation of Stalin, he was as much concerned to contain any possible social and political repercussions from inveighing against the once sacrosanct 'father of the peoples' as he was to expose Stalin's crimes. Khrushchev's entire explanation of Stalin's actions reflected this attempt at damage control.[68] The focus was purely on Stalin, divorced from the role of the party or its leadership, let alone any broader social forces. What analysis there was, was tantamount to a 'Great Man' theory of history, the 'cult of the personality', couched of course in Marxist–Leninist verbiage.[69] All the failings of and deviations from the ideals of October – terror, the parlous state of agriculture, the ignominy of defeats by Hitler's armies, the orgy of self-adulation – were laid at Stalin's feet. Conversely, the achievements became those of Leninism, the party or the masses; an 'inverted hero cult'.[70]

Almost immediately, however, the party leadership sought to put a cap on the destalinization process, reflecting the resilience of Stalinism, personified by Molotov, Kaganovich and Malenkov, behind the facade of 'collective leadership'. The 5 March resolution endorsing Khrushchev's report did not mention Stalin by name.[71] The 'heated discussions' about the Stalin period which subsequently took place both publicly and privately, nurtured by the millions who had returned from the gulags and the posthumous rehabilitation of millions of victims of the terror,[72] were denounced in the party press as pretexts for 'scandalous calumnies' against the overall course pursued by the party.[73] Particularly unnerved by disturbances in Poland, the leadership's retreat from the agenda of the Twentieth Congress, which had given the 'struggle' against the legacy of Stalin's regime an 'official political status',[74] was codified in the June 1956 Central Committee resolution 'On Overcoming the Cult of the Personality and its Consequences'. The resolution baulked at outright condemnation of Stalin and acknowledged his contribution to the party, the nation and the international revolutionary movement. Further, it was argued that the perseverance of a basic 'Leninist core' within the Central Committee had acted as a brake on his excesses. The same approach to Stalin remained, however. The resolution, straddling both determinism and contingency, pointed to both 'objective, specific historical conditions' and 'certain subjective factors, connected with Stalin's personal qualities' to explain the Stalin phenomenon. The stress, however, was on Stalin's 'mistakes'; the resolution pointedly repudiated any systemic explanation for Stalinism (a term that was not to enter the Soviet political lexicon for another three decades).[75]

This ambiguity on the part of the CPSU leadership concerning the Stalin phenomenon,[76] fuelled by the Polish and Hungarian upheavals of 1956 which particularly alarmed Khrushchev,[77] was a crucial element in the political environment of the revisionist historians during the late 1950s and the 1960s. As Ya. S. Drabkin, a specialist on the November 1918 German revolution and a key player in historical revisionism, has put it, in a comment coloured by the demise of the Soviet Union:

> We saw in the decisions of the Twentieth Congress a call to undertake research, but not with a view to reporting back to the Central Committee on the results of our inquiries. We hoped that we could raise those questions which concerned us; that we could critically interpret the historical path of both the Soviet Union and the world revolutionary process, which for us were closely connected phenomena. We hoped for this almost to the end of the 1960s. In that decade we placed our hopes on Khrushchev, although we saw that he by no means had a consistent outlook. On the one hand, he tried to overcome some things from the past; on the other, we saw that he was shaped by that very same past. On the one hand, he said that Stalin was a 'criminal', on the other, usually more vociferously, that he was a 'great Marxist'. Khrushchev, however, had no idea how to reconcile 'Stalin the criminal' with 'Stalin the great Marxist'. But we understood that these were irreconcilable notions. As a result, we increasingly diverged from the official party line, although we considered it our task to deepen and reinforce the line of the Twentieth Congress. We persistently requested – not demanded – that the party leadership meet us halfway and enable us to analyze the meaning of the 'cult of the personality'; a conditional term, a euphemism which glossed over the essence of the question. We requested documents and to be allowed into the archives. We complained that we were not being allowed to really research the question. We promised that

we would deal openly with the material they gave us; that we would not rush to publish it or broadcast it on foreign radio. But our request was denied. The answer was simple. The then director of our institute, Academician Khvostov, put it quite clearly: our task was to elucidate the C[entral] C[ommittee] resolution on the 'cult of the personality'. When we replied that this resolution already departed from the decisions of the Twentieth Congress, there was no response. We endeavoured to get into the archives, but we were not allowed. Had we been able to continue our work, then I think we would have been able to achieve some fundamental successes. In any event, we would not have had to wait for Aleksandr Solzhenitsyn to explain to us the meaning of the Gulag Archipelago. We ourselves wanted to find these documents to expose Stalin and Stalinism. Had we been able to do this then the outcome might have been otherwise for the durability of our society and state. What we attempted to do is reflected in our work at the time, though only a small part of it. The bulk of it remained either unpublished or unwritten. Because to write, knowing that no one will print it, is a very difficult thing to do. You always hope that you are writing for a reader and not simply for your desk.[78]

In sum, a half-open door on the past had been abruptly slammed shut in the faces of these 'children of the Twentieth Congress' – but they continued to knock. Soviet historical revisionism expressed this constant tension between what was historiographically possible and what was politically permissible in the 1950s and 1960s.

Nevertheless, for Soviet historians the Twentieth Congress was a veritable 'second October Revolution',[79] which unleashed a 'wave' of discussion throughout the higher educational institutions.[80] In the Institute of History meeting that gathered to hear Pankratova's report back from the congress there was an air of 'genuine liberation', 'repentance' and even 'forgiveness' as historians, some of whom had been the high priests of the 'cult of the personality', reminisced, recriminated and debated whether Stalin was a murderer or merely a tyrant and how they collectively had been reduced to falsifying the Stalinist past.[81] Though some historians, uncertain of Khrushchev's position, preferred a wait-and-see attitude, the political space provided by Khrushchev was soon occupied by historians anxious to come to grips with previously unassailable orthodoxies, albeit in the context of an ongoing contest between Khrushchevite and Stalinist politicians and historians.

In fact some historians, even if they were generally perceived as the most servile of academic minions, had helped to clear this space for Khrushchev, well before his 'secret speech'.[82] The thaw in literature that quickly followed Stalin's death in 1953 was accompanied by cracks in the intellectual ice in the Institute of History.[83] However, it was not so much the institute as its journal, *Voprosy istorii*, that was to lead the first and most spirited charge against the ossification of historiography (in itself confirmation of the less than homogenous nature of Soviet academic institutions). Ironically, it was the Central Committee itself, together with the presidium of the Academy of Sciences, that seeded this process by renewing the editorial board, especially by appointing Anna Pankratova as editor-in-chief of *Voprosy istorii* and Eduard Burdzhalov as deputy editor, less than three months after Stalin's death. In their first editorial, published in issue no. 6 of the journal in 1953, the new editors saw their primary task as one of struggling against the 'cult of the personality' and demonstrating the 'masses as the driving force of historical development'. However, in Yefim Gorodetsky's words, the editors were 'still far from understanding the scale of the task of the struggle with the cult of the personality in historical science'.[84]

Here we encounter, not for the last time, a paradox about the initial moving forces for the rejuvenation of historical writing: just as the vanguard of destalinization was made up of politicians who had been close allies of Stalin himself, so too some historians who had played an orthodox and even extremely reactionary role under Stalin laid the groundwork for the reinvigoration of historiography in the post-Stalin era. It was a measure of the importance that the new Soviet leadership attached to historical science that they appointed a Central Committee member, Academician Pankratova, to head up this process.[85] As noted above, Pankratova's speech at the Twentieth Congress had flagged the more thoroughgoing attack on Stalin by Khrushchev at the end of the congress. But in the three years before this more than a few indicators of the gathering storm in historical science were reflected on the pages of *Voprosy istorii,* as historians struggled to throw off Stalin's malevolent legacy and establish history as a discipline rather than as a mere agency for agitation and propaganda. Already, far reaching discussions had been initiated on economic and historical laws under feudalism, capitalism and socialism, on the periodization of the history of Soviet society, and on the colonial policies of the Tsarist empire.[86]

In response to the urging of the Central Committee for a more creative approach to history, particularly that of the USSR and CPSU,

Pankratova took the opportunity of the fiftieth anniversary of the 1905 revolution to publish articles that challenged the hitherto officially accepted view that in 1905 the Menshevik-dominated Petrograd soviet had played a completely reactionary role, in contrast to the Bolshevik-dominated Moscow soviet. More importantly, the journal became the vehicle for reestablishing the historical community by organizing large-scale discussions of historians – an event not seen since the Society of Marxist Historians organized an all-Union conference back in 1928.[87] It was these *Voprosy istorii* 'readers' conferences', coupled with the publication in the journal of some impermissible 'Trotskyite' views, that triggered the notorious 'Burdzhalov affair' of 1956–57.[88]

The Burdzhalov affair

The new editors of *Voprosy istorii* had set their sights on unmasking the individual shortcomings of Stalin. It quickly became apparent to them, however, that the roots of the stultification of historical science were deeper than this; eradicating them could not be achieved overnight. What was required was a reevaluation of methodology, of the democratic and national-liberation movements, of the role of the masses in history, of other classes, and of parties besides the Bolsheviks.[89]

Addressing the Twentieth Congress, Pankratova, rejecting the view that scholarship developed by 'edicts and votes', extolled the virtues of unfettered discussion for the development of historical writing. True to these convictions a month prior to the congress *Voprosy istorii* had already convened in Moscow the first of several readers' conferences that took place in 1956. At the January conference, 600 historians participated in three days of intense discussion. Pankratova lauded the increased size and distribution of *Voprosy istorii* in recent years (that is, since Stalin's death), which she hoped would become an 'international tribune of Marxist history'. She lamented, however, the shortcomings of many of the articles it published for their 'dogmatism, rote-learning, vulgarization, political fashionableness and black-and-white representation of the past.'[90]

Burdzhalov was even more forthright in his criticisms of the state of historical science. Among other things, he called for a reconsideration of the notion of feudalism in Eastern Europe and Russia, for more attention to the nature of Russian imperialism, for a reevaluation of both Plekhanov and Lenin as historians, for more thorough research into Soviet industrialization and the collectivization of agriculture, and for a closer look at the early years of the Great Patriotic War. As well, he condemned party historians, many of whom had yet to go beyond the pronouncements of the *Short Course*; testified to, for example, by the depiction of the Bolsheviks as the only progressive actor in 1905. Burdzhalov thus put on the agenda many of the issues that were to rack historical science over the next decade and a half. However, one question he raised was of particular political and historiographical immediacy: the denial of tsarist Russia as a 'prison house of peoples' and the concomitant damning of national movements as reactionary.[91] The sensitivity of Great Russian chauvinism in historiography can be gauged by the opposition of some of the conference participants to any reconsideration of this aspect of historical writing.[92] The Director of the Institute of History, Sidorov, chastised the journal for lack of vigilance against 'cosmopolitan views' in historiography, while his former student, Gefter, took the journal to task for, among other things, its 'imperious and negative' editorializing.[93] In his concluding remarks Burdzhalov responded vigorously to both Gefter and Sidorov, accusing the latter in particular of avoiding the 'fundamental questions' facing Soviet historiography.[94]

The Central Committee's Department of Science and Higher Educational Establishments also took a dim view of Burdzhalov's presentation and the tenor of the conference as a whole. In a confidential report to the party Central Committee, Burdzhalov was taken to task for encroaching in a 'free and easy' manner on a number of 'established views' concerning Soviet and party history, for example, the Mensheviks in 1905 and anti-tsarist national movements. At times, the report alleged, Burdzhalov's interpretations amounted to falsehood.[95] According to the report, Burdzhalov had 'embellished' the role of the Mensheviks in 1905–07 while his attempt to resurrect the role of the St Petersburg Bolsheviks, headed for a long time by Zinoviev, was 'irresponsible'. Further, many of the positive responses by the conference participants to Burdzhalov's repudiation of the textbook-depiction of tsarist Russia as a 'bulwark of national friendship rather than a prison house of nations' were condemned as 'politically incorrect'.[96]

What really seems to have aroused the ire of the Department of Science was that *Voprosy istorii* had taken upon itself the task of organizing discussions that went beyond the bounds of the role of the journal as they saw it. Thus Burdzhalov was criticized for concerning himself with questions other than the immediate ones of the past contents and future directions of the journal. In this context, a principle concern was that such a 'motley' audience of students, postgraduates, researchers and even retired military personnel, rather than 'leading historians', was apparently inimical to 'serious' scientific discussion.[97] Further, the editors had gone beyond their brief in arrogating to themselves the right to interpret the party's wishes in regard to historical writing and even presented the journal as if it, rather than the party, had resurrected Lenin's role in Soviet history.[98] Furthermore, the report complained that

> before the last session of the conference officers of the Department of Science ... advised comrade Pankratova to point out in her concluding remarks Burdzhalov's erroneous formulating of a number of questions. However, she declined to do this.

In view of Pankratova's unwillingness as editor-in-chief and a Central Committee member to rebut her deputy's errors it was recommended that the conference and *Voprosy istorii* editorial policy be the subject of an article in *Kommunist* and a special discussion in the Department of Science.[99] In short, Burdzhalov, with the support of Central Committee member Pankratova, had transgressed the doctrinal and organizational boundaries of historical science:

> Analysis of the condition of historical science, a self-critical approach, a willingness to listen to the writers and readers of the journal and to involve them in joint work in restructuring history invariably gained the sympathy of a large part of [Burdzhalov's] audience. It was precisely for this that he was to be accused.[100]

Parallel to the *Voprosy istorii* readers' conferences there were also discussions in the history faculty of Moscow State University and the Department of the History of the CPSU, Academy of Sciences of the Central Committee, that took the form of 'investigatory-accusatory tribunal[s]': '"Whoever speaks against Stalin speaks against our party", declared Professor D. I. Nadtocheev, for example. The journal was accused of anti-Sovietism and of "undermining the party".'[101]

If official disquiet about Burdzhalov's report before the Twentieth Congress might be expected, it is, at first sight, a little surprising that it was his activities after the congress that brought the wrath of the Department of Science down on Burdzhalov's head – until we look more closely at those activities. Almost immediately after the Twentieth Congress, a *Voprosy istorii* editorial,[102] personally written by Burdzhalov,[103] confronted the causes of the degradation of party history and proclaimed the journal's determination to revitalize historical science as a whole. Beria's notorious pamphlet on the history of the Georgian and Transcaucasian communist parties was singled out for reducing party history to a mere exaltation of Stalin as exclusive party theoretician.[104] From then on party history was chronicled by 'indifferent and unenterprising' scribes devoid of independent thinking, working only within the given 'line' and striving to 'conceal their scientific sterility by recourse to scientific authority'. The ensuing 'cult of the personality of I. V. Stalin led to the immediate distortion of historical truth'; but it was the 'task of historians', *Voprosy istorii* reminded its readers, 'to explain historical facts, not to hush them up'.[105]

Burdzhalov was as good as his word. Hard on the heels of his audacious editorial came his provocative article on the tactics of the Bolsheviks in March–April 1917, which had appeared in *Voprosy istorii* soon after the Twentieth Congress.[106] In his article, Burdzhalov took issue with the misrepresentation in party historiography of Bukharin, Kamenev and Zinoviev as treacherous opportunists in relation to the provisional government while, needless to say, extolling Stalin as the consistent advocate of Lenin's approach, even before the latter issued his famous April Theses.[107] Basing himself on hitherto inaccessible party archives,[108] Burdzhalov showed that in fact it was Kamenev who advocated a conciliationist approach towards the provisional government, while downplaying the revolutionary significance of the soviets, a position more or less shared by Stalin right up until Lenin turned the Bolsheviks towards the soviets in April 1917.[109] Contrary to the calumnies of the *Short Course*,[110] it was Zinoviev who was Lenin's most consistent ally on the soviets as the political basis for the bourgeois-democratic revolution 'growing over' into the socialist one.[111] Stalin was a belated convert to Lenin's theses.[112] Such criticism of Stalin went far beyond the 'secret speech'. Khrushchev had emphasized Stalin's failings only in the latter part of his career. There had been no hint that the 'Great Marxist' had strayed from the path of Bolshevism earlier in the piece. Above all, Burdzhalov's exposure of Stalin's role in March–April 1917 was perilously close to Trotskyism. It was precisely Stalin's cover-up of his conciliatory approach to the provisional government that lay at the heart of Trotsky's denunciation of the 'Stalin school of falsification'.[113]

Not content with this bold sally Burdzhalov, as a loyal party member, signalled in a memorandum to the Central Committee the sort of issues he intended to take up at the next readers' conference in Leningrad at the beginning of June. In his memorandum Burdzhalov identified five crucial problem areas in Soviet historiography: party history; tsarist colonialism and national-liberation movements; foreign policy and international relations; the history of social thought; and the administration of history itself.[114] Burdzhalov's wide-ranging comments about administration amounted to a programme for the renewal of the integrity and autonomy of the historical community. He complained that history was basically,

> restricted to the institutions of the Academy of Sciences and excessively bureaucratized. Many meetings, plans and reports are preoccupied with multi-volume publications. Historians do not have enough time for creative work and for writing individual monographs. There is no community of historians. Soviet historians need their own association and all-union academic conferences. A network of historical journals is required in which discussion and exchanges of opinion have pride of place. One general historical journal cannot meet the research needs of history; in the first place a specialist journal in party history is required. The circulation of historical literature needs to be increased, publishers however should not have the rights they currently have to interfere with an author's work nor should they take it upon themselves to elucidate specific historical questions (they should be limited to keeping an eye on the political line). It is vital to drastically reduce the so-called closed collections of literature in which even party documents are still held.[115]

Burdzhalov's identification of five problem areas registered the considerable step forward that had occurred in historical thought under the impact of both the Twentieth Congress and of the reemergence of a community of historians fostered by a constant 'dialogue' between the *Voprosy istorii* editorial board and its readership.[116] As Burdzhalov emphasized in his memorandum, he was articulating the concerns of the historical community at large, rather than of the *Voprosy istorii* editorial board.[117] For Burdzhalov these contentious questions were not just the outward signs of the falsification of history in the interests of party and state needs but of the deforming of 'historical memory' itself – a major impediment to genuine scholarship.[118]

In his three-hour presentation to the Leningrad conference held in June 1956, Burdzhalov voiced these and other concerns about historical science in no uncertain terms.[119] Welcoming the expansion of the journal and the enhanced contacts with non-Soviet historians (in Rome, in 1955, for the first time since 1933, a delegation of Soviet historians participated in the International Congress of Historians),[120] Burdzhalov acknowledged that the new, dual objectives of *Voprosy istorii* – to give direction to historiography while encouraging the freest exchange of views – had been poorly realized. The first readers' conference convened by the journal had, however, been very 'fruitful' because it took the discussion of the situation on the 'historical front' outside the narrow institutional boundaries of the Academy of Sciences and the universities. But even this fell far short of the possibilities and expectations opened up by the Twentieth Congress, the 'decisive turning point in every facet of our life – political, economic, international and scientific-ideological'.[121]

The realization of these possibilities could not be achieved instantaneously; on the contrary, it would require a serious and sustained campaign to overcome the customary inertia of historians used to awaiting directives from on-high before acting. Taking aim at the *Short Course*, which had long served as a 'handbook' for historians, Burdzhalov said it was now clear that its failings went far beyond partial inadequacies: the work as a whole, with its effective denial of Marxism, was discredited as a basis for scholarship.[122] However, while recognizing that Stalin's theory of the 'two leaders' of the party – Lenin and Stalin himself – no longer had currency, he cautioned against a substitute Lenin cult: 'Lenin was not alone; he was supported by an entire cohort of Bolsheviks. The cult of the personality', Burdzhalov reminded his enthusiastic audience, 'essentially highlighted one individual', at the expense of the rest. The result was an 'anonymous' history in which surnames were replaced by 'enemies of the people'. On this basis the real history of the St Petersburg Soviet in 1905 had been hidden, simply because at its head stood Trotsky.[123] (Trotsky was, of course, the *bête noire* in Stalin's demonology and this was certainly still the case in Soviet politics in 1956.)[124] Nevertheless, while Burdzhalov cautiously responded to several questions about Trotsky, acknowledging his errors in the civil war for example, he urged that Trotsky, along with Kamenev, Bukharin and Zinoviev not be treated simply as traitors of the revolution – the usual practice. '[I]deological struggle must not be reduced to simple treachery', he declared.[125] In his memorandum to the Central Committee Department of Science, Burdzhalov was even more forthright: 'The Trotskyites and Bukharinites were characterized not as tendencies hostile to Leninism but simply as paid foreign agents'.[126]

During the discussion of his paper Burdzhalov was forced to defend his controversial article on the tactics of the Bolsheviks in March–April 1917. In addition to his exposure of the crudest falsifications of party history, however, Burdzhalov challenged a dimension of the Stalinist historiographical paradigm that impinged on the very basis of Soviet historical consciousness, not only among historians but also political leaders, *apparatchiki* and ultimately the populace at large: Russian chauvinism. Here Burdzhalov advanced on a number of fronts. He deplored the neglect of the West European heritage of Russian social thought.[127] He decried the 'idealization' of tsarist foreign policy by Soviet historians; rather than an imperialist power with its own aggrandizing objectives, as Lenin had suggested, it was a semi-colony of Europe. Such sentiments by Soviet historians violated the internationalism of the Bolsheviks. But not satisfied with rationalizing the 'predatory' policies of the autocracy, some historians actually lamented the autocracy's inconsistent pursuit of such policies and even strove to establish 'continuity' between tsarist and Soviet foreign policy.[128] Similarly, tsarist policy towards the subject nations of its empire (Georgia, the Caucasus) was no longer colonial. Their annexation was not even a 'lesser evil'; as late as 1952 it was proclaimed a 'virtue'! Concomitantly, national liberation movements, such as that led by Shamil in the mid-nineteenth century in the Caucasus, became reactionary overnight.[129]

Burdzhalov placed much of the responsibility for this chauvinist prism through which the Soviet past was viewed onto Stalin himself. The putative continuity between tsarist and Soviet foreign policy owed not a little to Stalin's eulogizing of the ruthless policies of Ivan the Terrible and his *oprichina*.[130] Burdzhalov's concern here was not restricted to its historiographical implications; false analogies between tsarist and Soviet foreign policy only played into the hands of the USSR's adversaries.[131] Here was one of the sharpest political edges of historical revisionism: an honest and truly scientific historiography was one of the most effective weapons in the Soviet Union's ideological arsenal. The Stalinist falsification of the past could only dull such weapons. Such a stance, however, was not enough to save either Burdzhalov or Pankratova.

Public vilification of them erupted following the Leningrad and Kiev readers' conferences, but only after the adoption of the June 1956 Central Committee resolution 'On overcoming the cult of the personality and its consequences'. This resolution marked a definite retreat from the direction of the Twentieth Congress. In July the editors of *Voprosy istorii* were pilloried in the party press. *Kommunist* criticized the publication of articles that underestimated 'the danger of the opportunist, conciliatory, reformist politics of the Mensheviks' in 1905, as well as articles that, in dealing with 'problems concerning overcoming the cult of the personality in party history', drew 'hasty and unsubstantiated conclusions' while others were excessively 'vociferous and sensationalist.'[132] *Partiinaya zhizn'* took particular exception to Burdzhalov's treatment of events in March–April 1917. He was accused of a lack of *'obektivnosti'* in his selection of facts, thereby giving the erroneous impression that in these months in Russia 'there was no party of communists, essentially no Central Committee, and no *Pravda* to speak of.' The need for an 'objective' selection of facts had particular importance given the 'ongoing ideological struggle'.[133]

These criticisms were swiftly followed in early August by a scathing attack on Burdzhalov and several participants in the Leningrad conference published in *Leningradskaya pravda*. It is apparent that this offensive was triggered not only by Burdzhalov stripping away the myths surrounding Stalin's role in 1917, but also by the resonance *Voprosy istorii*'s campaign had within the historical community. Public support for Burdzhalov and protests against his misrepresentation in the press came from scholars working in the Leningrad division of the Institute of History, the Saltykov–Shchedrin Library and other higher education institutions.[134]

Striking evidence of party concern about the public impact of Burdzhalov's campaign is given by the hostile intervention during his address to the Kiev readers' conference held 28–29 June. Interrupting Burdzhalov's 'exceptionally ardent and enthusiastic' defence of Kamenev and Zinoviev as Leninists, the 'Secretary of the Kiev Obkom of the Ukrainian Communist Party, comrade Tronko, inquired "Tell us, please, on behalf of whom are you making all these pronouncements". Comrade Burdzhalov replied that he was making them on behalf of the editorial board of *Voprosy istorii*.' A report to Khrushchev on this event concluded that 'It turns out that comrade Burdzhalov, using his position [as deputy editor], at readers' conferences of *Voprosy istorii* held in the major cities of the USSR, basically attempts to mobilize academic opinion in favour of those who have already been unmasked by the party as enemies of socialism.'[135]

Moreover, as an active and proud party member, Burdzhalov took his destalinization campaign into the CPSU itself. Here, under the influence of the Yugoslav theoretician Edvard Kardelj, he advocated the democratization of the Soviet state apparatus. Reporting to a March 1956 meeting of the party members of *Voprosy istorii* editorial board, Burdzhalov spoke of the need to reduce the 'bureaucratized' party apparatus, citing as an example the Department of Science, whose 'instructors are apparently less qualified than academicians and therefore not entitled to supervise them.' Planning of research and of the work of *Voprosy istorii* he also saw as a sign of 'bureaucratism'. Burdzhalov's favourable comments about Kardelj's notion of 'merging the state apparatus and the workers' were raised in the context of his denunciation of Stalin's 'pack of lies' about the state, which had justified repression. Emphasizing the significance of the 'further democratization of party life', Burdzhalov suggested it would be expedient to have a broad party discussion on the state. In regard to the 'interrelations between party organs with social organizations and the creative unions', Burdzhalov maintained that the 'leading rule of the party must be take the form of intellectual guidance, not petty tutelage'.[136] It was further alleged that Burdzhalov had insinuated into his provocative March 1956 *Voprosy istorii* editorial, after its approval by the editorial board, the accusation that since the late 1930s 'in party and soviet organs had appeared dishonest careerists, who had striven to advance themselves by repressing ... cadres who were loyal to the socialist cause'.[137]

There were, therefore, good reasons – historiographical and party political – for the Stalinist stalwarts to rid themselves of Burdzhalov and his ally, Pankratova. Undeterred, encouraged by the response of their clientele, the editors of *Voprosy istorii* defended their campaign to refurbish historical science, despite the press barrage that grew especially intense in the wake of the Hungarian and Polish events of October 1956.[138]

The specific accusation levelled against Burdzhalov and Pankratova was their alleged departure from the principle of *partiinost'*; by this was meant their repudiation of several fabrications in the *Short Course*. Both, however, saw themselves as defending *partiinost'*, as they understood it. Their bold editorial pronouncements in favour of a 'truthful, Marxist elucidation'[139] of the past in order to overcome 'mistaken, simplified, anti-historicist views',[140] coupled with Burdzhalov's article about Bolshevik tactics in 1917, eventually attracted the most ominous political accusation – Trotskyism: 'At a [November 1956] meeting of the Departments of the History of the CPSU of the Academy of Social Sciences and Moscow State University my article was called Trotskyist and I a Trotskyite'.[141] These accusations were not without foundation. At a March 1956 editorial board meeting Pankratova had tabled a letter 'from that scoundrel Stalin to Comrade Trotsky'.[142]

Again and again during this period, Pankratova and Burdzhalov defended the new direction of *Voprosy istorii* as merely implementing the perspectives expressed in Central Committee resolutions, starting with the May 1953 resolution that criticized the journal for failing to provide direction in historical writing, and in relation to the Twentieth Congress in particular. Responding to the reproaches in the party press in July and August, for instance, Pankratova complained to the central party leadership that the unsubstantiated and even false accusations against the journal 'had created an unhealthy atmosphere that impeded it carrying out the tasks before it and hindered the journal reconstructing its work in the light of the resolutions of the XX congress'.[143]

Unfortunately, the fact that they sincerely believed that their campaign to regenerate historical science was fully in accord with the spirit of the Twentieth Congress was no defence. Indeed, given the political environment scarcely three years after Stalin's demise, an appeal to the decisions of that congress only made them more enemies among the still well-entrenched proteges of the late dictator. On the floor of the readers' conferences, within the academic and party institutions and at the very heights of the political apparatus the campaign against *Voprosy istorii* and its revisionist editors gathered pace, culminating in Burdzhalov's dismissal from the editorial board in March 1957 and Pankratova's premature death two months later: 25 May 1957.[144] According to Gorodetsky, Burdzhalov and Pankratova were casualties of the so-called 'anti-party' group's counter-offensive against the destalinization campaign unleashed by the Twentieth Congress.[145] It did not follow from this campaign, however, that they had reliable allies among Khrushchev's immediate circle.[146]

All the appeals of Pankratova and Burdzhalov to the highest echelons of the party, including Khrushchev himself, to defend *Voprosy istorii* and to repudiate the calumniation against them fell on deaf ears.[147] Despite Pankratova's status as a Central Committee member, she was not even allowed to speak at the 6 March 1957 meeting of the Central Committee secretariat that was to decide the fate of her journal. In her undelivered speech, while conceding certain 'errors, shortcomings and omissions', Pankratova reaffirmed her commitment to the ideals of the Twentieth Congress:

> We cannot accept the accusations ... according to which the journal had its own line which was maliciously anti-party ... We fought for the realization of the directives of the Twentieth Congress and the C[entral] C[ommittee] of the CPSU concerning the struggle with

dogmatism, for creative Marxism, with deep and sincere conviction, with great zeal and passion because we considered that only by pursuing this path could we guarantee the genuine flowering of Soviet historical science.[148]

Pankratova was admitted to hospital the next day, suffering from what she called a 'nervous breakdown', a victim of her contradictory commitment to both party and historical truth.[149] In the 9 March 1957 Central Committee resolution, 'Concerning the Journal *Voprosy istorii*', having failed to force Pankratova to denounce her deputy, Burdzhalov was singled out for condemnation, particularly for his alleged attempt 'under the pretext of criticizing Stalin's cult of the personality ... to inflate the role of Zinoviev in 1917'. This, together with several other articles and editorials, the resolution declared, was evidence of 'a tendency to depart from Leninist principles of *partiinost'* in history' in favour of 'bourgeois objectivism'.[150] This charge was echoed by the history faculty, Moscow State University. Burdzhalov had, of course, vigorously repudiated any departure from *partiinost'*:

> It is said that that we slipped up on the question of objectivism and departed from *partiinost'*. No! This was not so. Objectivity is not objectivism. A truthful, objective depiction of events is a party depiction of events.[151]

Despite his protestations of loyalty, Burdzhalov was removed from his post as deputy editor having foundered on the rock of *partiinost'*, the precise shape of which the party apparatus was determined it alone should decide. The newly-installed editorial board moved quickly to deal with the question of Stalin – 'in a spirit of neo-Stalinism':[152] Stalin should not be viewed 'purely through the prism of his mistakes'.[153]

It was not just *Voprosy istorii* that was brought into line by this resolution. It was used to snuff out any 'spark of dissent'.[154] A recommendation was made to review the teaching of the social sciences in higher education. For example, a resolution of 6 May 1957 by the Russian organization of the CPSU severely censured the Saratov party regional committee for its inadequate supervision of the teaching of Marxist–Leninist theory in the social science departments of the region. The teaching staff was accused of uncritically evaluating a number of 'erroneous' articles in *Voprosy istorii* and of failing to 'unmask' in their classes such manifestations of 'imperialist ideology' as glossing over the divide between Bolshevism and Menshevism. Similarly, a collection of documents on the revolution in Armenia which included previously unpublished non-Bolshevik sources, published in 1957 with the imprimatur of the republic's party, was viewed as a serious political error.[155]

More dramatically, in February 1958, a group of young, anti-Stalinist historians, led by K. N. Krasnopevstev, centred mainly in the faculty of history, Moscow State University, was condemned to up to 10 years in labour camps. They had been found guilty of 'counter-revolutionary revisionism', having accused Khrushchev of being an accomplice to Stalin's crimes, and calling for mass actions, the strengthening of the soviets and for further discussion at the next communist party congress.[156]

Despite this crackdown it is an exaggeration to conclude, as does a *perestroika* retrospective of the Khrushchev period, that the 'rout' of *Voprosy istorii* was so decisive that it 'retarded the rising trend of historical thought and – saddest of all for social knowledge – did not allow it to rise to a qualitatively new pinnacle of destalinization.'[157] Burdzhalov himself, despite being banished from the Institute of History to the Lenin State Pedagogical Institute in 1959, and having had his qualifications reexamined, went on to publish his masterpieces *The Second Russian Revolution* and *The Second Russian Revolution. Moscow. Front. Periphery* in 1967 and 1970, respectively;[158] works regarded as models of *'partiinost'*, objectivity and scholarly integrity' and vindication of the 'potential' of Soviet historical writing amidst the 'scholastic greyness' that prevailed on the 'historical front'.[159] It is true, of course, that with the Burdzhalov affair history, especially party history, had, once more, suffered a serious setback (the circulation of *Voprosy istorii* plummeted by more than a half over the next three years).[160] Nevertheless, as we shall see, even this was insufficient to halt the advance of historical thought in other branches of the discipline. We now need to examine the organizational initiatives that facilitated this advance in the decade after the Twentieth Congress.

The production of historical science

Prior to *perestroika*, Soviet authorities prided themselves on the planned nature of their society. This was no less true for historical science, where factory-like production was the order of the day. Ever since Stalin merged the prestigious Academy of Sciences with the Communist Academy in 1936,[161] historical writing had increasingly come under the superintendence of an elaborate academic and party bureaucracy. Its purpose was two-fold. Firstly, to maintain political control over historical writing. Secondly, to ensure that history remained in step with the socio-economic needs of Soviet society as determined by the party leadership. Despite the party's intentions, these could only be contradictory objectives. The need to develop a larger and more sophisticated community of historians could only run up against the subordination of their activities to party needs. It was Stalin who injected lethal meaning into the term *partiinost'*; but it was also Stalin who authorized the establishment of *Voprosy istorii* in 1945.[162] After the Twentieth Congress a virtual revolution in the organization and production of historical writing occurred, encouraged by the party itself. Despite some faltering, following the Burdzhalov affair, this revolution was given renewed impetus by the Twenty-second Congress of 1961, where the newly-adopted party programme proclaimed the transition from socialism to communism.

Party concern to professionalize history, if only to perfect it as an instrument of party policy, was embraced even by conservative historians such as I. I. Mints and Ye. M. Zhukov, who had been dismayed by the Burdzhalov affair. Over the next decade, the resultant quantitative expansion of research and the encouragement of new fields, such as historiography, stimulated the simultaneous 'co-existence of regressive and progressive tendencies' in history. At the same time it fostered an unprecedented 'dialogue' between the historical guild and the party,[163] that was rudely interrupted after the fall of Khrushchev.

The production and dissemination of history in the Soviet Union was marked by parallel party and academic centres of research and education – and an unceasing contestation between them. Alongside the Division of History of the Soviet Academy of Sciences stood the Central Committee's Institute of Marxism–Leninism and its Academy of Social Sciences. Both systems, academic and party, were entitled to award research degrees. Likewise, there was a pronounced demarcation between research and teaching within each system. The Academy of Sciences' Institute of History devoted itself purely to research, while teaching responsibilities fell to the universities and other Higher Educational Establishments (*Vuzy*), such as the pedagogical institutes. The *Vuzy* also took primary responsibility for postgraduate studies; the Institute of History taking at most some 12 to 14 *aspiranty* (graduate students) per year.[164] Control of the central party archives by the Institute of Marxism–Leninism, meant that it, together with the Academy of Social Sciences, tended to be research-oriented. In 1967 a

Central Committee resolution gave the Institute of Marxism–Leninism responsibility for coordinating all research on party history. The institute was also responsible for the publication of *Voprosy istorii KPSS*.[165] The Higher Party School was responsible for educating party officials.

Invigilating all historical writing on behalf of the party was the Central Committee's Department of Science and Higher Educational Establishments, which, under a slightly different name, was to achieve such infamy under S. P. Trapeznikov.[166] It is apparent that a considerable amount of the tension that existed between the Department of Science and the researchers and academicians of the Institute of History was professional. The most highly qualified historians, candidates and doctors of historical sciences, congregated in the Institute of History.[167] The revisionists amongst them obviously resented being overseen by ignorant 'Talmudists' graduated from the Higher Party School.[168]

Tensions between the 'intellectuals of quality' and the (pseudo) 'intellectuals of scope' were equally pronounced within the Institute of History during these years. These tensions derived from the fact that, often as not, party membership was a path to a privileged *nomenklatura* position, such as the head of a sector or institute director. Further, during the 1950s the relatively high wages of researchers in the Academy of Sciences encouraged many poorly-qualified *partrabotniki* (party officials) to seek a sinecure as a researcher in the Institute of History. Such *bezdelniki* (good-for-nothings) not only debased scholarship but fostered suspicion and uncertainty within the institute. Feeling threatened as they did by the emergence of serious scholarship after the Twentieth Congress, the 'party critics' set themselves up as overseers of genuine researchers. This powerful network of party 'incompetents' who administered the arts and sciences was, according to A. Nekrich, one of the 'most important props of the Soviet regime'. According to him, in 1958 Sidorov, then Director of the Institute of History, fell foul of this 'mafia'. His replacement as director, V. M. Khvostov, looked to this mafia of *bezdelniki* to police the institute.[169]

The years after the Twentieth Congress saw a dramatic expansion of the historical profession and its support infrastructure. The Institute of History grew from a mere 150 historians in 1946–47[170] to some 400 by the time it was divided in 1968.[171] They were the cream of a profession that totalled 17 000 in 1961.[172] Moreover, this elite was highly urbanized, congregated as it was largely in Moscow, Leningrad and Kiev.

Table 2.1 Numbers of candidates of historical sciences in *Vuzy* and research institutions

1950	2209
1955	5780
1960	6888
1965	7795

Source: Ye. N. Gorodetsky and G. P. Makhnov, 'Istoricheskoe obrazovanie v vyshei shkole', M. V. Nechkina and Gorodetsky, *Ocherki po istorii istoricheskoi nauki v SSSR*, Tom V (Moscow, 1985), p. 87.

As can be seen from Table 2.1, this expansion of the elite historians was fuelled by the sharp rise of graduate students and 'Candidates of Historical Sciences' in the early 1950s.

Many of these *kandidaty* were *frontoviki*: 'front-line' veterans of the Great Patriotic War. K. N. Tarnovsky, whose name was to become synonymous with historical revisionism, paints a vivid picture of the *frontoviki* and their attitude to their work:

> The make-up of the student body of Moscow University at the end of the 1940s and beginning of the 1950s was unique. Along the corridors went people in uniforms and military shirts, who had only recently removed their epaulettes and were still accustomed to wearing their decorations on holidays. The former *frontoviki* had become students. Generally five to ten years older than those in their same year who had come directly from school, they better understood why they had come [to university], what they were after and what they needed to do in order to attain more knowledge. Generally speaking, study came to them less easily. Not, however, because of the loss of schooling during their years of military service. It was simply that they approached their subject matter differently; they strove to comprehend it more profoundly, to analyse it more thoroughly, and to take from the university everything it could give them. Such students did not have to be compelled to study, to be watched over or supervised. They expected and demanded from their teachers something completely different – thorough knowledge, belief in the course they were presenting and uncompromising assessment of the results achieved. They particularly prized the breadth and novelty of their instructors' projects and the relevance of a problematic suggested by them that struck a chord with the principal, vital questions of the day.[173]

This picture of the *frontoviki* as enthusiastic, dedicated scholars concerned with the contemporary political resonance of their work helps to explain an apparent paradox of Soviet historiography: how did revisionism emerge from such a degraded discipline? It is apparent that those who were prepared to put life and limb on the line for their nation and the Soviet idea turned to history with enormous zeal and integrity, despite the toll of the Stalin experience. It was the *frontoviki* who went on to become the vanguard of the *shestidesyatniki* – the 'people of the 1960s'.[174]

The *shestidesyatniki* were defined both generationally and politically. Aged between 25 to 45 years at the time of the Twentieth Congress, they had usually graduated either just before the Great Patriotic War (such as Mikhail Gefter) or just after (such as Viktor Danilov). There were, however, those of the same generation who were waiting in the wings for a neo-Stalinist counter-offensive. So the *shestidesyatniki* were also defined *politically* as those scholars who identified with the aspirations of the Twentieth Congress. Burdzhalov was the most outstanding example of this; even though, being aged 50 in 1956, he belonged to an older generation of historians.[175] Thus it was the *frontoviki*, forged in the furnace of the Great Patriotic War and inspired by the Twentieth Congress, who formed the backbone of the revisionist historians.

The postwar expansion of trained historians, however, was an uneven process; and quantitative rather than qualitative. It was a frequent complaint at the 1962 all-Union conference convened to improve the quality of historical teaching and research, that nearly half of the *Vuzy* historians (3500 out of 7980) were still unqualified. Moreover, very few *Vuzy* historians, particularly party historians,[176] were professors or doctors of sciences (Table 2.2).

Table 2.2 Historians working in *Vuzy*, October 1961

Specialization	Total number	Prof./Dr	Percentage
CPSU history	5964	32	0.5
Soviet history	1211	64	5.3
World history	805	49	6.1

Source: B. N. Ponomarev, 'Zadachi istoricheskoi nauka i podgotovka nauchno-pedagogicheskikh kadrov v oblasti istori'i, *Vsesoyuznoe soveshchanie o merakh podgotovki nauchno-pedagogicheskikh kadrov po istorichekskim naukam 18–21 dekabrya 1962g* (Moscow, 1964), p. 44.

In this respect, a large proportion of the Soviet historical profession in the 1950s and early 1960s were 'barefoot' historians (a feature which might help explain the demand for textbooks by history teachers). This was symptomatic of the underdeveloped nature of Soviet society as a whole. An inadequate research infrastructure – a dearth of trained research assistance, of well-organized libraries and archives, of paper and microfilms[177] – coupled with the demands of daily life in a shortage economy, militated against productive scholarship. Moreover, history as a profession still had very poor status, despite the attempt of the party to overcome this particularly negative legacy of the Stalin period. Only 2 per cent of students chose to pursue history at tertiary level.[178] In fact, after 1956 the number of historian *aspiranty* actually declined,[179] while the market for history books and journals plummeted.[180] In both cases, this was a reflection on the poor social standing of historians rather than on history, in which there was an upsurge of popular interest after the Twentieth Congress.[181]

The party set out to redress this problem by committing more resources to history. But by building up the organizational support for history the party, wittingly or not, was setting the scene for confrontation with the elite historians. The years after the Twentieth Congress saw a marked increase in the number of specialist historical journals. Until 1957 *Voprosy istorii* was the flagship of the discipline, escorted by only two other journals: *Istoricheskie zapiski* (*Historical Transactions*), which specialized in medieval and modern Russian history, and *Vestnik drevnei istorii* (*Bulletin of Ancient History*), which specialized in ancient history. After 1957 these three were joined by a flotilla of specialist journals, including *Voprosy istorii KPSS* (*Problems of CPSU History*), *Istoriya SSSR* (*USSR History*), *Novaya i noveishaya istoriya* (*Modern and Contemporary History*), *Voennoistorichesky zhurnal* (*Journal of Military History*), *Vestnik istorii mirovoi kultury* (*Bulletin of the History of World Culture*) and *Ukrainskyi istorichnyi zhurnal* (*Ukrainian Historical Journal*).[182] By 1962 there were 81 Soviet periodicals devoted to history.[183]

Similarly, the raw materials for historical research – documents – were more readily available. Many more documents were published, especially by the Institute of Marxism–Leninism.[184] The archives themselves were somewhat better organized and access to them liberalized. In the decade between 1947 and 1957 the number of readers given access to documents by the State Archive Administration grew almost six times: from some 4000 to more than 23 000.[185] Meanwhile the regular publication of the journal *Istorichesky arkhiv* (*Historical Archive*), short-lived as it was,[186] signified an endeavour to raise the standards of archivist training and put them on a more a professional footing.[187] This bountiful publication of fresh materials went some way towards satisfying the 'permanent hunger for sources' by historians.[188] Nevertheless, the promised 'democratization' of the archives, proclaimed in formal resolutions in the late 1950s, was thwarted by reclassifying entire archives as 'secret' and by widespread shredding of their holdings. Above all, the vice-like grip of the party apparatus on the archives remained, even after the Ministry of Internal Affairs (MVD) finally relinquished its 22-year grasp in 1960.[189]

There also remained the problem of digesting the new materials. Crucial in this regard was the publication of the complete *Collected Works* of Lenin between 1958 and 1965 (purged of some his more violent utterances, as we now know).[190] Leninism was a two-edged sword within Soviet historical discourse. Citing from Lenin could be used to stifle discussion. According to an antagonist of revisionism, V. I. Bovykin, if Lenin's authority was invoked it was difficult to repudiate because it was not just an individual's opinion that was being repudiated but Lenin himself.[191] For other historians, however, Lenin's methodology provided the cutting-edge of revisionism.

It was a hallmark of Soviet historiography, in accordance with its status as a 'science', that research priorities should be systematically established. After the Twentieth Congress there was greater attention than ever to planning. The overriding criteria were political. Thus the seven-year research plan for 1959–65 adopted by the Presidium of the Academy of Sciences designated six 'key' research areas, among them the history of the October Revolution, of the CPSU and of the Great Patriotic War.[192] These areas were seen as integral to the needs of socialist construction and the 'struggle against bourgeois ideology', a continuous refrain in this period of 'peaceful co-existence'. To meet these expanded research horizons new forms of organization were adopted. Within the institutes of the Academy of Sciences sectors, groups and commissions proliferated. In 1956 there were 12 sectors within the Institute of History, organized according to their field, ranging from the History of the USSR: Feudal Period to that of World History. There were also two commissions dedicated to the history of historical science and the history of agriculture. These were supported by five auxiliary sections, which dealt with postgraduate training, editing and publishing, reference and bibliography, the library, and manuscripts and archives. Meanwhile, there was a growing number of institutes in which historical research occupied an important place:

between 1959 and 1961 the Institutes of Africa, of Latin America and of the Economy of the World Socialist System were established. The departure of Khrushchev did not halt this expansion of research institutions: 1966–67 saw the establishment of the Institute of the International Workers Movement and the Institute of Military History.[193]

A particularly important innovation, in the late 1950s and early 1960s, was the formation of *nauchnye sovety* (Scientific Councils). These councils, some Union-wide, coordinated research between institutions and collectives and concentrated inter-disciplinary research skills on the priority areas.[194] The results were reflected in multi-volume, collective works that appeared in this period which encouraged collaboration between scholars. A signal example of this was the 10-volume *Universal History*, which was published between 1956 and 1965. This massive work, running to almost two and a half million words, resulted from the combined labours of 400 writers, editors, consultants and assistants. It was edited by Yevgeny Zhukov, who chaired the Scientific Council on the Problem of the 'Laws Regulating the Historical Development of Society and the Transition from One Socio-economic Formation to Another'.[195] Mostly, the *nauchnye sovety* were not directly under the jurisdiction of the Institute of History nor of the Presidium of the Academy of Sciences. For this reason they were, in the words of M. V. Nechkina, 'not just institutions but social organizations'.[196] The relative autonomy of the *nauchnye sovety* from the party-state made them important rudiments of civil society in these years.[197] One other important realm of autonomy, which existed even in Stalin's day and was unique to Soviet academic institutions, was the *uchenye sovety* (Academic Councils). Senior researchers were elected, by secret ballot, to these councils for five years, or three in the case of junior researchers. These elected councils gave Soviet scholars considerable say in the research agenda.[198]

Thus during the late-1950s and early-1960s a growing network of institutions was set in place that gradually consolidated historians, along with other scholars, as a community, though a divided one. This process was spurred by the Twenty-second Congress that encouraged an increasing number of specialist conferences, many of them convened by the *nauchnye sovety*. The year 1962 saw several large conferences which climaxed with the 2000 strong all-Union conference of historians.[199] Thus the programmatic conviction that communism was on the horizon, plus the renewed onslaught against Stalin at the Twenty-second Congress, symbolized by the removal of his corpse from Lenin's mausoleum, led to *the party effectively mobilizing the historians*, although they remained carefully controlled, intellectually and organizationally.

This supervision was a systemic feature of the culture of Soviet historical research and writing, despite the relative liberalism of the Khrushchev era. Textbooks outlined officially-sanctioned perspectives on the past, and collective works were encouraged at the expense of individual monographs which were viewed with some suspicion.[200] The prohibition on non-state publishing houses prevented unauthorized publications and thereby impeded the development of independent 'schools' among historians.[201] Editorials in party and academic journals signalled the priorities and boundaries of research. Party committees within institutions were intended to ensure that these were adhered to, and if they did not there was the Argus-eyed Department of Science of the Central Committee. Its brief was not to decide what needed to be studied but what could not. Above all, there was an anonymous system of censorship administered by Glavlit, which authorized every text.[202] Relaxed somewhat under Khrushchev, censorship become increasingly harsh again under Brezhnev. The result was self-censorship – 'the most important of all forms of censorship'.[203] Historians, almost instinctively sensing the boundaries of the acceptable, often as not indulged in *dvoinoe soznanie* (dual consciousness): reserving one opinion for the public realm and another for the private.[204] Alternatively, a historian might resort to Aesopian or 'associative' thinking to evade censorship.[205] The intention of this regimen was to create a band of subservient court scribes. The outcome, however, was increasingly the opposite of this.

It proved impossible to completely stifle the developments in history unleashed by the Twentieth Congress, and given renewed impetus by the Twenty-second. A striking example of this was the posthumous, partial rehabilitation of M. N. Pokrovsky. In late 1961 he was reinstated as a Bolshevik and accorded guarded recognition of his achievements as a historian.[206] Sidorov, a former student of Pokrovsky, was instrumental in resurrecting his reputation. As Director of the Institute of History, he urged publication of Pokrovsky's selected works in 12 volumes, though he stressed that, 'Of course, this would not signify the rehabilitation of Pokrovsky'.[207] Sullied since the Stalin period as an 'economic materialist', restoration of Pokrovsky's reputation, if not that of his much-maligned 'school', was a shot in the arm for the proponents of destalinization.

The 1962 all-Union conference was a sequel to the anticipated transition to communism. Convened by the Central Committee and the Council of Ministers, the tone of the conference was set by the reports given by academic mandarins such as Central Committee secretary Boris Ponomarev and Academician V. M. Khvostov, Director of the Institute of History. While the formal agenda of the conference was the training of historians, the real agenda was to ensure that the historians served the immediate programmatic needs of the party.[208] Official calls to effectively bury the 'cult of the personality' in historical writing once and for all were coupled with cautions against those who would use this interment as a 'pretext' to undermine Marxism–Leninism.[209]

Nevertheless this did not prevent many of the historians present, including senior academicians, from publicly voicing their concerns in a way not seen since the *Voprosy istorii* readers' conferences six years earlier. Repeated complaints about unnecessary censorship, restrictions on access to archives, the doctoring of documents, the closure of *Istorichesky arkhiv,* the lack of opportunity to travel overseas, isolation from international scholarship, the lack of any professional organization, coupled with warnings about the need for an ongoing struggle against Stalinism, gave voice to the simmering discontent of an increasingly professional body of scholars resentful of party intrusion and the debasement of history as a craft.[210] Unfortunately, the furious struggle then being waged within the party leadership around destalinization prevented much of the potential of the all-Union conference from being realized, particularly in the field of party history.[211]

The intrepid Burdzhalov, speaking at the 1962 all-Union conference, reaffirmed the rightness of his stand five years earlier; his interpretation of Stalin's position in March 1917 had become more or less orthodoxy.[212] Despite official reconfirmation of the previous strictures against *Voprosy istorii,*[213] his confidence in the future of Soviet historiography had not diminished:

> It can't be said that there are no clouds on our horizon, nor that our skies are cleared of everything that brought us the cult of Stalin ... But the main thing has been done. The Twentieth Congress of the CPSU aroused our critical thought; it won't be stifled now. There may be zigzags and retreats; nevertheless Soviet historical science will move forward.[214]

Burdzhalov was right: historical science had already advanced down other paths, notably in the history of Russian imperialism under the tsars. An advance perversely facilitated by the revolution in the production of history unleashed by the Twentieth Congress. This progress undoubtedly registered the emergence of what Heer called 'professional group consciousness' among historians.[215] But the framework from Nettl adopted here enables us to see the growing professionalism of historians as but an element of their gradual crystallization into 'intellectuals of quality'. We are now in a position to examine the work of a particularly important group of them: the 'New Direction' historians.

Part II
Some Major Discussions

3
The New Direction Historians

> 'These new principles of the New Direction gave us the opportunity to move forward, to develop a more truthful picture of the pre-history of the October Revolution and, in general, to move towards a more profound, rounded understanding of the history of the development of the first quarter of the twentieth century – the most complex, contradictory, tragic and dramatic period in the history of Russia.'
>
> Academician P. V. Volobuev, Moscow, April 1992

It is an irony of Soviet historiography that some scholars who at one stage had been the staunchest Stalinists could be instrumental in generating new perspectives in historical writing. A particularly striking example of this was Arkady Sidorov. As we have seen, Sidorov had been a key player in the anti-cosmopolitan campaign and, as Director of the Institute of History, had vehemently opposed Burdzhalov. Yet Sidorov was the 'black sheep' of his generation;[1] he was also the patron of a group of young scholars who eventually formed the backbone of historical revisionism in the 1960s – the so-called 'New Direction' (*novoe napravlenie*) historians. The challenge to the prevailing historical paradigm that these scholars presented came not through rewriting party history, as it had with Burdzhalov, but more indirectly. Initially, it was through their reconsideration of the history of Russian imperialism; subsequently, it was through their application of the concept of 'multistructuredness' (*mnogoukladnost'*) to prerevolutionary Russian society, coupled with their challenge to existing interpretations of Russian absolutism.

The New Direction provides us with a neat case study of a paradigm shift in the making: what started out as an empirical inquiry into the economic preconditions of the October Revolution necessarily demanded new methods of conceptualizing this complex phenomenon. For this undertaking, the crude tools of the *Short Course* were far from adequate. It required a break with an approach that reduced October 1917 to a mere manifestation of the mono-dimensional productive forces/relations of production contradiction. These historians had to work their way through this question. It was an intense rereading of Lenin that provided the way forward, but even then the path was far from straight. The Twentieth Congress provided the space and stimulus to pursue this. In defiance of the 'intellectuals of scope', who merely reiterated the same received truths about the causes of the October Revolution, the New Direction 'intellectuals of quality' challenged the accepted explanatory framework, presaging thereby a paradigm shift. Ultimately, the result was a Marxism that located the causes of the revolution in a complex ensemble of contradictions. However, with the onset of the Brezhnevite reaction it was an increasingly risky academic enterprise to interrogate the fundamentals of Marxism–Leninism. The rise of neo-Stalinism drove these scholars and their cothinkers into a *public* defence of their principles. In other words, they gradually assumed the traditional role of the *intelligent* as an articulator of the public interest against bureaucratic tyranny. The vanquishing of the New Direction at the end of the 1960s signalled the final defeat of the aspirations of the 'children of the Twentieth Congress'. The dismissal of Pavel Volobuev, a key player in the New Direction, as Director of the Institute of the History of the USSR in 1974 was, at most, the last hurrah of this group of scholars.

Russian imperialism under the tsars

At the end of the 1920s the historiographical question of the socioeconomic status of prerevolutionary Russia had become an essential element of Stalin's political struggle with the reviled 'Trotskyite–Zinovievite bloc' over the nature of the October Revolution and the prospects for Soviet socialism. From the very beginning therefore it was no mere academic question.[2] Its political resonance was still palpable a quarter century later. These debates on Russian imperialism centred on whether the tsarist empire could be defined, in Leninist terms, as an imperialist power or a semi-colony. Resolution of this question revolved around three pivotal problems: the role of foreign capital in the Russian economy; the existence of state-monopoly capitalism; and the applicability of Lenin's term 'military-feudal imperialism' to the development of capitalism in Russia.[3] It was Stalin, as usual, who in the late 1920s intervened in the historiographical debate on the status of the Russian empire to shore up his doctrine of 'socialism in one country', and to consolidate his victory over the party opposition. The historiographical argument that absolutist Russia was a mere semi-colony of European imperialism seemed grist to the mill of the Left Opposition argument that Russian society was too immature for successful socialist construction.[4]

Stalin, however, having denounced the 'semi-colony' thesis as Trotskyist in his notorious 1931 letter to *Proletarskaya revolyutisiya*, in 1934 formally embraced the position that tsarist Russia was a semi-colony of the Western imperialist powers (a switch that coincided with a retreat from class to national perspectives formalized by the adoption of the Popular Front policy in 1935).[5] The 'semi-colony' thesis was formally incorporated into the *Short Course* in 1938.[6] It remained an unassailable orthodoxy until Stalin's death in 1953. Thereafter gradually challenged by researchers, it was not until after the Twentieth Congress that a frontal assault was made on the concept. But at this stage there was a contradiction; in repudiating Stalin's 'semi-colony' thesis, these historians embraced Stalin's earlier, anti-Trotskyist position that Russia was a full-fledged imperialist state, ripe for the construction of socialism.

For Konstantin Tarnovsky,[7] whose name was to become synonymous with the revisionist New Direction and who painstakingly chronicled this debate, a vital historiographical and political question was at stake. Stalin's endorsement of the semi-colony thesis violated the 'entire logic of the Leninist analysis of the lawfulness of the victory of the socialist revolution'. Lenin's theory of imperialism explained the existence of the necessary material and organizational prerequisites for the 'growing over' of the bourgeois-democratic revolution into a proletarian revolution, despite Russia's backwardness, and thus for the victory of the October Revolution. Stalin's approach, however, devoid as it was of any analysis of the 'internal lawfulness' of the revolution, necessarily resorted to extraordinary circumstances and/or exogenous factors, such as the destructive impact of the war on the Russian economy, to explain the October Revolution.[8] Accordingly, for Tarnovsky, 'the history of the elaboration of the problem of Russian imperialism by Soviet scholars [was] simultaneously the history of their ... gradual assimilation of the richness of Leninist thought' on imperialism and

Russian history.[9] But reappropriation of Lenin was no guarantee that they would be immune to the anti-Trotskyist political legacy bequeathed by this question.

The question of Russian imperialism reveals how much the renaissance in Soviet historiography in the 1960s was stimulated by a return to the debates of the late 1920s–early 1930s. It also reveals how much the nightmare of the Stalinist past weighed on the minds of these historians. At that time, Sidorov had been one of the principal proponents of the 'nationalizer' thesis, those that maintained that absolutist Russia was an imperialist state, against the 'denationalizers', like N. N. Vanag who argued for Russia's semi-colonial status. In the 1930s this was a life and death question: Vanag was eventually shot as an 'enemy of the people', having allegedly confessed to semi-Trotskyist errors in 1931.[10] Sidorov and his co-thinkers, such as I. F. Gindin, had wisely abandoned researching Russian imperialism during Stalin's heyday. But it was Stalin himself who facilitated the revival of research in this field by his last theoretical pronouncement, *The Economic Problems of Socialism* published in 1952. This brief tract, it will be recalled, reemphasized the economic problematic in Marxism–Leninism, an orientation with which Sidorov was comfortable. In the early 1950s, Sidorov set about reestablishing systematic research on the development of industrial monopolies in tsarist Russia. He gathered around him a 'brilliant' team of students to research this field, among them, V. V. Adamov, Valery Bovykin, Mikhail Gefter, Aleksandr Grunt, Kornely Shatsillo, Konstantin Tarnovsky and Pavel Volobuev. From the ranks of Sidorov's students were to emerge some of the most illustrious revisionist historians in the 1960s. The single exception is Bovykin, who eventually found himself in Trapeznikov's camp, a story that we shall return to.

The reconstitution of the 'nationalizer' thesis proceeded in two phases. The first, up until the mid-1950s, focussed on elaborating a number of key questions in relation to Russian imperialism on the basis of markedly increased primary research. The second phase, following the Twentieth Congress, witnessed researchers striving to make sense of the accumulated data, as well as moving towards a direct critique of the Stalinist 'denationalizer' formulation through a reconsideration of Lenin's approach to Russian imperialism.[11] Paradoxically, the motivation for this reconsideration had a conservative thrust. Sidorov and his colleagues, Gindin and P. G. Galuzo, were of that generation of historians whose outlook was steeled by the 'terrorist methods' employed against the oppositions in the 1920s and 1930s. They were intent on establishing, on the basis of detailed research, that the socio-economic prerequisites for full-fledged socialism, that is the highest forms of monopoly capital, existed in tsarist Russia.[12] In this sense, initially, they were giving succour to the original, anti-Trotskyist, tenets that underpinned Stalin's 'socialism in one country' doctrine. Ultimately, they would begin to undermine them.

It is apparent that Sidorov, despite his loyalties to Stalin, retained certain scholarly qualities instilled in him by Pokrovsky, which Sidorov passed on to his students. In this sense, Sidorov was a living link with the 1920s 'golden age' of historiography. One of his characteristics was a 'love of methodological questions';[13] the other, his conviction that archival research was the foundation of genuine scholarship: 'Archives – these are your future', he told the young Volobuev. 'You cannot be a historian without working in archives'.[14] In an environment in which historians were still viewed as 'archive rats', to use Stalin's unsavoury expression, this was a bold injunction indeed.

In the early 1950s, two of Sidorov's *kandidat* students, Volobuev[15] and Gefter, undertook intense archival research into the development of Russian monopolies in the production of sugar, oil and coal. From this research, and from his reading of Lenin, Gefter concluded that there was the 'basis for a critical reconsideration of the perceived absence in tsarist Russia of monopolies of the highest type'.[16] In drawing this conclusion, Gefter was reaffirming the arguments mounted against N. N. Vanag two decades earlier.

Meanwhile, the assault on the 'denationalizer' thesis advanced on another front: relations between the tsarist state and monopoly capitalism. Again, Gefter and Volobuev were in the front line. Their *kandidat* theses, defended in 1953, countenanced the previously discredited concept of the 'coalescence' of the tsarist state with the capitalist monopolies prior to the First World War.[17] This, together with research into the 'merging' of the state and monopolies fostered by the war, challenged Stalin's assertion that the tsarist state, allegedly the mere creature of feudal landlords, had impeded the development of monopoly capitalism. While strengthening the neo-'nationalizer' perspective, Gefter's and Volobuev's critique eroded Stalin's crude notion of the direct 'subjection' of the state to ruling class interests.

Thus, even before the Twentieth Congress, these historians were confident that the 'denationalizer' thesis had been seriously challenged by empirical research. But the *Short Course* concepts that underlay Stalin's caricatured version of the 'denationalizer' thesis had yet to be confronted. Without doing so, the historiography of Russian imperialism could not advance; yet few, if any, historians were conscious of the necessity to break with the Stalinist conceptions of this question. As long as Stalin was above reproach, it was extremely 'difficult to break with the routines' of research.[18] Given the real – not just imposed – weight of the *Short Course* paradigm, 'which pressed on the consciousness of the historian',[19] even more than Gefter and his colleagues were aware, it would take a fundamental rupture in the political realm to reorient the research environment. The Twentieth Congress provided that rupture.

At the January 1956 *Voprosy istorii* readers' conference Burdzhalov had bemoaned the journal's neglect of the history of tsarist imperialism. He called for research into the 'growing over of industrial capitalism into imperialism, the specific features of military-feudal imperialism in Russia and the character of the subordination of the state apparatus to the monopolies in various countries'.[20] Neither Sidorov nor Gefter in their contributions to the conference discussion took up Burdzhalov's remarks on Russian imperialism, which Sidorov at least seemed to interpret as a revival of Trotskyist errors. Burdzhalov's appeal was soon answered on the pages of *Voprosy istorii*, in an article candidly entitled 'Was Tsarist Russia a Semi-Colony?' Its author, B. B. Grave, squarely laid the responsibility for the 'semi-colony' thesis, and the chauvinist perspective on tsarism that accompanied it, at Stalin's feet.[21] However, the opportunity to finally demolish many of the Stalinist shibboleths on this question, if not recover the Trotskyist perspective, was lost with the counter-offensive against Burdzhalov. The incoming, neo-Stalinist editorial board of *Voprosy istorii* terminated debate around the dependent status of tsarist Russia.[22]

In the meantime, research on Russian monopolies continued, facilitated particularly by the publication *Istoricheskie zapiski* (*Historical Transactions*), of which Sidorov became chief editor in 1954. *Istoricheskie zapiski* consisted of 'collections of short scientific monographs devoted to various areas and problems of Soviet history', with a notable bias towards historiographical questions. But it was more than a research publication; it was also the vehicle for the 'crystallization' of many trends in Soviet historiography, above all, in the years 1954–57, the *'school of Professor A. L. Sidorov'*.[23] Mainly former *aspiranty* of Sidorov, this 'school' formed the 'kernel of a new scientific direction' that emerged in 1957, which was, according to Tarnovsky,[24] the 'crowning achievement of his life' (although almost another decade passed before its birth – in 1965 – was formally announced).[25] The presence of Volobuev among this cohort, as a former political instructor well-connected with the central party apparatus, also gave considerable impetus to its formation.[26]

The emergence of the New Direction was also facilitated by the formation at the end of 1957 of a scientific council, chaired by Sidorov, devoted to 'The Historical Preconditions of the Great October Socialist Revolution'. Concentrating the resources of historians and economists in Moscow and Leningrad, as well as 'tens' of researchers in the provinces, the council was well-equipped to take advantage of the considerably broadened source-base occasioned by the recent opening up of archives.[27] The next few years witnessed prodigious research, particularly by Bovykin and Shatsillo, on the formation of finance capital in Russian military industries during the First World War.[28] By the end of the 1950s these economic historians believed that they had firmly demonstrated that monopoly associations existed in Russia, just like those in other imperialist countries, and that there was a 'partnership' rather than a relationship of 'subordination' between Russian and foreign banking and industrial monopolies.[29] But, in so far as they erased the distinction between tsarist imperialism and that of other imperialist states, at this stage of their development the New Direction were still adapting to Russian patriotic sentiment, embellishing the Russian empire with a 'civilized, European appearance'.[30]

Nevertheless, they moved forward. Towards the end of the 1950s their research began to move away from a primarily *economic* problematic towards a *political* one. The prime movers here were Gefter, Volobuev and Gindin.[31] Their researches demonstrated that the tsarist state had actively fostered indigenous monopolies 'from above'. The long-standing 'subjection' thesis, that the tsarist state was simply subordinate to the Russian monopolies, a primitive version of Marx and Engels' view that the capitalist state was simply an executive committee of the bourgeoisie, had hindered research into modern day state-monopoly capitalism. It narrowed the Leninist understanding of the role of the state, which was depicted as merely serving to maximize monopoly profits. This purely passive, *economic* perspective on the modern capitalist state had been entrenched by Stalin's 'slating' in 1952 of Academician Eugene Varga's views of the active, interventionist state under postwar monopoly capitalism, which had encouraged renewed research into Russian imperialism.[32] But by the end of the decade Varga's perspective had established its credibility.[33] The evident conflict between the accepted notion of the simple subordination of the state to monopoly interests and the reality of capitalism in the 1950s, and the strategic importance of 'state capitalism' as an accelerator of economic development in Asia, India for example,[34] fuelled a state-monopoly capitalism perspective in which the state played an increasingly interventionist role. Thus contemporary developments in the capitalist world influenced historical research.

The study of tsarist government policy, particularly by Gindin, Bovykin and Tarnovsky, turned the research focus away from monopoly associations towards the autocracy's role in the latter half of the nineteenth century in promoting monopolies 'from above'. These three researchers repudiated the 'subjection' concept of state-monopoly relations in favour of the 'coalescence' of the tsarist state and monopolies. On the eve of the Twenty-second Party Congress, at the all-important session of Sidorov's scientific council held in Leningrad, the critics of the 'subjection' thesis were taken to task for deviating from Marxist–Leninist theory on the role of the state.[35] But the convergence between questions of history and those of contemporary political economy, such as Varga's, turned the tide. The debate over 'coalescence' versus 'subjection' had run its course.

At stake in this ostensibly terminological debate was a vital theoretical question: could the state play an active role in the formation of state-monopoly capitalism? (as we shall see, a harbinger of a subsequent debate in which the New Direction were to the fore: could a feudal-absolutist state foster a bourgeoisie?). According to Tarnovsky, victory for the proponents of the Leninist conceptions of the 'interweaving, coalescence and merging' of the state and monopoly capital was signaled by the inclusion of the 'state-monopoly capital' formula in the new party program adopted at the 1961 Twenty-second Party Congress.[36] Clearly, at this time, the historical perspectives of the emerging New Direction were largely in step with the party's political perspectives.

One other facet of the nationalizer/denationalizer debate remained to be addressed: Russian 'military-feudal imperialism', a question that exposed the contradictory tendencies inherent in the New Direction perspectives at this stage of their development. On the one hand, they strove to establish that Russian imperialism was essentially indistinguishable from its West European counterparts, and therefore provided the necessary preconditions for the October Socialist Revolution. On the other, they increasingly sought to elucidate the 'specific' conditions that triggered revolution in Russia in 1917. The former was essentially a conservative concern, flowing from the old nationalizer perspective; the latter hearkened back to the denationalizer thesis, which cast doubts that the prerequisites for socialist revolution were present in Russia. The New Direction sought to overcome this contradiction 'artificially – by recourse to the authority of Lenin'.[37]

Lenin had used the formula 'military-feudal imperialism' on a number of occasions to describe the tsarist autocracy. During the 1950s two competing interpretations of Lenin's formula developed within the neo-nationalizer school. Where Volobuev saw 'military-feudal imperialism' as defining the nature of Russian imperialism, Sidorov, Gefter and Tarnovsky saw it as defining the political superstructure of Russian imperialism, that is, the state; a stance that provoked a decisive debate about 'military-feudal imperialism' at the 1961 Leningrad session of the scientific council.[38]

For Tarnovsky, at stake in interpreting 'military-feudal imperialism' was the entire rationale for a proletarian revolution and the building of Soviet socialism. Lenin, he argued, had made a clear distinction between 'military-feudal' and 'capitalist' imperialism of tsarist Russia. The former applied only to the 'political superstructure' of autocratic Russia; to see it as a defining feature of Russian imperialism underrated the presence of the most advanced capitalist imperialism in Russia – and undermined the basis for the October Socialist Revolution.[39]

Tarnovsky tried to stave off the latter implication by distinguishing between 'the peculiarities of imperialism in Russia as elements of the capitalist structure (*uklad*), on the one hand, and the peculiarities of the economy of Russia of the period of imperialism on the other'.[40] The former, he argued, in Lenin's interpretation, was restricted to the finance capital component of the capitalist *uklad*; the latter, a much broader concept, embraced the 'exceptionally contradictory' character of the economy in the period of imperialism, based on Lenin's notion of the

> multistructuredness (*mnogukladnost'*) of the Russian economy. This multistructuredness arose from the combination of capitalism as the leading, defining *uklad* with remnants of feudalism and even patriarchy and, within the capitalist *uklad* – a combination of small domestic industries with big industrial concerns, highly concentrated and united by monopoly organizations.[41]

Tarnovsky argued that the error of the proponents of 'military-feudal imperialism' derived from their identifying 'feudal-serf remnants' in

84 *Some Major Discussions*

the economy as the defining feature of imperialism in Russia, rather than its political superstructure.

Given the historiographical-political significance of this alleged distinction between the peculiarities of the Russian economy and those of Russian imperialism, Tarnovsky hailed its elucidation as a 'major achievement of historico-economic literature in recent years'.[42] It was, but not in the sense that Tarnovsky maintained, that is, simultaneously safeguarding Russian ripeness for socialism while allowing for its specificities. Rather, it opened up a new problematic that would cast light on the specific features of Russian backwardness. Paradoxically, despite their intentions, in embracing 'multistructuredness' the New Direction were laying the groundwork for an approach that would give credence to the old 'Trotskyite', 'denationalizer' thesis, so reviled by Sidorov and Gindin. In doing so they were undermining the very notion that Russia possessed all the necessary prerequisites for Soviet socialism, although they themselves never explicitly acknowledged this.[43]

Rural Russia: capitalist or feudal?

Up until the early 1960s the research focus of the Sidorov school had been overwhelmingly on the development of imperialist monopoly capitalism in Russia, to the detriment of research on the question of the nature of socio-economic relations in the Russian countryside. What they mistakenly took to be the triumph of the 'nationalizer' argument in 1961 allowed attention to be turned to the development of capitalism in rural Russia in the latter part of the nineteenth century and the early twentieth century. This refocus on rural Russia by some of Sidorov's students during the 1960s raised the question of the interrelationship between the development of monopoly capitalism and parallel socio-economic developments in the countryside. It also turned the focus to Russia's backwardness, rather than its development.

The limited research on agrarian relations in imperial Russia undertaken between the late 1940s and the mid-1950s started from the presumption that by the 1890s the capitalist mode of production was 'completely victorious' in the countryside, notwithstanding the recognition that significant 'feudal-serf remnants' remained. In the early 1950s, however, considerable research was undertaken on the effects of Stolypin's reform on 'the socio-economic development of the Russian countryside' in the years after the 1905 revolution.

Overall, it was concluded, Stolypin's reforms had only 'sharpened contradictions in the countryside'. These researches in the early 1950s had a definite political concern. Just as the reevaluation of the development of monopoly capitalism raised the question of the preconditions for *socialist* revolution, so querying the degree of capitalist transformation engendered by the Stolypin reforms raised the question of whether they had eliminated the conditions for a *bourgeois-democratic* revolution in the countryside?[44]

According to Tarnovsky, the thaw in intellectual life occasioned by the Twentieth and Twenty-second Party Congresses was particularly conducive to the study of the agrarian history of imperial Russia. As well as the scientific council on the preconditions of the October Revolution, in 1958 the first of the annual symposia on the agrarian history of Eastern Europe convened in Tallin. Two generations of researchers took advantage of these openings: the first, survivors of the prewar generation, such as Galuzo and S. M. Dubrovsky, combined their talents with those who graduated in the 1950s, such as A. M. Anfimov and L. M. Ivanov. Together, they shifted the research problematic to a broad investigation of developments in agriculture at the beginning of the century.[45]

Andrei Anfimov (1916–95), who in 1956 defended his candidate thesis *The Russian Countryside During the First World War (1914–February 1917)*, concluded that estates operating on 'Prussian' capitalist principles (capitalist organization of the landlord's property combined with feudal exploitation of land worked by the peasantry) had actually retarded the development of capitalist agricultural production.[46]

In tackling this question, Anfimov simultaneously undertook an exegesis of Lenin's views. Anfimov argued that those who drew on Lenin to support their argument in favour of the dominance of capitalist relations in the countryside relied on isolated citations from Lenin, rather than the 'system of his views'. Armed with Lenin's 'system' of thought, Anfimov set out to establish 'to what degree' capitalist or serf features prevailed in Russian agriculture, bearing in mind that in the period of imperialism the rural economy was necessarily subject to the laws of capitalism. His preliminary conclusion was that up until the end of tsarism 'semi-feudal' relations had prevailed over capitalist ones in rural Russia.

Anfimov's conclusion raised an important political question: did this mean that the Russian Revolution at best could be only a bourgeois-democratic revolution and that there was no basis for the working peasantry supporting a socialist revolution led by the working class? In answering this Anfimov turned to Lenin, who, he argued, had repudiated the view that a socialist revolution was merely a 'direct result of the high development of capitalism'. Rather, Lenin considered it was the result of various social contradictions. On the other hand, the underdeveloped nature of Russian capitalism meant the peasantry *as a whole* had a vested interest in the nationalization of the land, that is, in a bourgeois-democratic revolution. On the other hand, agrarian capitalism was already deep rooted enough to drive the rural poor into an alliance with the urban working class towards a socialist revolution.[47]

By the end of the 1950s two distinct perspectives, largely reflecting a generational divide, had emerged within the new Soviet historiography in relation to the penetration of capitalism into the Russian countryside. At issue was the 'degree' of transformation of the feudal-serf agrarian system (*stroi*) into a capitalist one in the period of imperialism. One hypothesis, articulated principally by Dubrovsky, maintained that capitalist relations were victorious in 'agriculture as a whole, and in the agrarian system' in particular. The other, represented chiefly by Anfimov, argued that in the agrarian system capitalism had 'adapted the old property relations to its needs but had not managed to transform them; as a result, semi-feudal relations prevailed' in the countryside.[48]

These contrary perspectives looked beyond the *Short Course* to Lenin for their conceptual framework. Lenin had suggested that in Russia at the beginning of the twentieth century 'capitalist agrarian orders were still far from being formed'. According to Tarnovsky, the point of contention in interpreting Lenin's remark concerned the '*process* of the transformation of the feudal-serf agrarian system into the capitalist one'.[49] Such a contest of hypotheses could only be resolved by detailed empirical research. But their very existence testified how far the conceptualization of the debate on agrarian Russia had shifted since Stalin's time.

It is important to keep in mind, however, that shifting the terms of debate, even in Khrushchev's time, was more than just a benign intellectual exercise. Considerable political tensions were entailed in such a debate. According to Anfimov,[50] even in 1959 it was an audacious act on Sidorov's part, as editor of *Istoricheskie zapiski,* to publish an article by Anfimov in which he championed the 'seditious' thesis of the prevalence of semi-serf relations over capitalist relations.[51] Although little more than three years had passed since the Twentieth Congress, the 'Khrushchevite "thaw" had been left far behind as a new ideological offensive gained strength on every front of social life – from the natural sciences to cultural phenomena, such as art and sculpture.'[52]

When, in May 1960, an analogous formula to Anfimov's was presented to a session of the scientific council on the pre-conditions of the October Revolution it was met with 'angry condemnation' on the part of the reporters, such as Dubrovsky.

Underlying this academic tension was a generational conflict. Scholars, such as Dubrovsky, although he had suffered under Stalin, had continued to defend unequivocally the view that capitalist relations prevailed in the Russian countryside. The subsequent differentiation of the peasantry into the 'poor and the rich', provided a simple class explanation – rural proletariat versus bourgeoisie – for the 'lawfulness' of the socialist revolution in the countryside. The counterposition, according to Dubrovsky, was 'Menshevism', in as much as it admitted only a 'democratic revolution' under the hegemony of the bourgeoisie (Sidorov countered by likening Dubrovsky's position to the 'liquidationist' Menshevik position, which acknowledged the success of the Stolypin reforms in introducing capitalism). Such political 'labeling', a 'norm of social control' under Stalin, persisted in Soviet academic discourse long after the dictator's demise. At the 1962 all-Union historians' conference Gorodetsky condemned labeling as 'public informing'; but his protest, writes Anfimov, 'fell on deaf ears, informing remained a common practice',[53] despite the fresh impetus given to anti-Stalinism by the Twenty-second Congress.

Around this time the debate concerning the agrarian history of pre-revolutionary Russia began to merge with the research of scholars concerned with the history of Soviet agriculture; particularly that of Viktor Danilov. Danilov was not a member of the New Direction, but he owed his career to the patronage of Sidorov.[54]

In March 1960, Danilov presented a paper on the history of the peasantry and collective farming to the Scientific Council on the History of Socialist and Communist Construction.[55] Danilov differed from Dubrovsky on a number of crucial points. In particular, Danilov attributed much greater weight to the democratic tasks in the agrarian revolution than Dubrovsky. This difference derived from Danilov's critique of the *Short Course* omission of the 'two stages' of the October Revolution in the countryside: the bourgeois-democratic stage, up until spring 1918, and the socialist, beginning in the summer of that year. Dubrovsky, in Danilov's perspective, remained trapped within the *Short Course* thesis that the October Revolution had resolved the bourgeois-democratic tasks in the countryside 'in passing' – thereby dissolving 'an entire stage' of the rural revolution.[56]

This continuous dialogue between the specialists on pre-revolutionary, rural Russia and those on the Soviet agrarian revolution was indicative of a method of historical analysis that Sidorov had instilled in his students: in order to know if the conclusions about a given question were correct, it was necessary to look ahead to the outcome of a process, to 'the moment of its fullest development and resolution of its internal contradictions'. Only then could one go back to the early stages of the process and with confidence ' "discern" the main trends of development, as opposed to the purely contingent'.[57] In this case, the course of the October Revolution in the countryside would be a litmus test for the question of whether or not capitalist or pre-capitalist relations previously prevailed in the countryside. Those who advocated that capitalist relations prevailed argued that this alone could explain the 'swift growing-over' of the bourgeois-democratic revolution into a socialist revolution. The advocates of the dominance of feudal-serf relations stressed the 'two-stages' of the October rural revolution. For Danilov, the fact that the development of monopoly capitalism in Russia had actually strengthened feudal-serf remnants in the agrarian system provided evidence that the peasantry as a whole had supported the Bolsheviks up until summer 1918. Only after this had a (Bolshevik induced) 'split' occurred within the peasantry. In other words, the bourgeois-democratic revolution could only be realized, in the first instance, through a proletarian seizure of power.[58]

According to Tarnovsky, the May 1960 session of the Scientific Council on 'The Historical Preconditions of the Great October Revolution' was a 'turning point' in the study of the agrarian history of Russia at the turn of the century. The acknowledgement of the 'incompleteness' of capitalist development in agriculture up until October 1917, even by the staunchest proponents of the prevalence of capitalist relations thesis, marked a 'rapprochement' between the two tendencies.[59] The outcome of the session might, however, be better described as a 'truce'; within a decade the proponents of the predominance of capitalism would unleash their counter offensive– with a vengeance.

By the mid-1960s the revisionist historians had managed to confront, if not vanquish, the thesis of the preponderance of capitalist relations in the Russian countryside.[60] Nevertheless, the revisionists continued to share a fundamental conceptual error with their opponents: that the October Revolution involved an alliance between the proletariat and the *poor* peasantry, rather than with the peasantry as whole. The former, Stalinist perspective denied the 'two-stage' agrarian revolution; effectively asserting that the October Revolution in the countryside from the 'very beginning bore a socialist character'. Despite this, since the 1960s the 'Leninist principles' on the October Revolution as a proletarian 'bloc' with the entire peasantry and the 'two-stage' agrarian revolution had begun to reassert themselves in the literature. This opened the possibility of decisively resolving this contradiction within the research as well as establishing what it was about the socio-economic development of capitalism in Russia that shaped the 'originality of the historical situation in Russia at the time of the October Revolution'. But to do this required going still further beyond the research parameters established so far.[61]

The *political* stakes in these labyrinthine discussions about the socio-economic make-up of the countryside in pre-revolutionary Russia were very high indeed–as the fate of the New Direction was to testify. The case for the direct transition to socialist relations in the countryside, that is, full-scale collectivization of agriculture, ultimately rested on the view that capitalism already prevailed in Russia by 1917.[62] Exaggerating the weight of capitalist landlords in agriculture, as opposed to small producers and arguing that by October 1917 the basic rural conflict was between the poor peasantry and the 'Stolypin heritage' of rich, capitalist 'farmers' and not between the peasantry as a whole and the semi-serf landlords, justified the 'lawfulness and virtues of the future monstrous liquidation of this class'. Hence, the particularly 'heated arguments that flared up' around precisely who were the real allies of the proletariat in October 1917: the peasantry as a whole or only the poor peasantry.[63]

Russia's 'multistructuredness'

By the mid-1960s the question of the predominance of capitalist or semi-feudal relations in the agrarian system had 'ceased to be a *pivotal* issue'.[64] The problem of the level of capitalist development had been superseded by the question of

> a complex combination of semi-feudal ... early-capitalist and genuinely capitalist relations ... The study of the landlord economy as a composite ... [raised] the question of the *interaction* of Russian capitalist imperialism with other socio-economic structures.[65]

In other words, it raised the vexed question of 'multistructuredness'.

It was becoming apparent that previous research that focussed on two facets of the socio-economic history of imperialist Russia – the development of state monopoly capitalism and feudal remnants in the countryside – despite the considerable achievements, remained locked into a purely *economic* problematic. Major research undertaken in the mid-1960s, coupled with the 'conceptual' challenge of this work, generated a new model that focussed on the 'multistructuredness' of the Russian economy. On this basis, the question of the preconditions of the October Revolution began to be interpreted not simply in the light of the development of the *'highest* forms of capitalism, but also in the collisions and struggle of different structures'. Increasingly the question became one of 'the necessity of a multi-facetted study of the economic structures in their mutual interaction and influence'.[66]

A new approach of necessity required a new methodology; and this implied a new historical paradigm. In this sense, 1964 was a crucial year for historical revisionism. For historiography, it opened propitiously with the beginnings of an intense engagement with methodological questions. Politically, it ended ominously with the dismissal of Khrushchev as CPSU First Secretary. For the moment, however, the quest for a new methodology continued unchecked, spurring elaboration of the concept of 'multistructuredness'. Gradually formulated as the 'interaction' between different socio-economic 'structures', the Russian economy under the tsars came to be depicted by the New Direction revisionists as a complex, 'multi-structured' phenomenon. The generation of the concept of 'multistructuredness' reflected the increasing concern with methodological questions among Soviet historians, philosophers and economists towards the mid-1960s. The need to retool historical materialism, rather than replourhing the same fields with the flawed conceptual implements bequeathed by the *Short Course*, opened the way for a paradigm shift: not only the promise of new perspectives on Russian society in the period of imperialism and the driving forces of the October Revolution; but also the elaboration of a genuinely materialist conception of history in place of the ersatz version decreed by Stalin.

Such a potential paradigm shift, the result of the 'very logic of research', as Volobuev put it, was necessarily out of place with the political reaction that gathered pace after the October 1964 ousting of Khrushchev. This opened the way for the installation of the 'Brezhnev command' system, which took 'revenge' on the Twentieth Congress. The ensuing 'conservative restoration', overseen by Brezhnev's *alter ego* Sergei Trapeznikov, viewed such ideas as 'seditious'.[67] As we shall see in Chapter 6, they were to cost the scholars of the New Direction dearly; paying for their principles with their careers, health, and even their lives.

The concept of the interaction of a 'multistructured' society was deemed by its proponents to be distinguished from previous conceptions by being open-ended. It belonged, in Tarnovsky's words, to a 'class (or type) of *dynamically developing logical constructs*', which were open to refinement on the basis of further research and unfettered thinking and discussion. In this sense it reflected the relative liberalism accorded to historians during the 'thaw'. But it also reflected the increasing preoccupation of historians with methodological and theoretical questions during the early 1960s – a 'divide' for their intellectual life. The proliferation of research centres beyond Moscow and Leningrad and the increasing acceptance of broad-ranging discussions – rarities in the Stalin period – as the normal method of resolving contentious questions of scholarship, instead of administrative intervention, were powerful stimuli for reformulating research questions. The upshot was that the 'mid-1960s were characterized by a unique ferment of historical thought and by quests for new research methods and approaches, as well as for a new research problematic.'[68] Tarnovsky's characterization of this period well-accords with Kuhn's description of the 'pronounced professional insecurity' that accompanies a 'scientific crisis'.[69] Testimony to this ferment was provided by the growing awareness of the historical community, 'not [just] individual researchers', of the 'pressing need' for a 'multifaceted', theoretically sophisticated approach to research, which was heightened by the January 1964 conference convened to discuss methodological problems of 'history and sociology'.[70]

At the *Istoriya i sotsiologiya* conference the confluence of disparate streams of research, such as that into the developing countries of Latin America,[71] helped to refine the concept of the 'uneven' and 'multistructured' nature of socio-economic history in the twentieth century. Gindin emphasized the relevance which the refined interpretation of Russian imperialism had for the contemporary world: 'Instead of separate deviations from the "classical" capitalism of the West', by which Soviet orthodoxy had until recently measured developments in world politics,

> Russian capitalism as an object of research is far more immediate and instructive for today's developing countries; with its contradictions, multistructuredness, enormous landlord latifundia, adaptation of the big bourgeoisie to vestiges of serfdom, and its alliance of the landlords with big capital, coupling political dominance for the former with economic dominance for the latter.[72]

Tarnovsky's observations on the significance of the *Istoriya i sotsiologiya* conference make transparent the self-conscious striving of this cluster of revisionist historians for a new historical paradigm. For him, this conference revealed the 'trend of development of historical thought'. The discussions of 'multistructuredness' followed a period of intense, but separate, empirical investigations into the nature of monopoly capitalism in pre-revolutionary Russia on the one hand, and its agrarian structure, on the other. But the 'logic of the development of science' demanded that they begin to look at the links between these two social realms of imperial Russia. Increasingly this required a radical reconceptualization of the vacuous sociology provided for them by the accepted categories of orthodox historical materialism. Historians were driven to take up theoretical and methodological questions; hence the increasing championing of the 'comparative-historical method' and 'a multidimensional approach' to socio-economic research – 'above all', the 'interaction of different socio-economic structures within the same formation'. These developments were already well and truly established by 1964; the *Istoriya i sotsiologiya* conference gave an unprecedented opportunity to articulate them. In Tarnovsky's words, research of the socio-economic history of Russia at the beginning of the twentieth century, now heralded 'the formation of *new directions in science*'.[73] The old focus of the Sidorov school, Russia's similarity with the developed countries, with the formation of the New Direction had shifted to comparing Russia with the developing countries. For Tarnovsky, the Marxist historian of the modern world was by definition the historian of 'multistructuredness'.

If 'multistructuredness' and the New Direction were to become synonymous, then responsibility for the introduction of the term into the discourse of Soviet historiography in the 1960s is usually attributed to I. F. Gindin.[74] In 1963 Gindin published a major, two-part article on the development of the Russian bourgeoisie and its interrelationship with the autocracy after the 1861 reforms.[75] Almost in passing, Gindin observed that the 'incongruously' large role of trading capital in the Russian economy was symptomatic of its 'multistructuredness', a dimension that went a long way to explaining the 'complexity and the contradictoriness' of its socio-economic structure. Although the concept had been addressed 'in the most general terms' by Lenin in 1918, the 'multistructuredness' of the Russian economy, argued Gindin, had received scant attention in the Soviet literature, 'especially in relation to the period of imperialism. And no attention had been paid to the fact that "multistructuredness" was vividly reflected in Russian commerce'.[76] Although Gindin's proposition was tucked away in a mere footnote, he had reintroduced a concept that was to be fraught with political consequences for his co-thinkers in the emerging New Direction.

Gindin's introduction of the concept 'multistructuredness' marked in fact the beginnings of a paradigm shift in the study of the exemplar of Russian imperialism; a shift away from a 'purely economic approach in the study of the socio-economic problematic.'[77] Where hitherto the October Revolution had been explained as the necessary outcome of a 'dying, degenerating' capitalism in its imperialist stage,[78] now an explanation was sought in the contradictions of the interactions of its 'multistructured' economy.

Tarnovsky points to a second shift in the research focus that 'united' its two elements, specific research and the review literature, into 'one cycle'. Essentially this entailed the adoption of a 'new problematic' that went beyond a mere broadening out of the research on the socio-economic history of imperialist Russia. Rather, researchers began to refine their conceptions concerning the 'specific features' and 'type' of Russian capitalism and imperialism.[79]

In this regard, a very important methodological advance towards understanding the specific features of Russian capitalism was made with the publication of Tarnovsky's review of A. I. Levkovsky's 1963 study *The Specific Features of the Development of Capitalism in India*.[80] Tarnovsky's increasing enthusiasm for comparative analysis suggested the importance of examining the 'broader problem' of 'late' capitalist development.[81] Using Levkovsky's study, Tarnovsky argued that post-independence India 'roughly' corresponded to Russian capitalism after the 1861 reform. On the basis of this comparison, Tarnovsky identified 'two types of countries with similar features of capitalist evolution: countries of early capitalism and countries of late capitalism.' The latter were characterized by the absence of the archetypal 'free market' capitalism – but the presence of 'extremely significant remnants of feudalism, which impeded socio-economic development', together with accelerated large-scale industrial production. This belated industrialization was generated by the 'active intervention of the state into the economy, on the one hand, and by a massive influx of foreign capital, on the other'. This led to the emergence of a 'highly significant state-capitalist sector' in the second type of country; 'a phenomenon almost completely unknown in the first type'.[82]

For Tarnovsky, the heuristic value of Levkovsky's study was that it enabled historians of Russian imperialism to see that the peculiarities of the socio-economic development of Russia were not 'deviations' from the norm of capitalist development, as comparisons with Western Europe implied. Rather, comparison with newly-developing countries such as India confirmed, for example, the signal role of the state in fostering capitalist industrialization 'from above' as the 'lawful' path of countries belatedly embracing capitalism.[83] Tarnovsky's analysis of Russian imperialism was a far cry from that of Gefter and Sidorov a decade earlier who, comparing it to that of Western Europe, discerned the most developed forms of monopoly capital.[84] In this sense, it also registered a turn away from the pronounced Eurocentrism that coloured orthodox Soviet historiography.

Research in relation to the 'young capitalist' countries encouraged Gindin in particular to pursue another path of inquiry in relation to tsarist imperialism: the impact of 'multistructuredness' on the unevenness of capitalist development in Belorussia, the Urals and Central Asia.[85] In turn, increased attention to the geographical unevenness of Russian economic development led in the early 1960s to a provincial Soviet university emerging as one of the powerhouses of research into 'multistructuredness'. Under V. V. Adamov, The Department of History, at the Urals A. M. Gorky State University in Sverdlovsk, gathered together a *kollektiv* of *aspiranty* (graduate students) to study the socio-economic development of the Urals and the history of its working class in the inter-revolutionary decade 1907–17. Adamov argued that the standard literature misrepresented the penetration of finance capital into the Urals' mining and metallurgical industries as 'overwhelming and washing away feudal-serf remnants'. According to Adamov, penetration by Russian banks and monopolies of the backward Urals' mining and metallurgical industries on the eve of and during the First World War did not modernize these industries. Rather, there was a *'mutual adaptation* of finance capital to the semi-serf structure of the mining and metallurgical regions'; but this only sharpened the 'general crisis' of the socio-economic basis of Urals' industrial development.[86]

In a similar manner, Adamov gave short shrift to simplistic, schematic views of the Urals' working class. In a 1963 paper he took to task the false impression that in the Urals at the turn of century existed a 'pure' proletariat, identical with workers in the St Petersburg district. Examining the links of the Urals' mining and metallurgical workers with the land, and the role of handicraft industries among the Urals miners, Adamov concluded that both provided the mineworkers with additional income, while at the same time serving to tie them to the factory. Thus Adamov sought to breathe life into stereotypes about Urals' socio-economic development and the Russian empire as a whole by scrutinizing the contradictions of the latter through the 'prism' of the Urals.[87]

An extremely important contribution to the analysis of the 'multi-structuredness' of the Russian empire was made by P. G. Galuzo. His research on the socio-economic history of Central Asia is further testimony to the importance of pre-Stalinist historiography for the recrudescence of Marxism in the 1960s. Galuzo's work on Turkestan had been cut short in the mid-1930s. Apparently condemned as an 'enemy of the people', he only resumed his work a quarter of a century later, after his rehabilitation. His focus was southern Kazakhstan, an immense area characterized by variegated ethnic composition and social structure – from nomadic to settled peoples. Within five years of his rehabilitation Galuzo was reporting on the first results of his research. By 1965 he was defending his 'vast' doctoral thesis: *Agrarian Relations in the South of Kazakhstan, 1867–1914*.

Galuzo's study was the starting point for a new investigation into Russia's colonialism in Central Asia and the 'preconditions of the unification of the national movements with the proletarian revolution'. Tarnovsky hailed Galuzo's opus as one of the most outstanding achievements of Soviet historiography in its time. Galuzo's study was underpinned by an extremely 'high methodological level' of analysis of the 'interaction of different structures of the Russian economy':[88]

> In the system of exploitation of the region were intertwined the most diverse forms: the military-feudal exploitation of the peasantry by the entire tsarist state apparatus, the predatory dispossession of the local peasantry in the name of saving serf landholding in Russia, imperialist exploitation through unequal exchange of raw materials for the output of Russian industry, the penetration of the region by banking capital, and feudal and capitalist exploitation by the indigenous rich land-owners [*baistva*], Russian Cossack and immigrant kulaks.[89]

Galuzo drew from his analysis the '*socio-political*' consequences for the anti-colonial revolution of the mechanisms by which the industrial metropole retarded the development of the colonial periphery and pauperized, rather than proletarianized, the dispossessed small peasantry. He argued that the intrusion of capitalist relations, which utilized feudal mechanisms of 'servitude', gave the entire peasantry a vested interest in clearing away such corrupted capitalism, thereby opening the way to the 'pure', 'American path' to capitalism. But this also opened the way to the 'growing-over' of the anti-tsarist peasant movement into an anti-imperialist one. The increasing penetration of imperialist, industrial capital strengthened the

> forces of the peasant, national-liberation revolution and more closely allied the *peasant democratic national-liberation movement with the struggle of the working class for socialism*. The working class became the hegemon of the peasant, democratic national-liberation revolution.[90]

For Tarnovsky, Galuzo's research consummated the work of the New Direction at its current stage of development. Summarizing the achievement of the revisionists, he saw their analysis of the 'multi-structuredness' of the Russian empire as providing a scientific explanation for why it took a proletarian, anti-capitalist revolution in 1917 to eradicate the remnants and consequences of pre-capitalism, that is, to realize the bourgeois-democratic revolution. The New Direction historians had established that given the marked

> intertwining and coalescence of capitalist imperialism with outmoded and early-capitalist structures and forms of exploitation, the general democratic tasks [of the revolution], as the experience of February–October 1917 showed, could not be fully resolved within the limits of the bourgeois-democratic revolution. To resolve them it was necessary to go beyond these limits and strike directly at the system of *finance capital* – at Russian capitalist imperialism. Only the industrial proletariat was up to this task ... Thus the victory of the proletarian revolution was the indispensable condition of resolving the general democratic tasks, and, vice versa, the forces of the general democratic offensive created the necessary general political conditions for the overthrow by the proletariat of the capitalist mode of production as a whole.[91]

The driving forces of the revolutions in February and October 1917 were the focus of two international conferences held in 1967, their fiftieth anniversary. The New Direction historians argued strongly that the February revolution needed to be 'integrated' as the first stage of the 'revolutionary process' that culminated in October 1917. The *Short*

Course approach, they argued, had 'ruptured' that process, linking the February revolution simply to the First World War, thereby masking the fact that both the 1917 revolutions were induced by the profound inability of Russian capitalism to overcome its 'multistructuredness'. Volobuev designated the February revolution 'not only as a prologue but also a "guarantee" of [the] October' Revolution, in so far as it revealed the depth of Russia's crisis and 'created the fundamental socio-political prerequisites for its resolution'.[92] Moreover, the complex nature of the revolutions of 1917 could only be explained by a multi-causal analysis, not by recourse to the mono-causality of monopoly capitalism.

Towards a paradigm shift

If there was growing consensus that 'multistructuredness' provided the necessary conceptual key to understanding the socio-economic prerequisites of the February revolution, there was less than agreement on how to define the 'multistructuredness' of the Russian economy. It was noted that Lenin, who had chiefly referred to '*uklad*' in regard to the post-October transition to socialism, had not provided any precise definition of the term, especially in relation to imperial Russia. The diversity of views on 'multistructuredness' was more than apparent at the 1969 Sverdlovsk conference convened to discuss the topic.[93] Sverdlovsk marked the high tide of the concept, and it is apparent that by then 'multistructuredness' had established considerable currency among specialists of Russian imperialism. In effect, a tentative paradigm shift, in relation to the exemplar of Russian imperialism had occurred; but it was far from secure, politically at least.

Adamov, the Sverdlovsk University specialist on the Urals, emphasized not only the diversity of opinion on the content of such terms as 'structure' (*uklad*), 'multistructuredness' and 'ruling *uklad*' but the particular ambiguity concerning the 'mechanism of the interaction' of different 'structures'.[94] Disputation over the 'interaction' of *uklady* was evident in the exchange between Galuzo and his critics in relation to the Central Asian regions of Russia. Whereas Galuzo stressed the 'interaction' of different *uklady* as defining the social structure of these regions and the *conserving* impact of the intrusion of capitalism, his critics, still caught up in the old perspective, emphasized the importance of the capitalist *uklad* in eradicating the 'feudal relations and colonial dependence of these regions'.[95]

Any overview of the various perspectives on the 'multistructuredness' of prerevolutionary Russia at the Sverdlovsk conference is complicated by the fact that we are (prematurely) entering the thorny terrain of the politics of Soviet historiography in the *perestroika* period, in which the status of the New Direction was bitterly contested. According to Bovykin, who by 1969 was already out of step with his former colleagues of the 'Sidorov school' and who subsequently played a key role in vanquishing the New Direction,[96] at Sverdlovsk there were basically two different perspectives on 'multistructuredness': one argued for the dominance of the capitalist 'structure', the other for a multiplicity of 'structures', in which capitalism never became the dominant 'structure' capable of subordinating the other 'structures'.[97]

According to Bovykin, at Sverdlovsk in 1969 Tarnovsky occupied the latter position, departing from that which he had advocated back in 1964 when he defined capitalism as the 'leading and determining' *uklad*.[98] In this interpretation Bovykin was at odds with Volobuev, who maintained that his New Direction colleagues never repudiated the dominance of the capitalist *uklad*: 'For all of us', Volobuev stated in a letter to *Voprosy istorii* published in June 1990, 'the principle of the rule of capitalism, of the leading role of the capitalist *uklad* in the country was an axiom' on the basis of which different questions were pursued.[99] As V. V. Polikarpov put it at the time, in a spirited defence of the New Direction historians, 'despite Bovykin', none of them saw 'multistructuredness' as merely a combination of a 'monostructured' capitalism combined with the remnants of feudalism and patriarchy. This was to fall into the trap that Tarnovsky had warned about in 1964: that of confusing the capitalist *uklad* with the 'multistructured' *capitalist* economy as whole'.[100]

Whatever inconsistencies Bovykin discerned in relation to 'multi-structuredness', he missed the point of what was novel about the New Direction. They had shifted the focus away from the '*level*' of capitalist development in Russia to its '*type*' of development. Volobuev, as early as 1958, had dared to imply that it was not the high level of development of capitalism in Russia that was the motor of the Russian Revolution but its underdevelopment – in Lenin's words, 'Our backwardness propelled us forwards'.[101] Neither Volobuev nor the New Direction as a whole were simply counterposing Russian 'backwardness' to 'forwardness'. It was the peculiar 'combination of advanced forms of capitalism and backwardness', especially in the countryside where (as Anfimov later demonstrated) a 'sea' of primitive- and pre-capitalist relations remained.[102]

At the Sverdlovsk conference the implications of 'multistructuredness' were carried furthest by Gefter. Indeed, in his case the logic of 'multistructuredness' came almost full-circle, implying a resilient Russian serfdom that digested the capitalist *uklad*. The concept of 'multistructuredness' provided for Gefter both a way of filling in the 'gaps' of the 'purely' formational heritage bequeathed by orthodox historical materialism, and of overcoming its 'predeterminism' which allowed only one permissible path of development. The 'hybridness' which characterized capitalist development was a product not of the weight of a particular *uklad* but of their combination. Here Gefter was alluding to what he saw as the 'alternativeness' of historical development. Such an approach allowed not just for the forward movement of history but even for retrogression. The serf system of autocratic Russia, for example, far from succumbing to the capitalism unleashed by the great reform, had 'assimilate[d]' the latter, 'converting it into a source for itself.' Hence a 'paradox of history' whereby the 'one-sided accelerated growth of a new formation "returns" it again and again to the stage of genesis.'[103] This was not just characteristic of prerevolutionary Russia. Gefter seemed to be implying that Soviet society was not immune from this 'hybridness' – and perhaps not even from this 'paradox' of an apparently new formation succumbing to an old one. As Gefter noted in an aside, the October Revolution entailed *'the superseding of one "multistructuredness" by another.'*[104] In these circumstances, presumably, Soviet society could go either way: backwards towards some form of primitive capitalism or forwards to genuine communism.

While undoubtedly the concept of 'multistructuredness' had implications for the way the New Direction scholars reflected on their own society, their immediate concern was its implications for understanding not only the prerequisites for the October Revolution but also the international resonance of that momentous event. The re-focus on the 'multistructuredness' of prerevolutionary Russia saw it elevated to a 'peculiar *model of the world at that time, and as a focus of the contradictions of the new imperialist epoch*'.[105] To be more precise, the socio-economic structure of prerevolutionary Russia was recognized as a contradictory combination of the 'fundamental features of both the developed capitalist countries of the West and also of the states of the colonial and semi-colonial East.'[106] The fact that monopoly capitalism consolidated prior forms of exploitation helped to establish the significance of Russia and its revolution in world history.

In fact, the issue at stake was which characteristics of imperial Russia led to the revolutionary rupture of the imperialist chain at its weakest link, as Lenin had put it.[107] In 1967 Volobuev had assigned multi-structured Russia a 'middle position in the world capitalist system'.[108] Two years later, at Sverdlovsk, Gefter designated Russia a country of the 'second and third echelon' in as much as its 'abbreviated' capitalist development, compared to the classical European model, reflected not just the influence of the latter but a 'definite regularity': the 'world process' and Russia's place in it.[109]

This refrain of Russia as a 'country of the "second echelon" of capitalism'[110] became synonymous with the New Direction. For Volobuev, 'second echelon' defined pre-revolutionary Russia not as a Third World country but as a country whose complex, contradictory development (roughly comparable to the development of Latin America in the early 1960s) was explained by its belated entry into the capitalist path. The hallmark of this 'secondary' level of capitalist development was the need for deliberate, large-scale intervention by the tsarist state to implant capitalism from above and force the pace of industrialization.[111]

For the adversaries of the New Direction, designating Russia a mere 'second echelon' capitalism was a denial that the necessary social and economic prerequisites for the October Socialist Revolution existed. In this respect the opponents of revisionism remained mired in the 'traditional, apologetic', 'pseudo-patriotic embellishment' of the pre-revolutionary tsarist state. In other words, the striving of the New Direction to provide a more objective explanation of the Russian revolutions of 1905 and 1917 (and the 'attendant difficulties of socialist transformation after the revolution'),[112] entailed sloughing off the chauvinism that had coloured historical consciousness since the Stalin years. As we have seen, this struggle had been a vital element in the emergence of historical revisionism since the Twentieth Congress. Bovykin's position represented a capitulation to this chauvinism, but dovetailed con-veniently with the renewed emphasis on Russian nationalism which was actively fostered in the early Brezhnev years.

The political implications of a seemingly scholastic, terminological debate were rather more immediate, however, than the question of historical consciousness. They struck at the very foundations of the orthodox explanation for the origins and nature of the October Revolution – the cornerstone of the legitimacy of the Soviet oligarchy. As Volobuev put it, orthodox historical materialism explained the revolution as the 'lawful' outcome of the 'notorious conflict between the productive forces and the relations of production'.[113] Hence the emphasis on the maturation of the most advanced forms of monopoly capitalism and the prevalence of capitalism in the countryside. Without these, the necessary prerequisites for a socialist, proletarian revolution and the subsequent transition to socialism were presumed to be absent. Hence too the hostility of the 'fools' from Old Square (the Moscow location of the Central Committee apparatus) to the concept of 'multistructuredness', who perceived it as undermining the 'cruelly determined' nature of the October Revolution. It was precisely at this point that the question of *mnogoukladnost'* 'grew over from the field of science into politics'.[114]

For Volobuev, October 1917 'could not be simply explained by the objective laws of social development', although, 'in the specific historical conditions of Russia, it was historically necessary and even historically inevitable.' In the latter framework, it was possible to conceive of '*alternativy*' to the October Revolution itself – a proposition Volobuev discretely made in 1967 in a note to the liberal vice-president of the Academy of Sciences, A. M. Rumyantsev, to the effect that October was not 'programmed for one victorious outcome'. When Volobuev had the temerity to suggest publicly that Lenin had canvassed alternative directions of Russian agrarian development at the beginning of the twentieth century – along the American or the Prussian paths – and that indeed, the 'entire history of Russia was woven from alternatives, from a sharp clash of different possibilities and tendencies of development', he was vehemently criticized by the hardened Stalinists. One of the authors of the *Short Course*, the 'dyed in the wool dogmatist' Academician Pospelov, accused him of advocating the 'bourgeois theory of alternatives'.[115]

From a more complex interaction of *uklady* flowed a more complex interplay of class forces in the events of 1917. Whereas orthodox accounts portrayed the February revolution as merely a contest between two camps: the bourgeoisie and the proletariat, or, at most, the proletariat and the poor peasantry, the New Direction, drawing on Lenin, advanced a more nuanced analysis, arguing for three forces acting in the bourgeois-democratic revolution: the tsarist autocracy and the landlords; an 'intermediate force', the liberal bourgeoisie; and 'revolutionary democracy', the proletariat and the peasantry.[116] After the February revolution – the 'stage of the socialist revolution – with tsarism vanquished, the orthodox approach still admitted only two contestants: the bourgeoisie and the proletariat, this time leading only the poor peasantry. The New Direction, however, again argued for three contending forces: the urban bourgeoisie and the landlords versus the proletariat allied with the poor peasantry and the 'vacillating' middle (including the kulaks) and working peasantry. The only way the tiny proletariat could seize power in October was by championing the interests of the vast bulk of the populace of the former tsarist empire. Hence the 'combined' nature of the October Revolution and the conclusion of the New Direction that in the imperialist epoch,

> the radical resolution of a number of democratic tasks was impossible within the limits of the bourgeois-democratic revolution. Thereby only the proletarian revolution guaranteed the carrying through of the bourgeois-democratic revolution to a victorious conclusion.[117]

Thus, for the New Direction, the October Revolution triumphed because it alone could solve the preponderance of 'general democratic' tasks the revolution faced: the struggle for peace; the expropriation of the landlords and the transfer of their property to the peasantry; the resolution of the national question; the struggle to overcome economic collapse and the 'building of a democratic society' were the united tasks of a 'soviet, proletarian state'. This approach was construed by the stalwarts of Central Committee's Department of Science as a revisionist 'denial of the proletarian, socialist character of the October Revolution'.[118] Moreover, it was the 'democratic' content of the October Revolution realized through the victory of the proletariat that the New Direction identified as the basis of the universality of the October Revolution, rather than simply its 'socialism'. As Volobuev put it in 1967, 'precisely because the October Revolution performed this "dual function", its experience has a genuinely universal character, appropriate for the most socio-economically diverse regions of the world.' The Russian revolutionary movement, combining as it did 'three revolutionary forces – the workers' movement, the peasant agrarian revolution and the national-liberation movement' – therefore provided a prototype of revolutionary transformation to socialism in the twentieth century.[119] The model of the Russian revolution which those like Bovykin upheld, with its emphasis on the development of capitalism, was effectively a 'denial of the [revolution's] international significance'.[120]

Crypto-Trotskyism?

At first sight the conceptions of the New Direction appear to be Trotskyist. It was Trotsky, principal architect of the theory of 'permanent revolution', who wrote that this theory 'established the fact that for the backward countries the road to democracy passed through the dictatorship of the proletariat'.[121] Even more striking is the similarity between the concept of 'multistructuredness' and the concept Trotsky generated in the course of writing his *History of the Russian Revolution* in 1930–32: his 'laws of uneven and combined development'. With reference to backward countries in general, Russia in particular, Trotsky had rejected any universal laws of historical development. He stressed the necessity to analyze the peculiarities of national development on the basis of permutations of the economic, social and political factors which shaped a nation's history.

It would be temptingly convenient to see in 'multistructuredness' and its associated notions a resurrection of Trotsky's thought analogous to that resurrection of Bukharin's thought which Lewin discerned among the Soviet economists of the 1960s.[122] Alas, this is not the case. Trotsky's theory of 'permanent revolution' emphasized the socialist tasks of the proletarian revolution, and with it the differentiation of the peasantry – 'between village poor and village rich' – 'from the very first moment after its taking power'.[123] The New Direction, however, based on their re-reading of Lenin, concluded that the recipe for the success of the October Revolution had been an alliance between the urban proletariat and the peasantry as a whole against the autocracy and its landlords.

Similarly, the 'multistructuredness' of pre-revolutionary Russia was at most a 'parallel' conception to Trotsky's 'combined and uneven development'; not at all its direct offspring.[124] Volobuev, for example, while an instructor of the Central Committee, in the course of the Burdzhalov affair had read some of Trotsky's principal works (*My Life, The New Course, The History of the Three Russian Revolutions*), which were held in the closed section (*spetskhran*) of the library of the Institute of Marxism–Leninism. But he had put Trotsky aside.[125]

The concept of 'multistructuredness' was developed not only independently of, but indeed in opposition to, Trotsky. It will be recalled that in repudiating Stalin's 'semi-colonial' thesis, the 'Sidorov school' saw itself initially as substantiating the existence of the prerequisites for Soviet socialism, in defiance of Trotskyism. As time went on, however, it is evident their approach cast doubt on the existence of the prerequisites for fully-fledged socialism. Hence their increasing emphasis on the democratic content of the October Revolution. Nevertheless it is striking that the New Direction stopped short of directly posing the question as to whether in fact the necessary prerequisites for 'socialism in one country' existed, as Stalin and Bukharin had maintained against the Left Opposition.[126] It is as if for the New Direction, despite their close reading of Lenin, this crucial debate had been definitively settled in Stalin's favour. This may well have been the cost of rehabilitating Pokrovsky, who throughout the 1920s had been the most vehement opponent of Trotsky's historical conceptions.[127] This absence of any direct influence from Trotsky gives considerable credence to the traditional 'totalitarian' argument of the successful extirpation of the intellectual life that flourished before the triumph of the 'man of steel'.[128] Nevertheless, the prolonged endeavour of the New Direction to map the peculiarities of Russian historical development in the most concrete way almost necessarily generated concepts that even in the late 1960s were suspected of being 'Trotskyite'. A decade before, at the height of the Burdzhalov affair, they would certainly have been denounced as such.[129]

Whatever the limits of the reading of Lenin by the New Direction, whose observations they treated as self-evident truths, what has to be recognized is its distinctiveness in the Soviet context. For them it was more than just re-reading Lenin; it was a question of the *way* he was read and utilized. This meant more than mere formal citation to give credence and authority to their arguments, as was the practice of their opponents, but of understanding and applying Leninism 'as a system of thought'. Thus, on the basis of a few comments by Lenin, about the 'multistructured' nature of Russian society in 1918, they had deduced the 'multistructuredness' of its imperial predecessor. In short, the revisionists began to treat Leninism as a serious tool for research, not just as a set of pious, politically acceptable, platitudes.

It is true that the New Direction, like the revisionist historians in general, took Lenin's insights as axioms for their research; but it would be profoundly wrong to view their new-found enthusiasm for Lenin as a mere cloak donned to make their revisionism politically acceptable. Rather Lenin, together with Marx and Engels, provided them with a conceptual framework – in reality, the only one available to them – that they genuinely brought to bear on their research. This approach was symptomatic of the emergence of a more sophisticated, genuinely scholarly, generation of historians.

Such a re-reading of Lenin increasingly challenged the accepted verities of historical materialism. In particular, it displaced the general laws of the five-stage schema in favour of a multi-causal approach that emphasized the discreteness of historical developments rather than treating them as mere manifestations of universal laws. Hence the continual emphasis of the revisionists on the 'specific features' (*osobennosti*) of Russian historical development.[130] While they remained convinced Marxist–Leninists, the methodology of the advocates of the multistructural approach ran counter to that of orthodox adherents of historical materialism. Where the latter insisted on reconciling the world with the fixed categories of Marxism–Leninism, the revisionists gave primacy to facts about the world and the need to retool their Marxist–Leninist outlook in order to accommodate those facts.[131] In Nettl's terms, this was a classic clash between the 'intellectuals of scope' and those of 'quality'.

Russian absolutism

This clash burst into the public arena at a joint conference of Soviet and Italian historians held in Moscow in 1968. It was at this conference, it will be recalled, that the New Direction first officially declared their existence. The focus of the conference was Russian absolutism. While a less politically contentious issue than 'multistructuredness', in the sense that it did not strike directly at the legitimacy of the Stalinist conception of October 1917, the debate around the nature of Russian absolutism raised very important questions about some of the postulates of Soviet Marxism. It revealed clearly the methodological gap between the New Direction historians and the 'old', and the acute tensions between them (which also reflected the intense struggle going on within the Institute of History in 1968, then in the throes of being divided in two).[132]

Three fundamental theoretical issues were at stake. Firstly, was Russian absolutism the product of an equilibrium between a bourgeoisie and landed gentry, as Marx and Engels had explained the absolutism of Western Europe, or did Russian absolutism emerge on a different social basis from that of rising capitalism, as the New Direction scholars suggested? Secondly, was the absolutist state determined by the economic infrastructure of Russia or was it, as the New Direction argued, an autonomous political actor, capable of even 'getting ahead' of Russian socio-economic development? Finally, did Russian history conform to a set of universal laws (*zakonomernosti*), as Marxist–Leninist orthodoxy demanded, or was it *sui generis*?[133]

The key figures in this particular debate were Pavlenko, Gindin, Volobuev and, above all, Volobuev's friend, Aron Avrekh.[134] A 'talented' historian and a 'convinced communist' of 'aggressive' intellectual disposition, Avrekh was not afraid to tackle the big theoretical questions.[135] He devoted himself to the study of the autocracy in its dying days, at the end of the nineteenth century and the beginning of the twentieth. In particular, he researched the fate of the Russian parliament under Stolypin.[136]

The traditional Marxist–Leninist interpretation of absolutism was advanced in the main discussion paper on the 'Emergence of the Absolutist Monarchy in Russia in the XVI to XVIII Centuries', delivered by L. V. Cherepnin, a historian distinguished by his rudimentary knowledge of Marxism.[137] In this reading, the absolutist monarchy was the last form of the feudal state; a dictatorship of the nobility (*dvoryanstvo*) with an emerging bourgeoisie. He drew on Engels' famous aphorism that whereas the state was normally a political instrument of the ruling class, the absolutist state of seventeenth and eighteenth centuries Western Europe was an exceptional state that achieved a 'certain independence' due to the 'balance' between the 'warring classes' of the nobility and the bourgeoisie.[138] Cherepnin argued that Russian absolutism was a specific manifestation of Engels' universal model, which he linked in particular to the 'genesis' of capitalism with the emergence of an 'all-Russian market' under a serf dictatorship in the seventeenth century. Hand in hand with the first 'shoots of capitalism' occurred an 'unprecedented upsurge of class struggle'. Cherepnin defined absolutism as 'the form of state in late feudal society, in the womb of which the bourgeoisie was gestating'. In the case of Russia, absolutism was consolidated in the first quarter of the eighteenth century under Peter the Great, which conformed, Cherepnin stressed, to the European model of absolutism and not at all to 'Asiatic' or 'Eastern' despotism.[139]

Seeing Cherepnin's argument as riddled with inconsistencies, the response of the New Direction was scathing. The opening salvo was fired by Pavlenko: 'Often the less we know, the more views there are. There is no shortage of hypotheses concerning the emergence of absolutism in Russia.' He homed in on what he saw as Cherepnin's inconsistency with regard to class 'equilibrium', which, Pavlenko suggested, 'even the most experienced editor could not eliminate'. There was no evidence to sustain the thesis of a contest of interests between the Russian merchant class and the *dvoryanstvo*; on the contrary they were allies.[140] Speaking in Pavlenko's support, Avrekh derided Cherepnin's notion of equilibrium as 'empty noise'. Likewise, he dismissed the theory of the parallel development of capitalism and feudalism in Russia as a 'completely new approach to historical reality'. He drew attention to the fact that the notion of capitalist development in seventeenth-century Russia had been discredited in a paper delivered by Pavlenko in 1965 to a conference on the transition from feudalism to capitalism in Russia.[141] Volobuev was more circumspect. He pointed out that whereas the classic absolutism of England and France emerged on the basis of feudal decline and capitalist development, in Russia absolutism was based on a serf-feudal system, little connected with capitalism. Class equilibrium, which Volobuev did not see as essential to absolutism, appeared in Russia very late, only with the onset of capitalism in the mid-nineteenth century.[142]

The New Direction also rejected the notion that class struggle was in any way a determinant of Russian absolutism. There was no necessary correlation between class struggle and the 'form' a state took. It was not a factor that could be assumed. Rather, argued Pavlenko, it had to be demonstrated on the basis of historical analysis. In the case of Russia, absolutism was the product not of conflict between 'antagonistic' classes but of that between the dominant classes, a product of the 'liberation' of the autocracy from the Boyar *duma* (assembly) in the seventeenth century and its enlisting of the *dvoryanstvo* bureaucracy to govern the country.[143] Likewise, Avrekh argued that no link could be established between the peasant wars that erupted in the seventeenth century and absolutism. 'Simple synchronization of events' does not constitute a 'causal connection', he declared. Indeed, Avrekh stressed that far from Russian absolutism arising in response to the struggle of exploited classes, it was the relative absence of class struggle, compared to Western Europe, that sustained the absolutist monarchy. The peasantry, he insisted, provided the 'mass social support' of absolutism, right up until the 1905 revolution (a proposition that was to provide the pretext for severe censure when the tide began to turn against Avrekh and his colleagues). 'Facts should take precedence over schemas', he admonished Cherepnin.[144]

So saying, the New Direction scholars drove their methodological knife into the crude sociological reductionism that was orthodox Marxism–Leninism, severing the assumed deterministic connection between socio-economic and political developments, between 'base' and 'superstructure'. As a 'unique' manifestation of a general European phenomenon, argued Volobuev, the 'premature' appearance of the Russian absolutist state prior to the emergence of its socio-economic prerequisites (that is, capitalism) was possible. 'Such cases of getting ahead [*operezhenie*] are not rare', he declared. In Russia the 'non-correspondence' between a powerful superstructure and a weak economic base, a contradiction reinforced by the 'serf character' of Russian absolutism, saw state '*operezhenie*' compensate for economic backwardness.[145] Avrekh agreed: absolutism long preceded the appearance of capitalism, indeed the former was a 'powerful prerequisite' for the latter. But he found the 'basic cause' of absolutism 'getting ahead' in a factor external to Russia: 'the necessity to survive alongside the advanced West European countries'.[146] The perspective of Volobuev and Avrekh, emphasizing those features that distinguished Russian 'despotism' from West European absolutism, also exposed the unstated Eurocentrism of orthodox historiography, which was intent on demonstrating that Russia's development conformed to that of Europe.[147]

Consistent with his status as one of the leading theoreticians of the New Direction, Avrekh went further than any of his co-thinkers in revising Marxist–Leninist postulates about the state. Absolutism he defined as:

> A feudal monarchy which, due to its internal nature, is capable of evolving and transforming into a bourgeois monarchy ... The absolutist monarchy, appearing in advance of capitalism, is the prototype of the bourgeois state. It contains within itself all the constituent parts of the latter, right up to parliament ... Testimony to the contemporary nature of the absolutist state is the fact that the bourgeoisie, having seized power, does not destroy the state apparatus, but utilizes it as a whole – it is completely ready and adapted to bourgeois rule.

In proffering such a definition, which allowed for the absolutist state to 'evolve' into a bourgeois state and to pursue capitalist policies, 'prior to capitalism and without a bourgeoisie', Avrekh was repudiating primitive Soviet conceptions of the state as a mere instrument of class rule. The absolutist state, resting on a hierarchical bureaucracy, occupied a position of 'relative independence ... in relation to society as a whole including the ruling class'.[148] In arguing for the 'relative' independence of the state, Avrekh was not undermining Marxism.[149] Avrekh saw himself as refining and strengthening Marxism.

To this end, soon after the conference, Avrekh, with the support of Volobuev, initiated a discussion on the pages of *Istoriya SSSR* on 'Russian absolutism and its role in the establishment of capitalism in Russia'.[150] Elaborating the views he presented at the conference, Avrekh threw down the gauntlet to Soviet Marxist conceptions on the 'role of the state' and the 'evolution of the state apparatus'. A misreading of Engels' views on the state by Soviet historians was a source of 'serious errors', he charged. Soviet orthodoxy saw state autonomy as an 'exception' arising due to a 'balance of forces' between the 'warring classes', the state then seeming to mediate between them. Avrekh, however, argued precisely the opposite. He reread Engels as saying that 'the relative autonomy of the state is a universal rule, with no exceptions'.[151] The state was not therefore the mere creature of the ruling classes but acted as a 'mediator' of their particular and general interests. Moreover, in its relations with the subject classes, the state did not and could not rely solely on coercion to sustain itself. 'No state can exist without *mass* social support', he wrote.[152] The sophistication of Avrekh's analysis of the 'relative autonomy' of the state from the ruling classes (which in many respects anticipated similar discussions among Marxists in the West in the 1970s) is evident in his explanation of the contradictory role of Russian absolutism. How was it, he asked, that the 'bourgeois' absolutist state not only did not abolish serfdom, it actually strengthened it during the eighteenth century 'second serfdom'? Here he answered in terms redolent of the French structuralist Althusser (although there is no evidence he influenced Avrekh). Absolutism could not abolish serfdom in the eighteenth century because 'in the last instance' the economy always prevailed over the state. 'In the XVIII century serfdom was the *basis* of the economic development of the country and the strengthening of the state.' However in 1861 the same absolutism abolished serfdom 'despite the will of its class' for the 'very same reasons' it had strengthened serfdom a century earlier, because of the *'economic impossibility of preserving it*. Despite its serf sympathies, absolutism [was] not the *unconditional* champion of serfdom.'[153]

In the shadow of neo-Stalinism, attempts to refine Marxism–Leninism were viewed as seditious revisionism. Although a conference dedicated to the question of Russian absolutism was held in the Institute of the History of the USSR in 1971,[154] the discussion in *Istoriya SSSR* was summarily terminated that year. No editorial article summarizing and evaluating the debate, the usual practice, appeared.

Nevertheless, this was not the 1930s. The New Direction had indelibly placed their stamp on Soviet historical thinking. One of the most eloquent and succinct statements of the 'changes in the methods and tasks of historical research' which underpinned the 'powerful upsurge' in Soviet historiography represented by the New Direction was given by Gindin himself at the Soviet–Italian conference:

> The large shifts in methodology are seen first of all in the fact that the new research is being imbued with the historicism which is

peculiar to the methodology of Marxism–Leninism; [they are also seen in the fact] of the ever-broadening understanding of historical development as an evolution through contradictions. The same shifts have led to a deeper comprehension of the relationship between the economic basis and its superstructures; to the comprehension, that is, not only of the historical process being conditioned in the last analysis by the economic basis, but also of the uninterrupted interaction between that basis and the superstructural phenomena; [they have led] to a deeper penetration into the process of the reverse impact upon economic development of superstructures, that is, of the state and the institutions of public law and, aside from them, of the area of private law and, finally, of ideological currents.[155]

Such a relatively sophisticated, less-deterministic, model of Marxism, the product of prolonged, intense research not only into the history of pre-revolutionary Russia but also into the nature of Russian absolutism, was increasingly out of step with political developments in the Soviet Union of the late 1960s; it was to cost the New Direction dearly. Such a sustained, forthright challenge to academic orthodoxy could not but become a political challenge in a system where 'for the first time ever, a *theory of history* ha[d] been the official doctrine of the state and the foundation of social order'.[156]

4
Writing and Rewriting the History of Collectivization

> 'We wanted to write a genuine history of collectivization, not as it was in the *Short Course* or in the history of the party, but as it was in fact; not according to a preconceived formula, to which the facts are adapted, but to draw conclusions based on the facts, events and sources, not vice versa. The task was to resurrect the historical truth, within the limits possible at that time.'
>
> N. A. Ivnitsky, Moscow, January 1998

While the New Direction had been reconceptualizing the Russian countryside as 'multistructured', another group of historians was taking issue with one of the most contentious questions in Soviet history and historiography: the collectivization of Soviet agriculture. Stalin's triumphalist *Short Course* history asserted that with 'full-scale collectivization' and the 'elimination of the kulaks as a class', the basic problems of Soviet agriculture had been solved and the basis laid for socialist relations in the countryside and the Soviet Union as a whole.[1] As with so many other historical questions, the death of Stalin and the subsequent onset of the 'thaw' created the first opportunity for Soviet historians themselves to challenge this imposed wisdom. There was also a political imperative. Addressing the parlous state of Soviet agriculture bequeathed by Stalin was one of the first priorities. Between September 1953 and Khrushchev's ousting in October 1964, no less than 11 Central Committee plenums were dedicated to redressing the problems of agriculture. Registering considerable success during the 1953–58 five-year plan, the next 1959–65 seven-year plan saw agriculture 'gradually slide into stagnation',[2] a pattern mirrored in the rise and fall of revisionist history of collectivization.

The seeds for a radical rewriting of the history of collectivization were sewn by Viktor Danilov soon after Stalin's death.[3] In 1956 he published an article and the following a year his first book in which he demonstrated that on the eve of agricultural collectivization in 1929 the Soviet Union lacked the necessary material and technical prerequisites for the complete collectivization of agriculture.[4] Danilov's first book was not an attack on collectivization; rather it was intended to provide a more rational explanation for it. He maintained that 'full-scale collectivization' was the necessary outcome of the 'non-correspondence' of the rapidly developing productive forces and the relations of production in the countryside, characterized by small-scale farming.[5] In other words, collectivization was an objective necessity, not a political decision. In certain respects his argument was quite orthodox. Like the *Short Course,* he endorsed full-scale collectivization on the grounds that there was a hostile international environment coupled with the threat of a kulak 'counter-revolution', manifested by the presence of a 'right-opportunist' grouping within the party.[6] The sting, however, was in the tail of Danilov's conclusions about the lack of the necessary prerequisites for full-scale collectivization. While a 'massive' substitution of metal for wooden ploughs had occurred in the 1920s, there was a critical lack of sophisticated agricultural equipment, above all tractors, to sustain full-scale collectivization. In 1928 tractors were utilized to prepare a negligible 1 per cent of the spring-sewn area.[7] As he put it, the 'tempo of social reconstruction outstripped the tempo of technical reconstruction', putting a 'brake' on the accelerated collectivization at the end of 1929. Consequently, Soviet socialist agriculture was condemned to mere 'manufacturing development', largely dependent on manual labour and animal draught power, until the end of the second five-year plan (1932–37).[8]

Danilov's argument flew in the face of prevailing party orthodoxy. This held that prior to collectivization a powerful material-technical basis for socialist forms of agricultural production had been put in place. In accordance with rudimentary Stalinist Marxism, collectivization entailed bringing the relations of production into conformity with the new productive forces. It was a one-dimensional, technical approach to collectivization that ignored a number of other factors such as the disparity between individual farming and 'socialist' industrial development and the growth of capitalism in the countryside.[9]

The *Short Course* conception justified the 'spurring on' of the historical process that collectivization entailed.[10]

As a comparatively young, thirty-year-old, researcher in the Institute of History of the Soviet Academy of Sciences, Danilov had pursued this work for his *kandidat* degree, which was completed in 1955, as was the manuscript of his book. Thus Danilov's work preceded the March 1956 Twentieth Congress, which precipitated the anti-Stalinist 'thaw'. Despite the relaxation of intellectual controls, Danilov's book provoked a stream of protests to the Central Committee and he was forced to defend himself against charges that his work was 'anti-party'.[11]

Ironically, publication of Danilov's work was encouraged by the then Director of the Institute of History, Arkady Sidorov. Despite Sidorov's Stalinist credentials, in 1958 he appointed Danilov head of a Group on the History of the Soviet Peasantry and the Organization of Collective Farms. It was unprecedented to appoint a newly-graduated *kandidat* to such a position. However, according to Danilov, it was part of what had become Sidorov's personal campaign against the Stalinist generation of historians and against the influx of Stalinist bureaucrats then being purged from the Central Committee apparatus who were being appointed researchers in the Institute. An 'immense burden on historical science' they were to play a 'nasty role' in the defeat of the *shestidesyatniki* at the end of 1960s.[12]

Sidorov gave Danilov a specific brief to write a history of collectivization. To this end Danilov was joined by Maria Bogdenko, Nikolai Ivnitsky, Mikhail Vyltsan and Il'ya Zelenin, all researchers in the Institute of History (they were subsequently joined by Yury Moshkov from Moscow State University, who participated in the Group though he was not a formal member).[13] At that time mostly in their early thirties, these young historians were themselves mostly the offspring of peasants and were brought up in the countryside in the late 1920s and early 1930s. After the Second World War, these *frontoviki*, as all the men were, had embarked on scholarly careers, the study of the Soviet peasantry in particular. Some had directly experienced the trauma of forced collectivization. Ivnitsky, for example, saw his father arrested and his aunt's family expropriated and exiled as 'rich peasants' because they had an 'iron roof rather than the usual straw one.' As an eleven-year-old in the 'terrible' summer of 1933 Ivnitsky's stomach had swollen from hunger and he had witnessed starving peasants arriving in Voronezhskaya *oblast'* from the North Caucasus and the Ukraine desperately seeking food.[14]

But it was not only these personal experiences that motivated their research. It was also the fact that collectivization of agriculture in the newly-established Peoples' Republics of East Central Europe had been relatively successful, whereas collectivization in the Baltics in the 1940s had been implemented in the same brutal fashion as in the Soviet Union. From these experiences, Ivnitsky, for example, concluded that this process was not 'accidental' but the product of a 'system', the origins of which he wished to analyse.[15]

As members of Danilov's Group, each researcher concentrated on a different period. Danilov concentrated on the situation in the countryside in the 1920s up to the eve of collectivization. Ivnitsky focused on the abrupt turn to collectivization in the winter of 1929–30. Bogdenko and Zelenin looked at the immediate aftermath of collectivization and its consolidation. Vyltsan focused on the second five-year plan of 1934–37.

In 1958 Danilov provided further ammunition against premature, forced, collectivization in an article that 'single-handed[ly]'[16] resurrected the significance of the village commune (*obshchina*) in peasant life in the late 1920s, which had disappeared from the lexicon of Soviet historiography.[17] Working from Lenin's early views that the *obshchina* would be undermined by capitalism, Stalin's generation of historians viewed the *obshchina*, with its primitive strip-farming system perpetuated by its tradition of regularly distributing land to the peasant households, as a bulwark of the kulak and therefore an impediment to socialist agriculture. It was not mentioned in Stalinist historiography because it had no place in the allegedly socialist stage of the revolution deemed to have opened after October 1917.[18]

Danilov turned the spotlight on the *real* social relations in the countryside, in defiance of Stalinist generalizations about the prevalence of rural capitalism ripe for immediate collectivization. Danilov, basing himself on research rather than the injunctions of the *Short Course*, argued that peasant *obshchina* remained the 'most widespread' form of land use up until full-scale collectivization. At the beginning of the New Economic Policy (NEP), in the principal agricultural regions 98–9 per cent of all peasant lands were in communes.[19] The October Revolution had destroyed those elements of the commune Lenin had identified as 'reactionary, fiscal-feudal', leaving it as a 'landed, neighbourly organization of petty producers enjoying equal rights'.[20]

But for Danilov, the commune was a contradictory phenomenon that could develop either towards individual farming, favouring kulak, capitalist development or towards more collective forms, favouring the poor and middle peasantry. Although the Soviet state actively fostered the latter tendency in 1924–25, Danilov argued that the *obshchina* could not escape the grip of the kulak and was ultimately an obstacle to socialist agriculture. Therefore, in the context of the 'sharpening class struggle' in 1928–29, the need to move to full-scale collectivization necessitated the 'elimination' of the *obshchina*, as well as the kulak.[21] In short, Danilov supported collectivization, but not the pace nor the methods by which it was implemented. He was intent on establishing which social and economic institutions provided a bridge towards collectivization and which were obstacles to it.

Rural Russia in the 1920s

The first fruits of the collective researches of Danilov's Group were evident at a major conference, which it helped organize, on the Soviet peasantry and collectivization held in Moscow in April 1961. While at this stage Danilov took an orthodox approach to the kulak as the rural bourgeoisie, already he had repudiated 'simplified conceptions' of collectivization that reduced it merely to the 'form' in which was 'wrapped' the newly emerging productive forces.[22] To this end, he was interrogating clichéd Stalinist conceptions about social relations in the countryside. In this he was not unique. The 'socio-economic problematic' had become a focus of historians of the countryside, stimulated by the denunciation of the 'cult of the personality' at the Twentieth Congress.[23]

In a landmark paper Danilov criticized as 'inadequate' Stalin's proposition in his 1952 treatise *Economic Problems of Socialism in the USSR* that on the eve of collectivization capitalist relations of production prevailed in the countryside.[24] Rejecting such a broad, descriptive approach, Danilov argued that in order to capture the 'essence of the ruling socio-economic structure' in the countryside, it was necessary to analyse 'relations *between* different groups of the rural population, as well as the relations of these groups with the urban classes. In other words, it [was] necessary to study the system of relations of production of different groups of the peasantry.'[25] Characterizing rural relations of production prior to collectivization as 'petty-bourgeois', Danilov maintained that the nationalization of land after October 1917 meant that not land but the 'hiring and renting' of agricultural equipment and draught animals, the renting of land and 'exploitation of hired labour' shaped rural social relations. These, not land holdings, were the basis of kulak capitalism.[26] Further, by introducing 'group' as well as class analysis, Danilov depicted the Soviet countryside in the 1920s in categories similar to those of his New Direction colleagues, as a 'complex combination' of social relations: 'bourgeois (capitalist and especially petty-bourgeois), socialist and transitional to socialism', the correlation of which changed under the impact of NEP. According to Danilov, these 'transitional productive relations' developed only among the rural poor-proletarian and middle layers. The kulaks, which exploited labour, remained in irreconcilable antagonism with socialism.[27] Despite his orthodox views of the kulak, Danilov had made what one discussant called the 'first serious attempt' in Soviet historiography to establish the crucial role of 'transitional relations' in the Soviet countryside in the 1920s.[28] Not only did they develop in 'the exchange between the socialist town and the petty-bourgeois countryside but also within agricultural production'. They constituted an essential 'precondition for the triumph of socialist productive relations'.[29]

Lenin's 'cooperative plan' as an alternative to Stalin's draconian collectivization was an increasing concern of Danilov. According to him, cooperatives were an essential element of these emerging transitional relations during the NEP. Socialized commodity exchange was a way of unifying small peasant producers by means of marketing, supply and credit cooperatives. It freed the poor and middle peasantry from exploitation by private traders and speculators. By the end of 1927, 39 per cent of peasant households were members of consumer cooperatives; by 1929, 58.3 per cent were. A 'first breach in the private-property psychology of the peasantry', cooperatives were 'primary elements of collectivism', offering, in Lenin's words, the prospect of a 'simpler, easier and more accessible' transition to the new socialist order. In other words, declared Danilov, 'unification of peasant households on the basis of commodity exchange paved the way for collectivization of their production.'[30]

To a Western reader, Danilov's assertions about the 'transitional' nature of social relations and cooperatives might seem innocuous. But with the staunch Stalinist insistence that collectivization entailed the replacement of capitalism in the countryside with socialism, any suggestion that at most cooperatives were laying the ground work for a transition to socialism was beyond the pale.

Danilov's conceptual innovations in relation to the countryside in the 1920s were reinforced by an audacious assault on the postulates of Soviet historiography of collectivization presented to the conference by his colleagues Bogdenko and Zelenin.[31] They endorsed Danilov's critique of collectivization as a necessary, so-called 'objective' outcome of the development of the productive forces. Likewise, they emphasized the importance of cooperatives, especially trading cooperatives, as instruments for drawing the peasantry into collectivized agriculture. They, however, sharply criticized the orthodox literature's 'mechanical' treatment of the 'political' preconditions for collectivization, which 'extraordinarily' simplified and 'exaggerated the successes' of the increased role of rural soviets and lower party organizations. Claims that by 1929 the conditions for full-scale collectivization had been established completely ignored their absence in the more backward regions of the Union.[32]

Zelenin and Bogdenko noted that the 'overwhelming majority' of historians now accepted the view (Danilov's) that the material-technical prerequisites were not in place at the time of full-scale collectivization, indeed that five years elapsed after this social transformation before machinery became the basis of collective farming. In this regard they singled out for its failings the work of S. P. Trapeznikov, the future scourge of historical revisionism. Trapeznikov 'drew no conclusion' about the technical resources of the *kolkhozy* at the end of the first five-year plan.[33] The authors seemed to delight in using Trapeznikov to highlight the shortcomings of orthodox analyses of collectivization – which he no doubt remembered when he had the opportunity to put these revisionists in their place. Along with other authors, Trapeznikov was accused of a superficial analysis of the role of Machine Tractor Stations (MTS) in carrying out collectivization.[34]

Turning their attention to the 'tempo, forms and principles' of full-scale collectivization, the authors regarded the weak study of the 'dynamics' of collectivization as 'one of the most serious deficiencies' in the literature. Again, Trapeznikov was singled out; in this case in tracing the monthly dynamics of collectivization, 'for some reason' limiting himself to the first half of 1931 through to its 'completion' in 1932. In other words, Trapeznikov had bypassed the crucial turning point of 1929–30. But even in dealing with this crucial period, they argued, historians tended to skate over monthly and quarterly figures for collectivization. These would have shown the sharp fluctuations in collectivized peasants in this period. Zelenin and Bogdenko pointed to 'weak use of sources' and 'exaggerations' leading to 'premature and mistaken conclusions' about the numbers of peasants who left or joined the collective farms in the summer of 1930 in the wake of policies deemed 'leftist extremes'. As they pointed out, this period saw a net loss of collective farmers, which the literature turned into an influx by exaggerating the number of collective farms, conveniently ignoring the fact the newly created farms did not compensate for the old ones that had broken up. Trapeznikov was explicitly accused of claiming that the summer of 1930 saw an end to the exit of collective farmers and consequently the 'stabilization' of collectivization.[35]

In this regard, Zelenin and Bogdenko took issue too with what they saw as the tendency of many historians to see the acceleration of collectivization in January–March 1930 as an 'outstanding achievement' and on this basis to justify 'errors and extremes' in achieving it as even 'inevitable'. Others continued to accept that the first criticism of such errors had been made by Stalin in his 2 March 1930 article 'Dizzy with Success', even though it had long been established that this had followed a Central Committee resolution on this question adopted in February. Further, 'extremely contradictory' approaches had been taken by historians concerning when agriculture was actually completely collectivized. The hapless Trapeznikov was instanced as one who believed this had been achieved by the end of the first five-year plan.[36]

Some of their most trenchant criticism Zelenin and Bogdenko reserved for the failings of Soviet historians in relation to 'one of the most crucial questions': the expropriation of the kulaks and their 'elimination as a class'. They noted that the recent literature had for the first time, in 1958, brought to light the hitherto unpublicized Yakovlev Politburo commission, established in December 1929 to make important decisions in relation to collectivization and the kulaks.[37] They also noted certain distinctions in relation to expropriation of the kulaks, including the use of 'direct force'. However, they were more concerned with the time-scale within which expropriation of the kulaks was said to have taken place and whether their 'elimination as a class' had been entirely completed by the end of the first five-year plan as, for instance, Trapeznikov claimed, without a shred of evidence. Similarly, undocumented claims about a 'cruel class struggle' raging in the countryside exaggerated and 'schematized' the resistance of the kulaks to collectivization (slaughtering their cattle, subverting the kolkhoz), downplaying other factors such as extreme methods of collectivization. The failure of earlier Soviet historians to pay any attention to the decline of the rural economy in 1931–32 or, when they did, to verge on the 'falsification of history' by talking about increased grain output, Zelenin and Bogdenko saw as a direct 'reflection of the Stalin cult'. Even some more recent studies, while recognizing the decline of agricultural output, neglected to explore its causes. Here they noted, however, a positive contribution by Trapeznikov and their colleague Moshkov, both of whom had explored the 'objective difficulties' subsequently afflicting agriculture.[38] Finally, they rejected the periodization of agricultural transformation advanced in the *Short Course*, which asserted that socialist agriculture had been established in 1934. Zelenin and Bogdenko argued that 1932 and 1937 (the ends of the first and second five-year plans respectively) were the decisive turning points. Even after full-scale collectivization was achieved by the end of 1932, the peasantry remained imbued with the outlook of the 'petty commodity producer'. By 1937 not socialism, but merely socialist relations of production and the material-technical basis for collective farming were in place.

Zelenin and Bogdenko had undertaken a wide-ranging critique of orthodox Soviet interpretations of collectivization. At this stage, however, theirs was essentially a technical critique, which touched on but did not explore whether or not the social and cultural prerequisites for collectivization existed in the Soviet countryside. That question remained on Danilov's agenda.

Archival sources

While Danilov, Bogdenko and Zelenin were advancing on one historiographical front, Ivnitsky was advancing on another, using newly-accessible archival sources in particular. Focusing on the most dramatic and tragic period of full-scale collectivization, from the autumn of 1929 to the spring of 1930, Ivnitsky vigorously advocated the use of published sources and newly-accessible archives, such as The Central Party Archive (TsPA) and the Central State Archive of the National Economy (TsGANKh). Here Ivnitsky was particularly advantaged. Although he did not say so at the time, he had been authorized by the editor of the new edition of the *History of the Communist Party of the Soviet Union*, B. N. Ponomarev, to work on Politburo sources in the Kremlin archives.[39] Writing in the March–April 1962 issue of *Historical Archive*, of which he was an editor, Ivnitsky argued that inadequate use of statistics reduced the 'scientific-theoretical level of research' on the preparatory stage of collectivization in autumn 1929.[40] But in stressing the value of statistics, he exaggerated their shortcomings. He erroneously claimed that 'unfortunately' publication of statistical data on the kolkhozy themselves during this period had ceased in the 1930s.[41] He was correct, however, to claim that statistics on the national economy were inadequate for capturing the 'dynamic' of collectivization because they tended to cover a whole year, without providing monthly or quarterly breakdowns at least for autumn 1929. 'It is no wonder that the second half of 1929 is least studied. The statistical collections ... provide data for 1 June and 1 October 1929 but not for 1 January 1930.'[42]

In general, study of the onset of full-scale collectivization was impeded by the fact that the necessary archival materials were 'non-existent'. It was possible to research up to 1 October 1929 and from 1 January 1930, but the period October to December had remained 'outside the researcher's field of view' – the crucial period for understanding the 'problems' collectivization encountered in winter 1930: the 'rate', 'errors and excesses' and the 'elimination of the kulaks as a class'. Ivnitsky, however, was able to provide new insights into vital events in this period, such as the November 1929 plenum on the basis of archives from the Kolkhoztsentr, the Commissariat of Agriculture (Narkomzem) and the Central Committee. In the Narkomzem archive Ivnitsky unearthed previously neglected materials of the Yakovlev commission. These provided 'invaluable' figures on the scope of collectivization, collected by the commission in the course of preparing the 5 January 1930 Central Committee resolution 'On the rate of collectivization and measures of state support for the kolkhozy'. Materials from the commission, together with sources from the party archives, enabled Ivnitsky to provide a 'truthful picture' of collectivization, with all its 'difficulties and errors'. He lamented the neglect of these sources by Soviet historians.[43]

On the basis of 'hitherto unknown', 'inaccessible' sources, Ivnitsky devoted an entire article to the origins of the critical 5 January 1930 Central Committee resolution, which codified full-scale collectivization and 'explained the causes of the rampant errors and excesses' in its initial stages. Ivnitsky showed the crucial role of the Yakovlev commission and its sub-commissions in drafting the resolution in the course of intensive discussion on 14–15 December 1929. Clearly sympathizing with Yakovlev's cautious approach to the implementation of collectivization, Ivnitsky detailed how Stalin, acting on amendments to the resolution proposed by the deputy chairman of the Council of People's Commissars for Russia T. R. Ryskulov, substantially modified the Yakovlev commission's draft resolution put forward on 22 December. Submitted to the Politburo on 3 January, it was further edited by Stalin on 4 January. The 'final', edited resolution now reduced the period for collectivization of the major grain producing districts from two–three years to one–two, requiring the quickest possible development of the *artel'*, through the socialization of the basic means of production, as a transition to the *kommuna*, the highest form of collectivized agriculture. It also explicitly excluded kulaks from the kolkhozy.[44]

Ivnitsky used these archives to overcome what he derided as the 'recidivism' of even recent writings on this crucial period. These, he charged, often lapsed back into perspectives derived from Stalin and his *Short Course*, such as that the autumn–winter of 1929–30 was a period of unparalleled success and that errors and distortions only occurred in February 1930.[45] Ivnitsky showed that already by mid-December 'unjustified forcing' of the pace of collectivization was widespread, despite a timetable for collectivization over the course of the five-year plan that had been drawn up by G. N. Kaminsky's sub-commission on the rate of collectivization established on 8 December 1929.[46] In view of this, at the end of 1929 Yakovlev's Politburo commission set out a timetable for collectivization varying according to region from one to four years, much of which was incorporated into the 5 January Central Committee resolution. In no uncertain terms, Ivnitsky showed that in fact this timetable was already being violated by the 'connivance' of Stalin, Molotov, Kaganovich and People's Commissar for War K. E. Voroshilov. As early as mid-November 1929, Molotov had called for complete collectivization in the North Caucasus.[47]

Moreover, Ivnitsky condemned Stalin's attempts to shift responsibility for 'excesses' to local officials for being 'dizzy with success', as he did during the spring of 1930.[48] As Ivnitsky showed, Stalin and his circle were in receipt of regular regional reports almost every week from the end of 1929 indicating mass flight from the *kolkhozy*. Having 'underestimated' the cost to collectivization of the 'excesses' occurring at the end of 1929, they allowed them to reach 'threatening proportions' in the spring of 1930. 'It was not accidental therefore that, to cover himself, Stalin dated the emergence of the excesses from the second half of February 1930'.[49] Ivnitsky accused Trapeznikov of interpreting events in an outdated manner. Whereas Ivnitsky maintained that collectivization began to go astray at the end of 1929, Trapeznikov, like Stalin, dated the 'excesses' from the end of February 1930 and maintained the Central Committee had been quick to set them right. Trapeznikov, then on the editorial board of *Voprosy istorii KPSS*, took offence at Ivnitsky's article but did not have the numbers on the board to stop it being published.[50]

From the party archives Ivnitsky adduced damning evidence of Molotov's 'blatant attempt to artificially force the pace of collectivization'. He compared Molotov's speech to the November plenum, in which he declared the Northern Caucasus would be collectivized by mid-1930, with that of the Secretary of the Northern Caucasus district party committee who at the plenum predicted, correctly, that full collectivization would take at least another year, that is, until mid-1931. Ivnitsky concluded that in many regions Molotov's declaration had been interpreted as a 'directive', with 'disastrous consequences' in winter 1929–30. Yet, despite the fact that these speeches had been readily available to Soviet historians, 'not one' had paid attention to them nor to the responsibility of Stalin and his circle for the excessive pace at which collectivization was pursued in the regions.[51]

Ivnitsky was plainly anxious to use the archives to set the record straight on collectivization. But he was a historian of his time. Turning to the vexed question of the elimination of the kulaks, he was intent on using the new sources more effectively than Soviet historians had done to date to refute the depiction of this process by 'bourgeois falsifiers' as 'bloodthirsty and cruel'. Drawing on materials from the Yakovlev commission and from party central, regional and district committees, he maintained that the commission had advocated a 'differentiated' approach to the kulaks, according to their political attitude towards Soviet power, and that as a whole the communist party had been guided by 'humanitarian' considerations. The aim was to 're-educate' the kulaks, not 'physically annihilate them'. He concluded therefore that 'errors and excesses' in dealing with the kulaks had occurred 'in violation of C[entral] C[ommittee] directives' advocating 'partial confiscation of property' rather than the 'complete confiscation' that occurred, affecting even middle and poor peasants. Nevertheless, he noted that there was a serious gap in the available figures for 'dekulakization'; in the main they related only to 1930. 'Unfortunately', he wrote,

> there are no generalized sources on the elimination of the kulak as a class. It is only known that from the beginning of 1930 through to the autumn of 1932, 240,757 kulak families were evicted from the districts where full-scale collectivization occurred, less than one per cent of the total peasant households and around a quarter of all kulak households.[52]

Ivnitsky was talking of 'dekulakization' in terms of property, not life. While neither he nor his colleagues could have known precisely the scale of the human tragedy that had unfolded in those years,[53] Ivnitsky certainly had some suspicion of it. From his work on the secret 'special folders' of the Politburo in the Kremlin archives, he gleaned for the first time information on the numbers of exiled and special settlers, although he could not refer to these sources.[54]

A summary of the achievements of Soviet historians since the Twentieth Congress was published by Danilov in 1962. In it he laid bare the principles upon which the new cohort of historians had revisited the history of the Soviet countryside and begun to confront the pernicious consequences of the 'cult of the personality'. He argued that the focus on Stalin had been to the 'detriment of the role of the Communist Party' and in particular to the 'self-activity and the creative initiative of the popular masses'. In Stalinist historiography the peasantry was 'either ignored or presented as an object of measures implemented from above'.[55] Taking his cue from the Soviet historiography of the 1920s, Danilov sought to refocus Soviet historiography on the 'socio-economic' developments in the countryside prior to collectivization, to bring to life the real social changes that were occurring among the peasantry. These, he believed, made collectivization and the elimination of the kulak a 'law-governed', 'objective' process, not one driven by the 'general theoretical considerations' of the communist party leadership. He linked the imperative for collectivization to the sorts of changes in the countryside in the 1920s that had been unleashed by the October Revolution. Labouring under the burden of the *Short Course* approach, Soviet historians had neglected the social ramifications of eradicating the gentry estates and redistributing the land among the peasantry in 1917–18, a process that had promoted the middle peasantry by the averaging of land holdings. Stalin had compounded the *Short Course*'s neglect of changing rural social relations in the 1920s by his 'categorical' pronouncements in 1952 that purely 'capitalist' relations of production prevailed up until full-scale collectivization.[56]

A vital component of Danilov's resuscitation of the 1920s as a field of research was his call for recognition of 'the peasant household as the basic productive unit of agriculture'. The task, as Danilov saw it, was to locate the various households (poor, middle and kulak) in the overall system of relations of production. In this scenario, peasant 'land relations' became the focus of research, instead of being merely a passive 'background' to the 'measures of the state for the preparation and implementation' of collectivization, as it was in the standard Soviet interpretation. In this respect the April 1961 conference on agrarian history had been a landmark because it had established that the social structure of the Soviet countryside prior to collectivization was a 'complex combination' of relations – 'capitalist and petty bourgeois, socialist and transitional to socialism'. Accordingly, the priority of Soviet historians became the elucidation of changes in the 'correlation' of rural social 'structures' (*uklady*) and 'transitional' relations of production.[57]

In establishing these research priorities, Danilov was clearly echoing the 'multistructural' perspectives of the New Direction historians. The challenge of Danilov and his co-thinkers to the prevailing Soviet conceptions of collectivization lay not only in their critique of Stalin and the way he had implemented it, but in their reconceptualization of the driving forces of the agrarian revolution. In fact, Danilov gave collectivization legitimacy in so far as he argued that the poor peasantry had been an active proponent of collectivization; the committees of the poor peasantry (*kombedy*) had participated in the confiscation of the grain surplus of the kulak.[58]

The shift to a socio-economic problematic was part of a decisive break with the well-worn Stalinist view that the necessity for collectivization flowed from the necessity to overcome the contradiction between the socialist productive forces of urban industry and the relations of petty private production in the countryside.[59] It marked a break in Danilov's own evolution too. His first monograph had remained within the parameters of the productive forces/relations of production 'non-correspondence' paradigm, although he shifted the contradiction to that *within* the countryside, rather than that between the countryside and the cities. He had also demanded that analysis of the material-technical bases of socialist agriculture be based on 'specific-historical research' rather than mere 'exposition of theoretical principles illustrated by this or that example'.[60] This was clearly the guiding principle for his research group.

An unpublished manuscript

In 1964, Danilov's Group finally brought to fruition their combined researches and writing over a six-year period. The upshot was a massive 798-page history of collectivization during the first five-year plan: *The Collectivization of Agriculture in the USSR 1927–1932*.[61] This was the first of a planned two-volume study, intended to take the story up to 1937, that is, to the end of the second five-year plan. It was not to be. The proofs for the first volume were literally withdrawn from the publishers within 24 hours of the dismissal of Khrushchev as

CPSU First Secretary on 14 October 1964. The manuscript was never to see the light of day.

The preliminary page-proofs (*verstka*) of *The Collectivization of Agriculture* were produced by the publishers, *Mysl'* in autumn 1964. On 8 October 1964 Danilov signed for the initial printed version (*pervaya sverka*) to be produced. Six days later, at 4 p.m. on the very day that Khrushchev was ousted, Danilov was summoned by phone by the Deputy Director of the Institute of History, the 'inveterate Stalinist' Aleksei Trakov, to meet in his office next morning. Upon arriving Danilov was met by Trakov who leaped from his desk exclaiming '*Vot kto sevodnya opechalen!*' (Here we have somebody who is grieving today!). He was ordered to go to the publishers and withdraw the proofs.[62]

Danilov knew at once that this was the end of his Group's proposed history of collectivization. It was only the beginning, however, of the history of this history. The next two years saw an ongoing discussion and struggle over the fate of this book. According to Danilov,[63] after some disputation with the directors of the Institute, they decided to hold a discussion of the book in the Institute. They did so reluctantly, however, because they were concerned that an open discussion of the work would receive too much support from the Institute *kollektiv* (their concerns were justified: in November 1965 Danilov was elected to the Institute party committee by an overwhelming vote).[64] The discussion was scheduled for 2 July 1965. The discussion was based on a review of the work presented by Professor Valerya Selunskaya, head of the Faculty of the History of Soviet Society, Moscow State University. Leading the attack was F. M. Vaganov, representing the Central Committee, who was later to publish a critique of the Bukharinist 'right deviation'. As well as Selunskaya, the book was subject to criticism by Yury Polyakov, head of the Department of the History of Soviet Society in the Institute, to which Danilov's Group was subordinate.[65] The authors were entitled to invite their supporters to the discussion. Among those Danilov invited was Roy Medvedev.[66]

As a result of this discussion, Danilov and his co-authors prepared a second version of the proofs (*vtoraya sverka*). This version was the subject of a further discussion with the authors' collective in February 1966 in the Central Committee Department of Science, headed by the notorious Trapeznikov, by now Brezhnev's overseer of academic affairs. As a result it was decided to create an editorial board that, apart from Danilov and his nominee, included Trapeznikov himself. Further corrections were made by Danilov and his co-authors to create a third, more acceptable version.

Meanwhile Trapeznikov sent the proofs to the Faculty of History of the CPSU of the Central Committee's Academy of Social Sciences, having declared that 'the Central Committee will take control of this work. We need this work on collectivization. We will take the necessary measures to ensure it appears on the fiftieth anniversary of the October Revolution' [1967].[67] It was a hollow promise. In November 1966 the work was condemned as 'revisionist' and refused publication. It was finally withdrawn from the press in December 1966. In all the authors produced four revisions over two years – to no avail.[68] It was no accident, however, that in 1967 Trapeznikov published his own, extremely orthodox, two-volume history of collectivization.[69] Based on 'general-theoretical' considerations, unlike Danilov's banned volume which was the product of intense archival research, according to Ivnitsky it 'lacked any argument'.[70]

Overall, Danilov's unpublished monograph condemned forced collectivization, based on his view that the poor and middle peasantry, among whom traditional family ownership prevailed, were not ready for full-scale collectivization. Though a collective work, Danilov contributed the introduction, the first four chapters covering the period up to the eve of collectivization in 1929 and, together with Zelenin, the conclusion. The authors made much of the fact that the work was enriched by the access that they had to archives that were off-limits in the Stalin period.[71]

The structure of the work reflects the distinctive approach of Danilov and his colleagues to analysing the driving forces of collectivization. The first chapter dealt with the socio-economic structure of the Soviet countryside. Starting with the demographic make up of the peasantry, it moved to the peasant economy and the productive forces, socio-economic relations, and the development of agricultural production and the emergence of the grain procurement crisis.[72] In this it registered a distinctive departure from Danilov's first published work. There the starting point was the rural *economy*: the mode of production and the development of the productive forces – more or less Soviet orthodoxy in its time.[73]

Danilov's starting point was the need for utmost patience in dealing with the peasantry, particularly its middle layer. Russia, he emphasized was a 'transitional' economy made up of a 'complex, combination of five different socio-economic structures': socialist, state capitalist, private capitalist, petty commodity and patriarchal.[74] The numerical predominance of the middle peasantry made the socialist transformation of the countryside particularly fraught. Invoking Lenin, he cautioned against the expropriation of the middle peasantry and coercion to 'artificially accelerate' the reconstruction of agriculture. 'The slightest deviation' from the principle of voluntary collectivization could have 'pernicious consequences', as Soviet experience showed, alienating the peasantry, endangering its alliance with the working class and ultimately the 'dictatorship of the proletariat'. As Danilov dramatically emphasized in his introduction, during the winter of 1918–19, peasants had revolted against forced collectivization under the slogan 'Long Live Soviet Power, but Down with the Commune [*kommuna*]!' Stalin, ignoring these injunctions, had done 'great harm' to the development of collective agriculture.[75]

In his opening chapter, Danilov detailed the social basis of the peasant economy. He emphasized the 'commune system of land use' which 'absolutely prevailed' up until the onset of collectivization. But he did not idealize it. On the contrary, he emphasized the limitations of the *obshchina*. Under the impact of civil war, economic collapse and the famine of 1921 increasingly the peasantry had sought refuge in the commune. The periodic, egalitarian redistribution of land to each household discouraged soil improvement and long-term planting, so the Soviet state attempted to limit it. The commune was therefore ultimately an impediment to agricultural development and the development of the productive forces in the countryside.[76] For this reason, Danilov welcomed the move to collectivized agriculture.

Analysing the social and economic relations that defined the Soviet countryside before collectivization, Danilov maintained that 'no less than half' of all peasant farms were subject to exploitative, capitalist relations. The 'kernel' of these was the 'rent and hire' of the means of agricultural production (draught animals and tools) and land by the poor and middle peasantry from the wealthy kulaks, and the provision of hired labour by the former to the latter. The kulak therefore was the 'principal representative' of rural capitalism.[77] Pursuit of the New Economic Policy (NEP) had encouraged the development of the kulaks. However, it had also fostered contrary tendencies: the growth of the rural proletariat and, especially, of the middle peasantry. This 'class differentiation' of the peasantry meant that by the time of the Fifteenth Party Congress two possible paths for the economy were in contention: socialism or capitalism.[78] To this extent, Danilov was at one with the traditional explanation of the necessity for the move to collectivization in 1927.

But Danilov's Soviet countryside was not a seamless capitalist landscape. It was highly differentiated. Capitalist relations prevailed in its heartland, where 80–85 per cent of the peasantry lived, such as Russia, Belorussia and the Ukraine, and where in various forms the commune system was also preserved. But in Central Asia and the far East 'patriarchal-feudal' relations were predominant, necessitating a move to socialism, 'bypassing' capitalism.[79]

Danilov's explanation of the origins of the 1927–28 grain crisis was fairly traditional. The inadequacies of predominantly petty agricultural production led to a disproportion between industrial production and the countryside's capacity to pay. Forced procurement of the grain surplus in mid-1928 and the resultant kulak 'grain strike' forced the Soviet state to move decisively to reorganize agriculture 'along socialist lines' in order to eliminate the kulaks, 'the last and most numerous exploiting class', as both orthodoxy and Danilov would have it.[80]

In his treatment of the move to collectivization, however, Danilov focused on the faith that the Fifteenth Congress had placed in Lenin's cooperative plan as its basis. Envisaged by the party as the primary link between the state and small-scale peasant capitalism, after the Fifteenth Congress they experienced 'burning' development. The following year saw the poor and middle peasantry displace the kulaks, who hitherto had been admitted to the cooperatives, as a prerequisite for collectivization.[81]

Despite his commitment to Lenin's gradualist approach to collectivization, Danilov repudiated the critique of collectivization advanced by the Bukharinist Right at the Fifteenth Congress (he dismissed the Trotskyist–Zinovievist opposition as mere opponents of 'the victory of socialism in one country'). Danilov attributed Bukharin's call for 'economic' rather than 'extraordinary measures' against the kulak to his illusions in a 'peaceful transition' to socialism in the countryside. Counterposing Lenin's cooperative plan to that of Bukharin, he also endorsed Mikoyan's attack on Bukharin at the April 1929 plenum for giving cooperatives a secondary role in the transition to socialism. Mikoyan accused Bukharin of reducing cooperatives to mere instruments of commerce and trade, open to all classes, including the kulaks, rather than being vital mechanisms for the organization of production and the immediate precursors to collective farms.[82]

By the spring of 1928, according to Danilov, a 'broad network' of Soviet, party and cooperative organizations had laid the basis for the 'gradual growing over' of the 'simplest productive associations' into collective farms. But by the end 1929, the situation in the country had 'radically' changed: the 'immediate, direct' move to full-scale collectivization bypassed the productive associations. It was at this point that Danilov and his colleagues began to part company with party orthodoxy. They emphasized the lack of the necessary prerequisites for complete collectivization: the involvement of the mass of the peasantry in cooperatives, lack of MTS and of technically qualified personnel, such as agronomists.[83]

It was his thoroughgoing critique of the implementation of 'full-scale' collectivization that distinguished Danilov's approach.[84] While giving credence to the 'ousting' of the kulak from the collective farms and the use of article 107 of the Criminal Code against them to defeat the grain strike, Danilov shared the April 1928 plenum's condemnation of its application to the middle peasantry, which led, in the plenum's words, to 'forced procurement going off the rails'.[85] But in the true spirit of Khrushchevism, Danilov reserved his most scathing criticism for the personal role of Stalin. At the height of the grain procurement crisis in early 1928, Stalin had demonstrated 'mistrust' towards local party cadre and a predilection for 'administrative methods' and 'punishment' of those officials who failed to turn around grain procurement in the shortest possible time. This was most evident during Stalin's tour of Siberia in January–February 1928 when he recommended the dismissal and 'punishment' of local party and cooperative workers and 'repression' of judicial officials, whom he accused of consorting with kulaks. Stalin's approach was adopted in Central Committee directives and resulted in an attitude of 'its better to exceed objectives than to fall short of them' on the part of local officials. The result was 'distortions', 'exaggerations' and 'illegality' in dealing with the peasantry that continued despite their condemnation by the Central Committee.[86]

In counterposing the Central Committee to Stalin, Danilov was not really being that radical. Danilov's condemnation of Stalin's violations of Central Committee 'collective leadership' and Soviet law were consistent with Khrushchev's condemnation of the 'cult of the personality' and his attempt to reinstate collective party leadership and respect for the Soviet legal code during the 1950s and 1960s. But in this regard Danilov's approach was clearly out of step in the Brezhnev era. Danilov's position in relation to collectivization echoed the concerns of the more liberal technocrats at the end of 1928, such as K. Ya. Bauman, then head of the Commission of the Central Committee Department for Work in the Countryside. While expressing the opposition of the communist party to 'administrative arbitrariness', 'muddleheadedness' and 'dekulakization', Bauman called for merciless struggle against kulak counter-revolutionary terror,[87] a position Danilov and his colleagues undoubtedly shared.

In line with his emphasis on the need for gradual, voluntary collectivization, Danilov focused on the importance the CPSU itself had attached to transitional forms of collective agriculture, from the most simple to the most complex, as the basis for expanding the collectivization movement. For this reason he cited a Central Committee resolution of 26 December 1926 endorsing the development of the TOZ (Association for the Joint Cultivation of Land),[88] along with other simple production organizations such as for machinery, as 'the most widespread form of collectivization'.[89] By 1927, the TOZ had begun to displace the *artel'* as the primary form of collective agriculture in the regions where collectivization was most developed, such as the North Caucasus, the Lower Volga and the Ukraine. In both these forms of collective agriculture, particularly the TOZ, the peasants preserved a high level of individual ownership of the means of production as insurance against the possible failings of collectivization. Danilov acknowledged that even in its formative stage cooperative agriculture, utilizing existing 'manufacturing level' techniques, draught animals and manual labour, was already demonstrating its superior output over individual farming. But the further development of collectivization suffered from an acute shortage of tractors. Archival data from the files of TsGANKh showed that in the autumn of 1927 there were only 4988 tractors for 11 161 *kolkhozy* in the Russian republic, less than half the 10 349 required.[90]

Using the archives, Danilov also revealed that the obstacles to collectivization were as much organizational-political as technical. The Fifteenth Congress in December 1927 had proclaimed the 'immediate preparation of collectivization'. But TsGANKh files showed that by the middle of 1928 Baumann's commission found that a significant number of regional party organizations, Tambov, Stalingrad, Vologod and Ul'yanovsk, had resorted to 'shock campaigns' to achieve collectivization. Danilov argued these 'shock tactics' were symptomatic of the numerical weakness of rural party organizations that were out of touch with the mood of the peasantry. Telegrammed instructions to district agricultural departments ordering them to 'create kolkhozy' saw local agronomists, fearful of offending the authorities, even creating 'pseudo-kolkhozy', the commission reported. Danilov labeled such measures 'bureaucratic planning from above', which in the absence of effective party and Soviet grass roots connections with the peasantry, depended on a 'campaign-allotting method of work and defective agitation'. In some areas such 'bureaucratic distortions', as Danilov put it, led to the collapse of the kolkhozy. In others, kolkhozy that were planned to be established were not, while in others they sprang up spontaneously but local authorities were not in the position to provide them with the technical support that they needed to survive. But for Danilov, the 'main inadequacy' of the kolkhoz movement in the spring of 1928 derived not so much from the administrative methods of prosecuting it as from the inability of the state and cooperative bodies to cope organizationally with the burgeoning kolkhoz movement.[91]

Consistent with his view that the middle peasantry was essential to the viability of the kolkhoz, Danilov made much of the observations in the commission archives that already the kolkhozy were dominated by the poor peasantry at the expense of the middle peasantry. This included the TOZ, which allowed the highest level of private property and was therefore the most attractive form of collective for the middle peasantry. Kolkhozy that exclusively involved only one layer of the peasantry caused 'enormous political harm', Danilov argued, driving a wedge between the poor and middle peasantry. 'Without the broad participation of the middle peasantry the kolkhoz movement could not become a mass movement.' He found support for this proposition in the Central Committee resolution of 15 May 1928 that made the active participation of the middle peasantry in collectivization its first priority.[92]

It was part of Danilov's method to seek support for his conception of collectivization within the parameters of party discussions at the time of its implementation. Examining the discussion that occurred in June 1928 in Moscow at the First All-Russian Congress of Collective Farms, Danilov noted Yakovlev's conclusion that during 1925–27 the *artel'* and the *kommuna* were becoming serious competitors of kulak agriculture. Danilov, however, also noted Yakovlev's concern that to sustain this, collectivization would have to move as soon as possible to the *artel'* form of kolkhoz. But this would require 'large-scale machine production' and not just the 'simple' collaboration of a few small farmers.[93] Similarly, he drew attention to the report by Kolkhoztsentr chairman G. N. Kaminsky that reemphasized the importance of cooperatives as the mechanism for involving the mass of the peasantry in collectivization. But Danilov also pointed to a contradiction in Kaminsky's perspective that would augur badly for the full-scale collectivization that was yet to come. This was

Kaminsky's view that broadening the scale of collectivization might actually entail a short-term decline of agricultural output and productive capacity in order to ensure long-term growth. This position could serve as a '"theoretical" premise' for the use of 'administrative pressure' to implement collectivization, even at the expense of the productive forces. 'In the atmosphere of 1928', as Danilov put it, this notion was used polemically against these who argued for the need to consolidate the existing kolkhozy before establishing new ones, and their views dismissed as 'right-opportunist' (Danilov could have been talking about himself).

The 'danger' inherent in this notion was confirmed for Danilov by the subsequent appearance of the 'theory of the distinctive stages of collectivization – initially "extensive" (the stage of establishing kolkhozy) and then "intensive" (the stage of their organizational and economic reinforcement).' But Danilov stressed that despite the airing of these notions 'nobody assumed that full-scale collectivization would develop so quickly and stormily. Even the boldest proposals did not envisage the establishment of the conditions for full-scale collectivization before the end of the first five-year plan, which had just begun.' Even Kaminsky, like the 'overwhelming majority' of party members at the time, depicted the socialist transformation of agriculture as a 'transition', as an 'internal growing over' from 'one stage of the cooperative movement to another'. The notion of the peasantry 'bypassing' these stages to directly enter the kolkhozy 'still seemed impossible or even irrational', Danilov concluded. The unbridled revolutionary ardour of the small peasantry in dealing with the middle peasantry, effectively 'Who is not with us is against us', Danilov saw as extremely harmful to the collectivization movement. He emphasized that the final resolution of the congress avoided such 'extremes'.[94]

Detailing the expansion of the kolkhoz movement during 1928–29, Danilov was at pains to emphasize the cautious approach of party and other officials to the pace of collectivization. He emphasized in bold type Yakovlev's admonition in December 1928 that *'it will require decades to collectivize our country'*. Likewise, he quoted S. V. Kosior's condemnation of 'forcing of collectivization' and 'naked administrativeness' as a 'direct violation of party directives'. The general orientation of the party at this time, Danilov maintained, accorded with the 'objective and subjective conditions' as reflected in the figures for the national economy and the first five-year plan.[95]

Summarizing the outcome of the Sixteenth Party Conference in April 1929, Danilov noted the delegates' confidence that 'mass collectivization' would soon be a reality. He himself saw the conference, together with the adoption of the five-year plan, as an 'enormous' stimulus to collectivization. In his even-handed, loyal to the party fashion, he saw the conference, and the April 1929 plenum, as another 'defeat' for the view of Bukharin, Rykov and Tomsky that the expansion of collectivization was incorrect. Yet, at the same time, he endorsed Kalinin's concerns about the conference's 'neglect of the independent peasant'. At a time when only 2 per cent of the peasantry was in kolkhozy, this 'could lead to serious economic and political difficulties'. Nevertheless Danilov distinguished between the shortcomings of 'mass collectivization' and the 'serious economic and political consequences' of the 'unnecessary forcing' of 'full-scale collectivization' six months later, which outstripped the capacity for financial and technical support and expertise.[96] In Danilov's view this was compounded by the failure to involve the middle peasantry as collectivization accelerated in the summer of 1929. He saw a 'choice of forms of association' as a vital means of winning the voluntary commitment of the mass of the peasantry, especially the middle peasantry who wished to retain their economic independence. Confirmation of this Danilov found in the rapid expansion and predominance of the TOZ on the eve of 'full-scale collectivization'. He found further confirmation of the promise of the TOZ in the archives of Baumann's commission of the Department for Work in the Countryside. The commission deemed the TOZ as the 'most accessible, initial step along the path to collectivization'.[97]

But, according to Danilov, it was not the TOZ that was to be the basis of collectivization in the summer–autumn of 1929, it was the 'gigantic-kolkhoz' of five, ten and even 20 000 hectares. Under-resourced and disorganized, the '*kolkhozy-giganty*' did 'great harm' to cooperative production. This 'gigantomania' Danilov specifically linked to Stalin. Describing it as 'left infantilism' in the collectivization movement, Danilov argued that in the emerging 'cult of the personality' around Stalin, it was not only impossible to correct such gross errors, they were actually compounded. Without a demonstrably productive collective agriculture it would be impossible to win over the middle peasantry.[98]

The failure of the Stalin regime to draw the overwhelming majority of the peasantry into the collectivization movement was at the heart of Danilov's critique of collectivization. But he shared Kaminsky's conviction that there was no place for the kulak in the kolkhoz. 'The kulak is the enemy of the kolkhoz', he cited Kaminsky as saying at the First All-Union Congress of Collective farms in 1928. Danilov evidently agreed that the kulaks had to be 'eliminated' but not *'by simple measures of state force'*, as Yakovlev, whom Danilov cited at length, told the same congress, but by *'eradicating'* rural capitalism through the *'production cooperative'*.[99] But the question of the admissibility or otherwise of the kulak into the kolkhoz had still not been finally decided in mid-1929, on the very of eve of full-scale collectivization. That would only be decided, Danilov wrote, by the 'methods of the further struggle with the kulak and his elimination'.[100]

Censorship at work

A close comparison of chapters V and VI of the original (1964) proofs (*pervaya sverka*) of the unpublished monograph, written by Ivnitsky, with the second, revised version (*vtoraya sverka*), clearly reveals the critical thrust of this tome. These chapters dealt with the crucial turn to collectivization in September–December 1929 and the subsequent implementation of full-scale collectivization in January–February 1930. They were to be radically amended, under duress, after the discussions that took place in the Central Committee Department of Science in 1965–66. The amendments to the second version were introduced in early 1966 mainly by the publisher's editor, L. D. Petrov. It was done with care because ultimately the publisher, along with the author, bore responsibility for the finished work that would be presented to the censor, *Glavlit*, for final approval to publish.[101]

In his section of the unpublished history, Ivnitsky acknowledged the initial achievements of a new stage of collectivization that had been endorsed by the Central Committee in August 1929. He noted the spread of collectivization in the highest grain-producing regions. Already by autumn 1929 more than 60 per cent of farms in the South, South-east and East of the European part of the Union were collectivized. He noted too the importance of machine-tractor columns and stations (MTS) as providing the most effective material basis for encouraging the mass kolkhoz movement among the poor and middle peasantry. He wrote of the 'sharpening class struggle', including acts of terror, as the kulaks reacted to the growing kolkhoz movement. He hailed the importance of local party organizations and the mobilization of party members in promoting collectivization, combating kulak resistance and ensuring successful grain procurement.[102] In many respects, therefore, Ivnitsky's perspective differed little from official accounts. But this was not enough to satisfy academic orthodoxy.

The publisher's editor took exception to Ivnitsky's observation that prior to winter 1929 in the Black Earth regions, the kulaks took advantage of 'mistakes' of local party organizations enabling the kulaks to organize numerous 'anti-Soviet actions' that 'grew sharply' in response to full-scale collectivization.[103] The entire paragraph was deleted, as was a subsequent assertion that 'the further successes and failures of the socialist transformation of agriculture depended directly on how astutely defined were the paths, methods and period of the transition of millions of toilers into a new life'.[104] The latter assertion called in question the astuteness of party authorities in the implementation of collectivization.[105]

Not everything critical of party policy was censored however. Ivnitsky emphasized distortions of the party line by local organizations 'forcing the tempo' of collectivization. To this effect he quoted Ukrainian party secretary S. V. Kosior's condemnation at the November 1929 Central Committee plenum of 'tens of excesses' in the Ukraine, where resort to 'administrative methods' resulted in the 'collapse' of collectivized farms. Though Kosior's speech was not referred to in Trapeznikov's discussion of the November plenum, the publisher's editor did not erase it from Ivnitsky's account. But in general Ivnitsky's treatment of the crucial November 1929 plenum was heavily amended and/or censored. It was this plenum that had unleashed full-scale collectivization with the declaration that the 'optimal version' of the five-year plan could now become the 'minimal version' and condemned opposition to it by Bukharin, Rykov, and Tomsky.[106]

Ivnitsky agreed that the November plenum was 'of the greatest significance for the development of the kolkhoz movement and the successful building of socialism'.[107] He also quoted seemingly approvingly denunciation of the so-called 'right' oppositionists, Bukharin, Rykov and Tomsky who 'despite condemnation of their positions by the April [1929] C[entral] C[ommittee] Plenum and the XVI party conference, continued to struggle against the application of extraordinary measures, actually opposing the move to the liquidation of the kulaks as a class'. Ivnitsky later strengthened this by interpolating extracts from Stalin's speech in support of 'extraordinary measures'.[108] But he fell foul of the publisher's editor when he included a lengthy footnote directly citing, from the archives, a declaration to the November plenum from the right oppositionists that 'the application of extraordinary measures reflected a certain underfulfilment of the agricultural plan … We could achieve the desired results by a less painful path.'[109]

According to Ivnitsky he included this footnote because he wanted to show the 'mistakes' of the 'right deviation of the Bukharin group', but he did so by adducing documented 'facts' drawn from Kremlin and central party archives, where he had worked in the mid-1960s. In this respect his work differed markedly from that of Trapeznikov who calumniated the right and left oppositions, usually by referring to communist party resolutions, not archival material.[110] The Danilov grouping did not see themselves as latter-day Bukharinists, even though at first sight their gradualist approach to collectivization seems similar (in fact they had little knowledge of Bukharin's ideas, other than what Stalin had said, as Danilov informed R. W. Davies in 1963).[111] Nevertheless, Ivnitsky did not totally dismiss the Bukharin group's views either. On reading them for the first time he began to take seriously Bukharin's perspective that peasant cooperatives could 'grow over' into socialism. By citing the Bukharin group's views he was deliberately giving credence to them. This apparently was more than the editor could tolerate. Not only were Bukharin and his group not rehabilitated and still therefore 'non-persons' in the 1960s, but a reader might actually draw the same conclusions as Bukharin *et al.* that 'extraordinary measures' in relation to collectivization were 'superfluous'.[112]

Ivnitsky, noting that the November plenum had resolved that in several of the major agricultural regions the kolkhoz movement was in a position to move to 'full-scale collectivization', immediately added that several participants in the plenum (for example, Kosior) had drawn attention to 'excesses and distortions of the party line'. A letter from an official of the Kolkhoztsentr, Baranov, had warned about these excesses in relation to the Khoper region, on the Lower Volga, a region that had pioneered collectivization:

> However [Ivnitsky wrote], these warnings were ignored. I. V. Stalin, in replying 'Do you think that everything can be "organized in advance?"', in essence brushed aside the most urgent practical problems of collectivization. He not only did not adopt measures to forestall excesses and distortions in relation to kolkhoz organization, but, on the contrary, enabled them to spread.[113]

This direct attack on Stalin was obviously too much for the publishers. They softened the references to 'excesses', qualifying them by referring to undue 'hastiness' (*toplivosti*). The editor completely deleted, however, Ivnitsky's disparaging comments on Stalin substituting instead, in a handwritten note: 'I. V. Stalin, as general secretary of the C[entral] C[ommittee] of the VKP (b), naturally, had great influence on the direction and course of discussion concerning problems of collectivization'.[114] A masterful understatement, in keeping with the whitewashing of Stalin's status that the encroaching Brezhnev 'era of stagnation' required.

Ivnitsky continued on to lay much of the responsibility for false expectations about the achievements of collectivization onto Stalin himself, particularly in relation to its scope and the participation of the middle peasantry:

> The article of I. V. Stalin, 'The Year of the Great Turning Point', which appeared in the press on 7 November, had already called for an across the board acceleration of collectivization. It maintained that the bulk of the peasantry had already entered the *kolkhozy*, and that the turning point was past. 'Now even the blind can see – he [Stalin] wrote – that the middle peasant has turned towards the kolkhozy.' In fact [continues Ivnitsky], analysis shows that only in the leading grain-producing districts had the mood of the middle peasant masses begun to change. Stalin's article, however, has created the false ['false' was crossed out by the editor] impression that 'the decisive victory' … has already been won. In the article nothing was said of the necessity to take account of the actual mood of the peasantry, or of the necessity to correlate the rate of kolkhoz organization with the actual readiness of the peasantry to enter the kolkhozy.[115]

With the exception of the adjective 'false' to describe the 'impression' of victory created by Stalin, the paragraph remained intact. However, Ivnitsky's next paragraph was entirely deleted:

> Great damage was caused by the orientation formulated by Stalin for the establishment of 'big grain factories of 40 000 to 50 000 hectares'. In the conditions of the backwardness of the material-technical base and lack of qualified cadre, this orientation led to the organization of unviable state and collective farms, discrediting the idea of big, socialized production. As a consequence 'gigantomania' was doomed from the beginning in kolkhoz and then sovkhoz [state farm] organization.[116]

Ivnitsky went on to attack the 'negative' contribution at the plenum by V. Molotov, then secretary for agriculture, who predicted fundamental collectivization of the North Caucasus, and even beyond, by the summer of 1930 (that is, within six months). Taken together, Ivnitsky concluded, Stalin's article and Molotov's speech,

> thereby to the utmost extent encouraged the harmful pursuit of the highest percentages of collectivization. In circumstances where a cult of the personality had formed, Stalin and his closest associate were in a position to exert pressure on the course of discussion concerning problems of the kolkhoz movement at the Plenum.[117]

Once again, however, the hand of the editor is evident. In a marginal note he substituted for Ivnitsky's forthright condemnation of Stalin and Molotov: 'The article of I. V. Stalin and the speech of V. M. Molotov, thereby encouraged high rates of collectivization. This *influenced* the discussion ... at the Plenum'.[118]

Clearly the editor was alarmed by the negative observations about Stalin and his circle and their personal responsibility for the excesses and shortcomings of collectivization even before it got into full swing in early 1930. In the post-Khrushchev period, references to Stalin's 'cult of the personality' were rapidly falling out of favour. With the dismissal of Khrushchev a neo-Stalinist counter-offensive was underway which could not but impact on academic life and discourse, especially among historians. This did not mean, however, a complete resurrection of Stalin's role. Even Trapeznikov was critical of the role of Stalin for 'imprecise', 'mistaken' formulations which encouraged the premature 'liquidation' of the kulak class before full-scale collectivization was achieved. But he maintained that Stalin's disoriented approach was not reflected in the final decisions of the Central Committee, and that as an institution it served to correct the mistakes both of errant party leaders and misguided local party workers, as instanced by Stalin's 'Dizzy with Success' article, authorized by the Central Committee. Trapeznikov's stance was in keeping with the notion of 'collective leadership' that prevailed in the Brezhnev era. For Trapeznikov, except for the period January–February 1930, collectivization in the main had developed on a 'healthy', 'normal' basis. In a comment that could only have been directed at Danilov and his colleagues, Trapeznikov took issue with 'recent attempts in our historical literature to view the entire process of collectivization as a stream of rampant errors and distortions'.[119]

Ivnitsky, however, blamed central party bodies and the November 1929 plenum in particular for fostering unrealistic expectations, particularly at regional level, about what could be achieved, 'forcing' the pace of full-scale collectivization. The lower Volga district party committee, for instance, declared this would be achieved within one year. Regional party organizations vied with each other to collectivize in the shortest possible time, at least on paper if not in reality. The secretary of the Tambov regional party committee claimed that 25 per cent of the peasants in the district had been collectivized by 15 December.[120] The result of this race to collectivize was resort to 'administrative pressure' by local party organs. Again, Ivnitsky held Stalin personally responsible for this situation; he argued that Stalin had encouraged excessive 'haste' in his 27 December 1929 speech to the All-Union Conference of Marxist Agrarians in which he had dismissed as 'exaggerated cautiousness' Engels' admonition that the peasantry needed time to adapt to collectivization. Again, Ivnitsky's suggestion was rebuffed by the publisher, who erased it.[121] It should be noted, however, that Ivnitsky passed over in silence Stalin's menacing declaration in his speech of the shift in party policy to the 'liquidation' of the kulaks as a social class,[122] presumably because he, like other members of the Danilov Group, identified with the objectives, if not the means.

The publisher also found unacceptable Ivnitsky's charge that Stalin was personally responsible for the race to achieve the highest form of collective farming, the *kommuna*, in the shortest possible time and for the substitution of 'administrative methods' for voluntary collectivization. On the basis of painstaking analysis of archival material Ivnitsky demonstrated that the final form of the resolution adopted by the Politburo on 5 January 1930, which codified the call for the acceleration of collectivization and the 'liquidation of the kulaks as a class', was the work of Stalin. He had been principally responsible for amending the original resolution put forward for consideration by the Yakovlev commission on 22 December that had proposed a much more temperate pace of collectivization (and a more conciliatory approach to the kulaks). In Ivnitsky's words: 'Stalin's editing worsened the recommendations, put forward by the Politburo commission ... creating additional difficulties in the work of party, soviet and social organizations ... pushing them along the path of the forced implantation of the collective farms.'[123]

The publisher's editing of Ivnitsky's views certainly created difficulties for him. Deleting Ivnitsky's charge of Stalin's 'voluntarism' and his 'ignoring' of the opinions of well-informed local party workers, in a marginal note the editor called for 'special emphasis ... on the fact that the resolution contributed something positive'.[124]

140 *Some Major Discussions*

Analysing the frenzied collectivization in January–February 1930, Ivnitsky criticized attempts to achieve complete socialization of all peasant property in the shortest possible time, including cattle (which encouraged the destruction of livestock). Further, the drive for full-scale collectivization outstripped the necessary provision of tractors, machinery and credit. Moreover, in violation of the 'Leninist principle of voluntariness' in relation to collectivization, the peasantry were 'deprived of the possibility to experience new forms of economy and "think them through" '.[125] Despite the official line that both the poor and the middle peasantry had voted for collectivization with their feet, Ivnitsky charged that in the face of 'distortions and excesses' the poor peasantry alone were the real backbone of the kolkhoz movement. Ivnitsky specifically attacked the Stalin 'cult' for encouraging 'exaggerated reports' of local successes, while impeding 'democratic discussion' which might have averted gross errors. Moreover, he accused the Politburo, specifically Stalin, Molotov and Kaganovich, of wilfully ignoring the regular, weekly reports that they received from the end of January concerning the alarming situation in the countryside.[126] Ivnitsky did not, however, take issue with the declaration of intent to 'liquidate' the kulaks; but he did blame Stalin for derailing the recommendations of the Yakovlev commission and the Bauman sub-commission for a 'differentiated' approach to the kulaks. It was proposed to divide them into three categories: active 'counter-revolutionaries', who would be arrested or exiled in remote regions; those who resisted collectivization, who would be 'settled' outside their region; and those 'loyal' kulaks ('65 per cent' according to Ivnitsky) that would be accepted into the kolkhozy, though denied voting rights for three to five years.[127] M. P. Kim, Danilov's former supervisor, deleted this passage because it contradicted the official party line that no kulak was ever accepted into the kolkhoz.[128]

Overall, Ivnitsky concluded that in the winter of 1929–30 'violations of Leninist principles' of cooperatives, 'threats of dekulakization' and 'coercion of the middle peasant' were 'extraordinarily widespread' causing 'enormous harm to the whole cause of the socialist transformation of agriculture, undermining the very idea of socialism.' He even went so far as to suggest that 'arbitrary dekulakization' presented a 'mortal danger to the very existence of the dictatorship of the proletariat'.[129] In other words, it threatened the survival of the Soviet political system.

The publishers found the bulk of such criticisms politically unacceptable, deleting them.

Chapter VII of the proofs, written by Maria Bogdenko, focused on the spring and summer of 1930, when the task became one of correcting the 'distortions of the party line ... that had been allowed in autumn 1929–winter 1930 and which had caused enormous harm to the kolkhoz movement'. 'Mass dissatisfaction' was occasioned by the pursuit of dekulakization in isolation from the strengthening of collectivization, as the Central Committee acknowledged in a circular dated 30 January 1930. Thereafter a series of Central Committee directives set out to 'resurrect Leninist principles' of collectivization on a 'strictly voluntary basis'. It was on this basis that the Central Committee authorized Stalin to publish an article criticizing 'distortions' of the party line. The result was his (infamous) 'Dizzy with Success' article, published in *Pravda* on 2 March. Bogdenko condemned Stalin's article for shifting responsibility for 'errors and distortions' from the centre, and 'himself personally', to local party workers, thereby engendering 'bewilderment', 'despair' and even 'anger' in the party ranks and compounding an already 'difficult' situation in the regions.[130] Heavy censorship in 1930 subsequently gave a muted impression in the historical literature of the degree and extent of dissatisfaction in the party.[131] Bogdenko, however, set this right. She cited at length a letter to Stalin that captured the indignation of the rank and file:

> Comrade Stalin! I am an ordinary worker and regular reader of *Pravda*. Isn't the culpable person the one who has not listened to the hue and cry raised around the problem of collectivization of agriculture and who must manage the kolkhozy? All of us, the ordinary people and the press, overlooked this basic problem of the management of the kolkhozy, but comrade Stalin, undoubtedly, at this time slept a deep sleep and neither heard nor saw our errors, and therefore you also need to be called to account. But now comrade Stalin heaps all responsibility on the regions, while defending himself and the top brass.[132]

This 'interesting document', first published by Ivnitsky in 1962, had been kept in the Narkomzem archives.[133] There was certainly no reference to such responses in Trapeznikov's major work, for whom the chief significance of Stalin's 'Dizzy' article was that it 'put a stop to left-adventurist acts'.[134]

This is not the way Bogdenko saw it. Examining the speeches of regional and district party leaders in late March 1930, she concluded that they failed to analyse and redress the basic cause of the 'excesses' –

the pace of collectivization.[135] In April–May local lower party workers continued to bear the brunt of punishment for the excesses carried out by them on instructions 'from on high' – 'unconscionable punishments' which Bogdenko deemed 'one of the most odious features of the cult of the personality'.[136] Everywhere peasants continued to leave the kolkhozy, though the situation began to ease in March–April.[137] Notwithstanding these obstacles, by the summer of 1930 the kolkhozy were already the backbone of agriculture in the principle grain-producing regions. By then the mass exodus from the kolkhozy had ceased and the kolkhoz movement, while still declining, was 'gradually stabilizing'.[138]

Acknowledgment of these successes, despite everything, saw a marked tempering of the critical tone of Danilov's history. Backed by detailed statistics, it hailed the fundamental achievements of collectivization, notably the increased number of collective farms, the increased representation of the middle peasantry and even the predominance of the *artel'* at the expense of the TOZ. It is a measure of the relative moderation of their critique that they said nothing about the postponement of the Sixteenth Party Congress to June–July 1930, originally scheduled for May nor of the stifling of the last few voices of dissent in the lead up to the congress.[139] It is apparent that Bogdenko and her colleagues regarded the attempt by the party to correct its previous excesses, a policy given voice at the party congress in the report by the Commissar for Agriculture Yakovlev, as a desirable and effective basis for reinvigorating the movement towards socialist agriculture.[140]

Nevertheless, fundamental obstacles remained to the 'Establishment of Conditions for the New Rise of the Kolkhoz Movement', the title of chapter VIII, also written by Bogdenko. The 'backwardness' of the material-technical requirements, due to the lag in the production of agricultural machinery and tractors (the Stalingrad tractor factory did not reach peak output until spring 1932, nearly two years behind schedule), presented 'colossal difficulties'. The situation was compounded by a lack of technically qualified personnel, symptomatic of general illiteracy. Moreover, following the Sixteenth Congress, attempts to rebuild the cooperative movement, which had collapsed at the height of the collectivization offensive, were far from successful. By the end of 1930 the cooperative movement had been effectively abandoned as attention turned once again to full-scale collectivization. This entailed a new, more or less final, offensive against the kulaks; even those of the third, that is, 'loyal', category who remained were 'purged' from the kolkhozy and exiled. This was not an issue that separated Danilov and his colleagues from their orthodox opponents. This renewed assault on the kulaks they saw as 'one of the most important factors in the rapid growth of kolkhoz movement in winter 1930–31.' Despite the difficulties, the first harvest after full-scale collectivization was 'not bad', though animal husbandry was 'otherwise'. Most importantly for these scholars, the 'favourable results' in the kolkhozy had a positive impact on the mood of the middle peasantry; for Danilov *et al.*, this was the 'decisive condition for the further development of full-scale collectivization'.[141]

The 'New Rise of the Kolkhoz Movement' was the subject of chapter IX, the work of Zelenin. Working from archives in the Kolhoztsentr, he established that August–September marked a new influx of peasants into the kolkhoz. But fear among the peasantry of a repetition of the 'errors' that occurred at the beginning of the year was a 'serious' barrier to the party's renewed campaign.[142] Nevertheless, winter and spring 1931 saw 'new forms' of mass work – 'initiative groups' and 'recruitment brigades' – to organize peasants into the kolkhoz. Further, the December 1930 plenum set a slightly longer schedule for the completion of full-scale collectivization. Fifty per cent of peasant households in the USSR, 80 per cent in the chief grain producing areas, were to be collectivized by the end of 1931, and not by autumn 1930 or spring of 1931 as the 5 January 1930 resolution had envisaged. But the continued pursuit of the *artel'* form of collectivization rather than the TOZ, had its most pernicious effects on cattle-holdings. Resort to an 'artificially forced-pace' socialization of cattle from the summer of 1931 onwards resulted in their 'slaughter and selling off'. Zelenin laid responsibility for this at the feet of Stalin, with his 'line for the extraordinary forcing of collectivization.' In general, the TOZ suffered from the fact that it was subordinated to the *artel'* and the *kommuna;* in the main the TOZ was concentrated in the more backward regions and lacked the support of such institutions as the MTS.[143]

Nevertheless, Zelenin clearly felt some progress had been made compared with collectivization up to mid-1930. In the latest wave of collectivization, the middle peasantry predominated rather than the poor and labouring peasantry as in the previous period. Zelenin had no reservations about the Soviet state undertaking 'new decisive measures' in autumn 1930 to combat the 'cruel' resistance of the kulaks to the new collectivization drive. In August–September 1930, 'local organs of power' began to exile the remaining kulak families. The 'cruel class struggle' against this 'most implacable enemy' continued into 1931.[144]

The new collectivization drive, however, actually compounded the technical lag that afflicted the kolkhoz. The expansion of the kolkhoz system reduced the percentage of collective farms with mechanized fieldwork from 15.9 per cent to 4.2 per cent. 'Only from 1932, when full-scale collectivization was basically complete ... was machine-tractor technology gradually transformed into the fundamental element of the technical basis of agriculture.'[145] Despite the rapid expansion of the MTS in 1931–32, it was not enough to compensate for the shooting of draught animals during the first five-year plan. The overwhelming dependency of the kolkhozy on animal draught power impeded the growth of kolkhoz output.[146] But the impediments to the development of the kolkhoz system were not simply technical; they were also political and organizational. For example, in 1932 the ability of the rural soviets to take prime responsibility for 'mass work' in the kolkhozy fell foul of the

> regime of the cult of the personality, which was characterized by administrative methods, mindless, formal execution of directives and contempt for the voice and mood of the toiling masses. The administrative and forced methods resorted to in socializing cattle, planning kolkhoz production and in grain procurement, also characterized the work of the rural Soviets. Unfortunately, insufficient attention was given to the emergence of such methods of work, which contradicted the essence of Soviets as mass organs of the dictatorship of the proletariat. On the contrary, the atmosphere of the regime of the cult of the personality gave rise to and strengthened the retreat from Leninist norms and froze the development of soviet democracy.[147]

It was not only soviet democracy that was on the wane in 1932, so too was the kolkhoz movement, which Zelenin detailed. He drew up a table demonstrating that the first indications of the decline of the kolkhoz movement had appeared as early as autumn 1931, and continued throughout 1932, a development that he ascertained was 'unexpected by the leaders of the Kolkhoztsentr'. The 'fundamental causes' of this decline he found in the 'extremely difficult situation of many kolkhozy, brought on by drought and crop failure in the most important agricultural districts, by the organizational and economic disarray of the majority of the kolkhozy and by errors and distortions in kolkhoz building.' Inadequate payment in money and kind for labour on the kolkhoz triggered peasant departures from the kolkhoz.[148]

The famine

It was in the course of discussing the peasant mass abandonment of the kolkhozy that Danilov's history broached an ominous question: famine. During 1931–32, Zelenin noted, the Union and the Russian Central Executive Committees of Soviets received numerous 'complaints' about 'the inability of people with large families to exist'. Letters in the archives from collective farmers 'in the name of Stalin' recorded the 'serious food-supply situation' on kolkhozy in the Lower Volga, the Ukraine and Kazakhstan. Zelenin then made an unprecedented observation for a Soviet historian: 'In some kolkhozy starvation had begun'.[149] This he attributed to the exacerbation of a parlous situation by the 'grain procurement organs, striving to fulfil at all costs their prescribed objectives, acting according to the principle "seize grain down to the last seed", often forced the kolkhoz to surrender not only the seed gain but also the food grains'. Evidence for this he found in the archives of the Kolkhoztsentr grain procurement sector. These recorded the exit of the peasantry due to the 'extraordinarily high levels of grain surrender, completely out of proportion to the gross harvest of the kolkhozy.' 'It is completely understandable', Zelenin wrote, 'that when the kolkhoz began to surrender their grain, that the collective farmers began to leave'. From the TsGANKh archives Zelenin cited an unpublished letter from a delegate to a rural Soviet in the Central Black-earth region sent to *Izvestiya* at the beginning of 1932 that demonstrated that 'Stalin remained deaf to the signals coming from the countryside ... [and] that unlawful grain procurements were conducted with his knowledge and approval ... "Although You, comrade Stalin, are a pupil of Lenin", it read, "Your behaviour is not Leninist".'[150]

Similar letters addressed directly to Stalin provided further confirmation of his indifference to the fate of the peasantry in these years. Despite the disastrous harvest of 1931, the level of compulsory grain procurements rose dramatically, as did state seed and grain emergency reserves, while grain exports in 1930–31 were 'unprecedentedly high'. In such circumstances, Zelenin argued, consumption in both the countryside and the towns inevitably suffered, and collective farmers 'went without bread and starved (*golodali*).' 'I. V. Stalin scorned the needs of tens of thousands of peasants who found themselves in extraordinarily difficult circumstances due to harvest failure and [policy] excesses during the grain procurement'. He dismissed reports from the Ukraine at the end of 1932 of 'starving peasants' as 'fairy tales'.[151]

Zelenin found documented substantiation for his explanation for the exodus from the kolkhozy at the beginning of 1932 in the archives of the Central Executive Committee of the Soviets, authorized by Kalinin to investigate the complaints of certain peasants:

> The members of the commission concluded that the basic causes of the mass exodus were the uneconomic situation in the kolkhozy, unresolved problems of the organization and calculation of labour, the low payment for the work-day, the unsatisfactory living conditions for the kolkhoz farmers, compulsory socialization of cattle, and the anti-kolkhoz agitation of the kulak.

Kalinin 'daily' received 'hundreds' of letters confirming this conclusion. The archives also confirmed for the first time the 'extreme concern' of the central Soviet authorities over the 'departure' of the peasants into the towns, draining the kolkhoz workforce. A government resolution of 27 December 1932 to introduce a 'passport system … had as its main aim stricter control of population movement throughout the country'. The decline of the kolkhoz movement in winter–spring 1932 was not as serious as that in 1930 concluded Zelenin, but it may have become so had not the Soviet government distributed food, seed and grain.[152]

For the first time, Soviet historians had touched upon the taboo question of mass starvation in the course of collectivization. As mentioned above, from childhood experience both Ivnitsky and Danilov knew of starvation. But Ivnitsky, for instance, thought these were isolated instances. Not until thirty years later, when he looked into the Kremlin archives, did he realize the scale of the suffering. Then he was 'horrified' to discover that hunger affected 50 million people, driving some to 'cannibalism'.[153] There was no mention of this of course in 1964. Danilov and his colleagues had revealed only the tip of a macabre iceberg, but they did so 20 years before this question racked the Soviet historical profession in the *perestroika* period.[154]

Danilov's history depicted Soviet agriculture and the policies pursued by the party in 1932 in the bleakest of terms. Farming was jeopardized because the output of tractors was in no way sufficient to compensate for the 'catastrophic' decline of draught horses since 1930, as a member of the Collegiate of the Commissariat of Agriculture S. M. Buddeny put it.[155] While the area under kolkhoz cultivation increased over the previous year, the total sewn area actually fell in 1932 as a 'result of the extraordinarily difficult conditions' engendered for collective farms suffering from drought, lack of seed grain and food shortages. This situation was compounded by an 'underestimation' of the continued importance of the individual farmer, who had been denied credit, implements and seed. As a result, output per household was twice as low as before collectivization. 'The gravest situation existed in the Ukraine in the spring of 1932.'[156] The Ukraine, together with North Kazakhstan and the Lower Volga, despite severely depleted harvests and drought, had increased obligations to surrender grain to the state. This 'undermined' the motivation of the collective farmers. Coupled with agitation from 'hostile', anti-kolkhoz elements, all of this resulted in 'serious damage' to the principal grain producing areas. State grain procurements fell markedly in 1932.[157]

Once again, the revisionist authors placed prime responsibility for the demise of grain procurements onto Stalin. Ignoring the 'real situation' in the countryside in his pronouncements in late 1932–early 1933, Stalin looked to 'subjective causes' for the reduction in procurements. He blamed, variously, sabotage by 'anti-Soviet elements' or 'detachments' among the peasants themselves or the failings of Soviet and party officials, depending on the audience. Addressing the January 1933 Central Committee plenum he exonerated the peasants and blamed communists. In May, however, replying to the writer M. A. Sholokhov's 'angry protest' against 'mass repression of the grain-growers', Stalin again wrote of peasant 'sabotage'. According to Zelenin, the

> thesis of the 'war' of the grain-growers against the workers, the Red Army and Soviet power was put forward by Stalin as the basis for the most painful repression, which on his initiative rained down on the peasantry and party organizations of the North Caucasus.[158]

An investigation commission headed by Kaganovich sent to the North Caucasus in autumn 1932, 'in accordance with the specific instructions of I. V. Stalin viewed the non-fulfilment of grain procurement obligations as sabotage and kulak resistance. The commission sanctioned mass repression against the grain-growers of Kuban.' Yet in the historical literature from the end of the 1940s, the Kaganovich commission was 'extolled' for its role in the defeat of 'kulak sabotage'.[159]

Similarly, in the summer of 1932, Molotov and Kaganovich attempted to 'force the pace' of grain procurements in the Ukraine, despite the fact that grain output was a third less than in 1930, 'by means of repressive measures'. The party archives revealed that on

29 December 1932 the Politburo of the Ukrainian Communist Party, under pressure from Kaganovich, adopted a resolution requiring all kolkhozy that had not met the grain procurement targets to deliver within five to six days all their grain, including their seed grain. Failure to comply would be viewed, in the resolution's words, 'as sabotage of grain procurement on the part of the district leadership'. Despite these measures, the Ukraine could not meet its target, though it had been lowered three times. In this respect it was not unique. For the USSR as a whole, concluded Zelenin, grain procurement fell 'significantly' in 1932 compared to 1931. Likewise, the archives revealed the sharp reduction in meat products in 1931–33 wrought by the 'enormous' 'slaughter of cattle' during full-scale collectivization.[160]

In their concluding chapter Danilov and Zelenin hammered home the central lessons of the failings of full-scale collectivization. Chief among them was

> the vital necessity to observe the Leninist cooperative plan: definite material-technical and cultural conditions for large-scale, socialized production, widespread use of the simplest transitional forms of cooperation among the peasantry on the path to socialism, strictest observance of voluntary association among the peasantry, and the harmonious combination of social and personal interests as the basis of a successful collective economy. Retreats and violations of these requirements at various stages of full-scale collectivization, irrespective of local conditions, had negative results everywhere, but the more economically, politically and culturally backward the region the worse they were.[161]

Overall, Soviet collective farming, two-thirds of which at the end of 1932 relied on peasant manual labour, was doomed to a prolonged period of ' "manufacturing" development'. Stalin's 'theoretical discovery' that 'manufacturing' level collective farming was more productive than individual farming (a principle put forward by Yakovlev but attributed to Stalin) led to the 'voluntarist' policies adopted in autumn 1929. The bypassing of 'transitional forms of cooperation' was combined with Stalin's 'contempt for the needs of the masses, their experience, knowledge and moods':[162]

> The forcing of collectivization, the socialization of peasant livestock down to the last sheep and chicken, and the 'dekulakization' of part of the middle peasantry led to mass protests and upheaval, 'ebbs' in

the kolkhoz movement, the destruction of the productive forces (the shooting of cattle and so on) and damaged the entire cause of socialist construction in both the countryside and the towns. Compulsory grain requisitioning in such volumes that the kolkhozy and the kolkhozniki were left almost without bread undermined the material incentives of the collective farmers to develop production.[163]

Only the 'resolute struggle' to correct these errors 'saved the cause of socialist transformation in our country and averted the collapse of the economy and the political alliance of the toilers of town and country'. Even so, the authors concluded, these errors took a toll on agriculture, the definitive transformation of which faced the Soviet Union in the next five-year plan.[164] This was intended to be the subject of the second volume, but it was not even to reach the publishers.

Banning Danilov's book did not prevent it circulating in unpublished form, nor from having political resonance. Produced as it was against the background of Khrushchev's 1960–64 campaign against the party first secretaries in favour of new, educated, managers who it was hoped would re-energize agriculture, the manuscript

> passed from hand to hand among the new managers – one of the first swallows of the *samizdat* when no *samizdat* was supposed to exist ... There was no rural district where that sheaf of papers, like a Bible, [sat] on the desks of heads of production directorates ... Danilov's study was, as it were, a historical validation of the ideas of the new rural managers, who were actively seeking an alternative approach.[165]

Revisionism on the retreat

The suppression of Danilov's history was not entirely the end of revisionism in relation to the history of collectivization. But already in the close political atmosphere ushered in by Brezhnev it became increasingly difficult to publish critical material openly. A summary of the argument in Danilov's history, drawing on the unpublished research of his Group, appeared under his name in 1965 in the *Soviet Historical Encyclopaedia*.[166] Echoing the fate of his major monograph, the article was subject to censorious editing prior to publication.[167] Despite the pre-publication censorship, the article subsequently earned him public party censure. Danilov was accused of dwelling on the 'mistakes' made during collectivization and of falsely depicting it as being implemented in an 'administrative manner, "under pressure from above"'.[168] After Danilov's censure in the journal *Kommunist* he would undoubtedly have been expelled from the party, had he not been taken seriously ill.[169] But it did not save his academic career.

Danilov was dismissed on 15 April 1969 as head of the Sector of the History of the Soviet Peasantry, which had replaced his Group on the History of the Soviet Peasantry. Up until then Danilov had been shielded by the *kollektiv* of the Institute of History. After the division of the Institute, the presence of B. A. Rybakov as director provided a further stay of execution until he too, having fallen foul of Trapeznikov, was replaced by Khvostov.[170] At the time of his dismissal, Danilov was actively involved in the organization of a major conference on Soviet agrarian history held in June 1969.[171] His paper, in which he detailed the historiography of Soviet agriculture, became a public acknowledgment of his own mistakes. In the course of his presentation Danilov touched on works that had analysed the 'errors and excesses' incurred in collectivization. Noting that while all took into account the 'objective difficulties' in explaining these failings, others 'emphasized the role of subjective factors, particularly in the leadership of the kolkhoz movement'. Without any reference to his own suppressed volume, he cited 'sharp' party criticism of a recent study of the role of the communist party in collectivization which could just as easily have applied to his own tome. The work in question looked at collectivization,

> as if collectivization was conducted on the basis of unrestrained coercion and inordinate haste and as if all of this flowed from the official line of the party ... Instead of a rounded and thoroughgoing disclosure of the experience of the party in the field of collectivization the author concentrates on excesses and other inadequacies.

In a succinct addendum to this, Danilov noted that similar criticism by the party had been addressed in the past three years to 'other works, including those of the author of this report'.[172] This public self-criticism, however, was not enough for Trapeznikov's Department of Science. At his behest Danilov was called before the Director of the Institute of History, Khvostov, who demanded he write into the record of proceedings the confession that 'I consider it my duty to declare here that I take this criticism with utmost seriousness and as a communist I consider the demand for the raising of *partiinost'* incontrovertible.'[173] Danilov had never in fact made such an admission of guilt, but he was warned to do so, 'otherwise things might turn out badly'. While making this humiliating false confession, Danilov ensured he inserted a detailed footnote listing the articles in the party press in which he had been criticized so that future readers might know 'who criticized Danilov and how'.[174]

Despite the onset of the Brezhnev era, Danilov's revisionist colleagues continued their work. A number of ploys were used to escape the censor. One was to 'camouflage' their work by sprinkling it liberally with quotations from Lenin and even Brezhnev, 'otherwise it would not be published'.[175] Another was to provide misleading citations. An article summarizing many of the substantive accusations made against Stalin and his circle was published in *Voprosy istorii* in March 1965, based on a paper delivered to the Division of History of the Academy of Sciences in June 1963 jointly authored by Vyltsan, Danilov, Ivnitsky and Polyakov (the published version, however, did not include Danilov).[176] This particular article included for the very first time an extract from a letter to Stalin from the Middle-Volga district party secretary M. M. Khataevich that Ivnitsky had found in the Kremlin archives. Dated 6 April 1930, it protested Stalin's 'Dizzy with Success' article, accusing the centre of being equally if not more responsible than local officials for policy excesses. But it required subterfuge on the part of Ivnitsky to avoid the censor's scrutiny. He gave no precise reference to mislead the censor into thinking that this fragment had previously been published, and was not fresh from the archives.[177]

Other challenges were more direct. In 1965 Zelenin published a searching article on the role of the Political Departments (*politotdely*) in the Machine Tractor Stations (MTS), 'extraordinary organs of the party' established to deal with the tense situation in the countryside in 1933–34. The deputy heads of the *politotdely* were OGPU agents who played 'punitive' roles, purging the kolkhozy and the MTS. Often flouting local party authority, the OGPU were instruments of the erroneous policies of Stalin and Kaganovich, who was responsible for the *politotdely* in the Central Committee. Zelenin, however, also argued that the *politotdely* did actually play a significant role in increasing agricultural output over these two years.[178]

In 1966, Yu. A. Moshkov published a book (based on a paper first presented to the 1961 Moscow conference) in which he demonstrated that official claims that collectivization had solved the so-called 'grain problem' (the 'complete satisfaction of the country's bread requirements and the elimination of the divorce between the production of grain and its consumption'), fell far short of the truth. On the basis of archival sources, he showed that official figures exaggerated the 1930 grain harvest by up to 10 million tons. Indeed, not until 1935 were there significant steps towards resolving the problem, and even then not completely.[179] This was not Moshkov's only contribution to historical revisionism. In the course of a debate on the NEP in *Voprosy istorii KPSS* in 1966–68, Moshkov argued that the 'escape' from the NEP occurred in 1929. NEP did not last until the 'triumph of socialism' in 1936–37, as Stalinist historiography asserted. Moshkov's contribution was never published.[180]

The published materials of the revisionists increasingly reflected the daunting political atmosphere ushered in by Brezhnev. For example, Ivnitsky published an article in February 1966 in the party historical journal, which, while not uncritical, marked a definite retreat from previous positions.[181] By 1972 Ivnitsky was publishing a fairly standard history of collectivization, which passed over many of the previous accusations against the Stalin regime.[182] But even this was not enough in the period when Brezhnev was consolidating his position. Ivnitsky was still taken to task in the party historical journal for a conciliatory approach to the kulaks by suggesting, for instance, that forced expropriation was not a necessity and that up until mid-1929 the CPSU considered it permissible for kulaks to join kolkhozy.[183] The party ideologues were right to be suspicious. Even when Ivnitsky appeared to have fallen back into line with orthodoxy, he found ways to allude to the divorce between the official story and the terrible reality that he had encountered in the archives of the Central Committee, the NKVD, OGPU, the Commissariat of Agriculture and the Kolkhoztsentr.[184] He had secretly taken notes but had been unable to cite references.[185]

Meanwhile, Danilov continued to research social relations in rural Russia in the 1920s, despite his castigation by the party and his academic marginalization, and the pall that hung over intellectual life under Brezhnev. Though he skirted the contentious issue of full-scale collectivization, he sustained his methodological challenge to Stalinist orthodoxy. Though under continued siege from pro-Stalinist historians, Danilov remained unbowed. As late as 1977 he was arguing combatively against the bald assertions of his old antagonist Selunskaya about the 'petty-bourgeois' Russian countryside of the

1920s in favour of a 'multistructured' interpretation of the 'transitional relations of production' that shaped not only the economy as a whole but relations 'within each separate socio-economic structure' and 'even within each separate household'. By this time, too, he was giving more emphasis than ever before to the preservation of 'natural-patriarchal' residues of pre-capitalism, above all, the commune, in a 'multistructured' peasant society. Incorporation of the complex 'intertwining' of these socio-economic relations, past and present, were, he argued, essential for writing the history of the Russian countryside in all its specific complexity.[186]

Adhering to this approach in 1977 and 1979, Danilov published two major studies of the Russian countryside on the eve of collectivization, with a projected third on the way.[187] In his 1979 volume, which looked at the social structure of the pre-kolkhoz countryside, Danilov questioned whether in fact the kulaks could be considered a capitalist farming class, distinct from the bulk of the small holding peasantry: 'The Russian kulak of the 1920s was ... in large measure still the old Russian "*mir* [commune]-eater".'[188] In writing this, Danilov had moved a long way from the position held by himself and his colleagues in regard to the kulaks when his second book was banned. Then the kulaks were still the 'last exploiting class'. Danilov's questioning of the class credentials of the kulak flowed, however, from the views he had first enunciated back in 1961 that the Russian countryside was a transitional countryside characterized by social differentiation rather than class exploitation. In reply to an accusation by Selunskaya at a session of the biennial Agrarian symposium held in the mid-1970s, that Danilov considered the kulak as simply a 'peasant', he replied effectively in the affirmative that 'Marx called the kulak a *grossbauer*, that is, a big farmer and not a bourgeois'.[189] Such a position opened up the question of whether kulaks should have been 'liquidated as a class', or gradually incorporated into the collective farms as, for instance, Bukharin had advocated.[190]

Such a stance brought isolation to Danilov in the depth of the Brezhnev years. Returning to his seat after he finished his polemic against Selunskaya he looked up to find the hall deserted. Even his graduate students did not want to know him. 'This was a manner of behaviour that developed in Stalin's time.'[191] It would be ten years before he participated in the symposium again. Only with the arrival of *perestroika* in 1986 did the space open up for Danilov and his colleagues to at last consider publishing their long-lost work. But with the opening up of the archives and the subsequent revelations about the tragedy that had befallen the Soviet countryside under Stalin of which they, the leading Soviet historians in this field, had at best been partially aware, they decided against publishing their suppressed manuscript. Instead, they have turned to rewriting the history of these terrible years in their entirety.

5
The 'Hour of Methodology'

> 'One of the first problems ... I would call the problem of the possible and the actual in social development. However strange it may seem, these categories of dialectical materialism have least of all been studied on an historical basis. This can only be seen as one of the residues of the ideology of the cult of the personality. I have in mind Stalin's "straightening out" of history according to its outcome, his canonization of a given course of events as the only possible one, and his effective substitution of a Marxist determinism by the fatalistic inevitability of events (which incidentally, in recent times, has justified all his mistakes and what were more than mistakes – his crimes).'
>
> M. Ya. Gefter, in *Istoriya i sotsiologiya* (Moscow, 1964), p. 149

By the mid-1960s it is apparent that Soviet historians and other scholars were moving beyond the investigation of empirical questions towards a reconsideration of their own methodology, theory and philosophy of history. In the decade since the Twentieth Congress they had accumulated an enormous amount of data. It is equally apparent that they felt the need to refine the methods by which they made sense of this data. The primitive accumulation of anomalies across a broad spectrum of topics, from the nature of Russian imperialism to the structure of pre-capitalist societies, was palpable not only to historians but also to a host of allied scholars. The increasingly obvious inadequacies of the received categories of Marxism–Leninism fuelled the search for a new historical paradigm which converged around the problem of methodology.

Impetus to this quest was undoubtedly given by the communist party. Apart from the methodological concerns of the 1962 all-Union conference of historians, there were the injunctions of the June 1963 Central Committee plenum for greater emphasis on ideology to facilitate the alleged transition to communism and combat the pernicious influence of 'bourgeois ideology'.[1] As a result, a general meeting of the Academy of Sciences held that year emphasized the 'importance and immediacy of methodological questions'. A report on methodology in the natural and social sciences delivered by the neo-Stalinist ideological secretary Academician L. F. Il'ichev to the Presidium of the Academy of Sciences led to the authorization of discussions on these questions in all the research institutions.[2] Institutional initiatives followed in quick succession. In 1963 the 'Section of the Social Sciences of the Presidium of the Academy of Sciences' was established, followed soon after by the convening of a major conference and the establishment of organizations within the Institutes of Philosophy and of History dedicated to studying the methodology of history.

It would be wrong, however, to see these initiatives merely as responses to administrative directives. They plainly answered the felt needs of a growing number of scholars. Tarnovsky, it will be recalled, explained the sharp turn to methodological problems in the mid-1960s as flowing from the 'logic of research' itself.[3] Here lay the germs of conflict between the growing community of revisionist scholars and their academic and political overlords: the one anxious to shed the doctrinal baggage of Stalinism, the other increasingly intent on reappropriating it. At bottom this was a contest between pseudo-intellectuals of 'scope' and genuine intellectuals of 'quality', whose scholarly aspirations began to spill over into public life, especially as the neo-Stalinist offensive gathered pace under Brezhnev.

History and sociology

The newly-established 'Section of the Social Sciences' argued for a systematic consideration and discussion of methodological questions.[4] A major initiative in this regard, as we saw in Chapter 3, was the January 1964 gathering of historians, philosophers and other scholars, subsequently published as *History and Sociology*.[5] This gathering proved to be a 'vital step towards overcoming serious inadequacies in the methodology of history' in particular.[6]

In their position paper for the conference, Academicians P. N. Fedoseev and F. P. Frantsev drew attention to the shortcomings of Soviet historical writing and outlined several measures for overcoming them. Starting from the view that one of the negative consequences of the 'cult of the personality' on historiography was its debasement as a discipline, they admonished historians for being dogmatic, resorting to 'rote-learning', and simple-minded illustrating of preestablished principles. They also took to task the *Short Course* tendency to depict history as little more than the study of the development of production, a tendency more akin to 'economic materialism' than Marxism, which diminished the role of class struggle. They enjoined historians, following Lenin, to give a more rounded treatment to political and social life in their writings. Above all, they attributed the poverty of Soviet historiography to the divorce between history and sociology which, they argued, had led to a rupture between history and theory. To close this gap they advocated a nuanced alliance between sociology and history in which general sociological 'laws' (*zakony*) would inform the elucidation of 'specific historical regularities' (*zakonomernosti*) by studying the 'interaction of economic, political and ideological processes in social life ... under definite, specific conditions'. Further, the elucidation of such *zakonomernosti* would be a reaffirmation of the necessary historicism of Marxism, and thereby a powerful antidote to dogmatism. The key to the renovation of historical writing was then its methodological renewal, which would better equip historians to tackle the 'problems of the present'. And the best guarantee of history's methodological renewal was to forge an alliance between historians and philosophers.[7]

The paper presented by Fedoseev and Frantsev undoubtedly reflected the ambiguous objectives of the June 1963 plenum: on the one hand, to rearm historical science for the (illusory) transition to communism and the attendant, allegedly heightened, contest with 'bourgeois ideology'; on the other, to impose beforehand strict limits to this re-armament: 'The methodology of history – this is not composed of abstract theoretical constructs – this is a world view, this is an important field of ideological struggle', the reporters asserted.[8] They did not, however, go so far as to endorse the sweeping assertion of the Central Committee resolution that the negative consequences of the 'cult of the personality' had been completely overcome.[9]

Indeed, it is obvious this was not the conviction of most of the participating scholars – a good indicator that an important component of the scholarly community was less and less the willing minion of party resolutions. Sidorov, whose ambiguous attitude to Stalin we have noted previously, was adamant that the

> remnants of the cult of Stalin are significantly stronger and we are freed from them significantly slower than we might at times have imagined. For this reason I acknowledge that the posing of methodological questions is extraordinarily timely, necessary and useful.[10]

Likewise, the New Direction historian Gindin emphasized that success in overcoming 'dogmatism' on the sprawling 'historical front' was extremely limited, geographically and institutionally. The successes were concentrated in the 'centre'. Provincial teachers of history in the *Vuzy* and researchers in republican social science institutes remained apprehensive about challenging established conceptions. Where they did, often as not they were given no support or were 'even subject to intolerable pressure'.[11] Gindin's observations are a salutary reminder that historical revisionism was concentrated overwhelmingly within the community of scholars created in the metropoles, principally, Moscow and Leningrad. More importantly, his and Sidorov's statements suggest a gulf between the methodological agenda of the revisionists and that of mandarins like Fedoseev and Frantsev.[12]

Directly or indirectly, the discussion which followed the report touched on a myriad of unresolved concerns of method and philosophy in historical science. Among them were the role of the geographical factor in historical development; the application of dialectics to the history of the CPSU; the *partiinost'* of historical science; the meaning of historicism and of such terms as 'epoch', 'stage', 'period', 'phase'; historical truth and objectivity; scientific criticism and modes of combating 'hostile' ideology; the role of ideas in history; mathematical methods in historical research; the application of dialectical materialism to history, especially problems of causality, contingency and necessity; the interconnection of various countries and peoples in world history; the place of the great historians in scholarship; general and specific laws in history; and, the role of the 'history of social thought'.[13]

The range of contributions reflected the broad spectrum of institutional input into the discussion. Among the 33 contributors, apart from researchers from the Institute of History, were representatives from the institutes of philosophy, linguistics, ethnography, economics and Africa. Some of the most critical contributions came from unexpected quarters. Apparently emboldened by the reporters' appeal for a thoroughgoing reconsideration of the negative consequences of 'dogmatism', Academician M. V. Nechkina, who later lent her name to the reimposition of orthodoxy under Brezhnev,[14] resolutely denounced the grossest distortions of historical scholarship as a result of the Stalin phenomenon. At Stalin's feet Nechkina laid the blame for the demise of the embryonic Marxist sociology that began to take shape towards the end of the 1920s, fostered by the much-maligned M. N. Pokrovsky.[15]

Nechkina was not the only establishment figure from the Academy of Sciences to air grievances against the debasement of history under the impact of the 'cult of the personality'. Academician I. I. Mints, hardly in the van of historical revisionism, endorsed historicism as an invaluable 'compass' for Marxist history. Defined by Mints as a 'close nexus between general history, the habits of an historical approach and the necessity to place events in precisely defined historical conditions', historicism was a fundamental theme of both the report and the discussion. Similarly, he stressed the immediate relevance to the contemporary world of historical writing, its *'aktual'nost''*. Such stalwarts of academic orthodoxy usually tempered their remarks by reaffirming some orthodoxy that should be upheld or had been overlooked in the report or the discussion. Mints, for example, chastised the reporters for their neglect of *partiinost'* in historical science and 'the principle of repetition' in history which established the Soviet experience as the 'path for all humanity towards communism'.[16]

Nevertheless, recognition by even the most orthodox historians of the need to refine and hone the methods of history is a good indicator of a shift by historians as a whole towards more innovative approaches, and of their willingness to stretch the boundaries of formal party pronouncements about the need to reinvigorate their discipline. The problem arose when the dissenters began to transgress the bounds of what was academically and politically acceptable, which the conservatives set. For Mints, for example, the *aktual'nost'* of history resided in the political tasks it faced. Thus the *aktual'nost'* of the history of Kievan Rus' arose from the need by Soviet historians to repel attempts by 'anti-communist ... falsifiers' to depict Russia either as owing its origins to Western ('Normanist') influences or, after the Mongol invasions, as an 'Eastern despotism'.[17]

The *aktual'nost'*, and the historicism, of genuine Marxist historiography were taken up with enthusiasm by the devotees of 'multistructuredness' at the History and Sociology conference; but they invested these concepts with a critical cutting edge that was denied the conservatives.

The latter advocated rearming Soviet historiography to meet the challenge of its 'bourgeois' opponents – an agenda apparently aimed at containing domestic revisionism rather than foreign anti-Marxists. For the revisionists, however, the objective was a more critical reflection on the contemporary resonance of their work. The 'extremely uneven and multistructured way' in which history had developed, the Latin Americanist A. V. Yefimov argued, had direct implications for understanding the present world.[18] Conversely, as Tarnovsky put it, the 'present must permeate history'.[19] In this regard, the Africanist M. I. Braginsky, echoing the concerns of the Latin Americanists, decried the neglect of the 'stormy' collapse of colonialism and its theoretical implications for recent party programmatic statements about 'non-capitalist development' for underdeveloped nations. Here, again, this problem was posed as part and parcel of the larger question of the 'interaction of progressive modes of production on peoples that lagged behind in their socio-economic development'.[20]

The call for historians, as opposed to sociologists or philosophers, to study history in its most specific manifestations led to a clash over the meaning of and relationship between such fundamental categories of Soviet Marxism as the 'epoch' and the 'socio-economic formation'. Mikhail Gefter denounced as artificial any 'division of labour' between the 'philosopher-historical materialists who will elaborate the problem of the social formation, while it will fall to the historians to study historical epochs'. He saw any distinction between the abstract 'formation' and the actual 'epoch' as legitimizing the idealist counterposing of 'fact to law' in history. Such a distinction he deemed a threat to the 'specific in history', running the danger of rank empiricism.[21] For Gefter, 'universality' was the 'call of the times': the mid-twentieth century was witnessing tremendous movement by 'oceans' of people for whom everywhere socialism was becoming a 'living reality'. It was not possible for scholars using their old 'yardstick' to create the necessary 'historical synthesis' of these vast, complex processes. The first, major attempt by Soviet scholars to achieve such a synthesis, Zhukov's massive *Universal History*, had 'still not been subject to methodological analysis'. Hence, for Gefter, the particular urgency of a 'struggle with dogmatism'. But for him such questions were 'far from abstract'; they were part of an 'ideological struggle' and, as such, had a direct bearing on 'the spiritual development of our own society'.[22] If historical writing was to make any significant contribution to this process of 'spiritual' renewal then it could only be achieved by the 'internal, theoretical growth of science itself.'[23] Gefter's pronouncement makes crystal clear the linkage perceived by the revisionists between their intellectual agenda and their social aspirations – and the distance he had come since his hostile criticism of Burdzhalov.

A fundamental methodological question which was addressed repeatedly at the conference was the economism of orthodox historical materialism – a question facilitated no doubt by attempts to rescue the reputation of M. N. Pokrovsky, sullied since Stalin's time as an 'economic materialist'.[24] An ethnographer, Yu. P. Averkieva, bemoaned the cost to the international intellectual standing of Marxism that 'Stalinist dogmatism' had wrought by reducing the 'history of society to the history of productive forces and relations of production, to economic history'. Such an approach had made it easy for 'reactionaries' to depict Marxism–Leninism as a species of 'anti-humanist', 'technological', 'economic' determinism. As an antidote to this aspersion she called for Marxists to pay greater attention to 'ideology' and 'social, ethnic and national psychology'.[25]

In this call Averkieva was echoing the lament of a number of speakers concerning the long-standing neglect in Soviet Marxism of 'superstructural' phenomena.[26] Nechkina singled out Stalin's foray into linguistics for blurring the relations between basis and superstructure: 'He put forward a strange view, as if with the change of the basis the old superstructure was *annihilated*'.[27] But how then, she asked, could the continuity in human culture be explained? Stalin was found culpable by others too for this 'nihilistic' attitude to culture – 'social thought' in particular. Not only had it fallen outside his purview, but in 1946 he had specifically placed an embargo on the study of the history of pre-Marxist philosophy, which he saw as a 'heresy'. Such nihilism in regard to the history of social thought was seen as a serious obstacle to the writing of 'full-blooded social history'.[28]

The anaemia of social history was no more apparent than in the field of Soviet history, argued the historian I. B. Berkhin. This was particularly so in relation to those most politically-sensitive topics: industrialization and collectivization. The study of these had been reduced to the 'technical-economic, rather than the socio-economic, plane'. Moreover, modern Soviet political history – 'classes and class struggle, political parties, the development of economic policy, problems of the state and the construction of Soviet society' – was virtually a *terra incognita*. Undoubtedly a 'direct consequence' of the 'cult of the personality', Berkhin suggested, given the 'political significance' of this question.[29]

Berkhin's views were given credence by the redoubtable revisionist historian of Soviet agriculture, Danilov. He argued that the killing-off of a sociological perspective in history in the Stalin era had impeded a genuine characterization of the 'profile' and 'place' of classes in 'social life' under socialism. Such a characterization had been displaced by definitions about classes being defined by their relations to property and the means of production. While formally correct, such definitions impeded genuinely probing the real relations that obtained between classes in Soviet society.[30] Drawing on A. V. Venediktov, a scholar whose work constituted a living link with the discussions of the 1920s,[31] Danilov argued for the necessity to explore, in Venediktov's terms, the 'human collectives' that constituted the 'real economic relations' that underpinned the outwardly monolithic entity known as 'state, national property in the means of production'.[32]

Danilov's call to elucidate the real nature of class relations in the Soviet Union, inevitably encroached on the official image of Soviet society as an egalitarian society, well on the way to achieving classless communism. Criticizing the neglect in the literature of one of Lenin's criteria of class, 'their role in the social organization of labour', that is, the 'productive *function*'[33] of classes as opposed to their relationship to property, Danilov pointed out that differences in the two 'forms of socialist property' (state and collective), coupled with the division between mental and physical labour, gave rise to 'differences in the forms and levels of wages':

> The current literature deals only with differences according to the mode of appropriation (wages and the [collective farm] workday). However, differences according to the size of the appropriation of material wealth are not taken into account. Finally, a problem that has not at all been researched: the means and extent of the appropriation of material wealth by those groups of the population whose personal property, which exceeds the limits of the satisfaction of normal individual needs, is turned into an instrument of personal enrichment and speculation ... In order to combat such an undesirable phenomenon, it is necessary to know the paths of its emergence and growth.[34]

Besides drawing attention to pronounced social inequalities in Soviet society, Danilov pointed to the way in which the accepted sweeping sociological categories masked the 'internal' structures of classes in Soviet society. For example, lumping all 'workers of mental labour' under the rubric 'intelligentsia', glossed over 'groups which were extremely diverse in their social make up and objective situation', such as those who 'fulfilled a managerial organizational function'. The bulk of the latter were not differentiated in terms of income, however a 'completely special place is occupied by the so-called free professions, although in our literature they also are dissolved into the general mass of one "social stratum" '.[35] This was a direct challenge to the Soviet definition of the intelligentsia which, as we saw in Chapter 1, pointedly denied any separate status to the 'creative' intelligentsia. Concomitantly, while Danilov endorsed the orthodoxy that in Soviet society there was a 'unity' rather than an 'antagonism of class interests', he cautioned that a 'community of basic interests does not necessarily signify their complete identity'.[36] Thus Danilov signalled a nuanced approach to the structure of Soviet society that at least had the promise, more precisely the threat, of exposing inequalities based on power and privilege that were denied in official pronouncements.

However, such sociological insights generated less contention than the methodological issues. The proposition, advanced by A. V. Gulyga, convenor of the 'group for the elaboration of philosophical problems of history' in the Institute of Philosophy, that the 'historical fact' was a discrete category that could not be reduced to the status of facts in other sciences attracted intense flak.[37] According to Gulyga, who ventured that the writing of history was a 'creative activity' as closely allied with literature as it was with science, the task of the historian was to simultaneously follow the twin paths of gathering facts and giving shape to them in the light of general laws. For Gulyga, to avoid the dead-ends of pure 'ideographics' (the particular) or 'nomothetics' (the universal), primacy had to be given not just to reinterpreting facts but to the verification of the 'truthfulness' of facts themselves. 'The falsification of history', he observed, 'is a craft that has flourished in all epochs'[38] – an allusion to the Soviet experience that could scarcely have been lost on his audience in the mid-1960s.

Criticism of Gulyga came from several quarters. He was targeted for what was seen as his illegitimate attempt to establish a special status for facts in history: 'If history is a science, then facts play exactly the same role in it as in any other science.'[39] The importance attached to the defence of this vulgar, realist, epistemology is evident from the short shrift to subjective interpretations of the 'historical fact' given by Frantsev in his concluding remarks. He stressed the 'objective connection' between facts and the 'tendencies of the development of historical reality'.[40]

Here we begin to see the limits that the academic establishment set for the reconsideration of the methodological and theoretical underpinnings of Marxism–Leninism, as well as some forewarnings about the political storm clouds on the horizon. Methodological reconsiderations were acceptable, provided they did not drive a wedge between history and the logical categories by which it was interpreted. The indivisible 'unity of the historical and the logical' in such categories as the socio-economic formation was hammered by both reporters.[41] Likewise, any attempt to separate the methodology and/or philosophy of history from historical materialism, as both Gulyga and Gefter suggested, was not well received.[42] Given these concerns, it should come as no surprise that the custodians of historical orthodoxy should express more than a few reservations about the precipitous establishment of seminars and sectors dedicated exclusively to methodology. The lack of suitable 'leaders' for such seminars was the concern of Mints,[43] who was to play a major role in containing the challenge of methodological revisionism. Apprehension that was well justified, as it turned out. But it was a little too late. In the Institute of History the Sector of Methodology was already up and running.[44]

The Sector of Methodology

The Sector of Methodology within the Institute of History was, in every sense, the realization of the injunctions of the convenors of the History and Sociology conference that high priority be given to organizing seminars within and between institutes of the Academy of Sciences that would directly address questions of methodology in history.[45] Thus from the outset the sector was not an 'alternative' formation of dissident historians but an officially endorsed subdivision within the Institute of History. However, the aims and methods of work of the sector were largely decided by the collective of researchers that organized and participated in it, and they often went far beyond the bounds intended by their academic overseers, several of whom, notably the academic secretary of the Division of History of the Academy of Sciences, Ye. M. Zhukov, and the Director of the Institute of History, V. M. Khvostov, had been hostile from the outset to the establishment of the sector.[46] Their apprehension was justified, for the sector did not limit itself to the elimination of the 'negative consequences of the cult of the personality' in historical science. Rather, it sought ways to throw off the dogmatism and scholasticism which had encrusted Soviet historiography and to overcome the divorce between the theoretical disciplines, especially that of social philosophy, and actual historical research. In this regard the sector received active support from the 'democratic' party committee that was elected in the Institute of History in the autumn of 1965.[47] As we shall see below, the *partkom* was a bulwark in the arduous struggle of the Sector of

Methodology with the party–state bureaucracy that oversaw historical science. The sector proved to be a particularly crucial site of contestation between the academic apparatchiks and the resurgent intelligentsia. During its brief, five-year existence was concentrated a clash of unequal forces over the future direction of social science and ideology in the USSR.

At the first session of the sector, which convened in February 1964, its director and moving spirit Mikhail Gefter outlined the basic objectives of its work. They were by no means modest. The axis of Gefter's thesis was that 'entire epochs must be reread anew' since the 'contemporary world needs to be explained historically'. Moreover, the very 'meaning of the categories and concepts must change from the point of view of the progress of humanity as a whole'.[48] In this respect, Gefter noted the importance of the international context, particularly of the anti-colonial revolutions of the 1950s and 1960s which gave additional impetus to historical thinking. For scholars of Gefter's generation it had long been assumed that the dawning of independence in the colonial countries would signal the twilight of capitalism in its metropolitan citadels as well. This had failed to occur.[49] However, to make sense of this default and of the variety of the 'paths and forms of progress' which the post-colonial states were taking it was necessary to overcome the legacy of Stalinism in historical science, especially its 'dogmatism' and 'rote learning'. The elimination of this legacy however required more than just eliminating 'rote learning' because dogmatism had, according to Gefter, 'gnoseological roots': the confusion of relative and absolute truths, the absence of a dialectic and a fatalistic approach to the historical process, all of which debased and negated the 'creative essence' of Marxism. Accordingly, the fundamental objective of the sector was deemed to be the overcoming of the gulf between specific historical research and the theoretical disciplines, in which prevailed an abstract method divorced from historical reality.[50] The sector set itself the task of affirming the Marxist conception of abstraction as a means of reconstructing the movement of history specifically and comprehensively.[51] In short, the sector sought not to abandon Marxism but to find ways of reinvigorating it in its own terms.

Thus Gefter outlined three basic trends of research the sector should pursue:

- First, to elucidate the relationship between Marxism and the 'crisis of bourgeois historical thought' of the late-nineteenth and early-twentieth centuries.

- Second, to develop the 'comparative historical method' in historical science in order to grasp the 'specific forms of the world historical process'.
- Third, to develop the relationship between the method of historical materialism and 'specific historical science'.[52]

These objectives were reflected in the proposed organization of the sector's work. In particular, there was to be a conscious attempt to overcome the limits of 'petty specialities' which fragmented theory and specific research. Within the Institute of History the sector should not be, in Gefter's words, 'an isolated unit' but 'the active kernel of collaborative work for the entire institute'.[53] In this regard the sector exceeded its own expectations. It became a pole of attraction not only for theoretically-inclined, anti-Stalinist researchers from the Institute of History itself, but also for scholars from other research institutions: historians with a variety of specialities, philosophers, economists, ethnographers, orientalists, Slavists and linguists. Scholars from a broad range of institutes participated in the work of the sector including those from the prestigious Institute of World Economy and International Relations (IMEMO) and even the Institute of Marxism–Leninism and the Academy of Social Sciences of the Central Committee of the CPSU. In the main this community of scholars was drawn from Moscow but occasionally from other centres as far afield as Leningrad, Voronezh, Riazan', Tomsk, Saratov and Novosibirsk.[54] At any one time in excess of 100 scholars participated in its vigorous discussions. There were international participants as well. In 1967 Italian scholars presented papers, at least one of which concerned the legacy of Antonio Gramsci. There was also a report and discussion on the state of historiography and sociology in Poland, as well as a paper on structuralism by Pierre Vilar, a theme that was to be pursued by the Soviet scholar M. A. Barg.[55] Thus the sector also acted as a conduit for some major discussions among neo-Marxists in Western and East Central Europe.

In its brief life the sector facilitated discussions on a broad range of topics based on papers presented by some of the leading Soviet scholars of the day. Among these were A. S. Arsen'ev on 'Historicism and Logic in Marxist Theory',[56] Viktor Danilov on 'The Characteristics of Classes Under Socialism',[57] Lyudmila Danilova and N. B. Ter-Akopyan on the Asiatic mode of production and problems of the theory of social formations, Yakov Drabkin on the nature of social revolutions and the Leninist concept of world revolution[58] and B. F. Porshnev on the notion of the 'history of a single country.'[59] Considerable attention was devoted to problems of theory, methodology and epistemology in relation to the concept of socio-economic formations. Presentations along this theme by Barg and E. B. Chernyak[60] as well as Yu. I. Semenov[61] provoked lengthy discussions, particularly in regard to its applicability to pre-capitalist societies. It is important to note however that the sector looked beyond the traditional socio-economic concerns of official historical materialism, exploring such fields as social psychology and culture. For instance, towards the end of 1967 a group devoted to problems of social psychology was established under the supervision of Porshnev. The following year L. M. Batkin presented a paper on utopianism in the Renaissance.[62] However, such themes were examined not as rivals to Marxism, as they were later to become, but as a means of enriching the materialist conception of history.[63]

In March–April 1965 the sector conducted a conference on the question of the Asiatic mode of production. This politically sensitive concept, which had last been discussed at length by Soviet scholars between 1925 and 1931, was finally put back on the historiographical agenda in 1964 – three decades after it was officially ruled out of court.[64] 1964 saw the publication of Eugene Varga's writings on the political economy of capitalism. Since 1925 Varga had been a consistent champion of the concept of the 'Asiatic formation'.[65] In addition, papers on the Asiatic mode of production were presented by the French scholars Maurice Godelier and Jean Suret-Canale to the Seventh International Congress of Anthropology and Ethnography, held in Moscow in 1964. The upshot was a flurry of discussion during 1964–65 of the Asiatic mode of production within the Institutes of Philosophy, of the Peoples of Asia, and of History.[66]

Within the Institute of History the topic of the Asiatic mode of production, which drew a large audience, signalled the renewal of discussion on the general theory of the development of precapitalist societies. In his introductory remarks Gefter acknowledged the initiative of the 'late' Academician Varga in resuscitating this concept and stressed that its relevance arose from the 'very needs of the development of science.' [67] In a comment that reflected these needs, and what was novel for Soviet scholarship, the sector's unfettered discussion and open-ended approach,[68] Gefter emphasized,

> We have not set ourselves the task of a definitive resolution of the question. We merely want to define the circle of questions and indicate the paths and order of their resolution, since such a contentious question cannot be resolved at one blow.

He also called for 'restraint' by speakers, a reflection of the sensitivity of this issue in Soviet historiography.[69]

Three papers were presented. One, by Ter-Akopyan, surveyed the evolution of the concept in the work of Marx and Engels.[70] In reply to questions, Ter-Akopyan argued that reconsideration of the Asiatic mode of production was a manifestation of Soviet scholars 'bidding farewell to a certain dogmatism in our approach to this problem'. 'Marx viewed the universality of the Asiatic mode of production', he suggested, 'in the same way as capitalism. In the work of Marx and Engels the term "formation" does not have the same narrow meaning as it is understood and applied by our authors.'[71] The alleged 'universality' of the Asiatic mode of production was contested from an orthodox perspective by Ya. A. Lentsman. He argued that since in Marx and Engels' writings the Asiatic mode of production was 'not counterposed to the ancient and slaveholding modes of production', it would be preferable to 'speak of modes of production within the framework of the one slaveholding formation'.[72] Much of the criticism directed at Ter-Akopyan, by Lentsman and others, rested on the dearth of references to the Asiatic mode of production in the Marxist classics: it was not even mentioned in the *Communist Manifesto* or *The Origins of the Family, Private Property and the State*. Lentsman's approach was elegantly dispatched by Yu. M. Garushyants. He extolled as a 'merit' that Ter-Akopyan

> does not 'rip' this or that citation from the entire intellectual *oeuvre* but tries ... based on careful textual exegesis, to follow the developments of the views of Marx and Engels on the Asiatic mode of production in connection with the development of the study of formations.[73]

This exchange reveals quite clearly the gulf between the orthodox and emerging revisionist approaches to reading and utilizing the Marxist classics. The former, based on a rudimentary acquaintance with Marxism, resorted to the recitation of quotes; the latter, based on a much more extensive knowledge of Marxism, sought to capture and apply the logic of Marxist thought.

Another paper, by A. I. Pavlovskaya, looked at the treatment of the concept of the Asiatic mode of production in recent West European literature.[74] Denying that the discussion of the Asiatic mode of production had continued in the 1930s in a veiled form without recourse to the term itself, Pavlovskaya pointed out that, in the context of the upsurge of the colonial revolutions, the renaissance of the concept had been facilitated by discussions among scholars in Eastern and Western Europe. She also pointed to Marx's *Pre-capitalist Modes of Production* as a direct catalyst for discussion.[75]

Danilova's paper examined 'The Problem of the Asiatic Mode of Production in Soviet Historiography'.[76] Danilova revealed the latent potential of the Marxist conception of the Asiatic mode of production for a reconsideration of the generally accepted conception of the 'world-historical process' which, despite the formal repudiation of the *Short Course* history of the CPSU after the Twentieth Congress, retained the same general postulates that had been in place in Soviet historical discourse since the 1930s. The 'artificial termination' of the discussions on the Asiatic mode of production in the early 1930s, and their transformation into 'groundless political accusations', left a 'whole complex of unresolved questions', particularly in relation to the transition between pre- and early-class societies.[77]

Danilova, however, emphasized that the current discussion was not a mere repetition of the earlier one. The 'Mont Blanc of facts' in relation to precapitalist societies, as another speaker put it,[78] that had been accumulated in the intervening three decades defied assimilation by the established schema. 'It has now become completely obvious', declared Danilova, 'that the abundance of forms and types of the historical process is far richer and the unevenness of historical development far sharper than the schemas allowed for.'[79] Stalinist orthodoxy was incapable of capturing the 'extraordinarily varied paths' taken by history, the 'unevenness' of which varied according to the 'natural-geographical and historical environment'.[80] The traditional five-stage schema (*pyatichlenka*) was criticized in the paper for confusing the socio-economic formation as an 'abstract logical category' with 'actual social and historical epochs' and for 'fatalistically presuming' an uninterrupted, ascending, linear path of progress.[81]

Despite the markedly scholarly character of Danilova's paper, it undoubtedly had an implicit political dimension. Such criticism of the officially endorsed *de facto Short Course* paradigm constituted a direct challenge to the rigid, intellectual regime that existed in historical writing.[82] The *pyatichlenka* was effectively a teleology, in which Soviet-style socialism was depicted as the lawful culmination of the long march of humankind. This approach precluded any alternative paths or models of development to the Soviet-Stalinist model. In effect, Danilova's approach placed a question mark over the Soviet model of development itself and its relevance to the newly independent, ex-colonial nations.[83]

The subversive potential of such a rereading of Marxism for the prevailing ideology was reflected in the hostile response of several of the discussants. The medievalist Porshnev was particularly scathing. He viewed the resurrection of the concept of the Asiatic mode of production as a step backwards in Soviet historical science in as much as it 'counterpose[s] the liberation movement in Asia and Africa to the path of development in our country'.[84]

Danilova's overriding agenda, however, was the advancement of scholarship. She was determined to lift the discussion of the Asiatic mode of production above past practice of labelling exponents of the concept as 'Trotskyites or revisionists', as Porshnev had done.[85] For Danilova, the issue at stake was not even the validity of the Asiatic mode of production itself, rather it was the implications of the 'development of the concept' for the refinement of historical materialism. Here lay the 'general methodological' significance for historical science of the current discussion: 'The study on the comparative-historical plane of the paths and forms of transition from pre-class to class society, of the types of early-class societies and also the refinement of the specific schema of the periodization of world history – this', Danilova concluded, 'is one of the most important and pertinent tasks of Marxist science at present.'[86]

An important endeavour to do this, though with rather different outcomes from that of Danilova, came in the presentation two years later by Yury Semenov.[87] Danilova, responding to discussion of her own paper, had called for priority to be given to investigating the 'multistructuredness of social organisms' in relation to early-class societies.[88] In fact she was invoking a concept – 'social organism' – probably initiated, and certainly first elaborated, by Semenov.[89] He incorporated the category 'social organism' into his innovation in 1965 of a sixth socio-economic formation: 'servitude',[90] as one of three possible outcomes (together with feudalism or slaveholding) of the Asiatic mode of production for the ancient East in transition from pre-class to class society.[91] Semenov identified the social organism as 'one of the most important categories of historical science', which, he declared, was the 'science of the development of social organisms'. The failure of Soviet historians to clarify the relationship between the category socio-economic formation and generic categories, such as 'society', 'nation' or 'country', had blinded them to the specific relationship that existed between the socio-economic formation and the social organism. The latter was 'nothing more than the specific historical form of the existence of a given socio-economic formation'. Accordingly, the process of the development and superseding of socio-economic formations, that is, the process of world historical development, exists not in 'pure' guise, but in the form of the processes of the emergence, development and disappearance of an enormous number of social organisms.[92]

In his 1967 presentation to the sector, Semenov argued that it was the failure to differentiate between the social organism as such and 'society in general' that led to the erroneous view that the superseding of socio-economic formations occurs within each social organism. It was a projection of the European experience, France in particular, where the replacement of feudalism by capitalism occurred in the one social organism, onto ancient and Eastern societies, that led to the latter being viewed as 'exceptions to the rule, as anomalies' of the evolution of socio-economic formations. In reality, he maintained, the European experience was the exception, while what were previously viewed as exceptions, especially in pre-feudal epochs, turned out to be the rule.[93]

Semenov argued that the transition from pre-class to class society entailed not the transformation of an existing social organism but the 'emergence of entirely new social organisms'. Further, this process did not occur everywhere simultaneously. In the first instance it was restricted to the Nile valley and Mesopotamia, which were 'regional centres of historical development'. Here Semenov introduced a distinction which was crucial to his meta conception of world history: the transformation of 'regional centres of historical development' into centres of 'world historical development' which opened up a new 'epoch'. In the case of the ancient East 'one epoch of world history – the primordial – was definitively superseded by another, the epoch of the Ancient East. In this epoch the leading role in the history of humanity was assumed for the very first time by a socio-economic formation based on social classes: the '"Asiatic", servitudinal-antefeudal'. Thereafter human history pursued a geographical centre–periphery 'shift', with each new epoch emerging on the 'extremities' of the previous centre of world history: antiquity arose in the Mediterranean, on the periphery of the ancient Middle East; the fall of the 'slave-holding' social organism of Rome, occasioned by the invasions of the 'peoples of the pre-class historical periphery', gave way to feudalism on the north-west 'perimeter of the ancient centre of world-historical development'; the feudal formation in Western Europe then assumed the 'leading role' in history, giving way – this time on the same territory –

to capitalism. Finally, the centre of world history shifted again to the periphery, this time to Russia, ushering in a new 'socialist' socio-economic formation and a new epoch.[94]

Semenov's Hegelianized 'torch-relay'[95] view of history was far from uncritically received by his audience. His concept of the 'social organism' was lampooned from the floor by an anonymous wit as an 'undefined definition'.[96] Was the criterion of a social organism 'political or social'?, L. S. Vasil'ev asked. Further, Vasil'ev and his colleague I. A. Stuchevsky rejected Semenov's 'artificial' distinction between 'servitude' and 'antefeudal' relations; they were simply different names for the same substructures (*uklady*) within the Asiatic socio-economic formation.[97] Vasil'ev and Stuchevsky were merciless. Evidently they were stung by Semenov's contention that their thesis of three parallel paths leading from 'primordial society' suffered from the same methodological confusion between the 'logical' and the 'real', the 'general and the particular', the 'part and the whole', as the *pyatichlenka* 'template' they were reacting against.[98] They replied in kind: Semenov's conception was 'not history' but a multiplicity of social organisms that, like Toynbee's theory, lay 'outside history'. Stuchevsky dismissed it as 'speculative', 'dilettantish', Hegelian – a 'theological schema' based on a paucity of historical knowledge.[99]

Gefter was more polite, but no less critical. He started from the notion that the 'formation', as 'the Marxist-logical conception of the integrity of any historical phenomenon', was the 'only generalizing principle' that could provide the 'analytical key' to any element of human society. He argued that Semenov's approach had effectively stripped away the flesh from the 'skeleton' of the formation, which was the living embodiment of the social organism. For Gefter it was not the social organism that provided the lynchpin for history: it was the socio-economic formation. Where Semenov saw the formation as 'the ideal social organism, as a pure abstraction, found only in the minds of theoreticians', for Gefter it was the *formation* as the 'specific' stage of the 'world historical process' (itself a 'real category' not a construct), that was crucial – not 'separate societies'.[100]

At odds, here, were two divergent responses to the ossified paradigm of history bequeathed by Stalinism. Semenov was seeking to safeguard a *unilinear* conception of world history which, drawing on a centre/periphery 'displacement effect',[101] could purportedly contain the historical anomalies disclosed by recent research. Gefter was wary of the mere replacement of one schema by another. For example, he accused Semenov of 'absolutizing' one transition: that between antiquity and European feudalism.[102] Instead, Gefter sought a *multiplicity* of paths based on illuminating their specific manifestations within the course of world history. The latter position, which Gefter shared with Danilova, was ultimately the more threatening to Marxist–Leninist orthodoxy.[103] This became clear from the extremely hostile official response to an anthology published in 1968, edited principally by Danilova, dedicated to the study of the 'unevenness' of historical development.

Precapitalist societies

One of only two major works published by the sector, *Problems of the History of Pre-capitalist Societies* was to be the focus of sharp criticism in as much as it challenged the fundamental postulates of Soviet-style historical materialism. In many respects it summarized the motivation, intentions and methods of the sector's activities. Published as part of an intended series on 'The Laws of History and the Specific Forms of World History' the central thesis of this collection of essays was encapsulated in the title of Gefter's anonymously written introduction, 'The Problem of the Unity and Diversity of World History', a formula given more precise definition as the '*unity in diversity*' of world history.[104]

In his introduction, Gefter argued that the immediate stimulus for such an ambitious project was the enormous expansion of information concerning human society and the difficulty of assimilating it all; a situation brought about by the development of new tools of analysis – ethnography, linguistics, archaeology – that had the potential to facilitate a more profound analysis of an ever-broadening source base. But here the problem arose of the 'unevenness' of research engendered by the difficulty of incorporating the multiplicity of historical paths pursued by different peoples in different regions into the existing historical framework. What, therefore, was required was a 'new synthesis' of knowledge. 'At such critical moments' any science must reconsider its concepts and methods. Marxist historical thought is doing this not only to bring itself into line with the accumulated research but also to incorporate new resources into its classical heritage to enable its further development. Hitherto, researchers had relied on comparative analysis but this, despite its importance, had limited utility unless, Gefter argued, it entails '*strict scientific method of the correlation of various social forms with the stages of world-historical development*'. Creation of this methodology, '*the science of world history',* Gefter maintained, was Marx's great contribution.[105] This 'materialist historicism', which had captured both the inner dialectics of social change and the 'unity' of human history was not a 'monism', nor did it dissolve the peculiarities of historical reality into 'absolute, immutable sociological laws'. Marxism was both a 'philosophy of history and a theory of historical cognition, distinguishable not only from Hegelian apriorism but also from positivist anti-historicism and naturalism'.

In a direct tilt at the Soviet conceptualization of world history, which tried to ram every history into the Procrustean bed of the *pyatichlenka,* Gefter maintained that Marx and Engels did not downplay the distinctive features of the development of particular peoples and societies. 'On the contrary, they emphasized that one and the same economic base, depending on the natural-geographic, historical and other conditions, could lead to widely differing developments.' In a further tilt at the reification of social laws that underpinned official Marxism–Leninism, Gefter asserted that the Marxist 'law of the superseding of socio-economic formations, like any law, expresses only the *dominant tendency,* incapable of encapsulating the *entire* historical process'.[106]

Lenin, with his focus on the 'historically particular', had kept alive 'Marxist historicism'. This was more appropriate than ever in the epoch of the Russian Revolution, the hallmark of which was not so much the 'unity' of history as its 'diversity' which, as Zhukov's ambitious 10-volume *Universal History* demonstrated,[107] defied attempts to synchronize its diverse rhythms of development. The concomitant 'explosive' contradiction between the general and the particular necessarily meant for Marxists reevaluating the underlying precepts of the 'phasic method', subjecting the concept of the 'formation' in particular to an 'historical critique'. In this connection it was not enough to recognize the coexistence of a multiplicity of different modes of production and ways of life within a given epoch. The problem that had moved to the fore was to analyse the interaction of these elements that shaped the *'unity of humanity'* whose history, however, was a 'special organism' that could 'not be reduced to the sum of its parts'. The problem was to locate separate societies in the 'chain of human progress' while taking into account both the 'classical forms' and the 'exceptions' in history. In effect all this meant radically reconstructing the prevailing 'historical world view'. To do this, however, required the honing of theoretical tools and casting aside outmoded preconceptions.[108]

One such theoretical refinement proposed was to view the 'productive forces' as a 'social' category, broader than the 'instruments of production', in order to 'liberate historical thought from vulgar-technological interpretations', a distortion that had long held sway in Soviet historical writing. Similarly, it was to the 'social sphere' that researchers needed to look if the 'variation of "social organisms"', each developing according to their internal laws', was to be depicted historically. Here, the analysis of societies in terms of 'the interaction of structures', allowing for the influence of the substructures on the 'ruling structure', acquired particular significance 'defining not only the *trend* of development but also its *specific historical* type'.[109]

This complex, 'multistructured' model was, of course, a direct challenge to the notoriously vulgar conception of the 'base determining the superstructure' which in turn influences the base. This approach had proved incapable of capturing the '*asinkhronnost*' of economic, political and cultural changes within a society or of penetrating the 'internal, autonomous patterns of development of separate social institutions and forms of cultural activity'. Moreover, the multifarious types of interactions rarely coincided with the West European model on which they were based. Indiscriminately drawing from the latter had tended to iron out history, whereas in fact the real tendency in contemporary history was towards increasing 'diversity' and the changing '*nature of [that] diversity*'.[110] While Gefter repudiated the tendency of Western sociology to counterpose 'process' to 'structure' he acknowledged the tendency of human history towards 'stability' and 'intractability' together, however, with its simultaneous tendency towards 'renewal ... by means of a change of inherited social structures'. Thus '*struktura*' represents a 'moment of movement' which is not predetermined but the '*resultant* of social struggle, of a clash of human interests and wills, by means of which one of the objectively possible variants of a given path has been transformed into historical reality.'[111]

Danilova, in her preface to *Problems of the History of Pre-capitalist Societies*, stated that the anthology had two major concerns: the nature of 'primitive' societies and of early-class and ancient societies.[112] For 'primitive' society, the fundamental issue was the particular weight that should be given to the 'clan' (*rod*) and to the 'commune' (*obshchina*) in defining the social relations of these societies. The traditional position, a refinement of which was defended in the anthology by Semenov, gave primacy to the clan as the fundamental structure of primitive societies, defined essentially by its productive role.[113] In opposition to this, a 'new direction' in ethnography gave primacy to the commune as a cooperative that regulated both productive and social life.[114] For early-class and ancient societies the fundamental concern was the formation of classes and the state.[115]

Danilova's own essay exposed the implications of these revisionist perspectives for many of the received notions of orthodox scholarship. She saw these debates about the primary institutions of primitive society, in particular Ter-Akopyan's notion of primitive (pre-class) society as a 'non-economic formation ... in which the mode of production of material wealth was not determining', as a necessary corrective to the 'absolutization of the economic factor' which had so long prevailed in Soviet scholarship on pre-class societies. The latter she saw as the consequence of the mechanical projection onto pre-capitalist societies of concepts based on the political economy of capitalism.[116]

But the root of the problem confronting Soviet scholarship in this field lay in the previous abrogation of the concept of the Asiatic mode of production and the imposition of the *pyatichlenka* in the early 1930s. This had truncated discussion that had flourished in the 1920s on the Marxist concept of socio-economic formations and its correlation with the concept of 'mode of production'.[117] While 'for its time' the *pyatichlenka* was 'not an insignificant achievement' its legacy had been to divide precapitalist societies either into feudal or slave-owning. These were extraordinarily Eurocentric concepts, however, and neither was really encountered outside the bounds of Europe. In the case of slave-owning, it had proved to be an exception rather than the rule and even as a description of so-called slave-owning societies, in which the majority of the population were actually petty producers dependent on the state, it was inaccurate. Further, with the suppression of the Asiatic mode of production debate, Soviet scholarship proved incapable of establishing the status of societies that, having bypassed slave-owning, remained in transition (for example, the Germanic tribes that moved from primitive to feudal society after the collapse of the Roman empire).[118]

The real perniciousness of the *pyatichlenka*, according to Danilova, was that rather than the mode of production as a whole serving as the basis for formational periodization 'the *relations of property* to the conditions and means of production' defined the entire system of the social relations of production:

> In recent decades our literature on political economy, philosophy and history has virtually identified the relations of production with

property relations in the means of production. As a result, the division of post-primitive, pre-socialist societies into formations has been based on types of big private property.[119]

When applied to class society this approach was even more narrowed; here, monopoly of property by the ruling class became the exclusive criterion of a given formation. This not only blurred the classical Marxist distinction between actual relations of production and their juridical expression – property relations; it impeded conceptualizing what really defined the social relations of precapitalist societies. In ancient Eastern despotisms, for example, organizational functions rather than property relations were decisive.[120] In the case of West European feudalism the focus on juridical land ownership by the feudal lords, as opposed to real land-holding by the peasantry, obscured the fact observed by Marx that personal relations of subordination, in which ownership of land was merely an extension of proprietorship over the peasant producer, was decisive.[121]

What Soviet medievalists had lost sight of was that under feudalism political power over a subject peasantry, that was exploited by rent not profit, was primary rather than economic relations.[122] This trend had been reinforced by Stalin's emphasis, in his 1952 pamphlet *Economic Problems of Socialism in the USSR*, on large-landed property as the basis of feudalism.[123] As a result of Stalin's foray into medievalism, Soviet scholars had further diminished the role played by extra-economic coercion – the mechanism by which feudal lords extracted a surplus from the peasantry.[124] Overall, these trends in Soviet scholarship of precapitalist societies amounted to a modernization of history. Monopoly of the means of production by the ruling class and its complete separation from political power, in the guise of the state apparatus, occurs only under the capitalist mode of production, Danilova argued.[125]

In many respects Danilova's *Problems of Pre-capitalist Societies* represented the resurrection of important advances in Marxist concepts made during the 1920s that had been lost during the subsequent terrible decade. In particular, the notion of the 'unevenness' of historical development was at the heart of these explorations of precapitalist societies. In the 1930s the concept of 'unevenness' had been displaced by the rigid 'template' of the 'natural-historical process' according to which each society, people, region and even estate [!] had to pass through the *pyatichlenka*. Unevenness of development, however, a concept whose lineage could be traced back to Marx's draft letter to Zasulich on the prospects for Russian social development, and which was upheld in the 1920s by Bogdanov, Bukharin and Trotsky, stressed that no society had to follow the path of its predecessor. Indeed, given the influence of the 'centre' and its interaction with its 'periphery', whether it was Rome and the barbaric tribes or the capitalist metropoles and their colonies, the path to modernization was actually shortened by this interaction. Each society was not condemned to reinvent the wheel, so to speak. Stalinist dogma, however, never understood that 'unevenness of development' was governed by the epoch in which a given formation occurs. Further, for the contributors to the anthology such formations should be understood 'not as sequences but as equivalent stages' the 'form' of which, and even whether they occurred or not, depended on the epoch in which they emerged. It was this theory of the 'unevenness of development' that the anthology tried to resurrect on the basis of specific research.[126]

Within a year of publication, in 1969, Danilova's anthology was the object of fierce criticism in *Kommunist*. The most serious accusation was that there was a 'theoretico-methodological sub-text' to its 'structural analysis'. *Kommunist* charged that the denial of the paramountcy of the economic factor in both primitive and precapitalist class societies amounted to a 'dissolution' of the boundaries between them (an accusation that Danilova describes as 'convergence theory') and placed a question mark over the existence of classes under slavery and feudalism and, in essence, the materialist conception of history.[127]

There was more at issue here than even the credibility of Marxism–Leninism. During her discussion of the 'absolutization of the economic factor', Danilova referred explicitly to the relevance of relations of 'domination and subjection' not only to precapitalist societies but also to 'socialist' societies. As she concluded, 'the discussion concerning primitive and early-class societies is connected with contemporary discussions of economists, arising from the need to elaborate a political economy serving the practical requirements of socialist society'.[128] This was no mere sub-textual insinuation. As Gellner discerned, Danilova was saying quite explicitly that if we are to understand not only precapitalist but also postcapitalist societies, 'we must look at the relationships of power'.[129]

For Danilova the publication of *Problems of Pre-capitalist Societies* was most definitely a 'political act', and a courageous one – given the intimidating atmosphere of the times; it was a statement of protest against the October 1964 overturning of Khrushchev's 'Second October

Revolution'.[130] Notwithstanding the editors' declarations that revitalizing Marxism was the best defence against its adversaries and that enrichment of historical thought should be seen as enriching revolutionary thought,[131] the anthology was received by *Kommunist* as a repudiation of Marxism. The hostile review in the party's theoretical journal was in fact a serious political 'condemnation'. After this, to use Danilova's expression, 'all hell broke loose' for the Sector of Methodology's former participants.[132]

A paradigm in crisis

Within the sector, the revisionist challenge to orthodox historical materialism advanced on other fronts besides anthropology. A major assault on the technological determinism of orthodox historical materialism was the paper delivered in December 1965 by the archaeologist Aleksandr Mongait, 'Archaeological Cultures and Ethnic Communities', and the discussion that followed. In his paper Mongait cast doubt on the accepted Soviet definition of archaeological culture as a simple totality of the material instruments of production and the assumption of an immediate correspondence between them and the origins of a given ethnic community, that is, 'ethnogenesis'. Mongait argued that archaeological culture had to embrace 'spiritual' data as well, notably the artistic and, above all, linguistic forms through which communities expressed their identities.[133]

The real sting, however, in Mongait's paper was that he had the temerity to suggest that Soviet archaeologists, who during the 1940s and 1950s repudiated ideas of racial superiority advanced by Nazi scholars, were themselves unwittingly indulging in their own theory of Slav superiority. Mongait laid bare the theoretical premises that underlay the chauvinism of Soviet archaeology's attempts, on the basis of a restricted definition of material culture, to establish the unadulterated continuity of the Slav peoples. The response from the custodians of orthodoxy was predictably vitriolic. Then Director of the Institute of Archaeology, Academician B. A. Rybakov, a 'devotee of the idea of the singular predestination of the Russians',[134] was outraged and denounced Mongait's paper as a denial of the achievements of Soviet archaeology. For Rybakov, whatever inadequacies there were in Soviet archaeology, and whatever challenges that it faced in the 'new period' of its development, could be readily rectified by a 'synthesis' of the accumulated archaeological data with linguistics and other ancillary disciplines.[135] For Mongait, however, and Gefter, who spoke in his support, the principal problem facing archaeology in its current stage of development was a 'crisis' in archaeological science as such, brought about by the 'incompatibility between important partial conceptions and the way in which problems are theorized as a whole'.[136]

This theme of a 'crisis' in the historical and other social sciences was present in just about all the discussions that occurred in the sector. In essence this crisis amounted to the increasing inability of the dominant Soviet paradigm of historical materialism to make sense of either the complexities of the world in the 1960s or the Soviet past. It is no exaggeration to say that the sector derived its very *raison d'être* from the need to address and redress this paradigmatic crisis, which had reached its peak in the mid-1960s. All of the sector's activities were dedicated to a reevaluation of the 'fatalistic' Marxism that had so long held sway in Soviet social science and which, Gefter considered, had in essence eliminated Marxism's 'revolutionary-critical basis and harmed historical thought in particular'.[137] In a 1966 discussion in the sector on the development of party history, Gefter characteristically went to the heart of the question. According to him the *Short Course* method was a schema that 'straightened out' Soviet history, and 'drained [it] of blood' by reducing 'every nuance of thought' to a 'direct class interest'. Above all the *Short Course* method was an '*a priori* method':

> Every scheme is a reconstruction of the past, making it seem above all a preparation for the present condition of society, so that the beginning stages of a process are defined in one way or another by its result. Stalin turned this particular feature of historical cognition into an absolute. For him the result was the *one and only* important thing; the current result was turned from a criterion of historical truth into an instrument for constructing it. Hence such a characteristic feature of the *Short Course* as its self-evident style. Living reality served as an illustration of the obvious truth of some ideas and propositions and the obvious falsehood of others. Building the conclusion into the point of departure imparted the quality of predestination to historical development: *it could have happened only this way and no other*.[138]

The negative legacy of the *Short Course* paradigm extended to its inability to explain the phenomenon of which the paradigm itself was a product – Stalinism. The question of explaining the phenomenon of

Stalinism, judged by the minutes of the sector's discussions, was an underlying if not an explicit objective of its work, undoubtedly, with good reason, out fear of political retribution. For these historians, the *shestidesyatniki* who had been brought up and trained in the Stalin era, the question of Stalinism was not just an intellectual conundrum. Unlike the upheavals in the former colonial world, it had an agonizing, personal immediacy. According to Gefter, the crucial issue that faced this generation of historians was 'if Stalinism was not the lawful, inevitable, indispensable outcome of everything that had gone before', including the October Revolution, as the logic of the *Short Course* implied, then was it simply accidental, as official pronouncements about the 'cult of the personality' suggested? For scholars who wished to remain Marxists and true to the ideals of the October Revolution the notion of the 'fortuitousness' of Stalinism was inconceivable. However, once the question was posed in terms of Stalinism being neither 'inevitable' nor 'fortuitous' – then the 'hour of methodology' had arrived.[139] It was impossible to grapple with this monumental question without challenging a paradigm that depicted the October Revolution as simultaneously the endpoint and beginning of the historical process, nor to subject Marxism itself, which had effectively become an 'accomplice of the tragedy' of Stalinism, to the most searching scrutiny. To avoid this interrogation was to 'doom' Marxism itself. What was required was a '*new reading of Marxism*' in order to overcome the 'artificial', obstructive, divorce between historical materialism and historical research that reduced the latter to little more than 'illustrating' the general principles of the former. 'If theory is not internal to history itself then there can be no science of history'.[140]

Reporting on the work of the sector for 1967, Gefter endorsed the 'fundamentally Marxist' conception of the socio-economic formation that 'alone' provided a genuine basis for analysing the complexities of world history. However, simultaneously he argued that it was necessary to recognize the 'contradiction' between factual data accumulated in the course of research and 'the specific schema of the historical process', as he called it. 'Such a contradiction there is', Gefter emphasized, 'and in this schema have appeared enormous cracks which threaten to undermine the schema itself.'[141]

Faced with the apparent inability of the dominant historical-materialist paradigm to explain the complexities of the colonial and postcolonial world, which did not fit into its crude, received notions of slavery or feudalism, the tasks facing historical science were two-fold. Firstly, to bring the schema of socio-economic formations into line with the accumulated factual data (for example, as we have seen, by reintroducing a sixth formation such as the Asiatic mode of production). Secondly, to further refine the theory of formations itself in order to grasp the 'contemporary world' and the 'genesis of the new forms of the movement of humanity'. To realize these lofty aims it was necessary to develop a new problematic and method of studying world history that went beyond separate epochs together with the 'cognitive instruments' that would enable the eventual reconstruction of the process as a whole.[142] However, to encroach on the 'holy of holies' – Marxism–Leninism – as a theory, philosophy and methodology of history, was fraught with political consequences.

For the guardians of ideological orthodoxy, such as Academician Izaak Mints, there was no need to seek a special methodology of history separate from historical materialism; as one of Mints' colleagues put it, in a note to Gefter, 'This is one and the same science'.[143] For an 'intellectual of scope' like Mints, all that was required of Soviet historiography was simply to use the same instruments to reinterpret the world. It was never a question, as it was for the sector's 'intellectuals of quality', of reevaluating the research instruments themselves.

The sensitivity of party ideologues to the question of methodology in historical science was reflected in the severe criticism published in the party's theoretical journal directed at scholars who had been some of the sector's most active members and participants: Barg, Aron Gurevich and, as we saw above, Danilova. They were accused of a multiplicity of sins: revising Marxism, purveying the bourgeois methodology of structuralism, embracing Weber's 'ideal type', treating the socio-economic formation as a 'logical construct' rather than as a 'reflection' of social reality, and, worst of all, questioning the primacy of economic relations in primitive and precapitalist societies which, they also suggested, had a tendency towards 'homeostasis'. All in all, these tendencies were perceived as a direct assault on the fundamental category of historical materialism, the socio-economic formation, and with it the 'Leninist principle of *partiinost'* in historical science and philosophy.[144]

At issue here is not which was the more Marxist, the Sector of Methodology or the Central Committee's Department of Science, but an attempt by scholars to find new tools and techniques to break out of the iron cage of the *Short Course* approach to history. This trend, and the noticeable silence on the question of *partiinost'* in the sector's discussions, provided good reason for Trapeznikov and his Department of Science to feel threatened by, and to threaten, the very existence of the sector. Moreover, if drawing on non-Marxist traditions such as structuralism was seen as subversive, even more dangerous were attempts to revivify Marxism–Leninism from within its own traditions. This is glaringly obvious from the reaction to Gefter's endeavours to 'read Lenin anew'. For Gefter especially, Lenin was not simply a grand historical figure; far more important was Lenin's thought 'as a whole' as a key to understanding the contemporary world. For Gefter, Marxist social scientists and historians in particular ought to occupy an extremely important place in 'the struggle of ideas' concerning the significance of Leninism. In his opinion it was the 'duty' of Marxist scholars to 'defend the heritage of Lenin'. He cautioned that it had to be understood that this defence was only possible by the most penetrating investigation into this heritage, by considering it 'as it evolves' and by applying to it that 'criterion of social practice which Lenin, like Marx, considered decisive in the process of human cognition'.[145]

History and the present

'Who is our Lenin?', it was jocularly asked in the sector. 'It is Mikhail Yakovlevich [Gefter]'.[146] But Gefter's attempt to transform Leninist thought into a living tool of analysis, rather than an icon of state ideology, roused the ire of the party ideologues. Particular wrath was reserved for Gefter's essay on the relationship between Lenin's thought and nineteenth-century populism that appeared in the anthology *History and Problems of the Present,* published in 1969, the year the sector was formally dissolved.[147] Aleksandr Tvardovsky, editor-in-chief of *Novyi mir*, upon receipt of a signed copy from Gefter, welcomed it as a book which promised to be an 'event, and not only in the strictly academic sense'.[148]

In many respects this anthology represented a kind of manifesto of the sector, encapsulating many of the tasks the sector had set itself, triggered, it was said in Gefter's preface, by the Twentieth Congress. The congress had revealed the 'alarming' disparity between theory and historical research. The 'very indifference' of the notorious 'general laws' to the recent qualitative growth in historical research indicated a 'serious absence' of a 'theoretical synthesis' in Soviet historiography, a failing occasioned not just by the '*faktomaniya*' of historians or the divorce of philosophers from historical research, but by an 'unjustified counterposing of "law" to "fact" and of the theory of historical development to the depiction of the specific course of events'.[149] The 'momentous nature of the epoch' gave particular urgency to a 'new reading' of the Marxist classics and Lenin's heritage in particular as an antidote to the 'stultification and canonization' of the fundamental principles of Soviet historiography. It was not a matter of mobilizing a set of counter-quotes but of a historicist approach to the historical conceptions of classical Marxism. The methodology of Soviet historiography could only be rejuvenated from within, bridging the gap between history and philosophy, in this case at least, on the basis of particular problems being tackled by 'working' historians. However, the task was more than one of enriching the accumulated research by Marxist theory; particular attention had to be given to those questions most closely connected with 'social and revolutionary practice' in a fast-changing world, the dynamics of which were difficult to capture intellectually. At stake in this context was the 'type of Marxist research' and, accordingly, the 'type of historian that most answered the needs of the times and of method'.[150] Here we have an explicit statement of the changing self-perception of these scholars: of their movement from mere 'intellectuals of scope' to 'intellectuals of quality', challenging the imposed orthodoxies. And with this movement a growing sense of their role as *intelligenty*.

The pivotal question that this anthology sought to address was, as its title suggested, 'the nexus between history and the present'. This, it will be recalled, was the motivating passion of the *frontoviki* for history. The anthology formulated it as the 'problem of the genesis of the revolutionary changes of the contemporary world, changes that constitute the main content of the twentieth century, at the heart of which is October 1917'. Hence the focus on social revolutions and Lenin's contribution in this field with a view to grasping these developments as a 'united process' by overcoming the parochialism of what passed for Marxism in the Soviet Union and relocating national history in the broader sweep of human history. Hence too, the 'vital' task of investigating the precursors of Marxist socialism and their intellectual cross-fertilization with it, albeit in a new context.[151]

The articles, papers and discussion published in the anthology certainly reflected these concerns: in addition to Gefter's article on the populist impulse in Lenin's thought, there were, *inter alia*, considerations on the 'revolutionary creativity' of the masses, on the nature of 'social revolutions' and on the 'historicism' of Marxist theory, an abiding theme within the collective. Many of these contributions were subsequently singled out for criticism from various quarters, party and academic, but it was Gefter's essay, 'A Page from the History of Marxism at the Turn of the Twentieth Century', that attracted most flak. The reasons are not hard to discern. While much of Gefter's argument focussed ostensibly on the shortcomings of Plekhanov's Marxism, in rereading Lenin and the populist stimuli for his thought Gefter was effectively attacking the misrepresentation of the evolution of Lenin's thinking in Soviet scholarship and the methodology that underpinned it. Three years after the anthology's publication, Gefter was to be accused in the CPSU's theoretical journal of repeating calumnies last made in the 1920s, and repudiated at that time by no lesser lights than Ye. M. Yaroslavsky and M. N. Pokrovsky, that 'Russian social democracy had two theoretical founts: Marxism and peasant utopian socialism, thereby dissolving the principal, qualitative difference between scientific socialism and petty-bourgeois utopianism.'[152]

A close reading of Gefter's article suggests that this was a serious misrepresentation, willful or otherwise, of his explanation of the impact the populism of the 1860s and 1870s had on Lenin's approach to the agrarian revolution. For Gefter the question facing Lenin in 1905 was what 'type' of revolution did Russia face, that of 1789 or 1848, and, specifically, what form would it take? Lenin came to the conclusion that in Russia the democratic revolution that would clear the way to the flowering of capitalist relations in the countryside would be effected under the 'hegemony' of the proletariat, thereby simultaneously clearing the way for socialism. Gefter probed the intellectual processes that underlay such a 'break' in revolutionary theory. Soviet representations tended to reduce such processes to simple recognition of social change by the given theoretician (in this case Lenin); they then adjusted their theory accordingly. On this basis Lenin's thinking was often presented in contemporary literature as a 'straight line of Leninist creativity'. Gefter, however, stressed the autonomy of theory. He argued that recognition of such social changes requires the elaboration of a 'new view' which breaks out of the existing 'vicious circle' of thought, opening the way to the resolution of its internal contradictions.[153] It was precisely this task, we should add, that also faced the revisionists of the 1960s.

For Gefter, it was Lenin's re-evaluation of populism that opened the way to his recognition of alternative paths of development for Russian capitalism in the countryside: the Prussian path – a constitutional monarchy of landlords with private property in land – or the American path – a farmers' republic combining a bourgeois legal structure with direct popular power. Where Plekhanov saw only the 'bourgeois content' of the peasant economy, 'the economist' Lenin 'discovered' the peculiar 'intertwining of the old and the new' that shaped Russian agrarian capitalism: 'the remnants of serfdom and patriarchy largely adapting to themselves the bourgeois relations emerging within peasant society, thereby barbarizing the social development of the country'. Recognition of the possibilities of the American path, of a community of interests between a peasantry seeking radical redistribution of land on a capitalist basis (the programme of the populist group 'Black Redivision') and a working class struggling for socialism, was directly linked to Lenin's recognition of the contradictory nature of populism. Whereas Plekhanov, true to his deterministic conviction that history was essentially a 'blind' process, saw populism merely as a wholly reactionary obstacle to the imminent, purely proletarian revolution, Lenin recognized the janus nature of populism: while it was reactionary in its hostility to socialism and in its yearning to preserve the small land holder, it was progressive in its desire to clear away the vestiges of feudalism.[154]

Gefter's essay was really a celebration of Lenin's mastery of the dialectic; in elucidating the evolution of Lenin's thinking he highlighted its ability to capture the contradictory nature of specific social phenomena. When Gefter counterposed Lenin's approach to the one-sided, formalistic, doctrinaire Marxism that Plekhanov espoused, Gefter was obviously repudiating these same tendencies in Soviet Marxism itself. In contrast to the objectivist, unilinear conceptions of history espoused by Plekhanov (and it should be said, Soviet Marxism) genuine Marxism emphasized the 'meeting point between changing circumstances and human activity'. Here there was no divorce between theory and reality, between the 'educator and the educated'. Rather, 'historical creativity' always recognizes the necessity of deviations from 'the norms' of theory, always allows for the ebb and flow of progress. In contrast, argued Gefter, those who clung to the letter of Marxist theory 'apply only one criterion: the immediate coincidence of reality with theoretical conceptions and prognoses. Everything that coincides, is true, everything that does not, is deception.' 'Therefore', asked Gefter,

> aren't the advocates of a ready-made, 'royal road' of history prone to a dangerous self-confidence in regard to their own role as the mentors of history? Moreover, hasn't one of the most fundamental causes of the downfall of many orthodoxies, beginning with the Mensheviks, been that in aspiring to teach the revolution, they failed to see the necessity to learn from it?[155]

Though the implications of such propositions for Soviet Marxism must have been obvious to Gefter's critics, such innuendoes were not the focus of their attacks. Rather, they emphasized that the axis of the dispute between the Mensheviks and Bolsheviks at the Second Congress of the Russian Social Democrats was the organizational principles of the party not the agrarian question. Nor was there anything unique about the type of Russian social development, as Gefter's critics claimed he suggested. Above all, evidently taking their cue from the *Short Course*, they emphasized the discontinuties between Leninism and populism. The critics maintained it was a travesty on Gefter's part to suggest that Lenin drew his understanding of the form the Russian Revolution would take either from the narodniks or their Social Revolutionary successors.

Why was this point laboured in every critical review? On the theoretical plane it is apparent that Gefter's opponents, party and academic, wished to preserve the self-sufficiency of Marxism–Leninism. For them, Lenin derived his theory exclusively from within Marxism; to suggest otherwise, as Gefter did, was to open up the possibility that Marxism–Leninism might benefit from exposure to other schools of thought. But at the heart of the critique was a more pressing political issue: *partiinost'* – the intersection between historical science and the monopoly of political power by the CPSU.

In their prefatory remarks, the editors of *Istoricheskaya nauka* outlined their notion of *partiinost'* and its relationship to objectivity in historical writing. They declared 'a vested interest in scientific truth and serving progress'. Such a concept of objectivity was not divorced from *partiinost'*, they argued:

> The objectivity of Marxism is not secured by reference to laws of history that disfigure life and are counterposed to the interests of individuals and peoples – the living creators of the progressive movement of history. Objectivity entails both the heroic tradition of progress and condemnation of reaction in all its forms – open, as well as those disguised as progress. Objectivity is impartial both to the events and the personae of history.[156]

Such a watering down of 'partyness' in historiography could not go unchallenged, especially in the wake of the 1971 Twenty-fourth Party Congress which reaffirmed Marxism–Leninism and the CPSU's pronouncements as the arbiters of worthwhile research. Defence of *partiinost'* was the basis of a particularly hostile review that appeared in the journal of party history in 1972.[157]

In defence of *partiinost'*, the journal also took the field against a number of Gefter's colleagues, notably Ya. S. Drabkin. Drabkin's paper on 'Unresolved Problems in the Study of Social Revolutions' was singled out for attack in just about every review of the anthology.[158] The reasons are not difficult to discern. As an expert on the abortive November 1918 German revolution, Drabkin was alive to the question that had been at the heart of Stalin's and Bukharin's confrontation with Trotsky in the 1920s: 'socialism in one country' versus world revolution. In his paper Drabkin, though mindful of the peril that the heresy of 'Trotskyism' still carried four decades later,[159] came down unequivocally on the side of Lenin's – and *ipso facto* Trotsky's – conception of the Russian Revolution as merely the prelude to world revolution. Noting that Lenin's position on this question had disappeared at the end of the 1920s only to resurface 30 years later, Drabkin identified two closely-related 'postulates' in Soviet literature that required 'critical re-evaluation'. Firstly, a 'simplified formula' according to which Lenin had revised the classical view that the socialist revolution would occur simultaneously everywhere, in favour of its victory in one country. Secondly, that Lenin was 'not the champion of world revolution but of revolution in one country'. Flowing from these reservations, Drabkin broached an element of Lenin's thought that was crucial to any critical reconsideration of the viability of Stalin's model of socialism: the implications of the 'ripeness' or unripeness of Soviet society for socialist revolution. 'One of Lenin's greatest services', Drabkin opined, was to call on the Russian proletariat to begin the revolution; but Lenin never shrank from acknowledging the difficulties that would ensue should the revolution remain isolated, hence Germany was for Lenin the 'main link' in the world revolution.[160] Drabkin's perspective here was Trotskyist to the core; curiously, however, it did not attract that charge overtly. Only a hostile review in *Sovetskaya Rossiya* challenged Drabkin's interpretation of Lenin's stance on revolution in one country.[161] The main thrust of the criticism leveled at him was directed elsewhere.

The first attack concerned Drabkin's challenge to the received Soviet wisdom on the nature of the modern capitalist state. Drabkin, in the context of querying the relationship between reform and revolution in the transition to socialism, argued that it was no longer adequate to speak of the state in advanced capitalist societies simply as an instrument of coercion. Plainly influenced by the French and Italian communist parties' considerations on the possibilities of 'peaceful forms' of socialist revolution, Drabkin pointed to the growing political and ideological functions assumed by the modern state, as well as its enhanced role as economic regulator and planner. In this context Lenin's views about 'breaking' the old apparatus, while retaining certain elements of it, required reconsideration as to what precisely should be 'broken' and what should not in the modern state. It was precisely with this point that Rybakov took issue with Drabkin, and A. A. Galkin who went even further in denouncing the 'dogmatic approach' to smashing the state apparatus.[162] Far from any attempt to evaluate these propositions by examining the real record of the modern state, Rybakov took refuge in that reliable redoubt of orthodoxy: quoting Lenin, in this case, Lenin's proposition in *State and Revolution*.[163]

The central attack on Drabkin, however, came in response to his attempt to historicize the concept of 'social revolution' in Marxism. Drabkin maintained that Soviet historians had struck problems when they attempted to apply the concept of 'social revolution', on the basis of the *Short Course* definition as a 'law of transition from one social formation to another', to specific historical problems. The *Short Course* 'schemas' had effectively 'modernized' the concept, projecting the image of recent revolutions onto earlier societies. Attempts to establish the concept as a 'universal law' ran up against its geographical and temporal limitations. It could not, for instance, explain transitions from primitive-communal to class society or from slave holding to feudal society (as for example, the discredited, but still extant *Short Course* notion of the Roman 'revolution of the slaves' had attempted to do). Nor could it explain transitions that occurred, say from feudalism to capitalism, without a revolution, let alone revolutions that entailed less than inter-formational transitions, political revolutions for instance. Rather than broaden the concept's scope so that it embraced all transitions between social formations, which would effectively reduce it to a revolution in relations of production, Drabkin suggested that it would be more fruitful to recognize that 'social revolution' is peculiar only to a certain stage of historical development, namely, the advent of class society. Social revolution only reaches its 'apogee in the epoch of transition from capitalism to socialism'.[164]

In developing his argument Drabkin focused on the way in which Soviet historians, following, if not fetishizing, Marx's 'Preface' to the *Critique of Political Economy*, had so often reduced the causes of revolutions to the non-correspondence of the productive forces and the relations of production. Noting the distinction made by Marx and Engels between the 'epoch' of social revolutions and particular revolutions, Drabkin stressed that the former merely laid the groundwork for the latter, which, far from flowing 'automatically' from the nature of the epoch, could be triggered by a multiplicity of conflicts – political, social and ideological. Not least important here was the conscious willingness of the revolutionary classes to resolve these conflicts. In sum, Drabkin was arguing for an approach that captured both the unity of 'the world revolutionary process', shaped by the nature of the epoch, and the varied characteristics of specific revolutions which manifested it.[165]

In concert with his attempts to give more body to the concept of 'social revolutions', Drabkin called in question the usual antinomy between revolution and reform. Pointing to situations where the advent of capitalism had occurred without revolution, in Scandinavia for example, and of revolution effected 'from above', the 1861 reforms in Russia and the Bismarckian reforms in Germany, often as not under the impact of failed revolutions, Drabkin went on to pose two rather thorny questions: is a transition from capitalism to socialism by reform possible and what place is there for reform under the 'dictatorship of the proletariat'?[166] The first question had already been answered in the affirmative by Khrushchev. The second touched on issues that were not only violently ruled out of court by Stalin, but were distinctly out of place in the immediate aftermath of Khrushchev's failed 'reform from above'. Drabkin, however, referred to China's 'Great Leap Forward' and the 'tragedy' of the Cultural Revolution as putting the question of socialist reform immediately on the agenda, rather than more recent domestic events. Even so, Drabkin broached the question of socialist reform not from Chinese experience but in relation to the Soviet New Economic Policy which, he speculated, may well be regarded as a 'transition from revolution to reform'.[167] Rather more categorically, Drabkin suggested that the discovery and implementation of NEP was the 'greatest contribution' Lenin had made.

Drabkin's eulogy of NEP, a precursor to the vigorous reconsideration it received during the early period of *perestroika*, was made in the context of resurrecting a concept that had been proscribed since the defeat of the Left Opposition at the end of the 1920s: Thermidor. Following Ye. G. Plimak (a student of Gefter's and associate of the sector), Drabkin argued for the validity of comparisons between bourgeois and socialist revolutions and pointed to Lenin's mooting of a Soviet Thermidor at the Tenth Party Congress in March 1921. On this basis, Drabkin argued, somewhat defensively, that 'it was difficult' to categorically deny the possibility of 'Thermidor' in any socialist revolution.[168]

It was only a short step from this implicit conceptualization of Stalinism as the counter-revolution within the revolution to pointing to the silence in Soviet literature about the 'overheads and "cost" of revolution', and whether responsibility for them could be attributed exclusively to reactionary forces.[169] Again, however, rather than a frontal assault on the implicit Trotskyism of such notions, the apparently secondary question of the 'cost' of revolution was the focus of some of the harshest criticism directed at Drabkin. In suggesting that it was incumbent on Soviet scholars 'not to attribute all the difficulties and sacrifices of the revolution to the counter-revolution', Drabkin was accused of 'blasphemy'[170] against *partiinost'* – appropriate in the quasi-theological discourse that was Marxism–Leninism.

Hand in hand with the charge of blaspheming against *partiinost'* went a vigorous denunciation of historicist thinking in the anthology. This accusation was particularly pronounced in reports delivered in February 1971 by I. I. Mints and M. P. Kim to the Bureau of the Division of History of the Academy of Sciences. They reproached the anthology and its principal editor in particular for violating the 'integrity' and 'universality' of Marxism–Leninism in favour of a historicism which reduced Marxism to an 'essential kernel', restricted in its applicability in time and place. In this regard, Kim also took exception to Gefter's suggestion that 'contingency' played such a dominant role in history that contingency itself constituted 'a kind of lawfulness'. Kim saw this proposition as belittling 'the general laws that determine the historical process'. [171]

Such elevation of universal laws to the prime movers of history was the object of a sustained critique in the anthology in a paper by A. S. Arsen'ev entitled 'Historicism and Logic in Marxist Theory'. Arsen'ev took to task such textbook 'general phrases' in which 'the logic of the movement of the historical process and of thought in all epochs are considered synonymous'.[172] Soviet historiography had, he reasoned, treated the dialectic as a given, divorced from history; historical materialism, allegedly based on dialectical materialism, had been applied regardless of time and place. By denying the 'historicity' of the materialist dialectic, treating it as a 'closed' rather than an 'open' system, Soviet historians had approached 'history ahistorically (and consequently, illogically)'.

Strongly endorsing Arsen'ev's propositions, the philosopher Gulyga praised his exposure of 'pseudodialectics' which, often as not, had been formal logic masquerading as dialectics.[173] Gefter too praised it for at least identifying one of the obstacles to the self-renewal of Marxism: 'a reversal of the structure and logic of Marxism, whereby the materialist conception of history becomes a by-product of "diamat" [dialectical materialist] natural philosophy'.[174] Gefter, however, thought that Arsen'ev did not get to the root of the 'dogmatization of Marxism' which, he argued, was more than just 'primitive citation mania' or simply clinging to outmoded principles. It was a question of the 'dogmatization of forms of thought and of method'. Here was the significance of Lenin's contribution to Marxism. Lenin's innovation was, above all, that he viewed the problems of the Russian Revolution,

> not as a particular case of a general theory, but as a *special form* of historical reality, analysis of which required both a *special form of theory*, which gave specific content to old concepts and created new ones, capable of grasping and expressing the specific features of this reality ... No less important was that this reality contained new sources of activity and revolutionary creativity. Their theoretical anticipation and interpretation entailed the incorporation of all the *variables*. This changed the interaction of classes, and of separate layers and groupings within classes, *into a system of objective analysis of the process as a whole*: not lawfulness plus deviations, but lawfulness understood as conflict and the outcome of tendencies, which result in *various* possibilities of historical movement. Thus the organic thought of Lenin is a combination of polemical sharpness and even one-sidedness – focused on a definite event – with digressions and 'projects' that take in both the likelihood of other, including less favourable, variants of development, and possible ways of resolving those same problems and tasks, that is, Lenin's thought constitutes the philosophy and methodology of the *historical alternative*, without which Marxism is inconceivable in the twentieth century.[175]

In his reply to the discussion, Arsen'ev eloquently captured what was at stake in this abstruse discussion about the dialectic. Historicizing Marxism itself was a blow against the 'fatalism' that ensued from conceptualizing Marxism as a closed system of logic in which the present was a captive of the future. 'Real openness', he argued, 'is infinity, manifesting itself always as the spectre of possibilities'.[176] Such speculation was deemed beyond the pale by one of the staunchest practitioners of closed logic:

Academician Mints. He reasserted that the task facing Soviet historians was to analyse new phenomena in 'the light of the fundamental principles of Marxist–Leninist theory', not to reevaluate these principles themselves 'under the influence of new facts', as the editors of *Istoricheskaya nauka* had had the audacity to do.[177] The very way in which Mints formulated his injunction, separating fact from theory, revealed not only the unbridgeable gulf between Marxist–Leninist orthodoxy and its heretical critics, but the validity of Arsen'ev's claim that 'there are no facts outside of their theoretical interpretation'.[178]

Criticism of the anthology in the Division of History was part of a campaign that went on for almost three years, not only within the Academy of Sciences, but also within the CPSU and in the press.[179] In fact, the opening shot in this campaign, surreptitiously fired by the Central Committee,[180] had been the review of the anthology published in the paper *Sovetskaya Rossiya* 28 February 1970, under the sarcastic heading 'In the guise of a scholarly quest'. Gefter was accused of severing Leninism from Marxism for allegedly asserting that Lenin was a champion of the 'petty-bourgeois revolutionary outlook ... of the narodniks'.[181] The real significance of the review, however, lay not so much in its content as in what it signalled: the final 'liquidation' of the remnants of the Sector of Methodology collective and a prohibition on further publication of its research.[182]

As a result of the break-up of the sector, much of the important research carried out under its aegis remained unpublished. Specifically, the manuscript of the second volume of *Problems of the History of Precapitalist Societies*, which was ready for immediate publication, never saw the light of day. This particular volume, in addition to contributions from Soviet and East European scholars, such as T. Pokora from Czechoslovakia and F. Tokei from Hungary, contained many by prominent Marxist scholars such as Godelier, Suret-Canale, Jean Chesneaux and Charles Parain. Several of the latter group had contributed to the revival of the concept of the Asiatic mode of production in their native France in the mid-1960s.[183] Work on the third volume in this series, *Slavery in World History* (*Rabstvo v mirovoi istorii*) was terminated. An anthology on *V. I. Lenin and Problems of the History of Classes and Class Struggle*,[184] together with research on the role of social revolutions in world history (*Revolyutsiya v mirovoi istorii: istoriko-sotsialogicheskii ocherk*),[185] for both of which Drabkin was the responsible editor, were condemned to oblivion. Meanwhile a monograph by Danilova on *Theoretical Problems of Feudalism in Soviet Historiography* (*Teoreticheskie problemy feodalizma v Sovetskoi istoriografii*), a work begun in the Sector of Methodology and completed in the Sector of Feudalism in the newly-established Institute of World History, languished in manuscript form.

The principal players in the sector fared little better. Danilova was confined in a 'citadel of dogmatism': the Sector of Feudalism. She found herself immediately under the thumbs of the archconservative Academicians L. V. Cherepnin and V. T. Pashuto. They, together with Porshnev, worked overtime to prevent publication of her manuscript on the historiography of feudalism because, in her words, it 'exposed the dependence of historical concepts on politics'.[186] Gefter himself had been transferred to the same institute. Though quickly elected a senior researcher,[187] in 1971 he was subject to an official party reprimand for alleged 'mistakes of a methodological and ideological character'. Called upon to acknowledge his 'mistakes', Gefter, in the words of a supportive colleague,

> declined to go down this path – fortunately for himself and for our entire collective. With honour – I would even say with brilliance – he withstood the ordeal that befell him. I would hope that the conduct of M. Ya. in this question, as in all his scientific and public behaviour, serves our younger researchers as an inspiring example of civic courage, moral fortitude and devotion to science.[188]

Nevertheless, in 1973 Gefter became an active participant in the short-lived Sector of Economic History but once again, undoubtedly as a result of his pursuit of methodological questions, fell foul of party diktat, which eventually terminated his research career.[189] In 1976, on the grounds of ill-health, Gefter took early retirement from the institute.

What was the overall significance of the Sector of Methodology and the work it undertook? The sector was the institutionalized expression of the self-conscious transition of the post-Stalinist intellectual elite towards a new generation of *intelligenty,* reminiscent of the traditional Russian **intelligentsia**. Exactly what form that took depended to great degree on the particular fount of their intellectual reawakening. For all those scholars who genuinely identified with the objectives of the sector, it signalled the consolidation of historians characterized, in Gefter's words, by a 'new type of public behaviour',[190] who repudiated any 'dual consciousness' – any self-censoring disparity between private thoughts and public utterances – and who, while willing to defend their convictions, were prepared to subject their own precepts to criticism. Moreover, in so far as the sector as a whole was engaged in renovating the methodology and philosophy of history, the participants were picking up on a tradition that was deeply rooted in the Russian historiography of the late-nineteenth and early-twentieth centuries – *'istoriosofiya'* – whereby historical discourse was at once philosophical discourse. This was not only true of the 'culturologists', such as Bibler, Gurevich and Neretina, but also of the neo-Leninist, Gefter.[191]

In the context of the developments in Czechoslovakia in 1967–68 which, like Hungary a little over a decade before, saw intellectuals playing a leading role in the construction of a new model of socialism, the generation of an alternative world view by a wing of the intellectual elite was viewed with apprehension by the ideologues of the CPSU. In 1968 this apprehension was voiced concisely by Porshnev, who from the moment he entered the sector as a researcher was regarded as hostile,[192] in a question he put to Gefter: 'Don't you think the sector is similar to the Petöfi Circle and you to its chairman?' The implied threat in Porshnev's question was soon realized; within a year the sector ceased to exist.[193]

Ostensibly the break-up of the sector was merely a side-effect of an administrative need to divide the Institute of History into two independent institutions;[194] in reality it was to eliminate the sector as a source of research and discussion that refused to be contained within the parameters of the dogmatic discourse of Marxism–Leninism. For Porshnev, and those in the Department of Science who thought like him, such a challenge was tantamount to sedition whereas for the *aktiv* members of the sector it was more a question of taking the decisions of the Twentieth Congress 'intellectually' to their logical conclusion. Nevertheless, there was a consciously political facet to the sector's work. Besides the regular sessions of the sector there was Gefter's own, rather more discrete, theoretical seminar. This seminar met twice-monthly but, unlike the formal sessions, where detailed minutes were taken, no records were kept for fear of KGB informers. The seminar's themes were much more 'political': discussions, for example, about the fate of the French Revolution and Thermidor as well as three sessions devoted to the Brest Litovsk peace, world revolution, Lenin and Trotsky.[195]

The dissolution of the sector was part and parcel of a general campaign by the communist party to atomize and tame the anti-Stalinist intelligentsia; a story detailed in the next chapter. Looking back, however, we can see the roots of this conflict. An increasingly sophisticated community of scholars, nourished by the cross-fertilization of ideas facilitated by this tight-knit association as well as contact with the outside world, self-consciously striving to construct a new historical paradigm. Their mission was to replace the paradigmatic straitjacket bequeathed to them from a much more primitive, repressive and violent time. In a wistful retrospective on his own work, some five years after the dismantling of his sector when the cloud of Brezhnevism had already descended, Gefter expressed quite succinctly the agenda that scholars of his generation had set themselves in the mid-1960s:

> In recent years my output has not been markedly voluminous. Rather, this has been a laboratory period: the accumulation [of knowledge] and profound reflection ... The most intense period of the formation of my scientific views occurred during the life of the sector of methodology, particularly with the specific elaboration of a problem which could be defined as 'the movement of thought and especially revolutionary thought *within* world history' ... It remains to add, that the subject of the research and of its interpretation is difficult to separate from the method, the form, even the style and, if I may say so, from the conduct of the researcher. Here there is an obligation, not only on the personal but also the public plane. In recent years this has become especially obvious to me.[196]

Recognition that a principled quest for methodological renewal might have political as well as scholarly ramifications is indicative of the transformation of the *shestidesyatniki* from scholars to *intelligenty* – constantly relating their private scholarly concerns to their public stance. From the moment they embarked on this quest they were on a collision course with political authority.

Part III
The Political Consequences

6
Collision Course

> 'The *shestidesyatniki* were a generation of scholars who fervently grasped the ideas of the Twentieth Congress, adopted them, and, on the basis of them, began to construct and review their world outlook, their methodological principles and their approaches to research. They also began to review their social views.'
>
> Academician P. V. Volobuev, Moscow, April 1992

The dissolution of the Sector of Methodology was only part of an ideological offensive against the social sciences which had been unleashed soon after the ousting of Nikita Khrushchev as First Secretary of the CPSU in October 1964. That offensive had been led by the notorious S. P. Trapeznikov, head of the Department of Science and Educational Establishments of the Central Committee. It was no accident that this neo-Stalinist offensive coincided with a radical shift against Stalinism among social scientists in general and historians in particular. On one side of the barricade stood party bureaucrats anxious to stifle the anti-Stalinist wave unleashed in 1956 by the Twentieth Congress of the CPSU. Arrayed against them were a cluster of elite intellectuals on the road to reestablishing a critical philosophical and social outlook redolent of the classical Russian intelligentsia. This was an inherently unstable situation; in the end bureaucratic dictatorship was incompatible with an alternative outlook to official Marxism–Leninism, especially a critical outlook *within* Marxism, on the part of the intellectual elite. Such a precarious situation presaged a crisis of legitimacy for the bureaucratic apparatus that could only be resolved by the suppression of dissent and the imposition of a new orthodoxy.

The Trapeznikov offensive

The toppling of Khrushchev in the main did not lead to an immediate assault on the liberal intelligentsia. On the contrary, there was an initial attempt to woo them by the liberal wing of the party leadership. In February 1965 an article entitled 'The Party and the Intelligentsia' appeared in *Pravda*, written by its editor-in-chief and Central Committee member A. M. Rumyantsev.[1] Around Rumyantsev was clustered a small group of 'party democrats', including Aleksandr N. Yakovlev (later famous as an advisor to Gorbachev). Among those who identified with this distinct 'trend of socio-political thought', as Roy Medvedev has called it, were the editor-in-chief of *Novyi mir*, Aleksandr Tvardovsky, and the historians Danilov, Drabkin and Gefter.[2] Rumyantsev was intent not only on preserving the legacy of the Twentieth and Twenty-second Party Congresses but also on pursuing 'the causes and conditions of the emergence of the cult of Stalin and Stalinism'.[3] Rumyantsev's article argued the communist party should pursue a policy of enlightened benevolence towards the intelligentsia in order to maximize its creative potential. Rumyantsev reminded his readers of Lenin's opposition to 'commandist' approaches to the intelligentsia and extolled the virtues of competing 'schools and trends' in intellectual life.[4]

The overture to the anti-Stalinist intelligentsia, however, was short-lived. In late 1965 Brezhnev dismayed party workers and scientific researchers alike when he elevated his long-time crony Trapeznikov to one of the highest posts in the party hierarchy: head of the Department of Science. In his new post, Trapeznikov had responsibility for the Academy of Sciences and the Ministry of Higher Education. A product of the Higher Party School and the Central Committee's Academy of Social Sciences, distinguished only by his 'phenomenal ignorance coupled with extreme self-confidence', he was the laughing-stock of the anti-Stalinist intelligentsia whom he now set out to tame. In every respect the *alter ego* of the 'tedious, untalented bureaucrat' Brezhnev, Trapeznikov was the embodiment of bureaucratic reaction against the Twentieth and Twenty-second Congresses.[5]

The twentieth anniversary of the Soviet victory over Nazism provided the occasion for a neo-Stalinist counter-offensive, with the tacit connivance of Brezhnev and his supporters in the presidium. Spring

1965 saw Trapeznikov and the Director of the Institute of Marxism–Leninism, Pospelov, campaign to revive the myth of Stalin the 'Great Military Leader'. Pospelov's institute actually submitted theses to the Central Committee presidium that would have effectively rehabilitated Stalin. Though the theses were not adopted, at the twentieth anniversary victory celebrations Brezhnev gave renewed respectability to Stalin's wartime record as chairman of the State Committee of Defence.[6] Then came Trapeznikov's sinister proposal. At a conference of social science instructors, which met in November 1965 to consider the forthcoming third edition of the *History of the CPSU*, he proposed re-issuing the *Short Course*. A lone voice was raised against Trapeznikov's threat, that of the historian A. P. Kuchkin.[7]

The following year, with the Twenty-third Congress impending, the campaign to recoup Stalin's reputation gathered pace. An article published in *Pravda* in January 1966 repudiated the term '*period* of the cult of the personality' in relation to Stalin as 'un-Marxist'.[8] The signatories came from the highest echelons of the historical profession: the academic secretary of the Academy of Sciences' Division of History, Academician Zhukov, his deputy V. I. Shunkov and the editor-in-chief of *Voprosy istorii*, V. G. Trukhanovsky. According to Aleksandr Nekrich, this article was nothing less than a call to revise the relevant decisions of the Twentieth and Twenty-second Congresses.[9] The trial of the writers Daniel and Sinyavsky, which opened a month later, was both a 'watershed' in the neo-Stalinist offensive and for the liberal intelligentsia: it effectively triggered the rise of the human rights and dissident movement.[10] The threat of Stalin's rehabilitation at the forthcoming party congress was headed off by a letter of protest signed by some of the most illustrious representatives of the arts and sciences; among them Academicians Sakharov and Kapitsa. There was only one professional historian among the signatories, the medievalist, Academician S. D. Skazkin (Danilova's intellectual patron).[11] But within the Institute of History, steps had already been taken to defend academic autonomy and resist Trapeznikov's neo-Stalinist offensive.

The 'democratic' *partkom*

Khrushchev's dismissal, despite the fears of his opponents, had largely been received with popular indifference,[12] publicly at least. Khrushchev's 'carrot and stick' approach to the intelligentsia,[13] which had looked to him for reform, had taken its toll. Nevertheless, within the party committee (*partkom*) of the Institute of History a 'rearguard action'[14] to forestall the gathering neo-Stalinist offensive was undertaken by several historians who had been at the heart of historical revisionism.

Developments within the *partkom* reflected the changed generational balance of forces within the Institute of History that existed at the beginning of the 1960s. The younger anti-Stalinist historians promoted by Sidorov began to challenge the entrenched older generation of Stalinists. In 1962–63 a general 'deadlock' existed within the 15-member *partkom*, which virtually paralyzed it – much to the satisfaction of the director of the institute, Khvostov.[15] In these circumstances Tarnovsky and Danilov, then deputy *partkom* secretary, in spring 1964 declined to stand for re-election to the next *partkom*. Soon after, Khrushchev was ousted; it quickly became apparent that all the hopes for the continued liberalization of academic life had come to nought. As we saw above, the very first of the revisionist historians to feel the chill of neo-Stalinism was Danilov. He bore the brunt of the neo-Stalinist offensive against the *'ekstremisty'* that gathered pace after the overthrow of Khrushchev.[16] The campaign against Danilov's history of collectivization made it clear what lay in store for revisionism in general.

In this context, events spilled over into the party committee of the Institute of History. In November 1965 Danilov and Tarnovsky were elected to the committee by an overwhelming majority. Feelings ran high: 90 per cent of the 260 party members in the institute who voted, did so in favour of Danilov and Tarnovsky. Drabkin, Nekrich and Yevgeny Plimak, a student of Gefter and an active participant in the Sector of Methodology, were also elected. The generational balance that had hitherto existed in the *partkom* had now shifted decisively in favour of the 'young anti-Stalinist generation'.[17]

An exceptional situation had arisen where neither the director of the institute, Khvostov, nor his first deputy L. S. Gaponenko, had been elected to the party committee; indeed, their nominations had been rejected. Effectively, this was a vote of no confidence in Khvostov's administration by the institute's research collective. Matters were further complicated by the election of Tarnovsky as *partkom* secretary. Tarnovsky's outspoken critique of chauvinist conceptions of Russian imperialism under the Tsars as un-Marxist had not endeared him to the institute's director. The 'apprehensive' Khvostov conspired against Tarnovsky's election through an intermediary: the second secretary of the October *raikom* in Moscow: B. N. Chaplin. Chaplin spoke against Tarnovsky's election as *partkom* secretary. After two meetings the impasse was apparently resolved with the nomination of Danilov for the position by Tarnovsky, at the suggestion of Chaplin. Khvostov, according to Nekrich, reluctantly resorted to Danilov in the hope that he could keep Danilov under his thumb.[18] Khvostov was mistaken – as Danilov's principled research record should have told him.

In his capacity as secretary of the *partkom,* Danilov was scrupulously democratic in dealing with the attacks on it by its Stalinist opponents; according to Nekrich, to the detriment of the 'democratic' *partkom* itself. The progressive majority of the *partkom* saw as its principal agenda the establishment of an atmosphere in the institute that would be most conducive to creative intellectual activity, freed of the fear of being accused of 'political crimes'. In 1965 the 'authority of the *partkom* was at an all-time high'. According to Nekrich,

> these were wonderful months. A year after the departure of Khrushchev, the ideas established by the Twentieth and Twenty-second Congresses of the CPSU had become an integral part of the internal life of the institute.

In this atmosphere, feeling confident of support from the *partkom*, historians were emboldened to freely voice their opinions. This situation began to resonate throughout other institutes as well; the *partkom* was approached for advice on supporting a professor in Moscow State University who had been dismissed for refusing to testify in the Daniel-Sinyavsky trial. Danilov's name had become synonymous with a progressive approach in the social sciences.[19]

A vital step along this road was the decision of the 'democratic' *partkom* to undertake its own analysis of the state of the discipline. The upshot was the controversial report 'On the State of Historical Science', the principle authors of which were Danilov and Tarnovsky.[20] This report was presented by Danilov on 19 February 1966 to a closed meeting of 371 party members in the Institute of History.[21]

In many respects the report was a rejoinder to the mitigation of Stalin's crimes by Zhukov *et al.*, who in their *Pravda* article blamed Khrushchev's 'voluntarism' for the decline in the status of history. In the *partkom* report Stalin was personally held responsible for the degradation of historical science.[22] The report hailed the achievements in historical science since the Twentieth Congress, facilitated by the 'democratization' of both public and academic life. The 'right' to resolve academic argument by discussion, rather than administrative intervention, had been bolstered by a number of ideological, juridical and organizational measures. Two broad phases of the advancement of historical writing were distinguished. Initially, roughly to the end of the 1950s, it was a matter of dealing with 'specific questions', such as the status of Ivan the Terrible. But this had occurred essentially within the old framework. At the beginning of the 1960s, however, a number of questions were broached which impinged directly on themes 'forbidden' or falsely conceptualized in the *Short Course,* such as populism, collectivization and Russian imperialism. This had ushered in the 'lawful', 'second stage' of the development of history: the overcoming of outmoded conceptions, which was signified by an increasing emphasis on theory and methodology.[23] An overview which, not incidentally, accords with my argument that encounters by historians with an increasing number of anomalies in their research had paved the way for a paradigm shift.

According to the report, however, the very achievements of historical science had only exacerbated the tension between its development and its poor public standing; a tension given urgent expression in the report:

> It is hardly possible to name another period in the history of science as a whole, which has been so fruitful. Never before has there been such an efficacious struggle with dogmatism, rote learning and citationism, as has occurred during the years since the XX Congress of the party. Never before has our science witnessed such a broadening out of the research problematic. Never before, as now, has the practice of research led historians so earnestly to broaden and deepen the front of theoretical and methodological investigations and generalizations. Democratization of all public life in our country, of all ideological work and, in particular, the democratization of our research environment, such is the main condition for advancing from one conquest to another.
>
> Nevertheless, despite all this, probably never have there been such persistent cries concerning the decline of interest in history and of the 'prestige' of historical science. These assertions and reproaches come from writers and artists, publishers and booksellers, as well as secondary and tertiary history teachers ... Above all, such cries are far from infrequent among the historians themselves ... Why has this situation arisen? The most general answer to this question would be: *the tempo of the development of our science has turned out to be insufficient to satisfy the demands which our society is making on history.*
>
> The main task of our science, like any other science, is the cognition of truth. But in distinction from the exact sciences, historical science

also has a most important social function – the formation of the sociopolitical world-view of the members of our society.[24]

Here we see a self-conscious concern on the part of these revisionist historians with the social function of their discipline. Accordingly, we can discern their development not just as scholars but as intellectuals, in the sense that Nettl has defined them, whose collective voice has a public resonance above and beyond their immediate professional concerns.

The report identified the continued presence of the *figura umolchaniya* (the device of omission) in historical science as the immediate cause of the degradation of history and its educative function.[25] A central manifestation of the *figura umolchaniya* in historical writing was the silence, or at best negative treatment, accorded to the Bolshevik leaders who had allegedly strayed from Leninism. The *figura umolchaniya* was extended to scientific problems that Danilov's Group had been addressing: *viz.*, defining the relationship between the end of the New Economic Policy and the changes introduced in 1927–29, as well as 'errors' and 'distortions' incurred in the course of industrialization and collectivization. Of increasing concern, according to the report, was the recent tendency to 'apply the *figura umolchaniya* to Stalin himself' – a scarcely veiled reference to Zhukov's recent attempt to attenuate the nexus between Stalin and the 'cult of the personality':

> This might be seen as science taking its 'historical revenge', but in the end it would lose out. A view has developed that silence is the best method of struggling with the cult of the personality. But a positive outcome cannot be achieved by resorting to the methods engendered by the cult itself.

Finally, the report provocatively charged that behind the resilience of the *figura umolchaniya* in historical science lay not just the bad habits of Soviet historical practice, but a sinister conspiracy by unnamed forces: 'living people, who cannot and do not want to break with the *figura umolchaniya*, in so far as she has been their long-standing colleague and co-author.'[26]

The audacious challenge of Danilov and Tarnovsky to the gathering campaign to rehabilitate Stalin and his regime in historical science provoked an animated discussion. One contributor, Petr Lisovsky, captured perfectly the essence of the report when he described it as a 'programme of struggle for the transformation of Soviet historiography into a genuine science'.[27] Lisovsky and others saw the report as a necessary rebuff to the attempt by Zhukov *et al.*, contrary to the line of the Twenty-second Congress, to reimpose 'forbidden zones' in history – itself a manifestation of the notorious problem of 'conjuncturalism' in historical writing, whereby the academic agenda was determined by the latest party resolution. Once again history was threatened with being reduced to a mere 'appendage to politics'.[28]

In this respect, a central target of those who supported the report was the entire system of reviews and censorship which deprived the Institute's Academic Council, let alone the author, of the right to authorize publication; and thereby diminished the historian's self-esteem. Glavlit was singled out as crucial to the role of the *figura umolchaniya*: erasing the names of prominent Bolsheviks from the historical slate. It had even demanded that the 'cult of the personality' not be mentioned; thereby placing itself above the party.[29] Plimak argued that the bureaucratization of Soviet intellectual life impeded historians posing the bold questions; in this sense the *figura umolchaniya* was 'organically' reinforced by the '*figura vyzhidaniya*' (the device of wait-and-see): awaiting questions and solutions from on high.[30] Similarly, the prominent New Direction historian Avrekh saw 'political expediency' – adapting to the latest political formula – as a root cause of the demise of the status of historical science. He saw the 'word-play' around the formula the 'cult of the personality' as an obstacle to a serious investigation of the Stalin phenomenon. Should historians play Zhukov's renewed word-games, out of a misplaced sense of 'political expediency', then this could only be to the further detriment of their discipline.[31]

Hardly surprisingly, Khvostov was less than sympathetic to the tenor of the report and the discussion. For him the *figura umolchaniya* was an expression of the failure of historians themselves to treat the past consistently and 'scientifically'. Khvostov, defending the Zhukov article in *Pravda*, expressed particular concern about historians neglecting the impact of 'subjectivism' on historical writing, while overemphasizing the shortcomings of the 'cult of the personality', thereby losing sight of the 'positive' aspects of past 'mistakes'![32] Danilov, in his concluding remarks, answered this last piece of sophistry brilliantly: the 'mistakes of the cult of the personality and those of subjectivism' were not of a different order – they were 'one and the same'.[33]

For all Danilov's polemical skill, Khvostov held the trump card: the issues raised by the 'democratic' *partkom* would be decided by the forthcoming party congress, after which a new *partkom* would be elected.[34] This was confirmation of Lisovsky's incisive caution: the report's 'programme of action' was only the 'first step'; the *partkom* would need all the support it could get to ensure its implementation.[35]

The report itself argued that the only guarantee of addressing its concerns about the state of the discipline was the complete 'decentralization' and 'democratization' of the Institute of History.[36] According to Nekrich, the party committee hoped to 'free the institute's researchers from their humiliating dependence on the will of the administration'.[37] To this end, the party committee proposed a number of measures. Firstly, restricting administrators from 'monopolizing' more than one post. Secondly, extending the 'principle of elected positions' – which already applied to the director, heads of sectors, and research associates – to deputy directors, heads of departments and the Academic Council.[38] The latter proposal was crucial. Appointments to the Academic Council were usually made by the administration, reducing it to a mere 'consultative' role and, as the report tactfully put it, 'opening up the possibility for the administration to interfere in purely scientific questions in which it was not always competent'. It was proposed that this elected council have '*exclusive* competence' in academic matters – 'not subject to abrogation by the administration.'[39] Thirdly, the election of editors and editorial boards of journals by those competent in the field would place the editorial boards under the control of the appropriate research collective in the institute. Finally, it was argued that the institute party organizations have 'control' over both the Academic Council and the administration,[40] a suggestion that was opposed even by some of the *partkom*'s allies.[41]

The *partkom*'s proposals undoubtedly would have turned academic life upside down. They would have made the administration of the institute far more responsible to the research collective and the party organization. In fact the *partkom* attempted to demolish one of the pillars of Khvostov's authority in the institute: the 'do-nothings' (*bezdel'niki*) whom Khvostov, as part of his divide-and-rule approach, set upon recalcitrant scholars, intimidating them with political accusations. Khvostov fiercely resisted an attempt by the *partkom* to replace N. Samorukov, its secretary in 1962–63 and Director of the Sector of Contemporary West European History, which was a bastion of the *bezdel'niki*. However, the broad proposals for reorganization never came to fruition, as 'new ideological storms swept the party committee ship into a turbulent sea'.[42]

In March–April 1966, the Twenty-third Congress took place. The *partkom* report, though authorized for publication, was suppressed on

20 April 1966 by Glavlit as 'slanderous' to the CPSU.[43] Reporting back from the congress, Khvostov stressed the practical contribution that the party expected of the social sciences; and collective research as the most appropriate, effective means of achieving this. While paying lip-service to the costs of the legacy of the 'cult of the personality', he reemphasized the importance of *partiinost'* in history and the need for a 'rounded' Leninist approach which did not 'exaggerate mistakes' in isolation from other developments.[44]

While discussion around the report was more subdued than that which occurred in February, it was not without sparks. The revisionist historians endorsed Khvostov's concerns about organizational problems in history – though to rather different ends. Sof'ya Yakubovskaya called for an end to 'falsely understood collegiality', 'bureaucratism', 'over-cautiousness' and 'ugly traditions' whereby scientific polemic amounted to 'condemnation'.[45] As a prime example of 'disorganization' L. N. Shatrova cited the impediments to the publication of Danilov's two volumes on collectivization.[46] Danilov himself hailed recognition of the fact that history had more than 'propagandistic' importance, which he saw as an 'element of the ideology of the cult of the personality'. But the practical application of history required the elimination of the notorious *figura umolchaniya*. Danilov, however, took the question beyond the organizational obstacles to historical writing, such as censorship. In a speech that was punctuated by applause, he warned that the real obstacle was 'internal' to the historians themselves: the danger was that they would respond to the renewed 'threat' to critical research by 'timidity', 'conservatism of thought' and by shrinking from the thorny questions. Urging his colleagues to 'be on guard', Danilov argued that the best weapon for combating 'bureaucratism' and administrative interference was the 'public opinion of the party organization and of the entire institute collective'.[47]

In the two-year conflict between Khvostov and the *partkom*, the former relied on the support of the Central Committee's Department of Science, the Presidium of the Academy of Sciences and the *raikom*. The 'democratic' *partkom*, while trying to avoid a direct confrontation with any one of these organizations, looked to the collective and party organization of the institute.[48] In its first year – until November 1966 – the 'democratic' *partkom* received support from other party organizations; there were even attempts to organize resistance to Brezhnev's 'turn' within the Moscow party organizations.[49] The anti-Stalinists were rewarded by an overwhelming vote of confidence – six to one – in their favour for a second term. The original five in Danilov's detachment were now reinforced by Gorodetsky, who specialized in Lenin's contribution to historical writing, Yakubovskaya and the old Bolshevik, Mark Volin.[50] The neo-Stalinist tide, however, was already running strongly against them. They had lost the battle to publish the history of collectivization. Now it was a matter of holding the line: of maintaining their organization and securing whatever space remained for genuine research. This included 'extremely active support' for the Sector of Methodology.[51] The presence of Drabkin, who was Danilov's deputy in the *partkom*, together with Plimak, enabled direct cooperation around the shared concerns of both organizations; and there was close, regular consultation with Gefter, although he was not a member of the *partkom*.[52] The *partkom* also took up the cause of Nekrich – the revisionist historian of the Great Patriotic War. At this point the fate of the *partkom*, and that of historical revisionism as a whole, intertwined with that of Nekrich.

The Nekrich affair

The twentieth anniversary of the triumph of the Red Army over Hitler's forces was the occasion for a flood of articles hailing this feat of Soviet arms. The ideological ebb that followed Khrushchev's dismissal was, as we saw above, accompanied by an attempt to reevaluate Stalin's role in the war. This gradual reversal of the historical record was rudely interrupted in October 1965 when Nekrich published his revisionist *June 22, 1941*.[53] Nekrich's basic thesis was that Stalin's 'mistakes' were directly responsible for the disastrous military defeats inflicted by Germany following the undeclared attack on the USSR in June 1941. Stalin had ignored all the warnings he had been given in late 1940–early 1941, including by Soviet military intelligence, of an impending German attack on the USSR. Stalin had dismissed these warnings as an attempt by Britain to provoke a war between the Soviet Union and Germany.[54]

Nekrich's book was really only echoing the line of the Twentieth and Twenty-second Congresses and the Central Committee resolution of June 1956 which acknowledged Stalin's culpability for these mistakes. But in late 1965 there was a concerted campaign underway to reverse these judgements – and therefore the party line.[55] In fact, Nekrich's argument, in its final published form, was considerably softened under pressure from his editors: Hitler's attack, for example, became merely 'treacherous', rather than 'treacherous and sudden' (the latter formulation presumably implying that the Soviet leadership was caught off-guard).[56] Having run the gauntlet of five different censors, including that of the KGB which alone opposed publication entirely, *June 22, 1941* was finally published by the Academy of Sciences' press, 'Nauka', then headed by the liberal academician, A. M. Samsonov. Nevertheless, the storm that was about to break around Nekrich's text was intimated by the ominous silence with which was it was received in the academic journals. Tvardovsky's *Novyi mir* alone reviewed it, and very favourably – in these times the kiss of death.[57]

The trial of Daniel and Sinyavsky in February 1966, it should be remembered, was a watershed between the Khrushchev and Brezhnev eras.[58] That same month a discussion of Nekrich's book, instigated by Glavlit, was scheduled in the Institute of Marxism–Leninism's Division of the History of the Great Patriotic War.[59] Before a large audience, Nekrich faced his chief prosecutor, Professor G. A. Deborin. Deborin focused on three questions: the alleged unpreparedness of the USSR for the German attack; the non-aggression pact of 23 August 1939; and the prewar elimination of Soviet military leaders, such as Marshal M. N. Tukhachevsky.[60]

In relation to Soviet military unpreparedness, Deborin attempted to shift the blame away from Stalin and his circle to the secondary leadership: the General Staff's military intelligence unit and IMEMO for underestimating German economic and military capacity.[61] Deborin took exception to Nekrich's accusation, according to Nekrich made for the very first time in the literature, that the non-aggression pact was to the decided advantage of Germany. Usually this had been presented as an 'adroit manoeuvre' on the part of the Soviet leadership.[62] Finally, a storm was raised in the audience when Deborin tried to defend the Military Collegium of the Supreme Court against Nekrich's accusation that the sentences handed out to Tukhachevsky and his colleagues were based on fabrications.[63]

According to Nekrich's account, of the 22 contributors to the discussion, 21 spoke in favour of his book. Such an outcome was undoubtedly, as Nekrich himself has suggested, a victory for anti-Stalinist historiography.[64] But herein lay the political threat: Nekrich's analysis had exposed the entrenched inadequacies of the Soviet political and military leadership and the decision-making apparatus over which they presided.[65] It soon became apparent that those in the establishment who yearned to rehabilitate Stalin were intent on using Nekrich's monograph as a warning to anti-Stalinist historical revisionism in general.

The campaign was relentless. In mid-1966 the Chairman of the Committee on Press Affairs, N. Mikhailov, pressured the Presidium of the Academy of Sciences for further consideration of *June 22, 1941*. Though apparently nothing came of this, during a Central Committee ideological conference in October 1966 Nekrich's book was bitterly denounced by leading members of the Georgian and Belorussian communist parties. Apart from allegations that Nekrich had defiled the Soviet government and the communist party for their alleged concessions to Hitler's Germany, questions were raised about how it had come about that the minutes of the discussion in the Institute of Marxism–Leninism had been published in the Western press.[66] Despite reassurances to Nekrich from the Department of Propaganda and Agitation that the affair had been laid to rest in the Central Committee,[67] the campaign continued. During the December 1966 elections for the institute *partkom*, there was 'furious' opposition to Nekrich's nomination, especially from Khvostov's deputy, A. N. Shtrakhov. Though Nekrich was comfortably reelected – 200 votes for, 100 against – *June 22, 1941* itself was again severely criticized. In good part this was due to the sympathetic treatment it had received in the Western and East European press, especially the Czechoslovak, which Nekrich seems to have cultivated.[68]

In early 1967 the campaign gathered momentum. Following further attacks on Nekrich in the Moscow Party Committee, Khvostov urged him to acknowledge his errors, which Nekrich refused to do. Then came the heavy artillery: the Central Committee control commission. The pretext for this was the publication in March 1967 of an article in *Der Spiegel* about the Nekrich affair in which it was stated that Brezhnev had sought to rehabilitate Stalin. Alerted to this accusation by Trapeznikov, Brezhnev immediately ordered the control commission to inquire into *June 22, 1941*, the publication of the record of discussion about it in the Institute of Marxism–Leninism, and utilization of the book in bourgeois propaganda.[69]

Nekrich's first session with the control commission began on 22 May 1967. Apart from the two commission investigators, Nekrich was 'surprised' to find Shtrakhov present as an active witness for the inquiry. This was tantamount to the institute administration actively conniving with the control commission, that is, of bringing academic concerns into the political arena. The pivotal question that the commission addressed to Nekrich was: 'What ... is more important – political expediency or historical truth?' In effect, what was at stake was not the veracity or otherwise of Nekrich's views as a historian about the unpreparedness of the Soviet Union for a German attack, but whether it was politically apposite to raise this question now. In other words, at issue was whether 'conjuncturalism' should govern historical research and writing. 'Conjuncturalism', which was a hotly debated question around this time, had been vehemently opposed by the partisans of the 'democratic' *partkom*. Not surprisingly, then, Nekrich's attempt to avoid the question by replying that 'historical truth' was a prerequisite of 'political expediency' did not satisfy his interrogators.[70]

The gravity with which the party leadership viewed the Nekrich affair was confirmed by the decision to discuss it at a meeting of the control commission to be overseen by the chairman of the party commission himself, Politburo member A. Ya. Pel'she. At this session, which was attended by among others the Director of the Institute of Marxism–Leninism, Pospelov, and the editor-in-chief of *Voprosy istorii KPSS*, Kosul'nikov, the charges against Nekrich were presented in detail. He was accused of counterposing the total mobilization of Germany to the unpreparedness of the Soviet Union and 'whitewashing' the policies of Britain, France and the USA, conceptions that were similar to those of 'bourgeois' historians; including as German, territory that was actually occupied, thereby playing into the hands of German revanchism; slandering the Soviet government by depicting the non-aggression pact as advantageous only to Germany; claiming there was deliberate annihilation of the military leadership; asserting that the principal cause of the war was German fear of a coalition between the USSR, Britain and France, thereby justifying Hitler's thesis of a 'preventative' war and exonerating the real culprits – the 'monopolies'; relying on foreign rather than Soviet documentation; and implying that Soviet victory was 'not inevitable'. All of these lapses were compounded by Nekrich's failure to distance himself from anti-party remarks made at the Institute of Marxism–Leninism discussion, such as those of the old Bolshevik A. V. Snegov. In sum, Nekrich had capitulated to 'bourgeois ideology'.[71]

The party *coup de grâce* was not long in coming: 'Nekrich has lost his *partiinost'*. There is no place for him in the party'. He was expelled from the CPSU on 28 June 1967.[72]

In the course of the investigation Nekrich, by his own account, had boldly denounced the control commission accusations against him as nothing more than a 'camouflaged' example of recent attempts to exonerate the Stalin leadership for the disastrous reverses of June 1941. Nekrich saw his subsequent expulsion, quite rightly, as the act of those hardened Stalinists who, despite themselves, had been forced over the past decade to go along with the Central Committee's anti-Stalin campaign, although they had attempted to 'sabotage' it by construing it in their own interests.[73] Now they had their revenge.

Nekrich moved quickly to appeal against his expulsion. On 4 July 1967 he appealed directly to the Politburo to review the decision of the party control commission. When he received the written resolution of the commission, which accused him of 'premeditated distortion' of party and government policy in *June 22, 1941*, fearing this formulation opened the way to criminal charges he appealed directly to Brezhnev, protesting both the formulation and his expulsion.[74] It was precisely at this point that the Nekrich affair intersected with the fate of the 'democratic' *partkom,* in which Nekrich had been an active participant. But it was also the parting of the ways with his erstwhile allies.

According to Nekrich, from the very start he had seen the campaign against him as a mere cover for the real objective: the elimination of the 'democratic' *partkom* and its anti-Stalinist stance. Unable to vote them out, a pretext was required to remove them.[75] Confirmation of his suspicions was provided by the fifth point of the control commission decisions: it recommended establishing a commission to inquire into and 'assist' (*sic*) the activities of the party organization in the Institute of History.[76] Nekrich claims that his first priority had been to ensure the survival of the *partkom*.[77] The day of his expulsion Nekrich urged his colleagues not to defend him – for the sake of the party committee.[78] On 1 September 1967, however, he asked in writing for the *partkom* to support an appeal against his expulsion. Here, relations between Nekrich and his comrades began to sour. Here, too, Nekrich's interpretation of events begins to diverge from that of his former allies.

According to Nekrich's account, both Danilov and his deputy Drabkin promised to support his request in the *partkom*. However, neither kept their promise, on the grounds, as Danilov put it, that 'we cannot sacrifice the interests of the collective of the institute for the sake of one person'. Nekrich took this alleged '180 degree turn' by the *partkom* leadership as a personal betrayal and saw it as the 'beginning of the end' for the 'democratic' *partkom*, which, he says, subsequently lost credibility among its supporters in the institute. Danilov, in particular, was condemned for his shortsightedness.[79]

Danilov, however, argues that Nekrich's account downplays the support given to him by the *partkom* prior to his expulsion. In part, Danilov attributes this to Nekrich's concern, when publishing his account, for the well-being of those who remained behind after he departed for the West in 1976.[80] Further, the situation after his expulsion was, according to Danilov, rather more complicated than Nekrich presents it.

Only two courses were open to the *partkom*: either to protest the decision of the control commission, despite the party rules requiring a lower party body to accept the decision of a higher one, or to appeal to the party General Secretary to review the decision. Between July and September 1967 an acrimonious split developed within the party committee over which course to pursue. Drabkin, Yakubovskaya and Mikhail Al'perovich supported the first; Danilov and Tarnovsky supported the second (as did Volobuev),[81] fearing the consequences not only for the *partkom* but also for those who had supported it, and hence for the viability of the institute party organization as a whole. This would have only played into the hands of Trapeznikov and of the control commission, which was intent on destroying the 'democratic' *partkom* which it deemed to be 'ideologically bankrupt, and controlled by revisionist elements or groups'.[82] In the end the less-confrontationist course of Danilov and Tarnovsky prevailed; but this was not enough to save the 'democratic' *partkom*. It was dissolved at the end of January 1968; fresh elections in February saw a completely new *partkom*, with a new secretary, Volobuev, who seemed to offer the administration an end to confrontation within the institute.[83] As *partkom* secretary, Volobuev said, he sought 'to smooth over' the Nekrich affair. In his speeches at Moscow party meetings he argued that Nekrich's punishment was incommensurate with his alleged crime; after all, Nekrich had said nothing more in his book than in the sixth volume of *The History of the Great Patriotic War*.[84]

The ousting of the 'democratic' *partkom* was the end of a bold experiment; it had become synonymous with a new, principled approach to party office. Hitherto the post of *partkom* secretary, 'in the pocket' of the institute director, had been a stepping-stone to more privileged positions, such as a deputy directorship. This had been the reward given to the arch-Stalinist Shtrakhov, a hostile member of the *partkom*, for servility to Khvostov. The progressive *partkom* members, however, did not identify membership of the committee with personal advantage. In this respect Danilov was unique: he was the first *partkom* secretary whose career suffered as a consequence of holding this office.[85]

Above all, the 'democratic' *partkom* constituted one of those 'invisible colleges' that nurtured and encouraged innovative historical thinking and research; this microculture also provided a meeting place between the private academic concerns of the genuine scholars and their public concerns. There they could articulate the contribution they envisaged they as historians could make to the Soviet socialist ideal and Soviet society as a whole. As Gefter put it in a speech in support of the *partkom*'s reelection, which was received with 'prolonged applause':

> For the first time in a number of years our party organization has been transformed or, more precisely, has begun to be transformed – not in form but in essence – into the *leading, independent* factor of scientific and socio-political life of our Institute. This is a great conquest, which needs to be preserved and strengthened ... I think that our *partkom* knew in this regard how to make a definite step forward; it knew how to correctly ascertain the place which historians must occupy in the overall party structure, having pushed to the fore, in this connection, the *problem of historical experience*, and of its assimilation and inclusion in the real, present-day development of our country ... There is still one question which is exceptionally sharp and pressing, and I think, rightly so: this is the question of the influence of the results of our historical research on the populace at large, above all, on the youth; on that generation which grew up after the war, which remembers little but which experienced early in their lives the difficult spiritual catastrophe connected with the unmasking of the cult of the personality ... This is why the problem of [historical] experience cannot but remain one of the most central for historian-communists.[86]

In the course of his speech Gefter also called for the institute *partkom* to strengthen its links with the

> entire party organization, having thought through, in particular, the ripening question of the strengthening of local party organizations and the creation of more energetic and influential inter-sectoral [that is, horizontal] party collectives.

This question of the democratization of the party and Soviet society seems to have been increasingly on Gefter's mind. A year earlier, in the same speech to the party in which he had criticized Trapeznikov, Gefter urged the 'development of soviet democracy in all relations, from bottom to top' in order to counteract 'a certain danger of the problem of bureaucracy'. He even went so far as to suggest that unless the party embraced Lenin's injunctions on popular participation 'the movement of our society towards communism is impossible'.[87]

The *partkom* thus provided a dais for those who in every sense conformed to Nettl's criterion of intellectuals as the bearers of qualitatively new ideas capable, potentially at least, of being projected into 'socio-structural dissent'. For this reason, the existence of the 'democratic' *partkom* was incompatible with the Brezhnev reaction.

Danilov and Gefter agreed, between themselves, that the dissolution of the 'democratic' *partkom* constituted a decisive break in their lives.[88] Yet it was but a prelude to the break up of the Institute of History as a whole. For some time now there had been a commission of inquiry, set up by the Presidium of the Academy of Sciences, into the need to reorganize the institute, ostensibly on the grounds of its 'unmanageability'. In reality its objective was to 'atomize' the *kollektiv* within the institute,[89] which had generated such centres of anti-Stalinist history as the New Direction, Danilov's Group on the Soviet peasantry, the *partkom* itself, and the Sector of Methodology. All this took place against the background of the 'Prague spring', which directly impacted on Soviet historical revisionism. In 1967 M. Reiman's *The Russian Revolution* was published in Prague, with the authorization of the Czechoslovak party despite Moscow's dissatisfaction. Reiman drew heavily on the work of such luminaries of the New Direction as Gindin, Volobuev and Tarnovsky, to cast doubt on the unqualified definition of the October Revolution as socialist. Reiman's work was condemned by the Moscow Institute of Marxism–Leninism as a slur on the 'entire Soviet historiography of October'; no mention was made of the New Direction.[90]

Opinions on this proposed division of the Institute of History varied widely, even among the progressive and liberal historians. Volobuev, for instance, supported the proposal because he believed the Soviet Union required an institute dedicated exclusively to its own national history.[91] The 'democratic' *partkom*, however, had opposed division of the institute. It wanted to retain one institute as an integrating body in the face of the recent proliferation of research institutions usually organized according to the geographical focus of their research.[92]

Aside from the need to quash historical revisionism there were more personal factors at work here. Trapeznikov's support for the division of the institute, Nekrich suggests, was motivated by vindictiveness, following his failure to be elected a member of the Academy of Sciences in 1966, for which he blamed his arch-rival in the field of Soviet agrarian history, Danilov, in particular.[93] Trapeznikov gained support for his project from conservative historians by 'deftly' exploiting the 'bitter' competition to obtain highly-paid positions of institute directors and deputy-directors. In August 1968, at the very moment when Soviet forces were snuffing-out the Czechoslovak experiment in socialist democracy, Trapeznikov finally had his way. By a resolution of the Central Committee Secretariat and the Presidium of the Academy of

Sciences, the Institute of History was divided into two smaller, more manageable, institutions: the Institute of World History and the Institute of the History of the USSR.[94] The bitter clash between the New Direction and Cherepnin at the April conference with the Italian historians was symptomatic of the passions aroused by this issue.[95] Now, with the dissolution of the Institute of History, the research 'atmosphere' changed entirely.[96] Bovykin and D. A. Koval'chenko abandoned their former colleagues and went over to the conservative side in a 'furious "fight to the death"' against revisionism.[97] Fearful of losing their positions, the revisionist historians were on the defensive against the conservatives, who now occupied the administrative apparatuses. The situation was somewhat calmer in the Institute of World History, of which Zhukov became director, than in the Institute of the History of the USSR, where the new director was the former head of the Institute of Archaeology, Rybakov – infamous for his Russian chauvinism and anti-Semitism.[98]

The neo-Stalinist offensive within the institutes of history coincided with Soviet armed intervention in Czechoslovakia, which had a devastating impact on the liberal intelligentsia as a whole. For Neretina, for example, 21 August 1968 was a dark day, signalling the final 'collapse' of expectations raised by the Twentieth Congress.[99] Gefter, after 1968, considered that the 'potentialities within the party were virtually exhausted' – although he remained a member until 1982.[100] Both these comments bear out Kagarlitsky's view that 'on the morning of 21 August 1968 the entire ideology of Soviet liberalism collapsed in a few minutes, and all the hopes aroused by the Twentieth Congress fell to the ground'.[101]

The 'profound indignation' over the invasion of Czechoslovakia on the part of the progressive intelligentsia within the party manifested itself in different ways. According to Nekrich, some became cynical careerists (contributing to the corruption of the party apparatus under Brezhnev);[102] others, some of whom subsequently became dissidents, 'cursed' Soviet society; while others remained within the CPSU but severed their 'spiritual ties' with the system.[103] Though protests were largely *sotto voce*,[104] for Nekrich, the invasion of Czechoslovakia in August 1968 marked 'one of the turning points in the history of Soviet society. It meant the beginning of a genuine rebirth of the spirit of the intelligentsia in the Soviet Union.'[105] Nekrich's observation, however, rests on the view that genuine *intelligentnost'* was synonymous with intellectual alienation from state and society. To this extent it differs from the basic argument here: in mapping the emergence of historical revisionism we are witnessing the recrudescence of the *intelligent* tradition in Soviet society; and the decisive catalyst for this was the Twentieth Congress. Just how far intellectual consciousness had shifted in the decade after the Twentieth Congress is indicated also by the fact that there had been little opposition to Khrushchev's intervention in Hungary in 1956.

The evident insecurity of the state and party political elite in regard to the loyalty of the intellectual elite, which as I have suggested constituted an incipient crisis of ideological hegemony for the statocracy, provoked a witch-hunt against this new generation of *intelligenty*, spurred on by shrill cries for the 'purification' of Marxism–Leninism through a relentless struggle against revisionism.[106] This neo-Stalinist vendetta was at its most vicious in 1969–70. In March 1969 *Kommunist* published a barely disguised call for the repudiation of the anti-Stalinist line of the Twentieth and Twenty-second Congresses under the heading: 'For Leninist Party Spirit in the Elucidation of the History of the CPSU'.[107] December 1969 saw the last-minute retreat from the *de facto* rehabilitation of Stalin for fear of the outcry from fraternal communist parties in West and Eastern Europe: an article celebrating the 90th anniversary of his birth was withdrawn on the eve of its intended publication in *Pravda* on 21 December. Thereafter, ardent Stalinists such as Trapeznikov had to rest content with the mere 'whitewashing' of Stalin's reputation.[108]

Within the institutes of history the re-politicization of historical science, that is, to make it the dependent variable of the latest Central Committee resolution, proceeded apace; so too did the campaign to stifle dissenting scholarship. As we saw in the previous chapter, the rehabilitators of genuine Marxism and Leninism gathered around the Sector of Methodology felt the full force of this campaign. But it was not only the radical neo-Marxists; in mid-1969 there was an unsuccessful attempt to strip Nekrich of his doctorate. This was followed by an attempt to oust him from his position as a senior researcher in the Institute of World History. In 1970 Nekrich, together with Al'perovich, Gefter and the medievalist Gurevich, was refused permission to be a delegate to the XIII International Congress of Historical Sciences held in Moscow that year; the first three were only allowed to observe.[109]

That same year saw Gurevich arraigned by the Ministry of Higher and Secondary Special Education for his provocative analysis of the origins of feudalism in Western Europe, which challenged the accepted Soviet 'model' of feudalism.[110] Particular exception was taken to his assertion that under feudal society personal relations – of dependence, subordination, and mutual obligation – rather than relations of property and exploitation were paramount. Not surprisingly, Gurevich was accused of undermining the historical materialist conception of the primacy of socio-economic relations by introducing a structuralist-functionalist, idealist explanation for the origins and nature of feudalism. Concerned that Gurevich's book, which was intended as a teaching guide, would 'disorient students and teachers on theoretical questions' the ministry withdrew its imprint from the book in July 1970.[111] Such treatment of Gurevich, onerous enough, paled in comparison to that meted out to active party members such as Gefter or Nekrich; continual harassment eventually led the latter to emigrate in 1976.[112]

Meanwhile, in the Institute of the History of the USSR under Rybakov, Academician Nechkina, despite her ambivalent stance, was subject to sustained attack which ultimately forced her to resign as head of the Sector on the History of Historical Science. Meanwhile, publication of the fifth volume in the series the *History of Historical Science* produced by Nechkina's historiography sector was put on hold.[113] This particular volume, which was edited by Burdzhalov's old friend Yefim Gorodetsky, was not to appear until the advent of *perestroika*.

Volobuev appointed director

In the midst of this vengeful atmosphere a small breathing space appeared with the appointment in 1970 of Volobuev, then a corresponding member of the Academy of Sciences, as Director of the Institute of the History of the USSR in place of Rybakov. Nekrich provides a rather unflattering image of Volobuev as an unprincipled centrist who had failed to stand by him during his joust with the control commission. Volobuev, it will be recalled, had worked in the Department of Science for several years in the mid-1950s. According to Nekrich, because of Volobuev's well-established contacts in the party apparatus his appointment, after a 'prolonged struggle between the contenders', was supported by the arch-Stalinists Trapeznikov and Rybakov.[114]

Volobuev has told the story otherwise; there was no 'struggle' on his part to become director. There were other candidates, such as Samsonov, but he had been too deeply embroiled in the Nekrich affair.[115] Volobuev was already deputy director; having been invited by Rybakov to take up this post. When the position of director came up Volobuev said he accepted it,[116] in the belief that he would then be in the best position to shield his co-thinkers in the New Direction and others, like Danilov, from the 'neo-Stalinist restoration'.[117]

Volobuev's 'Achilles' heel', Nekrich suggests, was his 'professionalism'. Sooner or later, simply for drawing a few unorthodox conclusions about party history, Volobuev was bound to run foul of the conformist party historians ensconced in the Central Committee's Academy of Social Sciences, the Higher Party School and the Institute of Marxism–Leninism. Volobuev, however, was also 'ambitious', and this gave him a 'false sense of security' about his position. On this basis he pursued a course of 'simultaneously' struggling against both 'dogmatism and so-called revisionism', with a slight tilt against 'party conformism'. According to Nekrich, Volobuev even tacitly connived with a few of the researchers in his institute in fostering a 'legend' which portrayed him as 'virtually the defender of all historical science against the attacks of the Stalinists. In fact he played a role that was far different to that attributed to him.'[118] In short, Nekrich was saying, Volobuev played an opportunist role as institute director.

According to Nekrich, Volobuev's first clash with ultra-orthodoxy came during a discussion of *The Proletariat of Russia on the Eve of the February Revolution,* of which Volobuev was the responsible editor. Volobuev 'let slip' a remark that party historians had been 'asleep' for the past 30 years. This apparently raised the ire of hardened Stalinists like the past director of the Institute of Marxism–Leninism, Pospelov, now a secretary of the Central Committee and a member of the Presidium of the Academy of Sciences, and Ivan Petrov, a faculty head in the Academy of Social Sciences. They viewed Volobuev's indiscretion as a 'declaration of war'. Volobuev apparently compounded his situation by quoting from the record of the discussion which exposed the 'ignorance' of his opponents. According to Nekrich, Volobuev, in clashing with Pospelov and his ilk, had overestimated the support he could count on from two powerful ideologists in the Central Committee: Suslov and Ponomarev. When a veiled threat to his position appeared in *Pravda,* Volobuev allegedly sought to reestablish his credibility with his patrons in the political hierarchy by demonstrating his antipathy towards revisionism. He officially reprimanded the principal editor of his anthology, Kir'yanov, and reprimanded the other members of the editorial board, including Volin and 'his own *alter ego,* Tarnovsky'. Nekrich alleges that this was not the first time that Volobuev had resorted to such 'manoeuvres'; he claims that Volobuev had previously denounced the editorial board of volume VIII of the *History of the USSR* for Trotskyism, singling out the chapter on collectivization by S. Borisev, who as a result was forced to quit the Institute of History.[119]

This time, however, claims Nekrich, the tables were turned, and no amount of manoeuvring could save Volobuev. Volobuev's deputy director, Bovykin, who had been appointed from Moscow State University in order to shore up the conservatives, denounced his superior in a letter to the Central Committee. Bovykin accused Volobuev of 'conniving with the revisionists'. On the insistence of Pospelov, the Bureau of the Division of History adopted a resolution concerning the mistakes in the anthology and Volobuev's personal responsibility for them. Volobuev tried to defend himself in a letter to *Voprosy istorii KPSS*, but it was not published. Following a special party meeting convened by Trapeznikov's Department of Science, Volobuev completely 'repented' before the Central Committee. In the course of his confession Volobuev 'sharply criticized' his old colleagues Avrekh and, in particular, Tarnovsky, who had been publicly denounced as a Trotskyite and subsequently denied his doctorate. Following this alleged betrayal, Volobuev then 'requested he be relieved of his duties' as Director of the Institute of the History of the USSR. He was subsequently banished to the Institute of the History of Natural Science and Technology as a senior researcher.[120]

Volobuev, not surprisingly, gives a rather different account of events. He says that Nekrich's account is rather 'unobjective', downplaying as it does the extent to which the institute *kollektiv*, and Volobuev personally, defended Nekrich. Previously expulsion from the party had meant automatic dismissal from the institute. Volobuev maintains that he interceded on Nekrich's behalf with both Demichev, a secretary of the Central Committee, and Zhukov, to keep Nekrich on as a researcher – despite Trapeznikov, whose vendetta against Nekrich was motivated as much as anything by his virulent anti-Semitism. Volobuev says that he did not simply 'condemn' Nekrich for emigrating but pleaded with him to stay and defend those who had defended him, and were now under siege themselves.[121]

Nekrich's account of the demise of Volobuev and his colleagues is somewhat inaccurate. The *coup de grâce* for Volobuev centred on the anthologies *The Overthrow of the Autocracy* and, particularly, *The Russian Proletariat: Profile. Struggle. Hegemony.*[122]

The Overthrow of the Autocracy was, as the name suggests, a collection of papers on the February revolution first delivered at an all-Union conference held in Leningrad in 1967 to celebrate the fiftieth anniversary of the revolution. Many of the controversial contributions in the anthology were made by those associated with the New Direction. Likewise, *The Russian Proletariat* was the product of a conference held in November 1967 to celebrate the silver jubilee of the revolution. Both anthologies bore the stamp of L. M. Ivanov, who was the responsible editor of *The Russian Proletariat* and deputy editor of *The Overthrow of the Autocracy*. Ivanov, a former student of Pankratova, was an important historian who became associated with Sidorov's former students. His death in January 1972, on the eve of the disputation around these books, 'deprived his associates of a voice well known and influential in the Central Committee apparatus'.[123]

The Russian Proletariat might well be described as work-in-progress for a Soviet version of E. P. Thompson's *The Making of the English Working Class*. It was largely concerned with the culture, morality and daily life that shaped the Russian proletariat. These concerns reflected the rediscovery of social psychology by Soviet historians in the early 1960s – particularly by Ivanov, Volobuev and Danilov.[124] Once again, these revisionist historians were picking up a thread from the 1920s – the golden age of Soviet historiography – which had been severed in the early 1930s. There was specific reference to the work of Pankratova.[125] That these anthologies took three years to appear suggests some contention between their editors and the censors.[126] What is striking, however, is that another two years passed before the pogrom began in earnest. Apparently it was only after the 1971 Twenty-fourth Congress that the Brezhnevite apparatus felt confident enough to deliver the *coup de grâce* against the surviving detachments of historical revisionism.

A 'secret' report in June 1972 to the Central Committee from Trapeznikov and Yakovlev, respectively heads of the Departments of Science and of Propaganda, traced the protracted discussion that had taken place concerning these two anthologies. They were first discussed at an (undated) conference on the October Revolution under the auspices of the Institute of the History of the Party under the Leningrad *obkom* and the Ministry of Higher and Middle Specialist Education RSFSR. Discussions were also held in the Faculty of the History of the CPSU in the Central Committee's Academy of Sciences and 9–10 March 1972 in the Institute of the History of the USSR.[127]

The discussion in the institute, a joint session of the Sections for the pre-October and Soviet Periods of the Academic Council, was itself the focus of a resolution adopted by the Academy of Sciences' Division of History.[128] Yu. I. Kir'yanov and Volobuev were censured by name. Kir'yanov for his 'mistaken and confused' assertions that 'from the very beginning of the 1930s ... a schema established itself in the literature which exaggerated the level of consciousness and organization of the proletariat' and in which research of its history 'was to a great degree reduced to a study of its political pronouncements.'[129] Kir'yanov's endorsement of a 'new approach' which had taken hold during the 1960s, particularly in relation to 'spontaneity and consciousness' among the proletariat was condemned as the ' "depoliticization (or "deideologization") of the role of the Russian proletariat'.[130] In other words, he was belittling the decisive role of the Bolshevik party in the events of 1917.

Note was taken of critical remarks directed at Volobuev for his assertion in *The Overthrow of the Autocracy* that after the February Revolution the Russian proletariat 'naturally, was not ready for the role of leader of the new revolution'.[131] Volobuev was allegedly confusing the '*role* of the proletariat as the leader of the revolution ... with the establishment of a political army of the proletariat for the implementation of the revolution, which demanded time.'[132] The resolution censured Volobuev for his inadequate 'self-criticism' in relation to 'errors and confused reasoning' in a number of articles. But what really seems to have goaded Volobuev's academic overlords, was not so much his scholarship as his management of the institute and his shielding of the New Direction historians.[133] Among the recommendations adopted by the bureau to overcome 'serious inadequacies' in the work of the institute was a proposal to 'strengthen the leadership of the Sector of the USSR of the Period of Imperialism'.[134] That at least was to be implemented; with the dismissal of Volobuev the sector, then headed by Anfimov, was dissolved, and its researchers dispersed to other sectors.[135] Tarnovsky, for example, was sent to the Sector of Historical Geography, to help prepare an historical atlas of the USSR.[136]

The campaign against Volobuev and his institute continued unabated. Partial acknowledgement of isolated errors was not enough; total, unconditional surrender was required. Discussions concerning the 'shortcomings' of these works were next held in the Department of Science. Among the participants were Pospelov, in his capacity as Academic Secretary of the Academy of Sciences' Division of History; Fedoseev, vice-president of the Academy of Sciences, and Volobuev himself.[137]

Trapeznikov and Yakovlev had before them a report on the offending works from the rector of the Higher School of the Trade Union Movement (they had also been discussed in the council of this body). The report noted that 'in a number of books recently prepared by the Institute of the History of the USSR have appeared distorted interpretations of several fundamental principles of Marxist–Leninist theory on the characteristics of the working class and its role in the victory of the October revolution'. In particular, these books were marred by

> errors in their treatment of the problems of the hegemony of the proletariat, on the growing over of the bourgeois-democratic revolution into the socialist revolution and on the alliance of the working class and the poor peasantry in the October revolution, and on the leading role of the working class in Soviet society.[138]

In the report, *The Russian Proletariat* was singled out for 'mistakes of a methodological character, while the historical experience of the struggle of the working class was considered from non-party and non-class perspectives'. The attempts by a number of contributors to discuss questions that were allegedly 'resolved long ago' were viewed as 'alarming'. For example, the view of several contributors that 'for a long time in our literature in place of a social "portrait" of the proletariat has been substituted a schema that is devoid of specific content'.[139] The report viewed with marked disquiet Volobuev's assertions that after the February Revolution 'the proletariat, under the sway of petty-bourgeois influence, naturally, was not ready for the role of the leader of the new revolution'.[140]

Moreover, the report alleged there were attempts in the book to 'belittle the consciousness of the working class and its degree of organization, deliberately hushing up the enormous experience of the Russian proletariat in the conduct of the socialist revolution'. For example, statements that in the first decade and a half of the twentieth century 'the mass of the workers still knew little of the aims of socialism and of the means of attaining it, and had an inadequate socialist consciousness'. Similarly, a number of articles were alleged to 'labour' the notion of the 'passivity, backwardness and ignorance' of the Russian proletariat. Several instances of this were given: assertions that 'the proletariat of Russia, in comparison with its contemporary counterparts in the developed countries of Europe, was not only smaller, but less cultured, developed and organized'; that 'millions of proletarians everywhere remained illiterate' and that the 'urban proletariat was culturally backward'. The report took umbrage with characterizations of the working class, on the eve of the October Revolution, as 'still inadequately educated in socialism and inadequately conscious' and also references to various 'pre-revolutionary papers and journals (including those of the working class)' which suggested that 'there are numerous indicators that the workers were coarse and that there was widespread drunkenness'.[141]

The report went on to accuse 'individual authors' of

> ignor[ing] the fact that the centre of the revolutionary movement at the end of the XIX century shifted from Western Europe to Russia and of pass[ing] over in silence the most important factors characterizing the strength of the Russian proletariat: the presence at its head of a revolutionary Marxist party – the highest form of class organization of the proletariat which at the time of the victory of the October Revolution did not exist in any of the most developed countries of Europe and America, the creation in the course of the struggle of such political organizations as the soviets and the establishment of the closest connections between the proletarian and non-proletarian layers of the workers.[142]

In essence, the report maintained, the book 'hushes up the enormous experience of the class struggle of the Russian proletariat, attained in the course of three revolutions, a school of the education and shaping of the workers the like of which not one [other] of the detachments of the international proletariat passed through.'[143] In short, *The Russian Proletariat* was charged with casting a slur on the revolutionary attainments of the Russian proletariat and its revolutionary party.

The report singled out 'serious distortions' in several articles concerning the allies of the proletariat in the course of the October Revolution. Exception was taken to the contention (of Tarnovsky) that the proletariat took power 'with the support of the entire peasantry' and that the proletariat established an alliance with the poorest peasantry 'only after power was in its hands' and that consequently a 'split' occurred within the peasantry from summer 1918 onwards. More than once before, Anfimov and Danilov had also been accused of distorting the truth on this question, and the report made quite explicit why such exception was taken to this heretical view of this 'cardinal question': 'It seems as if the kulaks fought for the dictatorship of the proletariat'.[144]

Finally, two other errors in *The Russian Proletariat* were identified. Firstly, in the foreword it was suggested that on the periphery of Russia 'there were no preconditions for a socialist revolution'. Secondly, 'in contrast to the historical truth', it was asserted that 'not the Bolshevik party but the Soviets, which in the main during the first months after the February 1917 revolution were dominated by the Mensheviks and the Social Revolutionaries, were the "political centres, concentrating the revolutionary energy of the proletariat and its allies"'.[145]

This perceived neglect of the allegedly pivotal role of the Bolsheviks in igniting the entire revolutionary process in 1917 was also identified as the fatal flaw in *The Overthrow of the Autocracy*. Volobuev himself was singled out as the author of spurious propositions to the effect that the 'spontaneous upsurge of the masses' is the basis of any revolution:

> From the point of view of socio-economic and political development any revolution is the result of a spontaneous-objective process, independent of the will or desires of separate classes, parties and their leaders ... Only a small part of the proletariat fully consciously comes to revolution, guided by ideological convictions ... The February revolution, like the majority of genuinely popular revolutions, arose on the basis of a spontaneous revolutionary upsurge. The spontaneous revolutionary explosion, which occurred on 23rd February [1917] and marked the beginning of the revolution, *nobody prepared and nobody could have foreseen*.[146]

Volobuev's assertion was condemned in the report as 'distorting the role of the Bolsheviks and of the working class in the February revolution', a heresy that was compounded by Volobuev's 'conjectures' that 'the bourgeoisie was on side with the revolution and *became ... an ally of the workers and peasants*'.[147] The report even went back to a work of Volobuev's published in 1964, *The Proletariat and the Bourgeoisie in Russia in 1917*, to find ammunition against him. There, Volobuev had allegedly depicted the counter-revolutionary conduct of the Russian bourgeoisie during 1917 as a series of 'fatal errors' and 'political lapses' that resulted in it relinquishing power to the working class. Volobuev had hypothesized that 'had the bourgeoisie been more intelligent – it would have said to the working class: "We will give you a republic, an 8 hour day ... everything in order to help us win the war". But this was the highest "ceiling" of the Russian bourgeoisie', he wrote. The report described such an explanation for the counter-revolutionary role of the bourgeoisie as 'naive'.[148]

Volobuev's analysis made the bourgeoisie an active agent in the events of 1917. This approach gave the Russian bourgeoisie the possibility of opting for reform in 1917, and thereby the possibility of averting the revolution in October. His position was a far cry from that of official orthodoxy, which brooked no options for the Russian bourgeoisie, as history marched inexorably towards the proletarian seizure of power. It was, incidentally, precisely around the question of whether there were reformist options to the October Revolution that Volobuev had debated with his colleague, the 'uncompromising determinist', Avrekh.[149] Hard on the heels of the Twenty-fourth Congress there was little tolerance for Volobuev's perspective of the historical alternative. Trapeznikov and Yakovlev urged the publication of an article in *Voprosy istorii KPSS*, along the lines of the trade-union higher school report, under the bellicose title of 'Contrary to the Historical Truth', with a view to promoting a 'wide-ranging, scientifically argued critique' of these works.[150]

Further critical discussion did indeed take place; it was anything but 'wide-ranging', let alone scientific. On 4 July 1972 the Bureau of the Division of History met to discuss a resolution, prepared by a commission drawn from within its ranks, proposing guidelines for future research on the proletariat, the party and 1917.[151] Volobuev participated, and much of the discussion simply repeated earlier accusations about the shortcomings of the literature produced by his institute. A new voice, however, joined the chorus of accusers – that of Volobuev's deputy: Bovykin. He observed that these anthologies

> reflected, to a certain degree, that period when certain historians entered a very seductive path, which did not require a basic working through of the sources, of reviewing the existing, scientifically established views on the most important questions of history ... [Moreover] the fact that V. P. Volobuev, one of the authors of the books under discussion, is at the same time director of the Institute, complicates matters. This situation imposes a special responsibility on him.[152]

Volobuev, in reply to his critics, accepted responsibility both for the publication of the books and for their 'ideological-theoretical content'. In this regard he acknowledged certain deficiencies. In particular, he distanced himself from the 'erroneous' presentation in Kir'yanov's foreword to *The Russian Proletariat* of the proletariat being allied with the 'entire' peasantry in 1917 and with the 'poor peasantry only in the period of the Committees of the Poor Peasantry (*kombedy*). In fact, during the overthrow of the bourgeoisie and the landlords the proletariat was allied with the poorest peasantry. Only at a particular moment, for certain reasons, did it receive the support of the entire peasantry.'[153] In making this point Volobuev was differentiating himself from the position of Anfimov, Danilov and Tarnovsky.

Volobuev seems to have occupied a position halfway between theirs and the orthodox position that the October Revolution was effected by the proletariat in alliance with the poor peasantry alone.

Nevertheless, Volobuev rejected other criticisms. He re-stated his conviction that the events of 23 February 1917 amounted to a 'spontaneous explosion'. Yes, it had been the Bolsheviks' 'tireless work' that had prepared the proletariat 'to fulfil its role as hegemon in the February revolution. But an element of spontaneity there was.' He also denied that he had ever written of the proletariat 'losing hegemony after February'. He had

> something else in mind: the necessity of a *transition* from hegemony in the bourgeois-democratic revolution to hegemony in the socialist revolution, and the necessity *to prepare* the proletariat to fulfil its role in the new, that is, socialist, revolution. Hegemony – this is the *process* of consolidation of the leading role in the revolution, of the conquest of democratic allies and of leadership of them; and it is precisely this process that has its own stages. Immediately after February the working class could not begin to storm bourgeois power, since it was still not ready for this and had yet to achieve a regroupment of class forces. It had to pass from an alliance with all the peasantry to an alliance with the poorest peasantry. In my articles there are inadequacies ... but ideological-theoretical errors there are none.[154]

Volobuev's response did not satisfy Pospelov. He claimed that earlier Volobuev had acknowledged 'serious methodological errors'; now, however, in the course of discussion he had admitted only ' "imprecise formulations". This is formal acknowledgement of mistakes', railed Pospelov. 'It is not a question of "imprecise formulations", but essentially of pronouncements against some important principles of Marxism–Leninism.'[155]

The campaign became even more vicious. In September 1972 the article, secretly endorsed by Trapeznikov and Yakovlev, finally appeared in *Voprosy istorii KPSS*. Not content with misrepresenting Volobuev as a proponent of a spontaneist explanation for the Russian Revolution, they resorted to the technique of guilt by association: such views were akin to Menshevism. It was also alleged that he idealized the role played in the soviets by the Social Revolutionaries and the Mensheviks.[156] In October 1972 *The Russian Proletariat* was criticized in *Pravda*,[157] which had the satisfaction of reporting, the following January, that Volobuev had acknowledged the criticism as justified.[158]

Coup de grâce: Volobuev dismissed

This confession was not enough to save Volobuev. In March 1973 a conference of the Bureau of the Division of History of the Academy of Sciences convened in the Department of Science.[159] The session was chaired by no less than Trapeznikov himself. Volobuev, too, participated; but it is obvious this was a trial – and he was the defendant. These were dark days, antecedent to Volobuev's dismissal as director of the Institute of the History of the USSR.

The discussion took place in a context that was described by Rybakov as an 'intense struggle' with 'bourgeois and clerical' ideology outside the USSR and 'revisionism' within it. Pivotal in this struggle, declared Pospelov, was the history of the October Revolution. While making the usual *pro forma* acknowledgement of the achievements of Soviet scholarship in this field, he noted 'certain failures and even separate retreats from the Marxist–Leninist line', such as those that had appeared in *The Russian Proletariat* and *The Overthrow of the Autocracy*. Noting the intense discussion concerning these two books that had taken place during the last year, both within the Bureau of the Division of History and in the press, Pospelov singled out Volobuev's treatment of the role of the working class after February 1917 as an 'incorrect interpretation of questions of the hegemony of the proletariat in the socialist revolution'. He again took particular exception to Volobuev's assertion that after February the Russian proletariat 'was essentially not ready to assume the role of leader of the new revolution'.[160] For Pospelov, this error was based on an

> incorrect interpretation of the process of the conquest of political power by the proletariat, which was confused with the question of the hegemony of the proletariat in the socialist revolution. Nevertheless, the very fact that the proletariat could not immediately take power after the February revolution and that it required a certain time for the formation of the political army of the proletariat by no means signified that the Russian proletariat did not fulfil the function of the leader of the revolution in the period of the growing over of the bourgeois-democratic revolution into the socialist revolution.[161]

Returning again to the hoary question of the poor peasantry as the real allies of the proletariat in the October Revolution, Pospelov reminded his audience that this was an inviolable 'axiom of Bolshevism'. He did, however, reveal his uncertainty about one question at least: whether the historians who violated this axiom were 'careless or simply ignorant'.[162]

It soon became clear that it was Volobuev that Pospelov had in his sights, as the protector of those who were responsible for such gross departures from Marxism–Leninism. Citing Avrekh's contention, in his controversial 1966 book, *Tsarism and the Third of June System*,[163] that the Russian peasantry was the 'mass social basis of the autocracy', Pospelov asked rhetorically, 'How could such a monstrous thing be written?' It turned out that not only had it been recommended for publication by the institute administration but it had received the personal imprimatur of Volobuev himself. On its title page Volobuev was named as the 'responsible editor'. 'Surely it is not accidental', Pospelov surmised aloud, 'that P. V. Volobuev, at a recent session of the Bureau of the Division of History, resolutely defended A. Ya. Avrekh when his candidature was rejected by the bureau during a discussion of the make-up of the new academic council of the Institute of History?'[164]

For Pospelov, historians such as Avrekh, operating under the wing of Volobuev, were guilty of interpreting 'too broadly' the meaning of historical inquiry, during which emerged 'all sorts of surprising things'. Among these surprises were appeals for a 'new reading' of the key principles of Marxism–Leninism and proclamation of the establishment of a 'certain "new direction" in historical science'. Of considerable concern to Pospelov was that even though the 'so-called new direction' had been called to account, some scholars continued to defend its mistaken positions. A disreputable example was the doctoral dissertation of Tarnovsky. Pospelov found offensive Tarnovsky's argument that a 'qualitative' advance in historical science had required a break with previous approaches to the heritage of Lenin.[165] 'Only now have appeared the "bold innovators" who at last have found the truth'. Given the current state of the 'ideological struggle', when the antagonists of Marxism–Leninism would seize on any 'slipshod formulation', Pospelov thought it unwise to distribute works that would corrupt the minds of young historians and the reading public.[166]

Volobuev, in reply, was very much on the defensive, although he tried to hold his ground. He acknowledged that in the previous Institute of History 'serious mistakes' had been made by some historians of Soviet society, especially in relation to collectivization and the military preparedness of the USSR prior to the Second World War. But the situation in the institute had been turned around following what Volobuev called 'principled criticism' in the party press of 'serious errors by individual historians'. Now a 'business-like, creative' atmosphere in the institute encouraged scholarship based on 'firm party principles'.[167]

Further, Volobuev conceded that in 1968–69 (when, incidentally, Rybakov was director!) the institute administration had 'lost control' over the publication of anthologies of articles coming out of conferences held on the silver jubilee of the revolutions of 1917. These anthologies, the preface to *The Russian Proletariat* in particular, contained 'serious inadequacies' and 'mistaken principles concerning the loss of the hegemony of the proletariat after the February revolution and on the alignment of class forces in the October Revolution'. These errors, however, had been 'sharply' criticized in the party and academic press. Further, in order to prevent a repetition of this situation, the institute, Volobuev assured his superiors, had taken the necessary organizational measures to 'strengthen the control' of the administration over the 'ideological-theoretical content' of works intended for publication. 'Therefore it would be incorrect to say that the party organization, the institute administration and I in particular have not drawn the necessary conclusions ... All the *constructive* criticism', as Volobuev put it, 'had been taken into account'.[168]

Responding to Trapeznikov's concerns about publication of Adamov's *Problems of the History of Capitalist Russia: the Problem of Multistructuredness*, Volobuev defended the initial decision to publish material from the Sverdlovsk conference:

> The anthology represents the first attempt to analyse this complex problem both on a theoretical and a specific-historical plane. It has to be said that there are no works on this problem. When we were considering whether or not to publish this anthology, we decided that it would be better not to put this problem – of the *mnogoukladnost'* of capitalist Russia – on hold, because sooner or later it would have to be resolved.

It is clear, however, that Volobuev was under great pressure: 'Now it is apparent', he conceded, 'that we made a mistake. It would have been better not to have published it'.[169]

Similarly, responding to Trapeznikov's concerns about the New Direction, Volobuev was on the retreat; but he gave away nothing in principle. Referring to those who maliciously employed the term '*novoe napravlenie*', Volobuev maintained that

> it was not a question of a new, so to speak, anti-Marxist direction, but of a new scientific direction, though some may wish to inject other content into it. In the Sverdlovsk anthology, in particular, which was mentioned here, it is a question of a new direction in the sense of the study of the new problem of *mnogoukladnost'*.

As far as Volobuev was concerned, isolated errors by individual scholars gave no basis to the accusation that in the institute 'there are champions of a "new", i.e., *anti-Marxist direction*. There is no such direction in the institute', he declared. In relation to himself, Volobuev 'resolutely declared' that he

> never aspired to and, on the contrary, denied ever belonging to some sort of 'new direction'; moreover, as for multistructuredness, I have never really studied it. But, to my profound regret, there are continual attempts to place me at the head of a certain 'new direction', despite the fact that on more than one occasion I have categorically denied it.[170]

This confrontation with Trapeznikov and his allies in the Academy of Sciences was really the swan-song for Volobuev as director of the Institute of the History of the USSR – and for historical revisionism as a whole. In a spate of articles, the revisionist historians were admonished for failing to acknowledge the error of their ways; in the face of the challenge from 'multistructuredness', the 'superseding of socioeconomic formations' was reinstalled as the only acceptable interpretation of Marxism–Leninism; and Adamov's study of *mnogoukladnost'* joined the list of condemned books.[171] In June 1973, Vladimir Yagodkin made it clear that negative assessments of the Stalin period would not be tolerated: '*all*, and I repeat *all* – stages in the development of our Soviet society must be regarded as "positive".'[172]

As for Volobuev, although towards the end of March 1973 he had participated in an important gathering of high-ranking administrators of historical science,[173] within a year, at the annual meeting of the Division of History on 4 March 1974, he was dismissed as director of the institute for his failure to 'cope with the work'. He was replaced by Academician A. L. Narochnitsky.[174]

The most liberal of the revisionist historians but certainly not unprincipled, as Nekrich presents him, Volobuev's situation epitomized that of the liberal *intelligenty* of the 1960s: seeking to effect reforms by working within the existing institutions. As he himself put it in a retrospective on the aspirations of himself and his colleagues in this period:

> When the Twentieth Congress opened slightly the ideological curtain, so to speak, then naturally we tried to take advantage of the situation to draw it back as far as possible. In our circles we immediately said that we had to seize every opportunity. We knew that these would be short-lived. And as historians of revolution we knew, from the laws of Marxism, that if a revolution is to retain its conquests then it must run as far forward as possible, even further than the objective laws and conditions allow, before the inevitable reactionary counter-offensive begins. Thus, like any revolution, the Khrushchev thaw had to advance, in every sense, as far as possible; for when reaction assumed the counter-offensive, it would not stop halfway. We viewed the Brezhnev reaction like the Thermidor of the Great French Revolution, which did not immediately eradicate the conquests of the revolution. It only changed the regime in the political sphere. As Director of the Institute of the History of the USSR I, and all my colleagues, strove to maintain the previous gains; but I could already sense the offensive of the conservative forces. But I thought that while there were still possibilities, it was necessary to struggle and, where possible, even move forward so that we would not be forced back to where we started, back to pure Stalinism. Unfortunately, we did not entirely succeed.[175]

Volobuev's statement expresses perfectly the contradictory position of the genuine *intelligent* who was simultaneously both 'insider and outsider' in the Soviet system in the 1950s and 1960s. The defeat of the aspirations of these latter-day *intelligenty* was not only a precondition of the onset of *zastoi*; the 'period of stagnation' was symptomatic of the magnitude of that defeat.

7
From Zastoi to Perestroika

'The *shestidesyatniki* have suffered two defeats: one, at the end of the 1960s; the other, in 1990–91.'
V. P. Danilov, Moscow, February 1992

'Stalin deformed Lenin and Leninism. Now, however, a new stage has begun. They want to deny Lenin, to throw him out completely. But this is the same historical method, because history cannot be thrown out. It happened. It is still a question of a more profound understanding of the genuine role of Lenin.'
Ye. N. Gorodetsky, Moscow, April 1992

This book set out to investigate the *political* significance of the emergence of revisionist historical writing in the USSR in the 1950s and 1960s. It has long been accepted, even in the most recent sovietological literature, that these endeavours were at most isolated ripples on the surface of an historiographical swamp. This study, however, has revealed that a small, though important layer of historians, mainly concentrated in Moscow, were engaged in a very intense reconsideration of their own discipline that was stirring Soviet historiography deep below the surface.

Initially, even before the Twentieth Party Congress, it was a matter of challenging notions that had, by administrative fiat – or worse, been established as indisputable truths. For example the false portrayal of Stalin as one of the two principal leaders of the October

Revolution, on a par with Lenin, a fable that Burdzhalov had done so much to undermine; or the nature of Russian imperialism under the Tsars. But historical science quickly began to go beyond the bounds of correcting outright falsifications or even filling in the silences about the past. For some historians, many of whom had been ardent Stalinists, the death of Stalin and the experience of the Twentieth Party Congress was, to invoke Kuhn, akin to a gestalt switch,[1] which incited them to challenge the very premises of the *Short Course* paradigm so ruthlessly imposed upon them almost two decades earlier. The divide between those who became revisionists was, roughly, a generational one, though there were exceptions, such as Burdzhalov and, irony of ironies, his antagonist, Sidorov. In the main, those *frontoviki* who embarked on a research career after the Great Patriotic War formed the backbone of historical revisionism. Drawing principally on Lenin, they began to rethink the categories bequeathed to them by Stalinism, not only to make sense of the Soviet past but also of the relevance of the October Revolution in a world that in the 1950s and 1960s was being turned upside down by the anti-colonial revolutions.

No longer mere creatures of party resolutions, if they ever had been, the genuine scholars were driven, as they often said themselves, by the 'logic of science' on a methodological quest that would enable them to generate a new historical paradigm. Often as not, some of the decisive methodological gains were made in those fields that were farthest from the 'forbidden zone' of the history of the USSR; a process that expressed, in Gefter's words, 'the semi-conscious logic of the research process itself'.[2] An integral part of this process was a profound rethinking of their own part as historians in creating – or disfiguring – this past, of their place in the present and of their role in reshaping the Soviet future. In this sense they were engaged in generating a new paradigm – a new 'disciplinary matrix' in Kuhnian terms – that went beyond a mere reworking of the limited, primitive categories of the *Short Course* 'exemplar'. For the revisionist historians it was a question of discarding the old 'bouillon of primitive Marxism and the national-state idea' bequeathed by Stalinism,[3] in order to a create a new historical consciousness about the world and their place in it. At stake here was more than mere 'private', 'faceless' professionalism;[4] they were becoming intellectuals, in the three senses that Nettl defined them: they manifested a 'self-conscious' concern with questions of 'qualitative dissent'; their thinking went beyond the 'particularistic' concerns usually associated with professionalism to embrace 'universals'; and their ideas had, potentially at least, a popular resonance, capable of generating societal dissent.

The roots of the evolution of the *shestidesyatniki* from *intellektualy* to *intelligenty*, to use Kagarlitsky's distinction, lay in the thaw of Soviet intellectual life after the death of Stalin and the Twentieth Congress. In this climate journals, such as *Voprosy istorii* and *Istoricheskie zapiski*, the Institute of History, with its Group on the peasantry and its Sector of Methodology, and the 'democratic' *partkom* in particular, together with the proliferation of those 'social organizations' the Scientific Councils, provided the revisionist historians with crucial sites for the regeneration of intellectual life after the cruel winter of Stalinism. But more than this, they provided the institutional bases for the development of a self-conscious community of genuine scholars who were intent on reconstructing the officially sanctioned paradigm. But such a project inevitably set them on a collision course with the guardians of academic orthodoxy. Despite the best attempts of the party-state apparatus to keep a firm rein on the historians, the rhythms of politics and of historical science were increasingly out of step, and ultimately, by the mid-1960s, completely at loggerheads. Whereas the priority of the revisionists was the regeneration of their own discipline, political authority saw their endeavours as having a potentially subversive socio-political resonance. Any challenge to the postulates of the *Short Course* threatened to tarnish the ideological mirror which, hitherto, had provided such a flattering reflection for the *nomenklatura*; to ensure their stability Soviet-type political systems necessarily required a loyal intelligentsia to act as that mirror.[5]

It was in this context that the revisionist historians, like the *shestidesyatniki* as a whole, began to crystallize as a self-conscious stratum of the intellectual elite, redolent of the classical Russian intelligentsia – despite the vast social gulf that separated them. Those like Danilov, Danilova, Gefter, Tarnovsky and Volobuev, to name a few, who as 'children of the Twentieth Party Congress' sought to reinvigorate Marxism, did indeed fit Kagarlitsky's prototype of the Russian revolutionary-democratic intelligentsia of the 1860s: both 'insiders and outsiders', reformers and revolutionaries, though with varying degrees of confidence about the real possibilities for sustained reform. In this respect the revisionist historians gathered in the Institute of History found themselves in a similar situation to the literary journal *Novyi mir*, with which there was a great degree of cross-fertilization. Under the editorship of that archetypal *intelligent* of the 1960s, Aleksandr Tvardovsky, *Novyi mir*, whilst remaining loyal to Soviet society and socialist thought, did not hesitate to illuminate the darkest pages of Soviet history. It was no accident, therefore, that the public campaign against the remnants of the Sector of Methodology and the representatives of the *novoe napravlenie* had erupted in 1970 – the same year that Tvardovsky was dismissed as editor of *Novyi mir*.[6]

The revisionist historians of the 1960s, in so far as they became philosopher-historians, echoing the classical Russian historians, began to formulate an alternative, critical worldview counterposed to the positivistic, deterministic ideology of the party–state apparatus. The danger for the Brezhnev–Kosygin regime, then trying to roll back much of the space afforded by the Twentieth Party Congress, was that these historians might assume the mantle of champions of the people (*narod*), like their *intelligent* predecessors a century before.

In the case of the writers, notably Tvardovsky, such identification with the *narod* was manifest. In the case of professional historians, given the inherently more restricted nature of their audience, their *intelligentnost'* was manifested by their self-conscious concerns for the dignity of their craft and ultimately its capacity to contribute to popular consciousness and to the well-being of Soviet socialism (an engagement which, incidentally, contrasts strongly to the Anglo-Saxon academic tradition of objectivity and political detachment). It should be stressed, however, that theirs was a Soviet *intelligentnost'*. Though schooled in the Russian *intelligent* and historiographical tradition, it was a rereading of Marxism, above all Lenin, that directly fuelled their outlook. For this reason they identified with the promise of the Twentieth Congress, which they saw as being betrayed by Brezhnev and his cronies. They articulated their aspirations through whatever fora were available to them. If they could not find an outlet through their professional publications, then they turned to journals such as *Novyi mir*.[7] At the same time many of them took up arms in the principal 'public' arena – the communist party, and increasingly so in the face of the neo-Stalinist offensive.

Such manifestations of a civil society *in embryo*, both within and without the party, as Moshe Lewin's approach allows, were particularly threatening to the Soviet political elite in the late-1960s. The flowering of the 'Prague spring' in 1967–68, that 'glorious revolution' of the intelligentsia as Rudolf Bahro has called it, saw intellectuals playing a leading role in the construction of a new model of socialism – 'socialism with a human face' – with explosive political consequences.[8] In these circumstances especially, the very existence of an alternative worldview amongst a crucial sector of the Soviet intellectual elite constituted an incipient crisis of ideological hegemony for the CPSU.[9]

Unlike a socialist dissident such as Medvedev, who was not a professional historian by training and *ipso facto* was forced to snipe at the *apparatchiki* from the sidelines, these historians were ensconced just below the commanding heights of the intellectual apparatus: in the prestigious institutes of the Academy of Sciences, though only one, Volobuev, was an academician. Moreover, they were not alone; parallel processes of intellectual fragmentation and realignment were occurring among philosophers, economists, physical scientists and, of course, writers. The renegade intelligentsia formed a community, which counterposed itself to the mandarins and *apparatchiki* who stifled any manifestations of principled, independent, critical thinking. Further, working as they were essentially within the discourse of Marxism–Leninism, the methodological quests of the professional philosopher-historians threatened to explode that discourse from within. This was far more threatening, at least in these years, than those dissidents who began to repudiate the system as a whole and who could thus more easily be marginalized or, if need be, exiled.

By the mid-1960s the Soviet system was in a deep structural crisis. In part this was an expression of its inability to move from extensive to intensive growth. But this systemic crisis was compounded by the failure to realize the promise of the Twentieth Party Congress – reneged on by Khrushchev and suppressed by Brezhnev. The ensuing loss of confidence by the creative intelligentsia in the capacity of the system to reform itself, and the 'public apathy' which accompanied it, led to a profound 'crisis of social consciousness', the ultimate expression of which was the 'period of stagnation'.[10] Moreover, as William McNeill has suggested, only a strong, confident ruling class can afford the luxury of thoroughgoing, critical perspectives on the past – and then not for long.[11] The Soviet bureaucracy, a caricature of a class, was, despite appearances, anything but strong or confident. For these reasons it was vital for Brezhnev and the conservative apparatus, whose interests he embodied perfectly, to reimpose doctrinal consensus.

Key to this process was Brezhnev's underling, Trapeznikov, who actively set the agenda for the social sciences.[12] As Andrei Anfimov put it, tongue in cheek, Trapeznikov

> anticipated the danger of insidious bourgeois propaganda, insinuating 'convergence theory and pluralism' into our consciousness. We had to have 'unanimity of world outlook', whereas in fact [Trapeznikov complained], in science, we see 'differentiation' ... and the danger of mock differentiation – pluralism, which is 'the

differentiation of scientific knowledge and the appearance of new directions in research'. Trapeznikov condemned intellectual 'differentiation' outright on the grounds that it allegedly 'engenders a one-sided, narrowly empirical approach to the analysis of living social reality, leading researchers to lose general perspectives and attempting to substitute limited schemas for an integrated, living picture of the vital processes.'[13]

Moreover, continued Anfimov, in Brezhnev's era of 'developed socialism', 'pluralism of opinions' among social scientists was superfluous; it would only encroach on the new orientation and Trapeznikov's so-called 'unanimity of world outlook'.

In fact, the fiction of the USSR having established 'mature, developed socialism' was conjured up by Trapeznikov himself in 1972.[14] The very idea of developed socialism violated previous conceptions that communism, not socialism, was a distinct socio-economic formation.[15] Enforcement of a consensus around 'developed socialism' as the ideological underpinning of the 'period of stagnation' required bringing the recalcitrant revisionists to heel – and not just historians. The immediate organizer of these proceedings was the newly-appointed secretary for ideology of the Moscow *gorkom*, V. N. Yagodkin. The year 1973 had seen three conferences dedicated to this task conducted by Trapeznikov's Department of Science. That in March to deal with history was followed in May by one concerning philosophy, law, psychology and 'problems of scientific communism', which was capped off in November by a session on economics.[16]

In the field of history the task was to shore up the accepted verities of the socio-economic formation. Hence the belated rounding on such revisionist texts as the Sverdlovsk anthology on multistructuredness and the renewed attack on Gefter's *History and Problems of the Present*. Meanwhile, economists were enjoined by Trapeznikov to debunk the 'vacuous, reactionary conception of "market socialism", as petty-bourgeois, anarchist and syndicalist'. It was deemed a regression to the 'atomization of the economy to more or less "self-managing", isolated economic units, and to the elevation of individual and group interests over national interests'. The task for economists was to theorize the new stage of developed socialism, the onset of which had caught the economists 'unawares'. Yagodkin, echoing Trapeznikov, reminded the economists that their task was to answer the demands made by 'our party, its Leninist Central Committee and personally by Secretary comrade Leonid Ilich Brezhnev ... the great leader of all times and peoples' – a ritual flourish that was to become synonymous with the period of 'stagnation' (*zastoi*).[17]

A decade and half later, for the architects and advocates of *perestroika*, the very notion of *zastoi* was synonymous with Brezhnev himself. Initially restricted to the late 1970s and early 1980s in official assessments,[18] *zastoi* and the 'braking mechanism' that accompanied it, were extended by others, such as the political scientist Fedor Burlatsky, to encompass the entire period of the Brezhnev ascendancy.[19] Clearly, as this study has demonstrated, while *zastoi* might be the appropriate label for the political aspirations (or the lack of them) of Brezhnev and his ilk, it by no means defines all intellectual life, at least in the late 1960s. Moreover, it does not entirely define the later 'white period', as Danilov has referred to it, either.[20] For few of the revisionist historians, who were among the principal victims of Brezhnevism, did the concept of a 'period of stagnation' have any real content – though it had the most distressing consequences. For Gorodetsky, for example, *zastoi* was a 'political term' that related more to socio-economic development than to intellectual life because 'there is no direct correlation between a political regime and the development of art, culture or science'.[21] Similarly for Gefter, *zastoi* meant little more than the 'meaningless' formulation 'cult of the personality'. *Zastoi* was no more than an 'expression', a 'term' to designate a particular period, which was a 'complex combination of different factors'. In part *zastoi* was a 'reaction to the failure of Khrushchev, to the failure of the system to reconstruct itself ... as a system'. The failure of Khrushchev's partial *perestroika* stimulated a 'reflex action of the system, which attempted to recreate its integrity'. It was not inevitable that this recreation should take a reactionary path; but it did, including the attempts to rehabilitate Stalin. At the same time it was during this period that the USSR was 'transformed into a belligerent in a peaceful world, which entailed the gigantic development of everything concerned with war. Now we are paying for this. But this was not simply *zastoi*.' Finally, this was the period when 'a consumer society began to be established, on an extremely hasty, unhealthy basis'. For Gefter then *zastoi* was a period that was 'very unfavourable to intellectual endeavour, in every sense, because at this stage what was actually required was to review the system and reconceptualize a new integrity. But thought was still not prepared for this'. For historians this was, to put it mildly, a 'rather difficult period'. Those who remained in the profession generally could only pursue the most 'wretched' themes – methodological questions were completely beyond the pale.[22]

Likewise, for Gurevich, the appellation *zastoi* did not completely capture the Brezhnev period, though his perspective was somewhat more sanguine than that of Gefter: 'Intellectually a lot occurred during the period of stagnation'. The Brezhnev regime, despite the fears of the intelligentsia, was nowhere near as strong nor as total in its ideological control as its Stalinist precursor. 'We have a one-party policy, but there are many entrances', was a common expression at the time. The different departments of the Central Committee reflected the policies of those who oversaw them. It made a difference whether it was a Trapeznikov or a Yakovlev at the helm. And this gave the intellectuals room to manoeuvre. In Gurevich's case the 1970s and the early 1980s, were very productive. He was out of favour with the Institute of World History, so he worked at home. It was then that he wrote his 'best books'. Further, what he was unable to publish under 'Nauka' could be published by 'Iskusstvo'.[23]

Gurevich's more sanguine view of this period no doubt reflects his rather different experience from that of neo-Leninists such as Gefter, Volobuev and Danilov, all of whom, unlike Gurevich, had been party members and had directly engaged in politics. Gefter, having been hounded by Zhukov from the Institute of World History in 1976, found his way into the dissident movement. He became one of the principal contributors to the socialist, samizdat journal *Poiski* (*Quests*) that first appeared in 1979, edited by Gleb Pavlovsky, one of his students.[24] Eventually, in 1982, the year in which Pavlovsky was arrested and a Soviet invasion of Poland seemed threatening, Gefter finally left the CPSU. He was 'effectively a dissident. Outside the institute and outside the party'.[25]

Danilov never became a dissident but he was marginalized, able to publish only in minor journals and limiting himself to studying the safer field of the agrarian history of the 1920s. Though frequently the target of hostile criticism, and the belated recipient of his doctoral degree in 1982, he nevertheless had the good fortune to publish two major studies in 1977 and 1979 on the Soviet peasantry prior to collectivization.[26] His wife, Danilova, considered to have been 'infected by revisionism' in the Sector of Methodology, was less fortunate: the manuscript of her major study of the question of feudalism in Soviet historiography, which had first been approved for publication in December 1970, was finally returned to her in 1983 – unpublished.[27]

Volobuev, exiled for 16 years in the Institute of the History of Natural Science and Technology, and forbidden to study, let alone publish, anything on the preconditions of the revolutions of 1917, was reduced to studying the 'wretched' theme of the history of Russian science. Occasionally he published book reviews. In exile he found himself in familiar company. One-third of the institute was made up of outstanding, but disgraced, scholars – philosophers, sociologists, physicists, chemists – many of whom had protested or demonstrated against the maltreatment of such literary figures as Yevgeniya Ginzburg, author of *Journey into the Whirlwind*, and Andrei Sinyavsky. There, too, were confined his co-thinkers from the New Direction: Anfimov, Avrekh, Tarnovsky. Conveniently located a mere 200 metres from the Central Committee's headquarters on *Staraya ploshchad'* (Old Square), they worked under the duress of the 'ideological cowl' foisted upon them by the ideologues of the Department of Science. Though 'unrepentant', the constant pressure and the stress of battling to get anything published took its toll. Both Avrekh and Tarnovsky, like Adamov before them who had lost his position at Sverdlovsk University, went to an early grave.[28]

The blow delivered to historical revisionism arrested the development of historical thinking for the next decade and a half. Nevertheless, Brezhnev and his lieutenants managed to stifle, rather than completely stop, the intellectual energies accumulated during the thaw; and at some cost to the regime itself. For example, many former participants of the Sector of Methodology pursued their work, albeit by other means. A 'culturological seminar' continued in the flat of Vladimir Bibler for more than a decade after the sector's closure, while the methodological seminar of the Institute of Philosophy conducted by A. V. Gulyga and that of the sociologist Yu. A. Levada continued to meet, as did the circle convened by the philosopher L. B. Tumanova. Such seminars and 'domestic circles' provided fertile soil for the underground movement of dissidents in the 1970s which little by little eroded the enforced consensus of the so-called 'period of stagnation'.[29]

There was more than an echo of the concerns of the intellectual ferment of the 1960s among professional historians in one of the most renowned and searching studies of the Stalin phenomenon to emerge from this period – Roy Medvedev's *Let History Judge*, which finally surfaced in English translation in 1971. Apart from drawing liberally on many works, published and unpublished, including some from participants in the Sector of Methodology – Drabkin, Gefter, Levada and Semenov[30] – Gefter himself read this work in manuscript,[31] while one of his friends, A. Zimin, a former supporter of the Leningrad Opposition in the 1920s, under the pen-name L. El'konin, apparently supplied Medvedev's opus with much of its 'theoretical backbone'.[32] Medvedev's celebrated work is a prime example of my argument that it was legal dissent that fertilized the more visible illegal dissidence.[33]

Moreover, despite the severe strictures to which in the early 1970s scholars such as Danilova and Gefter and their interpretation of historical materialism were subject,[34] they had shattered the prevailing *Short Course* paradigm. What remained in place under Brezhnev was a hollow shell. While the *pyatichlenka* remained the orthodoxy of textbooks and conservative scholars, other scholars, notably those who had participated in the Sector of Methodology, continued to argue for alternative patterns of development, and the Asiatic mode of production in particular.[35] Similarly, the vulgar economism that had long been the hallmark of orthodox historical materialism had at least been tempered by a philosophy of history that allowed for a much more active human subject.[36] In this sense, the tiny, short-lived Sector of Methodology had proved to be not only a powerful catalyst for Soviet historiography, but also hastened the demise of Marxism–Leninism as a dogmatic ideology.

Similarly, the concept of *mnogoukladnost'* did not die completely; on the contrary, it gained a new lease of life. While proscribed in relation to the history of the Soviet Union and the Russian empire, during the 1970s 'multistructuredness' assumed a special place in the conceptual armoury of leading, progressive, Soviet Third World specialists such as Nodari Simoniya and Aleksei Levkovsky.[37] Meanwhile, the leading light of the *novoe napravlenie*, Tarnovsky, who it will be recalled had first recognized Russia as a prototype for contemporary revolutions in the colonial world, continued to investigate the social and political conditions which had enabled Russia to move to centre-stage of the world revolution. In particular, he researched the development of small-scale industry as a defining feature of Russian capitalism, with its peculiar polarity of advanced and backward development. Similarly, research for his second attempt at a doctorate concentrated on the role of the Bolshevik paper *Iskra* in the creation of a 'new type of liberation movement' in Russia, and the dialectics of its relationship to the particular type of capitalist development in that country.[38]

Above all, seen in the light of the ferment in Soviet historical science engendered by *perestroika*, it is clear that the *shestidesyatniki* played a crucial role not only in igniting these debates but in conceptually clearing the way for them. In so many ways the battles of the 1960s prefigured the *perestroika* process two decades later. The *variantnost'* and *al'ternativnost'* of the historical process and of a 'choice of paths of development' in general, and in the Soviet Union in particular, were at the heart of the discussions among historians that erupted in late 1987. Among the first voices from the ranks of the professional historians (who, as they themselves confessed, had been tardy in taking up the 'blank spots' of the past compared with film-makers and writers who had 'long ago overtaken historians in posing the sharp questions'),[39] were stalwarts from the New Direction, such as Volobuev and Tarnovsky. In this sense Danilov was correct to remind Yury Afanas'ev – a former defender of political correctness in the Institute of Marxism–Leninism often credited with rekindling the *perestroika* debates around history – that he had stormed through an 'already open gate'.[40]

For Volobuev, the onset of *perestroika* had by no means caught him, or those who thought like him, 'by surprise'. Indeed the 'work superintendent' of *perestroika*, as *Moscow News* called him, regarded the principles of the *novoe napravlenie* as a 'launching pad' both for the *perestroika* of historical science and the Soviet Union as a whole.[41] Volobuev, who was eventually elected a full academician in 1989, published a study of the 'choice of paths' in relation to Russia and the October Revolution which provoked intense and heated discussion.[42] Volobuev allowed that after February Russia had reached 'a historic fork in the road: to move towards capitalism and a bourgeois democracy; or toward socialism and proletarian democracy'.[43] However, during the course of 1917 the correlation of possibilities changed, narrowing the alternatives:[44]

> In the autumn of 1917 the people were presented with a choice: either the dictatorship of the proletariat in the form of Soviet power; or the dictatorship of a counter-revolutionary military clique (a 'second Kornilov coup'). Confronted with such alternatives, the people chose Soviet power.[45]

In a similar vein, Tarnovsky, engaged in drafting a new popular history of the CPSU following the April 1985 party plenum, had turned his attention increasingly to the 1920s as the transition period when the future of Soviet socialism was hammered into shape. He particularly focused on

> Lenin's conception of socialism, on elaborating alternatives for the construction of socialism in a country dominated by a small-scale peasantry, and on analysing the aggregate causes of the victory of the Stalinist model of socialism, which had led in practice to the

creation of an administrative-command system and the deformation of every facet of social life.[46]

Stalinism, and the related 'problem of choice', were questions for which his training in the 'diversity, multiformity and heterogeneity of development', together with his fate as an intellectual, had well-prepared him.[47]

Tarnovsky was not alone. Danilov, exuberantly riding the 'third wave' of the advance of historical science (following those of the 1920s and the decade after the Twentieth Party Congress),[48] turned his attention to the 1920s and the New Economic Policy in particular as an alternative to the Stalinist course pursued in the 1930s. Though at this stage his conception of the alternative concentrated on the 'Bukharin alternative'[49] (and to this extent he remained within the parameters of the Bukharin–Stalin conception of 'socialism in one country'), he urged serious consideration to be given to the Trotskyist alternatives, 'even if only to prevent the Stalin variant being attributed to them'.[50]

Many of the *perestroika* discussions saw historians and philosophers wrestling with the problem of alternatives to Stalinism and the 'regularities' (*zakonomernosti* as opposed to *zakony* – laws) of the historical process. For example, this was the focus of a 'round table' convened by *Voprosy filosofii* in 1988. Not by accident, at least five of the 19 scholars who participated in this round table had been associated with the Sector of Methodology: Danilova, Gurevich, Plimak, Loone and E. B. Rashkovsky.[51] Elsewhere, in an interview, Gefter himself went a little further. He interpreted Stalinism not just as a loss of alternatives but of its 'destruction'. For Gefter (unlike Volobuev), there was no alternative to the October Revolution; the choice came later, 'not of an historical path but of a choice within the "path"' laid by October 1917. In the years prior to the victory of Stalin there were a number of 'forks' in the path – 1923, 1928, 1 December 1934 – that could have been taken, but each also represented a *'growing narrowing of the field of choice'*.[52]

Soviet historiography, it was acknowledged in these turbulent days by more than one of the older revisionist historians, was in 'crisis'.[53] This was a crisis born of the incapacity of the official paradigm, which in its essentials was little removed from the Stalinist conceptions of the *Short Course*, to adequately explain the Soviet past, with all its fabrications and silences, its 'blank spots' and 'black holes'. The swift collapse of this hollow shell was retribution for the administrative suppression of a group of scholars at the end of the 1960s who had not only managed to discredit a bankrupt framework, but had been in the throes of generating an alternate, genuine, historical paradigm. What had been suppressed was an intellectually viable, and therefore *socially* more acceptable, paradigm in the making which would have been capable of addressing, if not definitively answering, some of the fundamental, torturous questions now being posed: 'Was the October Revolution historically necessary and inevitable?' 'Is the October Revolution responsible for the establishment of Stalinism?'[54] 'Was there a "Stolypin alternative" to the seeming disaster of the October Revolution?'[55]

In many respects this crisis was a re-run of events in the late-1960s. But it was more dramatic: the questions asked not only went deeper to the bone, but also were asked by the populace at large. However, they were posed in a different environment. And the disposition of forces was different: previously, radical revisionism had run up against conservative political authority; now political authority was fostering revisionism in the interests of reform.[56] To that extent, revisionism was less explosive during *perestroika*.

Moreover, the crisis of the prevailing paradigm during *perestroika* was compounded by the gulf between, on the one hand, historical consciousness and the popular thirst for knowledge about the past, and on the other, the inability of the historical profession to satisfy it.[57] This was a gulf that caused the revisionists particular *angst*. In part this was symptomatic of the self-conscious expectations of the Russian *intelligent* about their place in society, and their frustration with the lost opportunities of the 1960s. But this gulf also reflected a shift in the *locus* of the crisis; for historians no longer played such a 'decisive role in the development of historical consciousness'.[58] That role had shifted to the popular press and, above all, to film and television. The 'massmediatic' system of political domination had finally reached the other shore.[59]

But for Volobuev, for example, this was a crisis *sui generis*, a crisis within Marxism which should primarily be resolved within that tradition.[60] By now, however, not all those who two decades earlier had sought to reinvigorate Marxism shared Volobuev's opinion. Chief among these was the culturologist and medievalist Gurevich, who now made explicit what was probably always immanent in his work. Marxist formational theory, in its Stalinist or any other guise, was at best a species of nineteenth-century positivism – at worst a 'chiliastic eschatology'. The task of historians was to capture the discrete moments in history, the mentalities that shaped and expressed 'sociocultural' history, rather than imposing any grand schemes.[61]

Gurevich's repudiation of Marxism was not unique, though most of the *shestidesyatniki* stuck to their guns. In September 1991, after the August putsch and the demise of the CPSU, Danilov and Volobuev defended the October Revolution and called for the 'formation of a democratic party of socialist orientation'.[62] Once again, however, they were on the receiving end, often accused of being conservatives by those who, on the basis of the most superficial acquaintance with Marxism, had condemned them in the past as 'revisionists'. Those, especially the young, who threw out the Marxist baby with the Stalinist bath-water, began to embrace other orthodoxies, notably, and ironically, totalitarian theory – long discredited in Western social science.[63] In this sense, according to Danilova, 'the mentality of our society has not changed'.[64]

A new orthodoxy in both scholarship and politics, especially since the failure of *perestroika* and the collapse of the USSR, is the price that is being paid for the failure to reconceptualize Marxism, for which the *shestidesyatniki* had fought and argued in the 1960s. We might go even further and ask whether the defeat of the *shestidesyatniki* at the hands of Brezhnev, actually doomed *perestroika* to failure before it even started. After all, the best and the brightest of those who really believed in the ideals of the October Revolution and in the possibility of reforming the Soviet system lost confidence in the ability of the communist party to carry such reform through, especially after 1968. The politicians and *intellektualy* who unleashed the *perestroika* process, their convictions sapped by the careerist cynicism of the 'period of stagnation', were a pale reflection of the new *intelligenty* of the 1960s. Now in the successor states to the Soviet Union the flight from Marxism and 'totalitarianism' has been accompanied by a search for the elusive path that will take them to capitalism and democracy, whatever the social costs.[65] In this sense, the quest for a theory of history and society that opens up alternative paths and perspectives of development possesses as much *aktual'nost'* for the Soviet successor states in the new millennium as it did for the Soviet Union in the 1960s.

Notes

1 A resurgent intelligentsia

1. Stephen F. Cohen, 'Politics and the Past: The Importance of Being Historical (review article)', *Soviet Studies*, xxix, 1, January 1977, pp. 137–45.
2. Ciaran Brady (ed.), *Ideology and the Historians: Historical Studies XVII* (Dublin, 1991), p. 1. 'History and society' was an important theme of a discussion between Soviet and US historians at the height of *perestroika*. 'Perestroika, History and Historians' (Roundtable, Moscow, January 1989), *Journal of Modern History*, 62, 4, December 1990, pp. 782–830.
3. 'Konferentsiya chitatelei zhurnala "Voprosy istorii"', vi, 1956, 2, p. 213.
4. For example, R. W. Davies, *Soviet History in the Gorbachev Revolution* (Bloomington and Indianapolis, 1989); Joachim Hösler, *Die sowjetische Geschichtswissenschaft 1953 bis 1991 Studien zur Methodologie- und Organizationsgeschichte* (München, 1995); Takayuki Ito (ed.), *Facing Up to the Past: Soviet Historiography Under Perestroika* (Sapporo, 1989); Donald J. Raleigh (ed.), *Soviet Historians and Perestroika: The First Phase* (New York and London, 1989).
5. Stephen F. Cohen, 'Scholarly Missions: Sovietology as a Vocation', in Cohen, *Rethinking the Soviet Experience: Politics and History Since 1917* (New York and Oxford, 1985).
6. Konstantin F. Shteppa, *Russian Historians and the Soviet State* (New Brunswick, New Jersey, 1962), pp. xi–xiii.
7. John Keep (ed.), with the assistance of Lilliana Busby, *Contemporary History in the Soviet Mirror* (London, 1964).
8. *Ibid.*, pp. 14, 16–17.
9. On *partiinost'* see Chapter 2.
10. Novick, pp. 281–2, 293, 299.
11. Thomas Kuhn, *The Structure of Scientific Revolutions*, 2nd edn (Chicago and London, 1970), pp. 64, 151.
12. Robert Byrnes, 'Some Perspectives on the Soviet Ferment Concerning History', Ito, pp. 13–14.
13. John L. H. Keep, *Moscow's Problems of History: A Select Critical Bibliography of the Soviet Journal Voprosy Istorii, 1956–1985* (Ottawa, Carleton University, 1986, corrected edition 1988), pp. 8, 14.
14. 'Perestroika i istoricheskoe znanie', Yu. N. Afanas'ev (ed.), *Inogo ne dano – perestroika: glasnost', demokratiya, sotsializm* (Moscow, 1988), p. 498.
15. Nancy Whittier Heer, *Politics and History in the Soviet Union* (Cambridge, Massachusetts and London, England, 1971).
16. *Ibid.*, pp. 49, 243, 267.
17. Samuel H. Baron and Nancy W. Heer (eds), *Windows on the Russian Past: Essays on Soviet Historiography since Stalin* (Columbus, Ohio, 1977), pp. vi,

xiii. *Cf.* Baron and Heer, 'The Soviet Union: Historiography Since Stalin', George G. Iggers and Harold T. Parker (eds), *International Handbook of Historical Studies* (Westport, Conn., 1979), p. 291.
18. George M. Enteen, Tatiana Gorn and Cheryl Kern, *Soviet Historians and the Study of Russian Imperialism* (University Park and London, 1979), p. 44.
19. Baron and Heer, *Windows,* p. xv.
20. See Raleigh, p. x; Davies, pp. 1, 5.
21. John Keane (ed.), *Civil Society and the State: New European Perspectives* (London and New York, 1988), pp. 2–5.
22. Moshe Lewin, *Political Undercurrents in Soviet Economic Debates: From Bukharin to the Modern Reformers* (London, 1975), pp. ix, 262.
23. Moshe Lewin, *The Gorbachev Phenomenon: A Historical Interpretation* (London, 1988), pp. 2–8, 80–2.
24. *Cf.* Geoff Eley, 'History with the Politics Left Out – Again?', *The Russian Review*, 45, 1986, p. 390.
25. Gilbert Rozman, *A Mirror for Socialism: Soviet Criticisms of China* (Princeton, New Jersey, 1985).
26. Lewin, *Political Undercurrents.*
27. Alexander Gerschenkron, 'Soviet Marxism and Absolutism', *Slavic Review*, 30, 4, 1971, pp. 868–9; John Keep, 'The Current Scene in Soviet Historiography', *Survey,* 19, 1 (86), Winter 1973, pp. 13–4.
28. Roderic D. M. Pitty, 'Recent Soviet Development Debates: The "Third World" and the USSR', PhD thesis, Australian National University, 1989.
29. See Michael E. Urban, 'The Structure of Signification in the General Secretary's Address: A Semiotic Approach to Soviet Political Discourse', *Coexistence,* 24, 3, 1987, pp. 187–210.
30. Of all the scholars interviewed, Ye. N. Gorodetsky was the only one to emphasize the importance of Aesopian language as a means of avoiding censorship. Other scholars acknowledged a political facet to their work, but emphasized that they were first and foremost engaged in scholarly debate. Any attempt on my part to suggest a preponderantly political dimension was rebuffed.
31. Kuhn, ch. vii, esp. pp. 74–5.
32. *Ibid.*, pp. x, 7, 10, 92. Arif Dirlik, *Revolution and History: The Origins of Marxist Historiography in China, 1919–37* (Berkeley, Los Angeles and London, 1978), pp. 5–6 and n. 5, emphasizes the need to distinguish carefully between paradigms of natural science and those of social science; the latter are especially vulnerable to external factors.
33. David A. Hollinger, 'T. S. Kuhn's Theory of Science and its Implications for History', *American Historical Review,* 78, 1973, pp. 374, 378–9.
34. Kuhn, pp. 67–8, 167.
35. *Ibid.* (original emphasis).
36. Kuhn, 'Reflections on my Critics', in Imre Lakatos and Alan Musgrave (eds), *Criticism and the Growth of Knowledge* (London and New York, 1970), pp. 244–5.
37. Kuhn, *Scientific Revolution,* p. 103.
38. Hollinger, p. 377.

39. Regis Debray, *Teachers, Writers, Celebrities: The Intellectuals of Modern France*, intro. by Francis Mulhern (London, 1981, first published in French 1979), p. 13.
40. Kuhn, *Scientific Revolution*, p. 176, n. 5; Lewin, *Gorbachev Phenomenon*, p. 73.
41. Cited in Debray, p. 79.
42. Aleksander Gella, 'An Introduction to the Sociology of the Intelligentsia', in Gella (ed.), *The Intelligentsia and the Intellectuals: Theory, Method and Case Study* (London and Beverly Hills, California, 1976), p. 11.
43. M. P. Kim (ed.), *Sovetskaya intelligentsiya (Istoriya formirovaniya i rosta 1917–1965 gg)* (Moscow, 1968), p. 6.
44. E. A. Ambartsumov and L. K. Erman, 'Intelligentsiya', *Sovetskaya istoricheskaya entsiklopediya*, T. 6 (Moscow, 1965), cc. 115–6.
45. Kim, pp. 9–11.
46. I. G. Nikol'sky, 'K voprosu o strukture intelligentsii kak sotsial'noi gruppy v usloviyakh razvitogo sotsializma', in V. L. Soskin, *Iz istorii Sovetskoi intelligentsii* (Novosibirsk, 1974), p. 18.
47. Boris Kagarlitsky, *The Thinking Reed: Intellectuals and the Soviet State 1917 to the Present*, trans. by Brian Pearce (London, 1988), pp. 110–12; Debray, p. 29.
48. Rudolf Bahro, *The Alternative in Eastern Europe*, trans. by David Fernbach (London, 1978), pp. 225–7 (original emphasis).
49. V. V. Zhuravlev (ed.), *XX s"ezd KPSS i ego istoricheskie real'nosti* (Moscow, 1991), p. 22.
50. Bahro, p. 227.
51. Merle Fainsod, 'The Role of Intellectuals in the Soviet Union', in H. Malcolm MacDonald (ed.), *The Intellectual in Politics: Symposium* (Austin, Texas, 1966), p. 75.
52. V. A. Konev, 'K voprosu o sotsial'noi prirode intelligentsii', Soskin, pp. 8–10.
53. Gella, p. 19.
54. Lewis A. Coser, *Men of Ideas: A Sociologist's View* (New York and London, 1965), p. viii. For the classic statements on intellectuals from this perspective see Karl Mannheim, *Ideology and Utopia: An Introduction to the Sociology of Knowledge*, trans. by Louis Wirth and Edward Shils (London, 1940), pp. 9–11, 136–46, and Joseph A. Schumpeter, *Capitalism, Socialism and Democracy*, 5th edn, with a new introduction by Tom Bottomore (London, 1976), pp. 146, 151.
55. J. P. Nettl, 'Ideas, Intellectuals, and Structures of Dissent', in Philip Rieff (ed.), *On Intellectuals: Theoretical Studies, Case Studies* (Garden City, New York, 1970), p. 95, n. 45.
56. Talcott Parsons '"The Intellectual": A Social Role Category', in Rieff, pp. 3–26; Edward Shils, 'The Intellectuals and the Powers: Some Perspectives for Comparative Analysis', *ibid.*, pp. 27–52. *Cf.* Seymour M. Lipset and Asoke Basu, 'The Role of the Intellectual and Political Roles', Gella, pp. 111–50.
57. Nettl, pp. 58–9 (original emphasis), 62–3, 63 n. 5, 66–7.
58. *Ibid.*, pp. 69–71, 76.
59. *Ibid.*, pp. 87–90.
60. *Ibid.*, pp. 94–5.

61. *Ibid.*, pp. 92, 94.
62. 'Arakcheev' refers to the military-bureaucratic regime of Tsar Aleksander I, 1815–24. Roy A. Medvedev, *Let History Judge: The Origins and Consequences of Stalinism*, trans. by Colleen Taylor, edited by David Joravsky and Georges Haupt (New York, 1973, first published in 1971), Ch. xiv. On the bureaucratization of history see John Barber, *Soviet Historians in Crisis, 1928–32* (London, 1981).
63. J. P. Nettl, 'Power and the Intellectuals', in Conor Cruise O'Brien and William Dean Vanech (eds), *Power and Consciousness* (London and New York, 1969), pp. 15–32. Nettl's distinction between intellectuals and 'non-innovating bureaucrats' is the polar opposite of the argument mounted by George Konrad and Ivan Szelenyi that the Soviet intelligentsia of the 1960s constituted a highly educated 'class *in statu nascendi*', in the process of appropriating political power in their own interests. In their view, in the 1960s the differences between intellectuals and bureaucrats were gradually disappearing. Konrad and Szelenyi, *The Intellectuals on the Road to Class Power*, trans. by Andrew Arato and Richard E. Allen (Brighton, England, 1979).
64. Sheila Fitzpatrick, *The Cultural Front: Power and Culture in Revolutionary Russia* (Ithaca and London, 1992), esp. pp. 145–7. *Cf.* Vladimir Shlapentokh, *Soviet Intellectuals and Political Power: The Post-Stalin Era* (Princeton, New Jersey, 1990), pp. 10, 24.
65. Nettle, 'Ideas, Intellectuals', pp. 92–4.
66. *Ibid.*, pp. 124, 128.
67. Alvin W. Gouldner, *The Future of Intellectuals and the Rise of the New Class: A Frame of Reference, Theses, Conjectures, Arguments, and an Historical Perspective on the Role of Intellectuals and Intelligentsia in the International Class Contest of the Modern Era* (London, 1979), p. 45.
68. See the analysis in Debray.
69. Nettl, 'Ideas, Intellectuals', pp. 96–8.
70. *Ibid.*, pp. 102–3.
71. *Ibid.*, p. 101.
72. Gella, pp. 11–12. On the Soviet use of the term '*intelligentsiya*' as opposed to '*intellektualy*' see L. G. Churchward, *The Soviet Intelligentsia: An essay on the social structure and roles of Soviet intellectuals during the 1960s* (London and Boston, 1973), pp. 1–2.
73. Gella, pp. 10–15.
74. Fainsod, p. 87.
75. Leonard Schapiro, *Totalitarianism* (London, 1970), p. 118; Carl J. Friedrich and Zbigniew K. Brzezinski, *Totalitarian Dictatorship and Autocracy*, second, revised edition (Cambridge, Massachusetts, 1965), Ch. 24.
76. A point that Sheila Fitzpatrick has made in relation to the model's neglect of social processes: Fitzpatrick, 'New Perspectives on Stalinism', *The Russian Review*, 45, 1986, p. 359.
77. *Dictatorship Over Needs: An Analysis of Soviet Societies* (Oxford, 1983).
78. *Ibid.*, pp. 153, 191–3, 196–7, 291.
79. That 'the present dissidents are in many ways the intelligentsia's spiritual heirs' is the theme of Marshall S. Shatz, *Soviet Dissent in Historical Perspective* (Cambridge, 1980).
80. *Ibid.*, pp. 13, 140–1.

81. Marc Rakovski, *Towards An East European Marxism* (London, 1978), Ch. 3: intellectual 'non-conformism' was transformed into an 'embryonic counter-culture' from which emerged the 'counter-public sphere' of *samizdat* in the Soviet Union.
82. Boris Kagarlitsky, *Dialektika nadezhdy* (Paris, 1982, first distributed as samizdat 1980), pp. 209–10.
83. Elena Zubkova, *Russia After the War: Hopes, Illusions, and Disappointments, 1945–1957*, trans. and ed. by Hugh Ragsdale (Armonk, N.Y. and London, 1998), p. 193.
84. *Ibid.* p. 156. For the impact of writers on historians see L. A. Sidorova, *Ottepel' v istoricheskoi nauke: Sovetskaya istoriografiya pervogo poslestalinskogo desyatiletiya* (Moscow, 1997).
85. Kagarlitsky, *Thinking Reed*, pp. 14–7.
86. Kagarlitsky, interview.
87. Kagarlitsky, 'Lecture', Moscow State University, 27 February 1992.
88. Kagarlitsky, *Dialektika*, pp. 208–9.
89. Kagarlitsky, 'Lecture'. *Cf.* Kagarlitsky, *Thinking Reed*, pp. 162–4. Spechler's study of the writers around *Novyi mir* confirms their growing sense of identification with peasants and workers and the public at large, not least by the principal editor, Aleksandr Tvardovsky. Dina R. Spechler, *Permitted Dissent in the USSR: 'Novyi mir' and the Soviet Regime* (New York, 1982).
90. Shlapentokh, pp. 167–8.
91. Edward Shils, *The Intellectuals and the Powers and Other Essays* (Chicago and London, 1972), pp. 92–3.
92. Shlapentokh, pp. 167–8.
93. Sidney Robert Sherter, 'The Soviet System and the Historian: E. V. Tarle (1875–1955) as a Case Study' (PhD dissertation, Wayne State University, 1968), Ch. V.
94. Kagarlitsky, *Thinking Reed*, p. 95.
95. Richard Pipes, 'The Historical Evolution of the Russian Intelligentsia', in Richard Pipes (ed.), *The Russian Intelligentsia* (New York, 1961), pp. 54–5, 59–61.
96. Kagarlitsky, *Dialektika*, pp. 208–9. However, Shlapentokh, p. 168, gives a contrary impression of the new intelligentsia, attributing to them scepticism and contempt towards the masses.
97. I am not implying here opposition in the sense that Peter Reddaway has used it as an 'aspiration to rule in place of existing rulers'. Reddaway, 'The Development of Dissent and Opposition', in A. Brown and M. Kaser (eds), *The Soviet Union Since the Fall of Khrushchev* (London, 1978), p. 122.
98. Kagarlitsky, 'Lecture'.
99. Cited in Zhuravlev, p. 73 (emphasis added – RDM).
100. Bahro, pp. 313, 317, 321.
101. Zhuravlev, pp. 87–8, 142.
102. *Ibid.*, pp. 80, 142–3.
103. Kagarlitsky, 'Lecture'.
104. Shatz, p. 144 and nn. 9, 10, and pp. 147–8.
105. Kagarlitsky, *Dialektika*, pp. 149, 152, 154–5.
106. 'That Lysenko rose to a position at the commanding heights of Soviet biology, despite the questionable nature of his theoretical position, attests to the importance of the links between knowledge and power as criteria

for truth in the Soviet context.' Stanley Aronowitz, *Science as Power: Discourse and Ideology in Modern Society* (Minneapolis, 1988), p. 227.
107. Cohen, 'Politics and the Past', p. 139.
108. Kagarlitsky, *Dialektika*, p. 159; Kagarlitsky, *Thinking Reed*, p. 9; Rakovski, pp. 46–7.
109. Cohen, 'Politics and the Past', p. 139.
110. Aronowitz, p. 208.
111. Kagarlitsky, *Dialektika*, p. 152.
112. Zhuravlev, pp. 152, 184.
113. Kagarlitsky, interview.
114. L. V. Danilova, interview.
115. Kagarlitsky, *Thinking Reed*, pp. 101–3.
116. Rakovski (pseudonym of Bence and Kis), pp. 42–5.
117. *Ibid.*, pp. 43–4.
118. *Ibid.*, pp. 45, 48–9.
119. *Ibid.*, p. 48.
120. Karl Marx, 'Critique of Hegel's Doctrine of the State', in Bahro, p. 216 (original emphasis).
121. Rakovski, pp. 55–8.
122. *Ibid.*, p. 59.
123. Kagarlitsky, *Thinking Reed*, p. 101. *Cf.* Bence and Kis: 'defence of cultural autonomy' was 'transformed into political opposition'. Rakovski, pp. 58–62.
124. Julien Benda, author of the *Trahison des Clercs* (1927) cited in Tibor Huszar, 'Changes in the Concept of Intellectuals', in Gella, pp. 81–2
125. Huszar, p. 99.
126. Antonio Gramsci, 'The formation of the intellectuals', in Quintin Hoare and Geoffrey Nowell Smith (eds), *Selections from the Prison Notebooks of Antonio Gramsci* (London, 1971), pp. 5–14.
127. Gramsci, 'State and Civil Society', in Hoare and Smith, p. 238.
128. 'More than most modern intelligentsias the Soviet intelligentsia are "officials" of the ruling elite'. L. G. Churchward, 'The Intelligentsia Revisited', in Churchward, *Soviet Socialism: Social and Political Essays* (London and New York, 1987), p. 62.
129. Debray, p. 127.
130. Louis Althusser, 'Ideology and Ideological State Apparatuses (Notes Towards an Investigation)', in Althusser, *Lenin and Philosophy and Other Essays*, trans. by Ben Brewster (London, 1977), pp. 136–7.
131. Debray, p. 195.
132. Alastair Davidson, 'Antonio Gramsci', in Peter Beilharz (ed.), *Social Theory: A Guide to Central Thinkers* (Sydney, 1992), pp. 127–32.
133. Debray, p. 30. Likewise, Urban argues that Soviet political discourse erected a 'linguistic barrier *against* political thought' whereby 'ostensibly political terms' were 'depoliticized'. Urban, pp. 188, 203–4 (original emphasis). *Cf.* Urban, 'Conceptualizing Political Power in the USSR: Patterns of Binding and Bonding', *Studies in Comparative Communism*, xviii, 4, Winter 1985, pp. 217–8.
134. Eero Loone, *Soviet Marxism and Analytical Philosophies of History*, trans. by Brian Pearce (London and New York, 1992, first published in Russian in 1980), p. 228.

254 Notes

135. Debray, pp. 131–2.
136. Leon Trotsky, *The Revolution Betrayed: What is the Soviet Union and Where Is It Going?* (New York, 1972, first published 1937), pp. 254–6; Isaac Deutscher, 'The Roots of Bureaucracy', in Deutscher, *Marxism in Our Time* (London, 1972), pp. 195–208.
137. Michael Löwy, 'Stalinist Ideology and Science', in Tariq Ali (ed.), *The Stalinist Legacy: Its Impact on Twentieth-Century World Politics* (Harmondsworth, 1984), p. 168.
138. Gramsci cited in Ralph Miliband, *Marxism and Politics* (Oxford, 1977), p. 59.
139. Gianfranco Poggi, 'The State and Creative Intellectuals' (Colloquium, Department of Government, University of Sydney, 11 August 1992).
140. William H. McNeill, *Mythistory and Other Essays* (Chicago and London, 1986), pp. 3, 11–13.
141. Geoffrey Barraclough, *Main Trends in History* (New York and London, 1979), pp. 122, 128. History played a key role in consolidating the 'new national consciousness' that was integral to the Chinese revolution. 'From the beginning, advocates of political change turned to history as the clearing house of legitimacy'. Dirlik, p. 260.
142. Eric Hobsbawm, 'Introduction: Inventing Traditions', in Hobsbawm and Terence Ranger (eds), *The Invention of Tradition* (Cambridge, 1983), pp. 12–14 (emphasis added – RDM).
143. Jean Chesneaux, *Pasts and Futures or What is History For?* trans. by Schofield Coryell (London, 1978), pp. 3, 16.
144. Ian Green, '"Repulsives vs Wromantics": Rival Views of the English Civil War', in Brady, p. 149.
145. Heer, *Politics and History*, pp. 12–33. Cf. Heer, 'The Non-Bolshevik Left', in Baron and Heer, *Windows*, pp. 157–8.
146. *Ibid.*, pp. 30–3, 77, 112.
147. T. H. Rigby, 'Introduction', in Rigby and Ferenc Feher (eds), *Political Legitimation in Communist States* (London and Basingstoke, 1982), p. 16.
148 George Schöpflin, 'The End of Communism in Eastern Europe', *International Affairs*, 66, 1, January 1990, p. 6 (I have put the quote in the past tense – RDM).

2   The Twentieth Party Congress and history

1. *XX S"ezd Kommunisticheskoi Partii Sovetskogo Soyuza 14–25 Fevralya 1956 goda Stenographichesky otchet*, Vol. I (Moscow, 1956), p. 325.
2. *Ibid.*, pp. 621–2.
3. John Barber, 'Stalin's Letter to the Editors of *Proletarskaya Revolyutsiya*', *Soviet Studies*, XXVII, 1, January 1976, pp. 21–41.
4. John Barber, *Soviet Historians in Crisis, 1928–32* (London, 1981), pp. 1–2.
5. J. V. Stalin, 'Some Questions Concerning Bolshevism: Letter to the Editorial Board of the Magazine "Proletarskaya Revolyutsiya"', *Works* (Moscow, 1955), Vol. 13, pp. 86–104.
6. Barber, *Soviet Historians*, p. 10; Konstantin F. Shteppa, *Russian Historians and the Soviet State* (New Brunswick, New Jersey, 1962), p. 206.
7. Shteppa, pp. 88–9.

8. Barber, *Soviet Historians*, p. 9.
9. *Ibid.*, p. 8, citing Kaganovich's speech of 1 December 1931, the tenth anniversary of the founding of the Institute of Red Professors.
10. Stalin, 'Letter', p. 104.
11. Barber, *Soviet Historians*, p. 144.
12. *Ibid.*, p. 6.
13. N. I. Pavlenko, interview; Pavlenko, 'Istoricheskaya nauka v proshlom i nastoyashchem (Nekotorye razmyshleniya vslukh)', *I SSSR*, 1991, 4, pp. 93–4.
14. Shteppa, p. 23.
15. *Ibid.*, pp. 49, 90, 97–8, 146, 179. Pokrovsky, who died in 1932, was posthumously arraigned as an 'anti-Leninist' whose 'sterile sociology' had given comfort to the 'Trotsky-Bukharinist hirelings of Fascism' by one of his former pupils, Pankratova, who was also Grekov's party minder.
16. *Ibid.*, pp. 168–9; Medvedev, *Let History Judge* (1973), p. 223.
17. Ivan Mstyslav Myhul, 'Politics and History in the Soviet Ukraine: A Study of Soviet Ukrainian Historiography, 1956–1970' (PhD dissertation, Columbia University, 1973), pp. 15–18.
18. Shteppa, pp. 95, 100.
19. See Elena Zubkova, *Russia After the War: Hopes, Illusions, and Disappointments, 1945–1957*, trans. and edited by Hugh Ragsdale (New York and London, 1998), esp. Ch. 13.
20. M. Ya. Gefter (1918–95), interview. Born in Simferopol 24 August 1918, Gefter entered the history faculty of Moscow State University in 1936. In 1941 he volunteered for the front, where he was badly wounded. After the war he entered the Institute of History, Soviet Academy of Sciences, as an *aspirant*, going on to head the Sector of Methodology, 1964–9. After its disbandment, he was a researcher in the Institute of General History, until taking early retirement in 1974. In 1982 he resigned from the CPSU in protest against threatened Soviet intervention in Poland. After the events of August 1991 he became a member of the Presidential Council, from which he resigned in protest against Yeltsin's destruction of the parliament in October 1993. He died 15 February 1995 'in revulsion at the Chechen war, pseudo-democratic reforms, the collapse of the democratic movement, the false hopes of part of the intelligentsia and unbridled criminality.' Svetlana Neretina, 'Mikhail Yakovlevich Gefter', *Vek XX i mir*, 3, 1996, pp. 234–7.
21. A. L. Sidorov, Gefter's supervisor, was the key figure pursuing this campaign among historians. Aleksandr Nekrich, *Otreshis' ot strakha: Vospominaniya istorika* (London, 1979), p. 39.
22. A. Ya. Gurevich, interview. Gurevich's supervisor, the outstanding medievalist A. N. Neusykhin, was singularly humiliated during the anti-cosmopolitan campaign. At a December 1948 meeting of the Academic Council of the Institute of History 'old' scholars, such as Bakhrushin, were criticized by the 'new' Soviet educated historians such as V. T. Pashuto and L. V. Cherepnin: 'The star of the "old" scholars was obviously setting.' Shteppa, pp. 232, 246.
23. Ye. N. Gorodetsky, interview. Gorodetsky was also a victim of the anti-cosmopolitan campaign. He lost his position in the Central Committee apparatus and was sent to Moscow State University. Nekrich, p. 52.

24. Gefter, interview. The classic 'state-juridical' school of history, exemplified in the work of V. N. Chicherin (1828–1904), S. M. Solovev and, to a certain extent, V. O. Klyuchevsky, depicted the state as the 'demi-urge' of Russian history. N. L. Rubinshtein, *Russkaya istoriografiya* (Ogiz, 1941), pp. 303, 326, 468. Rubinshtein's book, incidentally, was denounced during the anti-cosmopolitan campaign.
25. Shteppa, p. 271.
26. Danilova, interview.
27. 'Historical consciousness' is an important element of Russian historical thinking, and for the revisionist historians of the 1960s. Gefter spoke of a 'definite interconnection between the processes that occur in the sphere of historical knowledge and historical consciousness, a notion that goes beyond the professional work of the historians. Historical consciousness is a more general factor, dictated by politics, public opinion, by the correlation of social forces and by the international context. The professional activity of the historian is an essential part of historical consciousness, but by no means exhausts it.' Gefter, interview.
28. *Ibid.*
29. *Ibid.*
30. Gefter, interview, whose assessment of this work contrasts markedly with that of Pavlenko. For Pavlenko, Nechkina was no more than a *politruk* (political instructor) who feted the Decembrists as 'prevolutionary members of the VKP (b)' (!), while jealously monopolizing this area of research. Pavlenko, interview.
31. In this regard, however, the Soviet Union was not unique. Japan too had a penchant for using textbooks to establish a single reading of history. In both cases an official textbook provided a strong state – Stalinist or military-fascist – with a vital ingredient for mobilizing the 'national idea' behind modernization. See R. J. B. Bosworth, *Explaining Auschwitz and Hiroshima: History Writing and the Second World War 1945–1990* (London and New York, 1993), pp. 180–1, 187.
32. Medvedev, *Let History Judge* (1973), p. 500, n. 5, p. 511.
33. Ye. N. Gorodetsky, 'Problemy velikogo oktyabrya', V. S. Lel'chuk (ed.), *Istoriki sporyat* (Moscow, 1988), p. 8.
34. V. D. Polikarpov, in 'Istoriki i pisateli o literature i istorii. Materialy konferentsii', *VI*, 1988, 6, pp. 95–6.
35. *Ibid.*
36. *KK*, pp. 342–3. According to Medvedev, *Let History Judge* (1973) p. 346, V. M. Molotov interpolated this panegyric of Stalin 'in his own hand'.
37. Gorodetsky, 'Problemy', pp. 7–8; Yu. N. Afanas'ev, in 'Istoriki i pisateli', p. 73.
38. Polikarpov, in 'Istoriki i pisateli', pp. 95–6.
39. D. K. Shelestov, in ' "Krugly stol": Istoricheskaya nauka v usloviyakh perestroiki', *VI*, 1988, 3, p. 35.
40. Afanas'ev, 'Perestroika', p. 498.
41. *KK*, p. 339.
42. *Ibid.*, p. 343.
43. Medvedev, *Let History Judge* (1973), pp. 499–500. Even in the revised, 1989 edition of *Let History Judge*, p. 810, n. 2, the name of the historian 'cannot yet' be divulged.

44. Herbert Butterfield, *The Whig Interpretation of History* (Harmondsworth, 1973, first published 1931), p. 9. This analogy was suggested by George M. Enteen, 'A Recent Trend on the Historical Front', *Survey*, 20, 4 (93), Autumn 1974, p. 123, n. 4.
45. Myhul, p. 18.
46. *KK*, p. 100.
47. *Ibid.*, p. 109. As Herbert Marcuse observed, the conversion of Soviet Marxism from 'theory to ideology' saw the 'petrification of the dialectic', resulting in 'a de-emphasis of history' which was 'reified into a second nature.' *Soviet Marxism: A Critical Analysis* (Harmondsworth, 1971, first published 1958), Ch. 7. *Cf.* James P. Scanlan, *Marxism in the USSR: A Critical Survey of Current Thought* (Ithaca and London, 1985), pp. 107 *ff.* and 182.
48. Helmut Fleischer, *Marxism and History,* trans. by Eric Mosbacher (New York, 1973), pp. 38–41.
49. *KK*, p. 118: 'The productive forces are not only the most activating and revolutionary element of production. They are also the determining element of the development of production ... Whatever the level of the productive forces the relations of production must correspond to them.'
50. A. Ya. Gurevich, 'Teoriya formatsii i real'nost' istorii', *VF*, 1990, 11, p. 37.
51. *Ibid.*, p. 36; A. A. Iskenderov, '"Krugly stol"', p. 5. Volobuev pointed to a 'braking mechanism' in 'historical science' the methodological and psychological bases of which were implanted in the 1930s by Stalin's schemas 'from which time began the depersonalization of the history of the party and the country.' 'Istoriko-partiinaya nauka: Puti perestroiki i dal'neishego razvitiya', *VI KPSS*, 1987, 7, p. 140; *Cf.* 'Perestroika, History and Historians (Roundtable)', p. 788.
52. Fleischer, p. 41.
53. Pavlenko, p. 19. This tendency of Soviet historiography to reduce history to the production of material wealth was subject to an important critique in 1964 by Gurevich, 'Nekotorye aspekty izucheniya sotsial'noi istorii (obshchestvenno-istoricheskaya psikhologiya)', *VI*, 1964, 10, p. 54. Volobuev, 'Istoriko-partiinaya', pp. 139–40, argued that the effects on historical writing of the reconsolidation of Stalinist 'dogmatism' in the Brezhnev era was a 'subjective vulgar sociologism and a primitive economic materialism'.
54. Gurevich, 'Teoriya', p. 33. Eeero Loone points out that the *Short Course* itself did not categorically exclude the possibility of other formations: 'Incidentally, Stalin himself *wrote* very cautiously: "Five *main* types of relations of production are known to history ..." The transformation of the "set of five terms" into the norm took place in the process of interpreting that sentence under the conditions of those days, when extra-scientific arguments played a palpable role.' Loone, *Soviet Marxism and Analytical Philosophies of History*, trans. by Brian Pearce (London and New York, 1992, first published in Russian in 1980), p. 255, n. 2 (original emphases).
55. V. A. Kozlev, cited in Lewis H. Siegelbaum, 'Historical Revisionism in the USSR', *Radical History Review*, 44, 1989, p. 50.
56. *KK*, p. 111; J. V. Stalin, *Marxism and Problems of Linguistics* (Peking, 1972, first published in *Pravda* 20 June 1950), p. 5. *Cf.* Scanlan, p. 267.

57. J. Stalin, *Economic Problems of Socialism in the USSR* (Moscow, 1952), pp. 5–13.
58. Shteppa, pp. 308–11.
59. *KK*, p. 116.
60. Gurevich, 'Teoriya', p. 36.
61. Isaac Deutscher, 'Marxism and Primitive Magic', in Ali, pp. 106–17.
62. On the accelerating urbanization after 1956, that rocketed in the 1960s, and its effects on the skills of the labour force see Lewin, *Gorbachev Phenomenon*.
63. *KK*, pp. 331–2; *Istoriya Kommunisticheskoi partii Sovetskogo Soyuza*, second, expanded edition (Moscow, 1963), p. 505. For a summary of the basic revisions in the 1959 *History* contrasted to the *Short Course* see Heer, *Politics and History*, pp. 109–10.
64. *Osnovy Marksizma Leninizma: Uchebnoe posobie*, 2nd edn (Moscow, 1962), p. 125.
65. 'Stenogramma zasedeniya kafedry istorii KPSS, Akademii obshchestvennykh nauk pri TsK KPSS. Obsuzhdenie maketa tretego izdaniya uchebnika "Istoriya KPSS"', TsKhSD, f. 5, op. 58, d. 37, l. 152
66. '"Krugly stol"', p. 18.
67. Afanas'ev objected to any proposal for yet another official history of the CPSU on the grounds that this would simply reinforce the concept of '"historical truth"' which had underpinned the *Short Course* approach: 'Our students need questions not answers'. Afanas'ev, 'Perestroika', p. 505.
68. V. V. Zhuravlev (ed.), *XX s"ezd KPSS i ego istoricheskie real'nosti* (Moscow, 1991), pp. 42–3.
69. Nikita Sergeyevich Khrushchev, *The 'Secret' Speech delivered to the closed session of the Twentieth Congress of the Communist Party of the Soviet Union*, introduction by Zhores A. Medvedev and Roy A. Medvedev (Nottingham, 1976). For background to the report and its aftermath see Yu. Aksyutin, 'N. S. Khrushchev: "My dolzhny skazat' pravdu o kul'te lichnosti"', Aksyutin (ed.), *Nikita Sergeyevich Khrushchev: Materialy k biografii* (Moscow, 1989), pp. 32–42.
70. Isaac Deutscher, 'Khrushchev on Stalin', in Deutscher, *Ironies of History: Essays on Contemporary Communism* (London, 1966), pp. 7–8, 14.
71. Zhuravlev, pp. 42, 46.
72. Roy A. Medvedev, 'The Stalin Question', Stephen F. Cohen, Alexander Rabinowitch and Robert Sharlet (eds), *The Soviet Union Since Stalin* (Bloomington, Indiana, 1980), p. 39.
73. Zhuravlev, p. 44.
74. *Ibid.*, p. 42.
75. 'Postanovlenie Ts KPSS o preodelenii kul't lichnost i ego posledstvii', 30 yuniya 1956 g.', *Khrestomatiya po istorii KPSS*, T. 2, 1925–mart 1985 g. (Moscow, 1989), pp. 413–30. Cf. Roy A. Medvedev and Zhores A. Medvedev, *Khrushchev: The Years in Power*, foreword by Stephen F. Cohen, trans. Andrew R. Durkin (New York and London, 1978), p. 71; Aksyutin, p. 38.
76. Khrushchev's 'dual evaluation' of Stalin is explored by Stephen F. Cohen, 'The Stalin Question Since Stalin', in Cohen (ed.), *An End to Silence: Uncensored Opinion in the Soviet Union from Roy Medvedev's Underground*

Magazine, 'Political Diary', trans. by George Saunders (New York and London, 1982), pp. 32–4.
77. Ya. S. Drabkin, interview.
78. *Ibid*. Born in 1918, Yakov Drabkin was a student in the history faculty, MGU, 1936–41. He then served on the front until 1945, subsequently serving in the Soviet military administration in Germany. In 1963 he became a researcher in the Institute of History, Soviet Academy of Sciences. In 1991 he edited an anthology of Rosa Luxemburg's writings. *Vek XX i mir*, 1996, 1, p. 96.
79. Danilova, interview.
80. Sidorova, p. 80.
81. Nekrich, pp. 141–3.
82. Hösler, pp. 15–16, 295.
83. Nekrich, p. 123.
84. Ye. N. Gorodetsky, 'Zhurnal "Voprosy istorii" v seredine 50–x godov', *VI*, 1989, 9, pp. 69–70; Nekrich, p. 90.
85. A. M. Pankratova (1897–1957) joined the communist party in 1919 and studied in Pokrovsky's Institute of Red Professors in 1922–5. Under Pokrovsky's patronage in the 1920s she established her reputation as the founder of the Soviet school of historians of the working class (Gorodetsky). Expelled from the party in 1936, she was readmitted in 1938. In 1939 she played a leading role in condemning the 'historical conceptions of M. N. Pokrovsky'. In 1953 she became an academician and was appointed principal editor of *Voprosy istorii*. Hösler, pp. 19–20, n 10. According to Gorodetsky, while of 'democratic and open' temperament, Pankratova was 'demanding' in relation to research and complemented her deputy, Burdzhalov. Gorodetsky, 'Zhurnal', pp. 69–70.
86. Hösler, p. 295.
87. Barber, *Soviet Historians*, p. 19.
88. Of Armenian nationality, Eduard Burdzhalov (1906–85) joined the Komsomol at the age of 14 and the communist party in 1923. A graduate of Moscow State University in 1938 he published his first book, *The 26 Baku Commissars*, a major study of their alleged massacre by British interventionist forces. As a member of the Central Committee apparatus he volunteered for the front in 1941. After the war he returned to the Central Committee administration until 1953 when he became a teacher in the Higher Party School and a researcher in the Institute of History until his appointment as *Voprosy istorii* deputy editor in 1953. Both Pankratova and Burdzhalov in the 1930s and 1940s, in Gorodetsky's words, 'contributed to the "cult of the personality". But as honest communists, having embraced the party's liberation from Stalinism, they never deviated from this course.' Gorodetsky, 'Zhurnal', p. 69; Ye. N. Gorodetsky, G. Z. Yoffe, G. S. Akopyan, N. D. Kuznetsov, 'E. N. Burdzhalov – Istorik fevral'skoi revolyutsii 1917 goda', *I SSSR*, 1987, 6, pp. 168–169. For an overview of Burdzhalov's life and work see the 'Introduction' to E. N. Burdzhalov, *Russia's Second Revolution: The February 1917 Uprising in Petrograd*, trans. and ed. by Donald J. Raleigh (Bloomington and Indianapolis, 1987, first published in Russian, 1967).
89. Gorodetsky, 'Zhurnal', pp. 70–1.

90. 'Konferentsiya chitatelei zhurnala "Voprosy istorii" ', *VI*, 1956, 2, p. 200.
91. *Ibid.*, p. 202; Gorodetsky, 'Zhurnal', p. 71, n. 5.
92. 'Konferentsiya chitatelei', p. 210.
93. Sidorov's remarks were not entirely negative, however. Apart from urging a reconsideration of the Shamil movement, a question that struck at the heart of Russian chauvinist historiography, he also urged the development of other specialist historical journals, annual all-Union conferences of historians and the establishment of a historians' association to promote discussion. *Ibid.*, pp. 207–8.
94. *Ibid.*, pp. 212–13.
95. '(Report to the) TsK KPSS', 7 February 1956, signed by the Director of the Department of Science and Higher Educational Establishments, V. A. Kirillin, and K. Kuznetsova, political instructor of the Department of Science. TsKhSD, f. 5, op. 35, d. 39, ll. 20–5.
96. *Ibid.*
97. *Ibid.*, l. 20.
98. *Ibid.*, l. 22.
99. *Ibid.*, ll. 24–5.
100. Gorodetsky, 'Zhurnal', p. 72.
101. Cited in *ibid.*
102. 'XX s"ezd KPSS i zadachi issledovaniya istorii partii', *VI*, 1956, 3, pp. 3–12.
103. Raleigh, 'Introduction', p. xiii.
104. 'XX s"ezd KPSS i zadachi', p. 4.
105. *Ibid.*, pp. 4, 7.
106. E. N. Burdzhalov, 'O taktike bol'shevikov v marte-aprele 1917 goda', *VI*, 1956, 4, pp. 38–56; Burdzhalov replied to his critics in 'Eshche o taktike bol'shevikov v marte-aprele 1917 goda', *VI*, 1956, 8, pp. 109–114.
107. Burdzhalov, 'O taktike', pp. 38–9; *KK*, p. 176.
108. Initially, the 'rough notes' of the minutes of the Bureau of the Central Committee of the Russian Social Democratic Workers' Party; later he had access to the actual minutes of several sessions of the Bureau of the Central Committee of the Russian Communist Party (bolsheviks). Burdzhalov, 'Eshche o taktike', p. 110.
109. Burdzhalov, 'O taktike', pp. 45–7; *KK*, p. 179.
110. *KK*, p. 181.
111. Burdzhalov, 'O taktike', p. 54; 'Doklad E. N. Burdzhalova o sostoyaniii sovetskoi istoricheskoi naukii i rabote zhurnala "Voprosy istorii" (na vstreche c chitatelyami 19–20 yuniya 1956 g. v Leningradskom otedelenii instituta istorii AN SSSR)', *VI*, 1989, 11, p. 127. This is a continuation of Burdzhalov's paper under the same title from *VI*, 1989, 9, pp. 81–96.
112. Burdzhalov, 'O taktike', p. 51.
113. Leon Trotsky, *The Stalin School of Falsification* (London, 1974, first published in Russian in 1932), pp. 146–50.
114. Memorandum to D. T. Shepilov, (Secretary of the) CPSU Central Committee, from E. N. Burdzhalov, 30 May 1956. TsKhSD, f. 5, op. 35, d. 39, ll. 88–94.
115. *Ibid.*, l. 93.
116. Gorodetsky, 'Zhurnal', p. 73.

117. Memorandum to D. T. Shepilov, ll. 93–4.
118. Gorodetsky, 'Zhurnal', p. 72.
119. 'Konferentsiya chitatelei zhurnala "Voprosy istorii" v Leningrade', *VI*, 1956, 7, pp. 184–90.
120. Barber, *Soviet Historians*, p. 177, n. 25.
121. 'Doklad E. N. Burdzhalova o sostoyanii sovetskoi istoricheskoi naukii i rabote zhurnala "Voprosy istorii" (na vstreche c chitatelyami 19–20 yuniya 1956 g. v Leningradskom otedelenii instituta istorii AN SSSR), *VI*, 1989, 9, pp. 82–4.
122. *Ibid.*, 9, pp. 85–6; 11, p. 116.
123. *Ibid.*, 11, pp. 117–19.
124. When the survivors from Stalin's camps returned to the Institute of History in the mid-1950s and encountered free-flowing discussion among the younger scholars they accused them of propagating Trotskyist and Bukharinist views. This, said Volobuev, was the 'contradictoriness' of the survivors of the camps: 'Having been imprisoned for 17 years, they remained the same people, with the same methods of polemic and argumentation. They, in fact, proved to be Stalinists. Paradoxically, while they were the victims of Stalinism, they criticized from the position of Stalinism.' Volobuev, interview.
125. 'Doklad E. N. Burdzhalova', 11, pp. 129–30.
126. Memorandum to D. T. Shepilov, l. 89.
127. 'Doklad E. N. Burdzhalova', 11, pp. 113, 115–16.
128. *Ibid.*, 9, pp. 89–91.
129. *Ibid.*, pp. 92–3. The theory of the 'lesser evil', first promulgated in 1937, rationalized Russian annexation of other nations by suggesting this was preferable to their annexation by other great powers. Shteppa, pp. 277–8, 282–3.
130. 'Doklad E. N. Burdzhalova', 11, p. 122 where Burdzhalov quoted at length from Stalin's famous conversation with the actor N. Cherkasov concerning the film *Ivan groznyi* (Ivan the Terrible). The Institute of History, Burdzhalov noted, had recently devoted a two-day conference to Ivan the Terrible, whose status was linked to the question of feudalism and the centralized state. *Ibid.*, 9, p. 87. These themes were taken up in S. M. Dubrovsky, 'Protiv idealizatsii deyatel'nosti Ivana IV', *VI*, 1956, 8, pp. 121–8.
131. 'Doklad E. N. Burdzhalova', 11, p. 122.
132. 'Za tvorcheskuyu razrabotky istorii KPSS', *Kst*,1956, 10, p. 24.
133. E. Bugaev, 'Kogda utrachivaetsia nauchnyi podkhod', *Partinaya zhizn'*, 1956, 14, pp. 69–72.
134. 'Zaveduyushchemu otdelom nauki TsK KPSS chlenu-korrespondentu Akademii nauk SSSR tovarishchu Kirillinu, zaveduyushchemu otdelom nauki Leningradskogo OK KPSS tovarishchu Bogdanovu, Otvetstvennomu redaktoru "Leningradskoi Pravdy"'. 1 September 1956, signed by 17 historians. TsKhSD, f. 5, op. 35, d. 39, ll. 135–42. A copy of a reply to A. Aleksandrova sent to N. S. Khrushchev by 7 researchers from Saltykov-Shchedrin Library, 5 September 1956. *Ibid.*, ll. 143–52.
135. 'Sekretariyu TsK KPSS tov. Khrushchevu N. S.', 18 September 1956, TsKhSD, f. 5, op. 35, d. 39, l. 74.

136. Report by A. Gavrilova to the Department of Science, 27 June 1956, TsKhSD, *ibid.*, ll. 95–107.
137. *Ibid.*, l. 97.
138. Gorodetsky, 'Zhurnal', p. 76. *Cf.* Zubkova, pp. 195–6.
139. 'XX s"ezd KPSS i zadachi', p. 12.
140. 'O stat'e tov. E. Bugaeva', *VI*, 1956, 7, p. 222.
141. 'Tovarishchu Shepilovu D. T.', Letter from Burdzhalov, 11 December 1956. TsKhSD, f. 5, op. 35, d. 39, ll. 153–4. Among those who criticized Burdzhalov for reviving Trotskyism in his articles were A. L. Sidorov and his student P. V. Volobuev. According to Volobuev, Sidorov, in criticizing Burdzhalov, was not only acting on conviction, but on the 'specific instructions of the Central Committee'. Volobuev himself (at the time an instructor of the Central Committee's Department of Science and Culture, a post he occupied for more than two years), was ordered to report on *Voprosy istorii* and the allegations against it to the Central Committee in letters written by 'conformists and conservatives'. In his report Volobuev, 'on the whole', gave a 'negative appraisal of the innovations of the journal and of Burdzhalov's articles in particular.' During the *perestroika* period Volobuev publicly 'repented' his role in the Burdzhalov affair which occurred, he said, at the beginning of 'the evolution of my Stalinist views and convictions. I was confused.' Volobuev, interview. *Cf.* Volobuev, letter, vi, 1990, 6, p. 183. In his final word on this issue, he categorically rejected allegations that he co-authored the March 1957 resolution. 'Intervyu s akademikom P. V. Volobuevym', *OI*, Nov-Dec 1997, 6, p. 112.
142. Sidorova, p. 12.
143. A. Pankratova, 'Chlenu presidiuma tsentral'nogo komiteta KPSS; tov. Suslovu M. A.', 23 August 1956. TsKhSD, f. 5, op. 35, d. 39, ll. 61–3.
144. Gorodetsky, 'Zhurnal', p. 80. Gorodetsky himself, then in the history faculty, MGU, was censured by a party meeting.
145. *Ibid.*, p. 73.
146. The Central Committee secretaries Shepilov and Pospelov, both of whom had contributed to Khrushchev's 'secret speech', and to whom Burdzhalov had directed his written appeals, lined up on different sides during the 'anti-party' affair. Pospelov supported Khrushchev, while Shepilov lost his secretaryship and was expelled from the presidium and the Central Committee. Zhuravlev, pp. 39, 50, 60.
147. 'Sekretaryu TsK KPSS tov. Pospelovu P. N, zav. Otdelom nauki TsK KPSS tov. Kirillinu V. A., zav. Otdelom propagandy i agitatsii TsK KPSS, tov. Konstantinovu F. V.', Letter from Burdzhalov, 8 February 1957, TsKhSD, f. 5, op. 35, d. 39, l. 161; Gorodetsky, 'Zhurnal', pp. 78–9.
148. Cited in Sidorova, p. 277.
149. *Ibid.*, pp. 155–6.
150. *Ibid.*, p. 78; 'Za leninskuyu partiinost' v istoricheskoi nauke!', *VI*, 1957, 3, pp. 4–5, 8. P. N. Pospelov, the main reporter at the 6 March meeting of the Central Committee Secretariat, was the head of the commission upon whose research Khrushchev's 'Secret Speech' was based. *Khrushchev Remembers*, Introduction, commentary and notes by Edward Crankshaw, trans. by Strobe Talbot (London, 1971), p. 345, n.15.
151. Cited in Gorodetsky, 'Zhurnal', p. 78.

152. *Ibid.*, p. 79.
153. 'Za leninskuyu partiinost' ', p. 10.
154. Zhuravlev, p. 252.
155. *Ibid.*, pp. 252–3.
156. *Ibid.*, p. 251.
157. A. B. Bezborodov, *Fenomen akademicheskogo dissidentstva V SSSR* (Moscow, 1998), pp. 29–31.
158. Raleigh, 'Introduction', p. xv.
159. Gorodetsky *et al.*, 'E. N. Burdzhalov', pp. 171, 173.
160. Sidorova, pp. 160–2.
161. Barber, *Soviet Historians,* p. 176, n. 5.
162. Gorodetsky, interview.
163. Hösler, pp. 296–7.
164. *Vsesoyuznoe soveshchanie o merakh podgotovki nauchno-pedagogicheskikh kadrov po istorichekskim naukam 18–21 dekabrya 1962 g.* (Moscow, 1964), p. 329.
165. M. V. Nechkina and Ye. N. Gorodetsky, *Ocherki po istorii istoricheskoi nauki v SSSR*, Tom V (Moscow, 1985), p. 70.
166. For a brief period, December 1962 until May 1965, responsibility for science and higher educational establishments was actually taken by the Ideological Department of the Central Committee. TsKhSD. f. 5, op. 35.
167. As several participants in the 1962 conference complained. *Vsesoyuznoe*, pp. 99, 380.
168. Volobuev, interview.
169. Nekrich, pp. 76–7, 83, 153, 162–3.
170. *Ibid.*, pp. 20–1.
171. Gorodetsky, interview.
172. This is the number of historians in *Vuzy* and research institutions as of 1 October 1961. *Vsesoyuznoe*, p. 43.
173. K. N. Tarnovsky, 'Put' uchenogo', *IZ*, 1967, 80, p. 229.
174. Danilova, interview. Zubkova, p. 112, distinguishes between the war veterans and the idealistic generation that grew up during the war.
175. Volobuev, interview.
176. *Vsesoyuznoe*, pp. 213–14.
177. *Ibid.*, pp. 40–1, 46, 88.
178. *Ibid.*, p. 106.
179. See Table 2.1 above. The number of graduate students of Moscow University History Faculty declined from 39 in 1956 to 14 in 1961. *Ibid.*, p. 44. Whereas in 1956 there 531 *aspiranty* who graduated from the *Vuzy*, in 1958–61 this had declined on average to 200–250, the majority of whom did not defend their theses in the allotted time. *Ibid.*, p. 329.
180. The average number of books published by Nauka per annum dropped from 6,303 in 1960 to 3,749 in 1961. *Ibid.*, pp. 189–91.
181. *Ibid.*, pp. 336–7.
182. S. V. Utechin, 'Soviet historiography after Stalin', in Keep, *Contemporary History*, p. 119.
183. Despite this growth, these figures compared unfavourably with the 437 historical publications in West Germany and 542 in the USA. Fedoseev, *Vsesoyuznoe*, p. 190. Nechkina and Gorodetsky, p. 104.

184. The imminence of the fortieth anniversary of the October Revolution occasioned the publication of such important materials as the 'Proceedings of the Russian Social Democratic Workers Party (bolsheviks). August 1917 – February 1918', the minutes of the Russian bureau of the Central Committee of the RSDWP (b) and materials relating to the March 1917 conference of the Bolsheviks. Zhuravlev, p. 243.
185. *Ibid.*
186. Previously an occasional publication, *Istorichesky arkhiv* appeared bi-monthly from 1955 to 1962. In the main it published documents on Soviet and party history. Publication of the journal was suspended in the first half of 1962. At the end of that year it ceased publication altogether. Utechin, p. 119 and n. 2. At the 1962 all-Union conference financial stringency was the excuse offered in response to the numerous complaints about its closure.
187. Nechkina and Gorodetsky, pp. 72–8.
188. Zhuravlev, p. 243.
189. The MVD was the successor to the NKVD (People's Commissariat of Internal Affairs) to which responsibility for archives was transferred in April 1938. T. Khorodina, *Istoriya otechestva i arkhivy 1917–1980–e gg.* (Moscow, 1994), pp. 239–40, 311–3, 316, 355. Nekrich was a member of a Department of Science group formed in 1956 to investigate the state of Soviet archives and prepare a Central Committee resolution on the question. The group's work was aborted in good part due to the resistance of the MVD. Many of the published documents were, moreover, 'doctored'. Nekrich, pp. 139–40.
190. Zhuravlev, p. 242. On recent revelations about Lenin see R. W. Davies, *Soviet History in the Yeltsin Era* (London, 1997).
191. V. I. Bovykin, interview.
192. Nechkina and Gorodetsky, p. 52.
193. Cyril E. Black, *Understanding Soviet Politics: The Perspective of Russian History* (Boulder, Colorado, 1986), pp. 52, 54.
194. Nechkina and Gorodetsky, pp. 52–3.
195. Zhukov played a key role in containing historical revisionism. In 1957 he was appointed to the 'critical position' of Academic Secretary of the Division of History of the Academy of Sciences, a position that made him 'the principal administrative officer and party guide for historical research in the Soviet Union'. Black, pp. 77, 85, n. 34.
196. Otdelenie istorii AN SSSR, 'Stenogramma zasedaniya kommissii po podgotovke materialov dlya TsK KPSS 6–go yuliya 1965 goda', ARAN. f. 457, op. 1, d. 491, ll. 72–3. Nechkina made this comment in the course of expressing her concern about the 'liquidation' of all the *nauchnye sovety*, except those overseen by the presidium.
197. T. H. Rigby, 'The USSR: End of a long, dark night?', in Robert F. Miller (ed.), *The Developments of Civil Society in Communist Systems* (Sydney, 1992), pp. 16–17.
198. Gorodetsky, interview. *Vsesoyuznoe*, p. 46.
199. *Ibid.*, p. 409.
200. Gorodetsky, interview.
201. During the readers' conferences convened by *Voprosy istorii* in 1956 there were calls for cooperative publishing houses and for the right to form a

historians' association, necessary organizational underpinnings for any sustained intellectual autonomy. As Debray, p. 72, argues: 'A school starts with a review ... There would have been no new French historical school without the *Annales.*'

202. 'Glavlit', originally derived from the acronym for Main Administration for Literature and the Press, in the mid-1960s became the Chief Administration for the Protection of State Secrets in Publishing. A major publishing house like the Academy of Sciences' *Nauka* had its own pool of permanent censors. Leonid Vladimirov, *'Glavlit*: How the Soviet Censor Works', *Index on Censorship*, 1, 3–4, autumn-winter 1972, pp. 31–43.

203. Alexander Nekrich, 'Rewriting history', *Index on Censorship*, 9, 4, August 1980, pp. 4–7.

204. S. S. Neretina, interview.

205. Kagarlitsky, *Thinking Reed,* p. 106.

206. S. M. Dubrovsky, 'Akademik M. N. Pokrovsky i ego rol' v razvitii sovetskoi istoricheskoi nauki', *VI*, 1962, 3, pp. 3–31; 'Obsuzhdenie stat' S. M. Dubrovskogo "Akademik M. N. Pokrovsky i ego rol' v razvitii sovetskoi istoricheskoi nauki" ', *VI*, 1962, 3, pp. 31–40; Harvey Asher, 'The Rise, Fall, and Resurrection of M. N. Pokrovsky', *The Russian Review*, 31, 1, January 1972, pp. 49–63.

207. 'Sekretaryu TsK KPSS, M. A. Suslovu', 13 December 1958, TsKhSD, f. 5, op. 35, d. 77, ll. 274–6. It was decided to publish only the 'most valuable works'. *Ibid.*, 5 March 1959, l. 277.

208. Hans Rogger, 'Politics, Ideology and History in the USSR: The Search for Coexistence', *Soviet Studies*, XVI, 3, January 1965, pp. 259–62.

209. Academician P. N. Pospelov, *Vsesoyuznoe*, pp. 200–1.

210. See the particularly forthright contributions of I. S. Smirnov and A. V. Snegov, *ibid.*, pp. 255–8, 266–75.

211. Nekrich, p. 171. Zhuravlev, p. 254, is even harsher, seeing bold pronouncements at the conference about historical science 'moving forward' despite Stalinism as utopian 'self-deception'.

212. Pospelov, *Vsesoyuznoe*, p. 204 noted the corrected interpretation of Bolshevik tactics in March 1917 in *Istoriya Kommunisticheskoi partii Sovetskogo Soyuza,* second, expanded edition (Moscow, 1963), p. 210. I. I. Mints too now acknowledged Stalin's position was false in March-April 1917. *Vsesoyuznoe*, p. 272.

213. *Ibid.*, p. 299.

214. *Ibid.*, pp. 369–70.

215. Heer, *Politics and History*, pp. 148, 161. See pp. 55–6, where she provides figures that point to the increasingly academic rather than apparat background of historians of the party.

3 The New Direction historians

1. V. P. Danilov, interview. The son of a peasant, A. L. Sidorov (1900–66) was a student of M. N. Pokrovsky whose lively seminars instilled in him a sense of the value of scholarship that, according to one of Sidorov's students, Volobuev, he never forgot, despite his loyalty to Stalin. Sidorov 'reflected in himself all the contradictions of the formation of Soviet historical science.'

Once condemned as a Trotskyist, 'by luck' Sidorov narrowly escaped execution in 1937–38. Yet, despite his doubts, he loyally carried out party directives – couched in the uncompromising idiom of the Stalin period. As such, he 'did not always express his own opinions'. In his denunciation of I. I. Mints during the anti-cosmopolitan campaign Sidorov was acting on a 'party directive' from the Department of Agitation and Propaganda. His subsequent attack on Burdzhalov, while at the behest of the Central Committee, was based on his firm conviction that Burdzhalov's criticism of Stalin's role in March–April 1917 was resurrecting 'Trotskyite conceptions of the October Revolution'. This tension between Sidorov's political loyalty and his 'professionalism', coupled with growing doubts about his outlook induced by the Twentieth Congress, produced what was discerned by the Central Committee as 'half-heartedness' in carrying out directives; this may have cost him his position as Director of the Institute of History in 1959. V. P. Volobuev, interview.
2. K. N. Tarnovsky, 'K itogam izucheniya monopolisticheskogo kapitalizma v Rossii', in N. M. Druzhinin (ed.), *Sovetskaya istoricheskaya nauka ot XX k XXII s"ezdu KPSS*, 2 vols. (Moscow, 1962), Vol. 1, Istoriya SSSR: Sbornik statei, p. 299.
3. Enteen *et al.*, p. ix.
4. K. N. Tarnovsky, *Sovetskaya istoriografiya rossiiskogo imperializma* (Moscow, 1964), p. 21.
5. *Ibid.*, pp. 53, 65–7. Enteen *et al.*, pp. 26–7.
6. KK, p. 156. Stalin's 'semi-colony' thesis was a one-sided caricature of Trotsky's position. Trotsky, emphasizing Russia's backwardness, argued that Russia was characterized by a 'twofold imperialism': 'Privileged colony' of Western Europe and exploiter of 'countries weaker and more backward than herself.' Leon Trotsky, *The History of the Russian Revolution*, trans. by Max Eastman, Vol. 1 (London, 1967, first published in English, 1932–33), p. 33.
7. K. N. Tarnovsky (1921–87) was born into a cultivated family of school teachers in Luchesa, near Smolensk. A much-decorated *frontovik*, he entered the history faculty of Moscow State University in autumn 1947. That same year he became an active party member, being elected party-bureau secretary. Tarnovsky later explained that the international upheavals of the post-war period determined the research that preoccupied him throughout his career. As he himself put it, 'After May 1945, October 1917 became for me the tangible basis of the new historical processes'. His decision to pursue the topic of state-monopoly capitalism in Russia during the First World War for his candidate thesis, which he defended in 1955, was a 'bold act', given the status of Stalin's 'semi-colonial' thesis. In 1959 he was brought into the Institute of History by Sidorov in order to save him from a 'very difficult' political situation in Moscow State University (Danilov, interview). In the institute he teamed up with Sidorov's scientific council 'On the Historical Preconditions of the Great October Socialist Revolution'. V. A. Emets, V. V. Shelokhaev, 'Tvorchesky put' K. N. Tarnovskogo', IZ, 1990, 118, pp. 202–31.
8. Tarnovsky, *Sovetskaya*, pp. 61–3.
9. *Ibid.*, p. 4.

10. *Ibid.*, pp. 66, 69–70; Barber, *Soviet Historians*, p. 140.
11. Tarnovsky, *Sovetskaya*, p. 77.
12. V. V. Polikarpov, '"*novoe napravlenie*" 50–70x-gg.: Poslednaya diskussiya sovetskikh istorikov', in Yu. N. Afanas'ev (ed.), *Sovetskaya istoriografiya* (Moscow: 1996), pp. 349–51.
13. A. L. Sidorov, 'Nekotorye razmyshleniya o trude i opyte istorika', *I SSSR*, 1964, 3, p. 124.
14. Volobuev, interview.
15. P. V. Volobuev (1923–97) was born in Evgenovka, Kazakhstan. He entered the history faculty, MGU in 1940, but the war, in which he was wounded, interrupted his studies. He joined the CPSU in 1944. He finally graduated from MGU in 1950. Having defended his *kandidat* degree in 1953, he worked in the Central Committee Department of Agitation and Propaganda for about two years. He joined the Institute of History in 1955 and in 1966 became head of the sector responsible for producing the multi-volume *History of the USSR*. In 1962 he published *The Economic Policy of the Provisional Government*. Elected a Corresponding Member of the Academy of Sciences in 1969, he was appointed Director of the Institute of the History of the USSR in 1970 – until his dismissal in 1974. Finally elected a full Academician in 1989, at the time of his death he was, among other things, president of the International Commission on the History of the October Revolution. Volobuev, interview; 'Volobuev, Pavel Vasil'evich', Borys Lewytzzkyi, *Who's Who in the USSR* (Munchen, 1984), p. 356; 'Intervyu s akedemikom', pp. 99–123.
16. Tarnovsky, *Sovetskaya*, pp. 117, 120.
17. *Ibid.*, pp. 125–6.
18. *Ibid.*, pp. 142–3.
19. Gefter, interview.
20. 'Konferentsiya chitatelei zhurnala "Voprosy istorii" ', *VI*, 1956, 2, p. 201.
21. B. B. Grave, 'Byla li tsarskaya Rossiya polukoloniei?', *VI*, 1956, 6, pp. 63–74; Tarnovsky, *Sovetskaya*, pp. 193–4.
22. Tarnovsky, *Sovetskaya*, pp. 195–6. 'Za leninskuyu partiinost' v istoricheskoi nauke!', *VI*, 1957, 3, p. 12, accused Grave of obfuscating the semi-colony question.
23. Tarnovsky, 'Put' uchenogo', pp. 233–5 (original emphasis).
24. *Ibid.*, p. 207.
25. Gindin, addressing the third conference of Soviet and Italian historians, Moscow, April 1968, referred to the formation in 1965 of the New Direction under the leadership of N. I. Pavlenko, a historian of Russian feudalism. Gerschenkron, p. 859. This seems wrong; Volobuev referred to himself as the titular 'head' of the New Direction but Tarnovsky was its actual 'intellectual inspirer'. P. V. Volobuev, letter to *VI*, 1990, 6, p. 181.
26. Polikarpov, p. 391, n. 12.
27. Between 1958 and 1961 the council sponsored four conferences on Russian imperialism. Enteen *et al.*, p. 30.
28. Born in 1924, K. N. Shatsillo defended his *kandidat* thesis in 1958, which had been supervised by Bovykin: Finance Capital in the Naval Industry of Russia, 1908–1917. Successful defence of his candidate degree led to his acceptance by Sidorov into the Institute of History where, in 1968, he

defended his doctoral thesis: The Development of the Armed Forces of Russia on the eve of the First World War. K. N. Shatsillo, interview.
29. Tarnovsky, *Sovetskaya*, pp. 160, 207.
30. Polikarpov, p. 353.
31. Born 19 May 1900, I. F. Gindin graduated from the Leningrad polytechnical institute in 1925. There, under Academician A. V. Venediktov, he had researched for his diploma 'The Banks and Industry in Russia before the War.' During the 1960s he was a member of the Sector of the History of the USSR of the Period of Capitalism in the Institute of History. 'Yubilei I. F. Gindina', *I SSSR*, 1970, 5, pp. 231–2.
32. Varga's *Changes in the Economy of Capitalism as a Result of the Second World War* appeared in 1947. Polikarpov, p. 352; Tarnovsky, *Sovetskaya*, pp. 95, 101, 107–8, 189–90.
33. Tarnovsky, *Sovetskaya*, pp. 180, 191, n. 87. In Varga's last work, *Essays on Problems of the Political Economy of Capitalism* (1964), there was a thoroughgoing critique of the 'subjection' thesis.
34. Tarnovsky, *Sovetskaya*, p. 191, n. 86.
35. *Ibid.*, pp. 177–80.
36. *Ibid.*, pp. 189–90. '1961 Programme of the Communist Party of the Soviet Union', in Jan F. Triska (ed.), *Soviet Communism: Programs [sic] and Rules, Official Texts of 1919, 1952 (1956), 1961* (San Francisco, 1962), p. 40.
37. Polikarpov, p. 353.
38. Tarnovsky, *Sovetskaya*, pp. 224–5.
39. *Ibid.*, p. 226.
40. *Ibid.* Cf. Polikarpov, p. 392, n. 20.
41. Tarnovsky, *Sovetskaya*, pp. 226–7.
42. *Ibid.*, pp. 228–9.
43. Polikarpov, pp. 355, 357, who notes, p. 391, n. 17, that none of Vanag's critics, including the New Direction, challenged his data on the 'dwarfish' nature of the Russian monopolies, preferring instead to attack (Stalin's) dubious 'semi-colony' concept.
44. K. N. Tarnovsky, *Sotsial'no-ekonomicheskaya istoriya rossii nachalo XX v.: Sovetskaya istoriografiya serediny 50-kh--60-kh godov*, ed. with a preface by V. P. Volobuev (Moscow, 1990), pp. 22–3, 25–6. This is the text of Tarnovsky's first doctoral thesis, written at the end of the 1960s and 'brilliantly' defended in October 1970. The degree was not confirmed by the Higher Qualifications Commission (*VAK*).
45. Tarnovsky, *Sotsial'no*, pp. 92–3.
46. *Ibid.*, pp. 95–7.
47. *Ibid.*, pp. 103–4.
48. *Ibid.*, pp. 107–8, 111, 118.
49. *Ibid.*, p. 111 (original emphasis).
50. A. M. Anfimov, 'Neokonchennye spory', the sixth, and final, chapter in 'P. A. Stolypin i ego agrarnaya reforma' (Unpublished manuscript, 1990), p. 1.
51. A. M. Anfimov, 'K voprosu o kharaktere agrarnogo stroia Rossii v nachale XX veka', *IZ*, 65, 1959, pp. 119–62.
52. Anfimov, 'Neokonchennye', p. 1.
53. *Ibid.*, pp. 1–3.

54. On V. P. Danilov, see Ch. 4.
55. V. P. Danilov, 'K itogam izucheniya istorii sovetskogo krest'yantsva i kolkhoznogo stroitel'stva v SSSR', *VI*, 1960, 8, pp. 34–64.
56. Tarnovsky, *Sotsial'no*, pp. 116–7; Danilov, 'K itogam', p. 38.
57. Tarnovsky, 'Put' uchenogo', p. 215.
58. Tarnovsky, *Sotsial'no*, pp. 122–3.
59. *Ibid.*, pp. 128–9.
60. *Ibid.*, p. 180.
61. *Ibid.*, pp. 200–1.
62. Personal communication from A. M. Anfimov, 5 May 1992.
63. Anfimov, 'Neokonchennye', p. 40.
64. Tarnovsky, *Sotsial'no*, p. 180 (original emphasis).
65. *Ibid.*, pp. 180–1 (original emphasis).
66. *Ibid.*, p. 221 (original emphasis).
67. Volobuev, 'Ot redaktora', Tarnovsky, *Sotsial'no*, pp. 3–5.
68. Tarnovsky, *Sotsial'no*, p. 211.
69. See Ch. 1.
70. *Istoriya i sotsiologiya* (Moscow, 1964). This conference is dealt with in more detail in Chapter 5.
71. Tarnovsky, *Sotsial'no*, p. 215; *Istoriya i sotsiologiya*, pp. 74, 76.
72. Tarnovsky, *Sotsial'no*, p. 218; *Istoriya i sotsiologiya*, pp. 309–10.
73. Tarnovsky, *Sotsial'no*, pp. 219–20 (original emphasis).
74. James P. Scanlan, 'From Historical Materialism to Historical Interactionism: A Philosophical Examination of Some Recent Developments', in Baron and Heer, *Windows*, pp. 14–5.
75. I. F. Gindin, 'Russkaya burzhuaziya v period kapitalizma, ee razvitie i osobennosti,' *I SSSR*, 1963, 2, pp. 57–80. This article is continued under the same title in *I SSSR*, 1963, 3, pp. 37–60.
76. *Ibid.*, 2, p. 58, n. 9. See V. I. Lenin, ' "Left-Wing" Childishness and the Petty-bourgeois Mentality', 9–11 May 1918, *Collected Works*, fourth ed. (Moscow, 1965), Vol. 27, February–July 1918, pp. 335–6; 'Report on the Tax in Kind', 9 April 1921, Vol. 32, December 1920–August 1921, pp. 295–6. Lenin's comments on the five *'ukladov'* describing Soviet society were reproduced in the *Short Course*. KK, p. 306.
77. Tarnovsky, *Sotsial'no*, p. 221.
78. Shatsillo, interview.
79. Tarnovsky, *Sotsial'no*, p. 222.
80. K. N. Tarnovsky, 'O sotsiologicheskom izuchenii kapitalisticheskogo sposoba proizvodstva', *VI*, 1964, 1, pp. 120–132.
81. *Ibid.*, p. 123.
82. Tarnovsky, *Sotsial'no*, pp. 222–3; Tarnovsky, 'O sotsiologicheskom', p. 132.
83. 'O sotsiologicheskom', pp. 125, 127.
84. By the mid-1960s the New Direction were not alone in acknowledging the backwardness and peculiarity of Russian capitalism. This perspective was shared by other leading historians, some of whom subsequently 'actively' contributed to the 'eradication' of the New Direction, notably I. D. Koval'chenko. Polikarpov, p. 354 and p. 392, n. 23.
85. I. F. Gindin, 'O nekotorykh osobennostyakh ekonomicheskoi i sotsial'noi struktury rossiiskogo kapitalizma v nachale XX v.', *I SSSR*, 1966, 3,

pp. 65–6; I. F. Gindin, L. M. Ivanov, 'Neravnomernosti razvitiya rossiiskogo kapitalizma v nachale XX veka', *VI*, 1965, 9, pp. 125–35.
86. Tarnovsky, *Sotsial'no*, pp. 233–4 (original emphasis).
87. *Ibid.*, pp. 234–5.
88. *Ibid.*, p. 239.
89. Cited in *ibid.*, p. 240.
90. *Ibid.*, pp. 245–6 (Tarnovsky's emphasis).
91. *Ibid.*, p. 249 (original emphasis).
92. I. F. Gindin, 'Sotsial'noe-ekonomicheskie itogi razvitiya rossiiskogo kapitalizma i predposylki revolyutsii v nashei strane', I. I. Mints *et al.* (eds), *Sverzhenie samoderzhaviya sbornik statei* (Moscow, 1970); Gindin, 'Problemy istorii fevral'skoi revolyutsii i ee sotsial'no-ekonomicheskikh predposylok', *I SSSR*, 1967, 4, pp. 31, 36.
93. V. V. Adamov *et al.* (eds), *Voprosy istorii kapitalisticheskoi rossii: Problema mnogoukladnosti* (Sverdlovsk, 1972), p. 4. This anthology was the subject of severe criticism. See Ch. 6.
94. *Ibid.*, p. 5.
95. *Ibid.*, p. 8.
96. See Ch. 6.
97. V. I. Bovykin, 'Problemy perestroiki istoricheskoi nauki i vopros o "novom napravlenii" v izuchenii sotsial'no-ekonomicheskikh predposylok Velikoi Oktyabr'skoi Revolyutsii', *I SSSR*, 1988, 5, pp. 81–2.
98. *Ibid.*, p. 82; Tarnovsky, *Sovetskaya*, pp. 226–7.
99. Volobuev, 'letter', pp. 182–3.
100. V. V. Polikarpov, ' "Novoe napravlenie" – v starom prochtenii', *VI*, 1989, 3, pp. 50–1.
101. P. V. Volobuev, 'Voprosy dialektiki v rabotakh V. I. Lenina o Velikoi Oktyabr'skoi sotsialisticheskoi revolyutsii', VF, 1958, 4, p. 34.
102. Volobuev, interview.
103. Gefter, in Adamov *et al.*, pp. 84–6, 91, 93, 97–9.
104. *Ibid.*, p. 98, n. 28 (original emphasis).
105. Tarnovsky, in Adamov *et al.*, p. 41 (original emphasis).
106. *Ibid.*
107. Volobuev, 'Voprosy dialektiki', p. 35.
108. Cited in Tarnovsky, in Adamov *et al.*, p. 41, n. 48.
109. Gefter, in Adamov *et al.*, p. 87.
110. Volobuev, 'Ot redaktora', Tarnovsky, *Sotsial'no*, p. 6.
111. Volobuev, 'letter', p. 183, and interview.
112. Polikarpov, 'starom prochtenii', p. 44.
113. Volobuev, 'letter', p.184.
114. Volobuev, interview.
115. *Ibid.*
116. *Ibid.*
117. Tarnovsky, *Sotsial'no*, p. 281.
118. Volobuev, interview.
119. Cited in Tarnovsky, *Sotsial'no*, p. 281.
120. Polikarpov, 'starom prochtenii', p. 51.
121. Leon Trotsky, *The Permanent Revolution and Results and Prospects*, third edition (New York, 1972, first edition 1931), p.132.

122. See Lewin, *Political Undercurrents*.
123. Trotsky, *Permanent Revolution*, pp. 76–7.
124. Volobuev, interview.
125. *Ibid.* He had also read Rosa Luxemburg's criticism of the October Revolution, but could not refer to them. 'Intervyu s akademikom', p. 104. In the *perestroika* period Volobuev identified with the Bukharinist alternative to the Stalinist model of socialism. See P. V. Volobuev, 'Ot otvetsvennogo redaktora', *Akademik N. I. Bukharin: Metodologiya i planirovanie nauki i tekhniki Izbrannye trudy* (Moscow, 1989).
126. Volobuev, 'Ot redaktora', Tarnovsky, *Sotsial'no*, p. 6, remarks that Tarnovsky's monograph is tempered 'by an economic problematic and in this regard a certain exaggeration of the maturity of the economic prerequisites for socialism in Russia, which was characteristic of that time [that is, the end of the 1960s].'
127. Leon Trotsky, *The Stalin School of Falsification* (London, 1974, first published in Russian in 1932), p. x.
128. Confirmation of the depth of the ' "anti-Trotsky syndrome of Soviet consciousness"' is provided by V. P. Danilov, 'We are Starting to Learn About Trotsky', *History Workshop Journal*, 29, 1990, pp. 136–46.
129. Volobuev recalled that one of the first attacks on the New Direction was an article that was scheduled to appear in *Voprosy istorii KPSS* under the title 'Against the Resurrection of Trotskyism', although it never did so. Volobuev, interview.
130. Baron and Heer, 'Historiography Since Stalin', p. 288.
131. Scanlan, 'Historical Materialism to Historical Interactionism', pp. 18–20.
132. Polikarpov, '"*novoe napravlenie*" 50–70x-gg.', p. 375 (see Ch. 6).
133. For an overview see Gerschenkron, pp. 853–69.
134. A. Ya. Avrekh (1915–1988) graduated from the historical faculty of Moscow State University in 1940–41. *A frontovik*, he joined the CPSU in 1942. In 1954, having defended his *kandidat* thesis, he joined the Institute of History, where, in 1967, he defended his doctoral dissertation 'The Third Duma and the Collapse of Stolypin Bonapartism'. 'Aron Yakovlevich Avrekh', *VI*, 1989, 3, p. 190. For a survey of Avrekh's work see Robert H. McNeal, 'The Fate of Imperial Russia', in Baron and Heer, *Windows*, pp. 134–5, nn. 5, 6.
135. S. V. Tyutyukin, interview.
136. For example, *Stolypin i sud'ba ego reformy* (Moscow, 1991).
137. Cherepnin was a product of the Soviet school of feudalism which in the 1930s was schooled on the basis of a collection of Marxist quotes on feudalism which they could cite to justify their analyses. L. V. Danilova, interview.
138. *Dokumenty sovetsko-ital'yanskoi konferentsii istorikov, 8–10 aprelya 1968 goda: Absolyutizm v Zapadnoi Evrope i Rossii; Russko-Ital'yanskie svyazi vo vtoroi polovine XIX veka* (Moscow, 1970), p. 12.
139. *Ibid.*, pp. 15–6, 34–5, 160.
140. *Ibid.*, pp. 179, 181–2.
141. *Ibid.*, pp. 219–20. See N. I. Pavlenko (ed.), *Perekhod ot feodalizma k kapitalizmu v Rossii: Materialy dlya obsuzhdeniya* (Moscow, 1965). The school of B. D. Grekov, of which Cherepnin was an adherent, attempted to

establish that capitalism had appeared in Russia as early as the fifteenth or even fourteenth centuries, further evidence that Soviet Russia was just as ready for socialist revolution as Western Europe. Danilova, interview.
142. *Dokumenty*, pp. 193–5.
143. *Ibid.*, p. 186.
144. *Ibid.*, pp. 221, 223–4.
145. *Ibid.*, pp. 194, 196.
146. *Ibid.*, p. 222.
147. Danilova, interview.
148. *Dokumenty*, pp. 222–3.
149. As Gerschenkron, p. 862, suggested.
150. A. Ya. Avrekh, 'Russky absolyutizm i ego rol' v utverzhdenii kapitalizma v Rossii', *I SSSR*, 2, March–April 1968, pp. 82–3.
151. *Ibid.*, pp. 82, 90.
152. *Ibid.* (original emphasis).
153. *Ibid.*, p. 96 (original emphasis).
154. 'K diskussii ob absolyutizma v Rossii', *I SSSR*, 4, 1971, pp. 65–88.
155. *Dokumenty*, pp. 224–5, following the translation in Gerschenkron, pp. 858–9, who notes the 'deliberate echoes' in Gindin's statement 'from Engels's celebrated "four letters"' to J. Bloch and Hans Starkenburg.
156. Ernest Gellner, 'Foreword', Loone, p. viii.

4 Writing and rewriting the history of collectivization

1. *KK*, pp. 290–8.
2. Zhuravlev, pp. 106–8.
3. V. P. Danilov was born in 1925 into a peasant family in Orenburg, near the Urals mountains. He served as an artillery officer in the Great Patriotic War. This was a transformative experience. He wanted to know 'how it was that people could conduct themselves as they did in war, particularly those from such a highly cultured country as Germany.' But it was 'clear' to him that it was 'impossible to grasp all history. In the first place, a historian must understand his own country; and the history of my country is above all the history of the peasantry and the countryside.' Therefore in 1946 he entered the history faculty of Orenburg teachers' college, from which he graduated in 1950. He then joined the Institute of History as a graduate student. He was a *Komsomol* secretary in the institute and a 'respected' member of its party cell. Two 'invisible colleges' helped to shape Danilov intellectually: early on, his teachers in Orenburg, several of whom had been exiled there from Leningrad University in 1935; later, from the mid-1950s on, the contact he established with major British historians – E. H. Carr, R. W. Davies, Teodor Shanin and Orlando Figes. In 1954 Danilov had intended to write his *kandidat* thesis on 'socio-economic relations in the Soviet period'. Informed on to the Institute of History party organization, he was forced to abandon this project in favour of an inquiry into the material-technical basis of Soviet agriculture. Only his standing as a *frontovik* saved him from a party reprimand. Danilov and L. V. Danilova, interviews; Orlando Figes, 'Introduction', V. P. Danilov,

Rural Russia Under the New Regime, trans. and introduced by Figes (Bloomington and London, 1988, first published in Russian 1977), p. 17; Huw Richards, 'Soviet Agrarian Guru Comes in from the Cold', *Times Higher Education Supplement*, 1 April 1988, p. 16.
4. Danilov, 'Material'no-tekhnicheskaya baza sel'skogo khozyaistva SSSR nakanune sploshnoi kollektivizatsii', *VI*, 1956, 3, pp. 3–17; *Sozdanie material'no-tekhnicheskih predposylok kollektivizatsii sel'skogo khozyaistva v SSSR* (Moscow, 1957).
5. Danilov, *Sozdanie*, pp. 15, 395.
6. *Ibid.*, p. 9.
7. Danilov, 'Material'no', p. 15.
8. Danilov, *Sozdanie*, pp. 390–6.
9. Danilov, 'Material'no', p. 4.
10. Danilov, interview.
11. *Ibid.*
12. *Ibid.*
13. Yu. A. Moshkov was born in 1922, the son of a co-operative member in the province of Tverskaya. In the 1930s his family moved to the outskirts of Moscow to survive. Upon finishing school in 1940 he joined the army, serving on the Kalinsky front. Finally demobilized in 1947, he joined the MGU Faculty of History as an *aspirant*, going on to become a professor, which he remains to-day. Moshkov, interview.
14. N. A. Ivnitsky, interview. Ivnitsky was born in 1922 into a poor peasant family in the south of the former Voronezhskaya *oblast'* in the Central Blacksoil Region. In 1930 his father was arrested by an OGPU troika under article 58 of the Criminal Code on the false accusation of concealing 'hard cash'. He was condemned to labour on the White Sea-Baltic Canal for three years. Completing school in 1940, Ivnitsky held various administrative posts in the collective farm system, including director of a state farm. He fought as a sapper in 1943–4 at the Kursk Bulge and Stalingrad. In 1945 he entered the Historical-Archive Institute in Moscow. Accepted as an *aspirant* in 1949, in 1953 he successfully defended his *kandidat* dissertation: 'The Kolkhoztsentr 1927–1932. The Structure of its Organization and Activities'. In January 1953 he took the post of junior researcher in the Institute of History, Academy of Sciences, where he remains today. From 1954 to 1960 he was deputy editor of the journal *Istorichesky arkhiv*. A communist party member, without which he could not have held these posts, he was 'never a dissident'. Despite his personal sufferings as a child, he blamed the local OGPU, not Stalin nor 'Soviet power' which had enabled 'the son of a poor peasant to become a Doctor of Sciences.'
15. *Ibid.*
16. Figes, 'Introduction', pp. 21–2.
17. 'Zemel'nyie otnosheniya v sovetskoi dokolkhoznoi derevne', *I SSSR*, 1958, 3, pp. 90–128.
18. Figes, p. 22. It was not just Stalinist historians who had a negative opinion of the commune: 'All schools of thought within the Soviet communist party in the 1920s – from Trotsky and Preobrazhensky on the Left to Bukharin on the Right – regarded the strip system and communal tenure as inherently inefficient and unprogressive'. R. W. Davies, *The Socialist*

274 *Notes*

      Offensive: The Collectivisation of Soviet Agriculture 1929–1930 (London, 1980), p. 7.
19. 'Zemel'nyie', p. 100.
20. *Ibid.*, pp. 99–100.
21. *Ibid.*, pp. 124, 126–8.
22. 'K itogam izucheniya sovetskogo krest'yanstva i kolkhoznogo stroitel'stva v SSSR', *VI*, 1960, 8, p. 45.
23. According to M. P. Kim, 'Predislovie', Kim *et al.* (eds), *Istoriya sovetskogo krest'yanstva i kolkhoznogo stroitel'stva v SSSR. Materialy nauchnoi sessii, sostoyavsheisya 18–21 aprelya 1961 g. v Moskve* (Moscow, 1963), p. 4.
24. V. P. Danilov, 'O kharaktere sotsial'no-ekonomicheskikh otnoshenii sovetskogo krest'yanstva do kollektivizatsii sel'skogo khozyaistva', in Kim *et al.*, p. 50.
25. Danilov, 'O kharaktere', pp. 52–3 (emphasis added – RDM).
26. *Ibid.*, pp. 56, 58–62.
27. *Ibid.*, pp. 79–80.
28. Kim *et al.*, p. 142.
29. Danilov, 'O kharaktere', p. 80; Kim *et al.*, p. 142.
30. Danilov, 'O kharaktere', pp. 66–7. Danilov now admits that his analysis of the cooperative movement in 1928–29 'exaggerated its successes because we were unaware of secret materials that showed the peasantry had been driven into the cooperatives'. Danilov, interview.
31. M. L. Bogdenko, I. E. Zelenin, 'Osnovnye problemy istorii kollektivizatsii sel'skogo khozyaistva v sovremennoi sovetskoi istoricheskoi literature', in Kim *et al.*, pp. 192–221.
32. *Ibid.*, pp. 198–9.
33. *Ibid.*, p. 200, n. 37.
34. *Ibid.*, pp. 201–2.
35. Bogdenko, Zelenin, pp. 206–7.
36. *Ibid.*, p. 207 and n. 61, p. 208.
37. *Ibid.*, p. 211. The Yakovlev Politburo commission was established on 5 December 1929 to draft a decree on the rate of collectivization. It was chaired by Ya. A. Yakovlev, appointed three days later People's Commissar for Agriculture. One of its eight sub-commissions, that headed by K. Ya. Bauman, was concerned with policy towards the *kulak*. Davies, *Socialist Offensive*, pp. 185–6.
38. Bogdenko, Zelenin, pp. 212–15, 218–19 and n. 83.
39. Ivnitsky, interview.
40. N. A. Ivnitsky, 'O kriticheskom analize istochnikov po istorii nachal'nogo etapa kollektivizatsii (osen' 1929–vesna 1930 gg)', *Istorichesky arkhiv*, March-April 1962, 2, pp. 191–202.
41. Statistics on the *kolkhozy* continued to be published in the 1930s in the *Yearbooks on Agriculture*, based on the monthly returns from *Narkomzem*. Davies, *Socialist Offensive*, Table 17, pp. 442–4, used them to compile regional data on the percentage of collectivized households in 1928–31.
42. Ivnitsky, 'O kriticheskom', pp. 191–2.
43. *Ibid.*, pp. 192–3, 195–6.

44. N. A. Ivnitsky, 'Istoriya podgotovki postanovleniya TsK VKP (b) o tempakh kollektivizatsii sel'skogo khozyaistva ot 5 Yanvarya 1930 g.', *Istochnikovedenie istorii sovetskogo obshchestva* (Moscow, 1964), pp. 265–88.
45. N. A. Ivnitsky, 'O nachalnom etape sploshnoi kollektivizatsii (Osen' 1929–vesna 1930 gg)', *VI KPSS*, 1962, 4, p. 55. *Cf. KK*, p. 294.
46. Ivnitsky, 'O nachalnom', pp. 62–4; Ivnitsky, 'O kriticheskom', p. 194. His criticism did not prevent Ivnitsky from depicting Bukharin, Tomsky and Rykov in the crudest Stalinist terms, as was done at the November 1929 Central Committee plenum. They were reviled as 'anti-marxist', 'right opportunists' defending the '"peaceful growing over" of the *kulak* into socialism' and seeking to extend Lenin's cooperative plan from the middle peasantry to the *kulak*. Ivnitsky, 'O nachalnom', pp. 57–9.
47. *Ibid.*, p. 65.
48. *KK*, pp. 294–6.
49. Ivnitsky, 'O nachalnom', pp. 65, 71.
50. Ivnitsky, interview.
51. Ivnitsky, 'O kriticheskom'', pp. 194–5.
52. *Ibid.*, pp. 198–201.
53. See the revelations in Davies, *Soviet History in the Yeltsin Era*, Ch. 13.
54. Ivnitsky, interview. Ironically even today, with the passing of the Soviet Union, Ivnitsky has been denied the right to return to the Politburo archives. Hence the continual references to 'Former archive of the Politburo CC CPSU', without details of files, in his 1996 study of collectivization: *Kollektivizatsiya i raskulachivanie: nachalo 30–x godov* (Moscow). On 'special settlers' and also continued denial of access to the secret police and presidential archives under Yeltsin, see Davies, *Soviet History in the Yeltsin Era*, pp. 96–114, 167.
55. V. P. Danilov, 'Izuchenie istorii sovetskogo krest'yanstva', in N. M. Druzhinin (ed.). *Sovetskaya istoricheskaya nauka ot XX k XXII s"ezdu KPSS*, 2 vols. Moscow, 1962. (T. 1) *Istoriya SSSR: Sbornik statei.*, p. 449.
56. *Ibid.*, pp. 454–9, 462–4, 471.
57. *Ibid.*, pp. 466–7.
58. *Ibid.*, p. 451.
59. *KK*, pp. 273–5. The same approach was retained in the new official history: *Istoriya Kommunisticheskoi partii Sovetskogo Soyuza*, second, expanded edition (Moscow, 1963), pp. 414–15.
60. Danilov, *Sozdanie*, pp. 13–16.
61. V. P. Danilov (ed.), Kollektivizatsiya i kolkhoznoe stroitel'stvo v SSSR: Kollektivizatsiya sel'skogo khozyaistva v SSSR 1927–1932 (Moscow: Mysl', 1964). Unpublished proofs (*pervaya sverka*), PD.
62. Danilov, interview. The *pervaya sverka*, the first, corrected, printed version of the proofs, was actually completed by 26 December 1964.
63. *Ibid.*
64. See Chapter 6.
65. Why Polyakov would have played such a role in the discussion is unclear, given that he had co-authored a revisionist report on collectivization (see below).
66. Danilov, interview.
67. Ivnitsky, interview.

68. Danilov, interview.
69. S. P. Trapeznikov, *Leninizm i agrarno-krestyansky vopros*, 2 vols (Moscow, 1967).
70. Ivnitsky, interview.
71. Danilov, Kollektivizatsiya (*pervaya sverka*), p. 20.
72. *Ibid.*, p. 796.
73. Danilov, *Sozdanie*, p. 451.
74. Danilov, Kollektivizatsiya (*pervaya sverka*), p. 10.
75. *Ibid.*, pp. 11–12, 18.
76. *Ibid.*, pp. 32–8.
77. *Ibid.*, pp. 56, 62–3, 65.
78. *Ibid.*, pp. 66–7.
79. *Ibid.*, pp. 40–3, 67–8.
80. *Ibid.*, pp. 81–5, 87.
81. *Ibid.*, pp. 91, 121, 128.
82. *Ibid.*, pp. 85, 92–3.
83. *Ibid.*, pp. 132, 135, 151–2.
84. See Davies, *Socialist Offensive*, p. 114, n. 22, regarding different categories of collectivization.
85. Danilov, Kollektivizatsiya (*pervaya sverka*), p. 195.
86. *Ibid.*, pp. 195–6.
87. *Ibid.*, p. 204.
88. 'Small and informal farm collectives retaining a high level of individual ownership of the means of production', Figes, p. 18.
89. Danilov, Kollektivizatsiya (*pervaya sverka*), p. 218.
90. *Ibid.*, pp. 224, 228.
91. *Ibid.*, pp. 243–5, 247.
92. *Ibid.*, pp. 255–6.
93. *Ibid.*, pp. 257–8.
94. *Ibid.*, pp. 258–9, 262–3.
95. *Ibid.*, pp. 275–6 and n. 2.
96. *Ibid.*, pp. 281–3.
97. *Ibid.*, pp. 290–2. Danilov cited a commission report from archives in TsGANKh.
98. *Ibid.*, pp. 297–8.
99. *Ibid.*, p. 299 (emphasis in Danilov's text).
100. *Ibid.*, p. 309.
101. Ivnitsky, interview. Each publishing house had its own resident *Glavlitchik*: A *Glavlit* plenipotentiary.
102. Danilov, Kollektivizatsiya (*pervaya sverka*), pp. 312, 314–5, 320–2, 327–9.
103. Danilov, Kollektivizatsiya (*vtoraya sverka*), p. 321, and n. 2, from the personal archive of N. A. Ivnitsky. This observation, like much of Ivnitsky's work, referred directly to statistics drawn from TsGANKh.
104. *Ibid.*, p. 327.
105. Ivnitsky, interview. Ivnitsky subsequently replaced this assertion with a much blander observation, but this too was erased.
106. *Ibid.*, pp. 324–5. Trapeznikov, *Leninizm*, pp. 158–62. Cf. Davies, *Socialist Offensive*, pp. 155–74.
107. Danilov, Kollektivizatsiya (*vtoraya sverka*), p. 333.

108. *Ibid.*, pp. 335–6.
109. *Ibid.*, p. 335, n. 2. Yet passages from this document were published by Vaganov in 1970. Davies, *Socialist Offensive*, p. 158, n. 54.
110. Trapeznikov, pp. 158, 186–90.
111. Danilov, interview.
112. Ivnitsky, interview.
113. Danilov, Kollektivizatsiya (*vtoraya sverka*), p. 338.
114. *Ibid.*
115. *Ibid.*
116. *Ibid.*, p. 339.
117. *Ibid.*
118. *Ibid.* (emphasis added – RDM).
119. Trapeznikov, pp. 251–61.
120. Danilov, Kollektivizatsiya (*vtoraya sverka*), pp. 355, 358.
121. *Ibid.*, p. 361 (typed interpolation).
122. Davies, *Socialist Offensive*, p. 197.
123. Danilov, Kollektivizatsiya (*vtoraya sverka*), p. 370.
124. *Ibid.*, p. 373.
125. *Ibid.*, pp. 377, 383, 387, 406.
126. *Ibid.*, pp. 381, 410, 413, 417.
127. *Ibid.*, pp. 426–7. Ivnitsky, interview.
128. Ivnitsky, interview.
129. Danilov, Kollektivizatsiya (*vtoraya sverka*), pp. 386, 442.
130. Danilov, Kollektivizatsiya (*pervaya sverka*), pp. 443–4, 449, 452–4.
131. Davies, *Socialist Offensive*, pp. 318–19.
132. Danilov, Kollektivizatsiya (*pervaya sverka*), pp. 454–5.
133. Ivnitsky, 'O kriticheskom', p. 197.
134. Trapeznikov, p. 257.
135. Danilov, Kollektivizatsiya (*pervaya sverka*), p. 457.
136. *Ibid.*, pp. 468–9.
137. *Ibid.*, pp. 458, 469.
138. *Ibid.*, pp. 487, 490.
139. See Davies, *Socialist Offensive*, pp. 323–36.
140. Danilov, Kollektiuizatsiya (*pervaya sverka*), pp. 500–4. The congress hailed party policy for 'setting the objective of the realization of the five-year plan in four years.' *Ibid.*, p. 499.
141. *Ibid.*, pp. 506, 520–6, 535–41, 547–68.
142. *Ibid.*, pp. 569–71. Davies, *Socialist Offensive*, p. 377, and n. 20, citing Bogdenko, suggests that there was a net decrease of peasant households in the kolkhozy in July-August 1930.
143. Danilov, Kollektivizatsiya (*pervaya sverka*), pp. 581–2, 591–3, 599.
144. *Ibid.*, pp. 599–602.
145. *Ibid.*, p. 611.
146. *Ibid.*, p. 631.
147. *Ibid.*, p. 641.
148. *Ibid.*, pp. 645–9 and Table: 'Dynamika kollektivizatsii krest'yanskikh khozyaistv v 1931–1932 godakh', pp. 646–7.
149. *Ibid.*, pp. 649–50.
150. *Ibid.*, p. 650.

151. *Ibid.*, pp. 712–15. This was Stalin's response to a plea for grain for 'starving peasants' from the secretary of the Kharkov *obkom* and the Ukrainian communist party, R. Terekhovym. This particular account was published in *Pravda* on 26 May 1964.
152. *Ibid.*, pp. 653–6.
153. Ivnitsky, interview.
154. See *VI*, 3, 1988; Davies, *Soviet History in the Gorbachev Revolution*, pp. 54–5, 177.
155. Danilov, Kollektivizatsiya (*pervaya sverka*), p. 722.
156. *Ibid.*, pp. 725–6.
157. *Ibid.*, p. 730.
158. *Ibid.*, pp. 734–5. Sholokhov's famous letter of 4 April 1933 to Stalin was not cited by the authors. Ivnitsky claims that he first discovered it in the Kremlin archives, to which he gained access in 1964, and copied out in its entirety. It is now published in full under the title 'I saw things I shall never forget as long as I live', Yu. A. Afanas'ev (ed.), *Sud'by rossiiskogo krest'yanstva* (Moscow, 1996), pp. 535–57.
159. Danilov, Kollektivizatsiya (*pervaya sverka*), p. 735, n. 3.
160. *Ibid.*, pp. 735–6, 738, 740.
161. *Ibid.*, p. 773.
162. *Ibid.*, pp. 782–4.
163. *Ibid.*, p. 784.
164. *Ibid.*, pp. 785, 795.
165. Alexander Yanov, *The Drama of the Soviet 1960s: A Lost Reform* (Berkeley, 1984), p. 90.
166. V. P. Danilov, 'Kollektivizatsiya sel'skogo khozyaistva SSSR', *Sovetskaya istoricheskaya entsiklopediya*, V. 7, (Moscow, 1965), cc. 484–99.
167. *Ibid.* (*vtoraya sverka*), cc. 484–96. PD.
168. A. Gukovsky, A. Ugryumov, V. Kul'bakin, 'Po stranitsam Sovetskoi istoricheskoi entsiklopedii: Zametki istorikov', *Kst*, 1968, 4, pp. 109–10; *Cf.* Richards, 'Soviet Agrarian Guru'. A second article criticized Danilov by name: V. Golikov, S. Murashov, I. Chkhikvishvili, N. Shatagin, S. Shaumyan, 'Za Leninskuyu partiinost' v osveshchenii istorii KPSS', *Kst*, 1969, 3, pp. 78–9.
169. Figes, p. 19.
170. Danilov, interview.
171. M. P. Kim *et al.* (eds), *Problemy agrarnoi istorii sovetskogo obshchestva: Materialy nauchnoi konferentsii 9–12 yuniya 1969 g* (Moscow, 1971).
172. Danilov, 'Osnovnye itogi i napravleniya izucheniya istorii sovetskogo krest'yanstva', *ibid.*, p. 242.
173. Danilov, *ibid.*, p. 348.
174. Danilov, interview. See *ibid.*, p. 242, n. 107.
175. Ivnitsky, interview.
176. M. A. Vyltsan, N. A. Ivnitsky, Yu. A. Polyakov, 'Nekotorye problemy istorii kollektivizatsii v SSSR', *VI*, 3, March 1965, pp. 3–25.
177. *Ibid.*, p. 7, n. 12. Ivnitsky, interview.
178. I. E. Zelenin, 'Politotdely MTS (1933–1934 gg.)', *IZ*, 76, 1965, pp. 42–61.
179. Yu. A. Moshkov, *Zernovaya problema v gody sploshnoi kollektivizatsii sel'skogo khozyaistva (1929–1932 gg.)* (Moscow, 1966). *Cf.* Kim *et al.*, *Istoriya sovetskogo*, pp. 255–72, p. 366.

180. Moshkov, interview. See *VI*, 1988, 9, September 1988, p. 4.
181. Ivnitsky, 'Opyt KPSS po pretvoreniiu v zhizn' leninskogo kooperativnogo plana', *VI KPSS*, February 1966, 2, pp. 97–107 (original emphasis).
182. N. A. Ivnitsky, *Klassovaya bor'ba v derevne i likvidatsiya kulachestva kak klassa (1929–1932 gg)* (Moscow, 1972).
183. B. A. Abramov, Tk. Kocharli, 'Ob oshibkakh v odnoi knige', *VI KPSS*, 1975, 5, pp. 134–41.
184. Ivnitsky, *Kollektivizatsiya*, p. 5.
185. Ivnitsky, interview.
186. *Materialy XV sessii mezhrepublinskogo simpoziuma po agrarnoi istorii*, vyp. 3 (Vologda, 1977), pp. 149–66.
187. *Sovetskaya dokolkhoznaya derevnya: naselenie, zemlepol'zovanie, khozyaistvo* (Moscow, 1977), published in English as *Rural Russia Under the New Regime*; *Sovetskaya dokolkhoznaya derevnya: sotsial'naya struktura, sotsial'nye otnesheniya* (Moscow, 1979). See Figes, p. 25, n. 1.
188. Cited in Figes, p. 24.
189. Danilov, interview.
190. Figes, p. 24.
191. Danilov, interview.

5 The 'hour of methodology'

1. Zhuravlev, pp. 285–7.
2. *Istoriya i sotsiologiya* (Moscow, 1964), p. 8.
3. See Chapter 3.
4. '*Sovetskaya* istoricheskaya nauka i zadachi partiinoi organizatsii Instituta istorii AN SSSR' (unpublished manuscript produced by the Party Committee of the Institute of History, 1965), pp. 16–17. PD.
5. *Istoriya i sotsiologiya*, p. 3.
6. 'Sostoyanie i perspektivy razrabotki metodologii istoricheskoi nauki' (unsigned, undated manuscript, probably written by Gefter in 1969/70, PN), p. 2.
7. *Istoriya i sotsiologiya*, pp. 9–11, 16, 23, 25–6, 28, 37.
8. *Ibid.*, pp. 37–8.
9. Zhuravlev, p. 286.
10. *Istoriya i sotsiologiya*, p. 174.
11. *Ibid.*, p. 305.
12. This tension between the objectives of the ideologists and the historians was recognized by Arthur P. Mendel, who asked 'who is using whom'? 'Current Soviet Theory of History: New Trends or Old?', in Donald Cameron Watt (ed.), *Contemporary History in Europe: Problems and Perspectives* (London, 1969), p. 270.
13. *Istoriya i sotsiologiya*, pp. 326–7. More than two decades later V. P. Volobuev lamented that 'the impending period of stagnation for a long time arrested the working through of the majority of these questions'. Tarnovsky, *Sotsial'no*, p. 272, n. 5.
14. See Chapter 6.
15. *Istoriya i sotsiologiya*, pp. 226–7.
16. *Ibid.*, pp. 65–9, 71–3.

17. *Ibid.*, p. 72.
18. *Istoriya i sotsiologiya*, pp. 74, 77.
19. *Ibid.*, p. 316.
20. *Ibid.*, pp. 265–6.
21. *Ibid.*, pp. 146–7.
22. *Ibid.*, pp. 148–9. Gefter and L. V. Danilova had written a conclusion to this work which was diluted by Zhukov. A segment of what was eliminated was subsequently published in M. Gefter, Ya. Drabkin, V. Mal'kov, 'Mir za dvadtsat' let', *Novyi mir*, 1965, 6, pp. 206–30. Danilova, interview.
23. *Istoriya i sotsiologiya*, p. 151.
24. See Chapter 3.
25. *Istoriya i sotsiologiya*, p. 249.
26. *Ibid.*, pp. 135, 186–7.
27. *Ibid.*, p. 239 (original emphasis).
28. *Ibid.*, pp. 186, 202–3.
29. *Ibid.*, pp. 197–8.
30. *Ibid.*, pp. 244–5.
31. Danilova, interview. Venediktov, it will be re-called, supervised I. F. Gindin's research in the 1920s.
32. *Istoriya i sotsiologiya*, p. 257.
33. *Ibid.*, p. 259 (emphasis added – RDM).
34. *Ibid.*, pp. 259–60.
35. *Ibid.*, p. 261.
36. *Ibid.*, p. 264.
37. *Ibid.*, pp. 81, 83.
38. *Ibid.*, p. 84.
39. *Ibid.*, p. 105.
40. *Ibid.*, p. 334.
41. *Ibid.*, pp. 331, 334–5.
42. *Ibid.*, pp. 80–1, 144.
43. *Ibid.*, p. 73.
44. *Ibid.*, p. 102.
45. *Ibid.*, pp. 336–9.
46. Danilova, interview. According to Danilova the head of a sector was usually a *nomenklatura* appointment, but apparently Gefter's appointment as director of the sector was an exception to this rule, which only increased the trepidations of Zhukov and Khvostov.
47. Danilov, interview. See Chapter 6.
48. Protokol No. 1: Zasedanie sektora metodologii. Gefter, 'Plan raboty sektora na 1964 g.', 3 February 1964, AIRI, f. 1, d. 2188, l. 267.
49. Gefter, interview.
50. Gefter, 'Plan', ll. 267–8.
51. According to Scanlan, *Marxism in the USSR*, pp. 166–7, the principle of 'ascent from the abstract to the concrete', an expression used by Marx in his *Grundrisse* to describe his method of analysing capitalism, received particular attention in Soviet philosophy following the publication in 1960 of E. V. Il'enkov, *The Dialectics of the Abstract and the Concrete in Marx's Capital*.
52. Gefter, 'Plan', l. 268; S. O. Shmidt, 'Otchet o rabote sektora metodologii istorii na 1964 g.', AIRI, f. 1, d. 2187, l. 47.

53. Gefter, 'Plan', l. 268.
54. It is apparent that the Sector of Methodology was only the hub of an emerging, institutionally and geographically widespread, discussion; as the document cited above, 'Sostoyanie i perspektivy', p. 4, stresses 'this work is intensively pursued not only in the institutes of the Soviet Academy of Sciences (besides the Sector of the Institute of History also in the group on methodological problems of history led by A. V. Gulyga in the Institute of Philosophy), but in a number of the Union republics (Ukraine, Armenia), but also in the universities (Moscow, Leningrad, Kiev, Novosibirsk, Tomsk, Tartu and others).'
55. S. S. Neretina, 'Istoriya s metodologiei istorii', *VF*, 1990, 9, pp. 152–3.
56. 'Istorizm i logika [v] marksistskoi teorii', 2 December 1966, AIRI, f. 1, d. 2396, ll. 1–55. Arsen'ev's paper and the discussion were published in the controversial 1969 anthology *Istoricheskaya nauka i nekotorye problemy sovremennosti* (see below).
57. V. P. Danilov, 'K voprosu ob osnovnykh kharakteristikakh klassa pri sotsializme', 11 November 1964, AIRI, f. 1, d. 2188, ll. 41–3, 47–51.
58. Ya. S. Drabkin, 'Nekotorye aspekty leninskoi konseptsii mirovoi revolyutsii', referred to in M. Ya. Gefter 'Ochet o rabote Sektor metodologii istorii za 1965 g.', AIRI, f. 1, d. 2293, l. 4.
59. 'Myslima li istoriya odnoi strany?', (discussion dated) 25 November 1964, Archive, IRH, f. 1, d. 2188. Porshnev's paper and the discussion were also published in *Istoricheskaya nauka* (see below).
60. 'Obsuzhdenie doklada M. A. Barga i E. B. Chernyaka, 'Tipologiya sotsial'no-ekonomicheskikh formatsii', 21 February 1966, AIRI, f. 1, d. 2395, ll. 1–133.
61. Yu. I. Semenov, 'Teoriya obshchestvenno-ekonomicheskikh formatsii i mirovoi istorichesky protsess', 30 May 1967, AIRI, f. 1, d. 2507, ll. 1–58. A later (1976) version of Semenov's paper was subsequently translated and discussed in Ernest Gellner (ed.), *Soviet and Western Anthropology*, introduction by Meyer Fortes (London, 1980), pp. 1–58. Gellner, *State and Society in Soviet Thought* (Oxford and New York, 1988), p. 122, hailed Semenov as a 'virtuoso of the global Marxist vision of history'. Gellner was apparently in contact with the sector which planned to publish an essay of his comparing the historical development of the West and the East in the second volume of *Problems of the History of Pre-capitalist Societies* (see below).
62. L. N. Chernova, 'Khronika raboty sektora za 1964–68 gg.', PN. Chernova was academic secretary of the sector, 1965–68.
63. V. S. Bibler, interview.
64. In 1933 the view of V. V. Struve that ancient Eastern civilizations belonged to slave formations was officially adopted. Struve effectively eliminated Marx's notion of the Asiatic mode of production by ascribing a slave stage to the ancient East and a feudal stage to the medieval East. Marion Sawer, *Marxism and the Question of the Asiatic Mode of Production* (The Hague, 1977), pp. 80, 191.
65. *Ibid.*, pp. 79, n. 145, 81, 193. The text referred to is E. Varga, *Ocherki po problemam politekonomii kapitalizma* (Moscow, 1964).
66. Sawer, p. 193; L. V. Danilova, 'Diskussiya po vazhnoi probleme', *VF*, 1965, 12, pp. 149–55.

67. 'The time has come to discuss this remaining unresolved question in our science', Varga wrote in his 1964 essays. Cited by N. B. Ter-Akopyan, 'Razvitie vzglyadov Marksa i Engel'sa na Aziatsky sposob proizvodstva i zemledel'cheskuyu obshchinu', AIRI, f. 1, d. 2294, l. 7, n. 4.
68. A point emphasized by a participant in the sector, A. Ya. Gurevich, interview.
69. Gefter, 'Vstupitel'noe slovo o prichinakh postanovki voprosa na obsuzhdenie, programma i poryadke raboty zasedanii', AIRI, f. 1, d. 2294, l. 4.
70. Ter-Akopyan, 'Razvitie', ll. 5–75.
71. 'Otvety dokladchika', AIRI, f. 1, d. 2294, l. 77.
72. AIRI, f. 1, d. 2294, ll. 81–2.
73. *Ibid.*, l. 80.
74. A. I. Pavlovskaya, 'Novyi etap diskussii ob Aziatskom sposobe proizvodstva', AIRI, f. 1, d. 2294, ll. 98–116.
75. *Ibid.*, ll. 99–100, n. 2. Part of the *Grundrisse*, Marx's *Pre-capitalist Modes of Production*, was apparently first published in Russian in 1940 as K. Marks, *Formy, predshestvuyushchie kapitalisticheskomu proizvodstvu*.
76. O. A. Afanas'ev, 'Obsuzhdenie v Institute istorii AN SSSR problemy "aziatskogo sposoba proizvodstva"', *Sovetskaya ethnografiya*, 1965, 6, pp. 122–6.
77. L. V. Danilova, '(Tezisy doklada) Problema aziatskogo sposoba proizvodstva v sovetskoi istoriografii', AIRI, f. 1, d. 2294, l. 90.
78. L. S. Vasil'ev, AIRI, f. 1, d. 2294, l. 147.
79. Danilova, '(Tezisy doklada)', l. 84.
80. *Ibid.*, ll. 91–2. Here Danilova was advancing the notion of geography as a determining factor in history, not just one that accelerated or retarded social development as the *Short Course* had maintained. *KK*, p. 113. This was a proposition that both undermined the Asiatic mode of production as basically geographically determined and, given the overwhelming emphasis on social factors, encouraged voluntarist attitudes to Soviet development. Though reconsideration of the concept was evident from 1957 onwards, it was formally repudiated in October 1963 in a report to the Academy of Sciences by L. F. Il'ichev. See Sawer, Ch. III. During the discussion on the Asiatic mode of production in the Institute of Philosophy, Gulyga argued that geography should be considered as a 'productive force having a fundamental impact on the form of the productive process'; a perspective opposed by Semenov and Yu. A. Levada on the grounds that similar geographical conditions could give rise to vastly different economic structures. Danilova, 'Diskussiya', p. 155.
81. Danilova, '(Tezisy doklada)', l. 91.
82. In June 1965 Ye. M. Zhukov chastised younger scholars who called into question 'the validity of Marxist historiography concerning the progressive superseding of five socio-economic formations in the course of the world historical process'. V. I. Shunkov *et al.* (eds), *Perekhod Rossii ot feodalizma k kapitalizmy: Materialy Vsesoyuznoi diskussii* (Moscow, 1969), pp. 105–6.
83. In the late 1950s an unexpected and unorthodox radicalization among newly independent countries, above all Castro's Cuba, had already challenged Khrushchev's assumptions at the Twentieth Congress that socialism was the only path to third world progress. Acknowledgement of

other possible paths was first registered in an official discussion on 'the non-capitalist path of development' in November 1960. Jerry F. Hough, *The Struggle for the Third World: Soviet Debates and American Options* (Washington, D.C, 1986), pp. 71, 156–8.
84. Porshnev's contribution to discussion of Danilova, 'Problema aziatskogo sposoba proizvodstva', ll. 121–22.
85. Danilova, 'Zaklyuchitel'nye slova' (9 April 1965), l. 152. During the lively discussion that followed Danilova's report one contributor, Yu. M. Garushyants, repudiated Porshnev's attempts to politicize the debate: 'There is no need to emphasize continually that this (Asiatic mode of production) is only the conception of our political enemies ... Such an indiscriminate approach whereby anybody who dares to speak of the concept is an enemy is nothing more than voluntarism. Such speculation was encouraged to a certain degree by the Stalin cult, and we all know about this.' Garushyants went on to argue that the question has to be dealt with on an 'historiographical plane' and that it was incorrect to think that all the problems of precapitalist societies have been resolved in the writings of Soviet historians – not even 'in the basic works of B. F. Porshnev'! Discussion, 'Problema', ll. 128–133.
86. Danilova, 'Zaklyuchitel'nye', ll. 153, 157, 159.
87. Semenov, 'Teoriya'.
88. 'Zaklyuchitel'nye', l. 156.
89. Yu. I. Semenov, 'Kategoriya "sotsial'nyi organizm" i ee znachenie dlya istoricheskoi nauki', *VI*, 1966, 8, pp. 88–106. Gefter too, during the Asiatic mode of production discussion, referred to Marx's concept of the 'formation' as a 'social organism as whole with all its relations and mediations, on the basis of a given mode of production.' AIRI, f. 1, d. 2294, l. 171.
90. Yu. I. Semenov, 'Problema sotsial'no-ekonomicheskogo stroiya drevnogo vostoka', *Narody Azii i Afriki*, 1965, 4, pp. 69–89. *Cf.* Scanlan, 'Historical Materialism to Historical Interactionism', p. 15; Sawer, p. 212.
91. According to Danilova, '(Tezisy doklada)', l. 90, n. 1, Semenov advanced this third tendency argument during the discussion on the Asiatic mode of production in the Institute of Philosophy.
92. Semenov, 'Kategoriya', pp. 90–2.
93. Semenov, 'Teoriya obshchestvenno-ekonomicheskikh formatsii ... (Tezisy)', ll. 145–7.
94. *Ibid.*, ll. 145–8. Semenov's grand perspective was later elaborated in 'Socio-Economic Formations and World History', Gellner, *Soviet and Western*, pp. 29–58.
95. *Ibid.*, p. 64.
96. 'Obsuzhdenie doklada Yu. I. Semenova', 30 May 1967, AIRI, f. 1, d. 2507, l. 41.
97. *Ibid.*, ll. 65–7, 79, l. 82.
98. Semenov, *ibid.*, ll. 5–7, 26–8. On the significance of Vasil'ev's and Stuchevsky's work see Sawer, pp. 100, 211–13.
99. 'Obsuzhdenie doklada Yu. I. Semenova', ll. 61–2, 70, 76–7.
100. *Ibid.*, ll. 109–10, 112–13 (emphasis added – RDM).
101. Gellner, *State and Society*, pp. 146–7.

102. 'Obsuzhdenie doklada Yu. I. Semenova', ll. 112–3.
103. In his 1976 paper Semenov took issue with Danilova's contention in relation to the *pyatichlenka* that '"there turned out to be more deviations and exceptions, than cases falling under the rule, and secondly – and this is the main point – the regularities operating here showed themselves to be so specific, that they could not be explained by the influence of the historic environment alone." (L. V. Danilova *et al.* (eds), *Problemy istorii dokapitalisticheskikh obshchestv*, Kniga 1 (Moscow, 1968), p. 30.) All this led her to the conclusion that in human society exist not one, but several diverse lines of development. In this way Danilova, without clearly realizing it herself, arrives at the repudiation not merely of a five-stage, but more generally of any given scheme of the evolution of human society, that is, to the rejection of the very core of the theory of socio-economic formations.' Semenov, 'Socio-economic formations' (1976), in Gellner, *Soviet and Western Anthropology*, pp. 53–4; *Cf.* Gellner, 'One Highway or Many', in *State and Society*, pp. 151–2
104. Danilova *et al.*, *Problemy*, pp. 5–20 (original emphasis). While authorship of the introduction was given as the Sector of Methodology, in fact it was written by Gefter, in order to raise the profile of the sector. Gefter, interview.
105. *Ibid.*, p. 6 (original emphasis).
106. *Ibid.*, pp. 7–8 (original emphasis).
107. See Chapter 2.
108. Danilova *et al.*, *Problemy*, pp. 9–10 (original emphasis).
109. *Ibid.*, pp. 11–12 (original emphasis).
110. *Ibid.*, pp. 12–13 (original emphasis).
111. *Ibid.*, pp. 16–17 (original emphasis).
112. *Ibid.*, p. 23.
113. *Ibid.*, pp. 156–222.
114. *Ibid.*, pp. 33–4.
115. *Ibid.*, p. 23.
116. *Ibid.*, pp. 30, 38–9.
117. *Ibid.*, p. 46. For a summary of the 1920s debate see Marian Sawer, 'The Politics of Historiography: Russian Socialism and the Question of the Asiatic Mode of Production 1906–1931', *Critique*, 10–11, 1978–79, pp. 15–36.
118. Danilova *et al.*, *Problemy*, pp. 28–30, 41–2, 44–5.
119. *Ibid.*, pp. 49–50 (emphasis added) and n. 37. According to Danilova, it was an economist who headed the Department of Political Economy in the Central Committee's Academy of Social Sciences, I. I. Kuz'minov, who first resurrected the achievements of Soviet political economy of the 1920s. Kuz'minov published a political economy in 1963 that reviewed the concepts of historical materialism, particularly those of A. A. Bogdanov who emphasized this distinction between relations of production and their derivative, property relations. Danilova, interview.
120. Danilova *et al.*, *Problemy*, p. 52.
121. It is apparent that the publication in Russian of the introduction to Marx's *Grundrisse* was instrumental in enabling more sophisticated analyses of precapitalist societies such as that by Danilova, who frequently cites this text in her footnotes.

122. Danilova *et al.*, *Problemy*, pp. 58–9.
123. J. Stalin, *Economic Problems of Socialism*, p. 47.
124. Danilova *et al.*, *Problemy*, pp. 50–1, and n. 41. Danilova notes that in the 1920s Soviet medievalists had focussed on 'real' peasant proprietorship of land, even where it was 'completely deprived of juridical rights to landed property (as occurred under serfdom)'.
125. *Ibid.*, pp. 63–4.
126. Danilova, interview.
127. A. Danilov, 'K voprosu o metodologii', pp. 80–1.
128. Danilova, 'Diskussionye', pp. 48, 66.
129. Gellner, *State and Society*, p. 11.
130. Danilova, interview.
131. Danilova *et al.*, *Problemy*, pp. 15–16.
132. Danilova, interview, according to whom, Gefter was rather apprehensive about publishing the sector's work.
133. A. L. Mongait, 'Arkheologicheskie kul'tury i etnicheskie obshchnosti (k voprosu o metodike istoriko-arkheologicheskikh issledovanii)', *Narody Azii i Afriki*, 1967, 1, pp. 60–1.
134. Neretina, p. 152.
135. Stenogramma zasedaniya sektora metodologii Instituta istorii, 28 December 1965. Doklad: d.i. n. A. L. Mongait, 'Arkhaeologicheskaya kul'tura i etnicheskie obshchnosti' ', AIRI, f. 1, d. 2294, l. 20.
136. Mongait, 'Arkheologicheskie kul'tury', p. 75.
137. 'Otchet o rabote v 1964–1968', 9 April 1969, p. 2. Unpublished report, PN.
138. From Gefter's speech to the joint meeting of the historiographical group and the Sector of Methodology of the Institute of History, 29 April 1966, devoted to the report of N. N. Maslov, 'Sostoyanie i razvitie istoriko-partiinoi nauki v 1935–1955 gg.' (original emphasis). Medvedev, *Let History Judge* (1973), pp. 517–8. Unfortunately, and curiously, this important quote from Gefter is omitted from the second revised and expanded edition of this book (New York, 1989).
139. Gefter, interview. This was the logic underlying Gefter's forthright criticism in a party meeting of an article by S. Trapeznikov, 'Marksizm-Leninizm – nezyblemaya osnova razvitiya obshchestvennykh nauk', *Pravda*, 8 October 1965, pp. 3–4. Trapeznikov, while acknowledging 'mistakes and shortcomings' in the party's past, maintained that 'neither the cult of the personality itself nor its consequences to any degree flowed from the nature of the socialist system, nor could they have changed its character'. Gefter declared that this article 'not only does not open up the possibilities of a profound theoretical and scientific study of the problem (of the 'cult of the personality'), but, as it were, closes this possibility with the aid of a very simplified formula, which in essence is reduced to a prescription for proportions: What to say more, what to say less, where to whitewash, and where to add colour. If the research historian knows beforehand that he has no right to deviate even a millimetre from this proportion, then the question arises: Can he arrive at independent conclusions?' Gefter, 'Vystuplenie na partsobranii instituta istorii po dokladu A. M. Rumyantseva ob itogakh Oktyabr'skogo plenuma TsK KPSS 1965 goda'. 30 October 1965. PN. This clash of opinions deepened Trapeznikov's personal enmity towards Gefter. Trapeznikov's position

harked back to the ambiguous pronouncement on Stalin, the June 1956 Central Committee resolution 'On overcoming the cult of the personality and its consequences'. Joravsky, in his introduction to the 1973 edition of *Let History Judge*, pp. xi–xii, states that Medvedev basically shared the official view of Stalinism as 'accidental deformations of a fundamentally sound system' and points to the tensions induced by Medvedev's attempt to juggle a deterministic Marxism with a voluntaristic explanation for Stalinism.

140. Gefter, interview (emphasis added – RDM).
141. Gefter, 'Nekotorye voprosy metodologii istorii'. Report presented to the sector, 2 November 1967. PN.
142. Gefter, 'Otchet ... 1964–68 gg.', pp. 3–4.
143. Cited in Neretina, p. 150.
144. A. Danilov, 'K voprosu', pp. 71–2, 77, 81. Danilov took particular exception to Gurevich's challenge to the 'objective content' of the concept of the socio-economic formation. *Ibid.*, pp. 70–1. A. Ya. Gurevich, 'Obshchii zakon i konkretnaya zakonomernost' v istorii', *VI*, 1965, 8, pp. 14–30; 'K diskussii o dokapitalisticheskikh obshchestvennykh formatsiyakh: Formatsiya i uklad', *VF*, 1968, 2, pp. 118–29. Gurevich's view that this concept should be treated as a 'logical contruct' rather than as a 'specific social phenomenon' was perceived by Danilov, not incorrectly, as an adaptation to Weber's ideal-type. Gurevich now says that he was obliged to conceal the 'pathos' of his article, 'Obshchii zakon', which was his 'protest against the foisting on historians of general historical laws.' Influenced by Western ethnography, the *Annales* school and especially the neo-Kantianism of Heinrch Rickert and Max Weber, Gurevich deliberately counterposed to general laws his notion of 'specific historical *zakonomernost*', understood 'not as a series of repeated regularities but as an outcome of the particularities of given factors in a given moment in a given society. That is, the study of the specific – here resided the pathos of this work.' Gurevich, interview.
145. Gefter, 'Lenin, revolyutsionnaya teoriya i praktika revolyutsii'. Undated, PN.
146. Neretina, interview.
147. M. Ya. Gefter *et al.* (eds), *Istoricheskaya nauka i nekotorye problemy sovremennosti* (Moscow, 1969). According to Gefter he went over the entire anthology, aware that it would be very controversial. It was only published thanks to the support of then vice-president of the Academy of Sciences, A. M. Rumyantsev, in opposition to Zhukov and the Department of Science. Gefter, interview.
148. Note to Gefter, 3 September 1969, cited in Neretina, p. 158.
149. Gefter, *Istoricheskaya nauka*, p. 7.
150. *Ibid.*, p. 8.
151. *Ibid.*, p. 9.
152. A. Smirnov, 'Za stroguyu nauchnost', dostovernost' i istoricheskuyu pravdu', *Kst*, 1972, 16, p. 120. Smirnov's accusation harked back to that of the *Short Course*, which depicted Leninism arising from an irreconcilable struggle with populism. *KK*, p. 20.
153. *Istoricheskaya nauka*, pp. 16–19. Gefter published a very similar analysis of Lenin, 'Iz istorii leninskoi mysli', *Novyi mir*, 1969, 4, pp. 135–6.

154. *Istoricheskaya nauka*, pp. 20–1, 24–7.
155. *Ibid.*, p. 37.
156. *Ibid.*, p. 10.
157. M. B. Rybakov, 'O nekotorykh neopravdannykh pretenzyakh', *VI KPSS*, 1971, 7, pp. 123–33.
158. *Istoricheskaya nauka*, pp. 209–300.
159. Drabkin, interview.
160. *Istoricheskaya nauka*, pp. 231–5.
161. A. Kornilov, N. Prokopenko, A. Shirokov, 'Pod vidom nauchnogo poiska', *Sovetskaya Rossiya*, 28 February 1970, 49, p. 3. In fact, Pospelov, Director of the Institute of Marxism–Leninism, attempted to pressure Volobuev, apparently unsuccessfully, into denouncing Drabkin as a Trotskyite. Drabkin, interview.
162. *Istoricheskaya nauka*, pp. 225, 244.
163. Rybakov, pp. 132–3.
164. *Istoricheskaya nauka*, pp. 213–15.
165. *Ibid.*, pp. 216–20.
166. *Ibid.*, p. 224.
167. *Ibid.*, p. 227.
168. *Ibid.*, pp. 229–30.
169. *Ibid.*, p. 228.
170. Rybakov, p. 133.
171. On 10 February 1971 the Bureau of the Division of History of the Soviet Academy of Sciences convened to discuss 'current questions of the Marxist–Leninist conception of socialist revolution' and the anthology in particular. G. P. Shurbovany, 'Obsuzhdenie nekotorykh problem metodologii istorii', *VI*, 1971, 10, pp. 159–60.
172. *Istoricheskaya Nauka*, p. 330.
173. *Ibid.*, p. 348.
174. *Ibid.*, p. 354.
175. *Ibid.*, pp. 354, 358 (original emphases).
176. *Ibid.*, pp. 391–2.
177. Shurbovany, p. 161.
178. *Istoricheskaya nauka*, p. 392.
179. A. Kosul'nikov, A. Pedosov, 'Ovladevat' bogatym opytom leninskoi partii', *Pravda*, 13 October 1972, p. 2.
180. 'An organ of the C[entral] C[ommittee]' is the way Ye. M. Zhukov saw *Sovetskaya Rossiya*, as he frantically opposed Drabkin publishing the anthology *V. I. Lenin and Problems of the History of Classes and Class Struggle*. Drabkin, interview.
181. Kornilov, Prokopenko, Shirokov, p. 2.
182. 'Vitse-prezidentu AN SSSR akademiku A. M. Rumyantsevu'. Unpublished letter from Gefter, 3 January 1971. PN.
183. Centre d'Etudes et de Recherches marxistes, *Sur Les Sociétiés Precapitalistes: Textes choisis de Marx, Engels, Lenine*, preface de Maurice Godelier (Paris, 1978), p. 9.
184. Approved for publication 9 June 1969, *V. I. Lenin i problemy istorii klassov i klassovoi bor'by* was the subject of several commissions established within the Institute of World History to oversee corrections that would make it more in keeping with the 'current stage of the class struggle'. 'Otchet o

nauchno-issledovatel'skoi rabote Instituta vseobshchei istorii za 1970 g.' ARAN, f. 1900, op. 1, d. 29, l. 3; 'Protokol zasedaniya direktsii Instituta vseobshchei istorii AN SSSR', 30 March 1970, ARAN, f. 1900, op. 1, d. 30, ll. 11–2.
185. Preparation of this work is referred to in Gefter, 'Ochet o rabote Sektor metodologii istorii za 1965 g.', AIRI, f. 1, d. 2293, l. 4.
186. Danilova, interview. Cherepnin and Pashuto, it will be recalled, made their careers as historians as a result of the anti-cosmopolitan campaign. See Chapter 3.
187. 'Protokol No. 2 zasedaniya Uchenogo soveta Instituta vseobshchei istorii AN SSSR', 22 April 1969. ARAN, f. 1900, op. 1, d. 16, l. 2.
188. 'P. Lisovsky, 'Za svobodu tvorcheskoi nauchnoi mysli (vystuplenie na partiinom sobranii Instituta vseobshchei istorii).' 28 June 1971. PN.
189. The Sector of Economic History survived only for 1973. A proposal originating in the sector's party group to establish a methodological seminar in the 1974 academic year never eventuated. Gefter himself was the subject of renewed attack, both within the Institute of World History's party organization and from the CPSU's theoretical journal, *Kommunist*. Smirnov; 'Protokol No.2 partiinogo sobraniya sektora ekonomicheskoi istorii instituta vseobshchei istorii ANSSR ot 29 yanvarya 1973 g.', pp. 1, 4. PN. At this meeting an unidentified participant, noting that the original hostile review in *Sovetskaya Rossiya* had been repudiated by the Central Committee, asked why was the question of Gefter's article in *Istoricheskaya nauka* being raised yet again and 'once more not as a scholarly debate but as a denunciation? ... (when) M. Ya. Gefter had already been subject in 1971 to a party reprimand for an incorrect attitude to criticism.'
190. Gefter, interview.
191. The expression '*istoriosofiya*' is Neretina's. According to Neretina (interview), in pre-revolutionary Russian historiography history was not only a political question, it was also a philosophical one. The question of Russia's historical status became closely intertwined with the pre-revolutionary political debates about Russia's future. On the 'culturological school' and M. M. Bakhtin, see Kagarlitsky, *Thinking Reed*, pp. 278–82. We can discern another link here with pre-revolutionary historiography through Gefter's supervisor A. L. Sidorov, a former student of M. N. Pokrovsky, himself a student of Klyuchevsky. From reading the latter Sidorov developed an inclination towards philosophy, while from Pokrovsky's free-thinking historiographical seminar he imbibed a 'love of methodological questions'. A. L. Sidorov, 'Nekotorye razmyshleniya o trude i opyte istorika', *I SSSR*, 1964, 3, pp. 119, 124–5.
192. According to Danilova who recalls that Porshnev, addressing her from the rostrum during the Asiatic mode of production debate, declared 'In the 1930s we used to shoot people like you! Nowadays, unfortunately, we have to bring you up!' Danilova, interview.
193. Neretina, pp. 150, 157.
194. See Chapter 6.
195. Gefter, interview.
196. Gefter, 'Otchet o rabote na zasedanie partburo, instituta vseobshchei istorii', 8 yunya 1974 (original emphasis). PN.

6 Collision course

1. A. Rumyantsev, 'Partiya i intelligentsiya', *Pravda*, 21 February 1965, pp. 2–3.
2. Roi Medvedev, *Lichnost' i epokha: Politichesky portret L. I. Brezhneva*, Kniga 1 (Moscow, 1991), pp. 167, 223–4, 260–1.
3. *Ibid.*, p. 261.
4. Rumyantsev; Medvedev, *Lichnost' i epokha*, p. 223; *Cf.* Spechler, pp. 213–14.
5. Medvedev, *Lichnost' i epokha*, p. 143. Trapeznikov (1912–84) was a typical *vydvizhenets*. Born into a poor, Astrakhan, working class family, after five years in the Komsomol (1929–34), he spent the next decade (1935–45) in middle-ranking posts in the Penzensky regional party committee. In 1946 he graduated from the V. I. Lenin Moscow Pedagogical Institute and the Higher Party School and two years later from the Academy of Social Sciences of the Central Committee. According to Medvedev, 'Five years of intense training in the Higher Party School and the Academy of Social Sciences in the mid-1940s could not have given to a young party worker any serious knowledge in Marxism, the social sciences, history or philosophy; but they could foster a stubborn, self-opinionated dogmatist and Stalinist, such as Trapeznikov showed himself to be throughout his scientific and political career.' In 1948 when he was head of the Kishinev Higher Party School in Moldavia he became acquainted with Brezhnev who 'found in Trapeznikov not only an aide but also a distinctive ideological mentor. Brezhnev never considered himself an expert in the social sciences and willingly consulted with such a great scholar, by Kishinev standards, as Trapeznikov.' *Ibid.*, pp. 10, 64–5, 143, 166.
6. *Ibid.*, pp. 168–9.
7. P. Volobuev, 'Takie lyudi byli vsegda!', *Sovetskaya kul'tura*, 6 May 1989, p. 4. Earlier, on 5 September 1965, Trapeznikov attacked as a 'Trotskyist ... who collaborated with Whiteguard and facist filth' the recently rehabilitated F. F. Raskol'nikov – author of the famous 1939 'Open Letter to Stalin', a copy of which was then circulating in Moscow. Medvedev, *Lichnost' i epokha*, p. 169; Davies, *Soviet History in the Gorbachev Revolution*, p. 173.
8. Ye. Zhukov, V. Trukhanovsky, V. Shunkov, 'Vysokaya otvetstvennost' istorikov', *Pravda*, 30 January 1966, p. 2 (emphasis added – RDM).
9. Nekrich, *Otreshis' ot strakha*, pp. 257–8.
10. *Ibid.*, pp. 240–1; Medvedev, *Lichnost' i epokha*, pp. 240–2.
11. Medvedev, p. 170; Andrei D. Sakharov, *Progress and Intellectual Freedom*, Introduction, Afterword and Notes by Harrison E. Salisbury (Harmondsworth, 1969), pp. 17–8. The letter is reproduced as 'Establishment Intellectuals Protest to Brezhnev' in Cohen, *An End to Silence*, pp. 177–9.
12. Medvedev, *Lichnost' i epokha*, pp. 100–1.
13. Zhuravlev, p. 208.
14. Danilov, interview.
15. *Ibid.* There was one signal achievement of this partkom: It published N. M. Druzhinin (ed.), *Sovetskaya istoricheskaya nauka ot XX k XXII s"ezdu KPSS*, 2 vols. (Moscow, 1962), primarily due to the initiative of K. N. Tarnovsky. According to Danilov, this important publication was

produced in the spirit of 'our communist attitude to labour': It was not part of the institute's research schedule, nor did its authors receive 'one kopek' for its publication. Danilov, interview.
16. Ibid.
17. Ibid. Cf. Nekrich, pp. 249–50.
18. Nekrich, pp. 250–1.
19. Ibid., pp. 252–3.
20. 'O sostoyanii sovetskoi istoricheskoi nauki i nekotorye voprosy raboty partiinoi organizatsii Instituta istorii Akademii nauk SSSR'. What follows is actually based on 'Sovetskaya istoricheskaya nauka i zadachi partiinoi organizatsii instituta istorii AN SSSR' (1965). PD. This manuscript, which has annotations by Ye. N. Gorodetsky, is apparently the draft of the document presented by the *partkom* to the party meeting in February 1966.
21. 'Stenogramma obshchego zakrytogo partiinogo sobraniya Instituta istorii Akademii nauk SSSR.' 19 fevralya 1966 goda. PD. This is a transcript of the discussion of the *partkom* report.
22. 'Sovetskaya istoricheskaya nauka', p. 31.
23. Ibid., pp. 3–6, 11, 13–15.
24. Ibid., pp. 27–8 (original emphasis).
25. Ibid., pp. 36–8. Drawn from Russian literary tradition, '*figura umolchaniya*' meant not so much 'a lie as leaving the truth unsaid'. *Slovar' sovremennogo Russkogo yazyka*, T.16 (Moscow and Leningrad, 1964), p. 625. The term was resuscitated by Aleksandr Tvardovsky in his controversial 40th jubilee article for *Novyi mir*, 'Po sluchayu yubileya', *Novyi mir*, 1965, 1, p. 12. Danilov and Yakubovskaya planned to publish an article, 'O figure umolchaniya v istoricheskoi nauke', in the second issue of *Novyi mir* for 1966. Trapeznikov, however, on the advice of Glavlit, ensured it was consigned 'to the archive'. TsKhSD, f. 5, op. 35, d. 223, ll. 63–71. In their article Danilov and Yakubovskaya intended to make public many of the questions raised in the *partkom* report: 'Silence' concerning such major figures as Trotsky and Zinoviev and the institutions they had headed, such as Trotsky's Revolutionary Military Council; 'hushing-up' the 'exit' from the NEP into forced industrialization and collectivization; and the spurious 'conception of "two truths"'. The last-named provided the '"theory" of the *figura umolchaniya*', which justified, for instance, 'false[ly] and blasphemous[ly]' depicting the initial disasters in the Great Patriotic War as a preconceived, '"wise" "plan of active defence"'. In May 1965 Danilov, A. L. Sidorov, L. M. Ivanov and a 'large group of prominent' historians had attempted to publish an 'open letter' in *Izvestiya* supporting Tvardovsky's article: 'Pis'mo gruppy vidnykh istorikov v gazetu "Izvestiya"', *Politichesky dnevnik*, 1964–1965 (Amsterdam, 1972), pp. 83–8. This was in reply to criticism of Tvardovsky's article by E. Vuchetich in *Izvestiya*, 15 April 1965, in which he advanced the notion of 'two truths': The 'truth of the event and the fact' versus the '*truth of the life and struggle of the people*' (Vuchetich's emphasis). Danilov *et al.* attacked this as a spurious distinction between 'suitable and inconvenient facts' by someone who passed over the Twentieth Congress in silence. Ibid., pp. 84–5. Their reply was suppressed by the Department of Culture. TsKhSD, f. 5, op. 35, d. 223, l. 66. Many of these documents have been published in *Arkheograficheskyezhegodnik*, 1995, pp. 324–36.

26. 'Sovetskaya istoricheskaya nauka', pp. 31, 32a, 33–4, 37.
27. 'Stenogramma', p. 58.
28. *Ibid.*, pp. 41–2, 59–62.
29. *Ibid.*, p. 42, 63–4, 71–3, 223–4.
30. *Ibid.*, p. 114.
31. *Ibid.*, pp. 91–100.
32. *Ibid.*, pp. 186–8.
33. *Ibid.*, p. 201.
34. *Ibid.*, p. 181.
35. *Ibid.*, p. 66.
36. 'Sovetskaya istoricheskaya nauka', pp. 47–8.
37. Nekrich, p. 253. Nekrich's summary of the *partkom*'s proposal is somewhat inaccurate. He says the *partkom* proposed the 'democratization of the entire life of the institute, from top to bottom, including changing the method of electing the director of the institute, his deputies, heads of sectors and the senior and junior researchers.'
38. 'Sovetskaya istoricheskaya nauka', p. 49. According to Nekich, p. 253, the election of the institute director was a 'pure formality'. While an institute director was nominally elected by secret ballot of the relevant division of the Academy of Sciences, and then confirmed by the presidium, in reality the vote in the Academy of Sciences merely ratified an appointment already made in the Central Committee.
39. 'Sovetskaya istoricheskaya nauka', pp. 49–50 (original emphasis). In discussion Khvostov pointed out that the Academic Council was not appointed by the director but by the Presidium of the Academy of Sciences as a 'sufficiently representative collective organ.' He was clearly uncomfortable with the *partkom* proposal: 'Who would elect it [the Academic Council]? A general meeting of the research associates? I don't know, there is a lot of confusion here.' 'Stenogramma', pp. 196–7.
40. 'Sovetskaya istoricheskaya nauka', pp. 49–50.
41. Yakubovskaya, 'Stenogramma', p. 76.
42. Nekrich, p. 254.
43. Danilov, in 'Stenogramma otkrytogo sobraniya instituta istorii AN SSSR "XXIII s"ezd KPSS i zadachi istoricheskoi nauki" ', 17 maya 1966 goda, pp. 54–5. PD.
44. V. M. Khvostov, 'XXIII s"ezd KPSS i zadachi instituta istorii AN SSSR', 17 maya 1966 goda, pp. 4, 8–9, 35–8. PD.
45. 'Stenogramma otkrytogo sobraniya', pp. 36–7.
46. *Ibid.*, pp. 43–4.
47. *Ibid.*, pp. 50–3.
48. Nekrich, p. 255.
49. Danilov, interview.
50. *Ibid.*; Nekrich, p. 341.
51. Danilov, interview.
52. *Ibid.*; Drabkin, interview.
53. A. M. Nekrich (1920–93) was born in Baku of Jewish parentage. He was a student of the history faculty, MGU, from 1937 until he joined the army in 1941. He joined the CPSU in 1943. He entered the Institute of History in 1945, defending his *kandidat* degree in 1949. Specializing in the history of the Second World War, he went on to become a Senior Researcher in

1956. After his expulsion from the CPSU in 1967, he became a researcher in the Institute of General History until emigrating in 1976, taking up a position at Harvard University, which he held until his death. M. S. Al'perovich, *et al.* (eds), *Otreshivshiisya ot strakha. Pamyati A. M. Nekricha: Vospominaiya, stat'i, dokumenty* (Moscow, 1996), p. 211.

54. Nekrich, pp. 214–15, 217, 221. *Cf.* Vladimir Petrov, *"June 22, 1941"*: Soviet *Historians and the German Invasion* (Columbia, S.C., 1968), according to whom the significance of Nekrich's book was that it 'went further than anybody else' in absolving the 'fighting marshals' of blame for the disasters in the first years of the Great Patriotic War, when, in the mid-sixties the neo-Stalinists were trying to re-embellish Stalin's role. *Ibid.*, pp. 10, 13.
55. Nekrich, pp. 212–13; Medvedev, *Lichnost' i epokha*, p. 168.
56. Nekrich, pp. 214–15; *Cf. June 22, 1941* in Petrov, p. 226.
57. Nekrich, pp. 215, 226, 228–9; Petrov, p. 21 and pp. 264–70: G. Fedorov, 'A Measure of Responsibility', *Novyi mir*, 1, 1966.
58. Nekrich, p. 241; Medvedev, p. 240.
59. Nekrich, pp. 230–1. For a transcript of the discussion see Petrov, pp. 250–61.
60. Nekrich, pp. 233–4. There is no mention of the non-aggression pact in the transcript, Petrov, pp. 250–2.
61. IMEMO is not mentioned by Deborin in the transcript, Petrov, pp. 250–2.
62. Nekrich, p. 234; *Cf., June 22, 1941*, Petrov, p. 43.
63. Nekrich, pp. 234–5. According to the transcript, Petrov, pp. 251–2, there was 'excitement in the hall' around Deborin's attempt to defend the 'honour' of those like Voroshilov and Budennyi who condemned Tukhachevsky and others at their trial, knowing they were innocent.
64. Nekrich, p. 235. Petrov, p. 249, concludes from the transcript that the audience overwhelmingly condemned Stalin and his associates and that 'resistance to anything suggesting Stalin's rehabilitation is strong among Soviet historians.'
65. Nekrich, pp. 235, 237.
66. *Ibid.*, pp. 238–40, 264–5.
67. *Ibid.*, p. 265. Nekrich claims, however, that A. N. Yakovlev, in his capacity as Deputy Head of the Department of Propaganda and Agitation, refused to deal directly with him.
68. *Ibid.*, pp. 259–60.
69. Nekrich, pp. 261, 266–70. *Cf.* Petrov, pp. 246–7.
70. Nekrich, pp. 270–2.
71. *Ibid.*, pp. 275, 280, 290. Almost all these accusations were publicized in a hostile review of *June 22, 1941* by G. A. Deborin and B. S. Telpukhovsky, 'In the Ideological Captivity of the Falsifiers of History', *VI KPSS* September 1967. See Petrov, pp. 277–302.
72. Nekrich, pp. 287–8; Petrov, p. 22, who claims that in June 1966 Nekrich was elected a corresponding member of the Academy of Sciences. Nekrich, pp. 265–6, however, states he was nominated but not elected to the academy.
73. Nekrich, pp. 281–2, 287–8.
74. *Ibid.*, pp. 292, 295–6.

75. *Ibid.*, pp. 270, 296–7.
76. *Ibid.*, p. 292.
77. *Ibid.*, pp. 270, 291.
78. *Ibid.*, p. 291.
79. *Ibid.*, pp. 298–300.
80. Danilov, interview.
81. Volobuev, interview. M. S. Al'perovich was a Latin Americanist.
82. Danilov, interview.
83. *Ibid*. Nekrich, however, p. 300, states this occurred in autumn 1967.
84. Volobuev, interview.
85. Danilova, interview.
86. Gefter, speech, 27 December 1966, pp. 1–2, 5, 7. PN. 'Vystuplenie na partsobranii instituta istorii po dokladu A. M. Rumyantseva ob itogakh Oktyabr'skogo plenuma TsK KPSS 1965 goda'. 30 October 1965, pp. 1, 3, 4. PN.
87. In a similar vein, Tvardovsky looked to the 'democratic backing of public opinion' to counter the resurgence of Stalinism; in 1969, in *Novyi mir*, he advocated the democratization of the USSR. Spechler, pp. 212, 227.
88. Danilov, interview.
89. Nekrich, p. 337.
90. Polikarpov, ' "*novoe napravlenie*"' 50–70x-gg', pp. 373–4.
91. Volobuev, interview.
92. 'Zadachi istoricheskaya nauka', pp. 46–7.
93. Nekrich, p. 318, and pp. 291–2 on Trapeznikov's personal grudge against Danilov. S. S. Neretina, 'Istoriya s metodologiei istorii', *VF*, 1990, 9, p. 150, links the division of the Institute of History to the Nekrich affair itself. After Trapeznikov's initial failure to be elected to the Academy of Sciences, Academicians Rybakov and Khvostov spoke in favour of a second, also unsuccessful, ballot. Trapeznikov finally became an academician in 1976. Medvedev, *Lichnost' i epokha*, p. 144.
94. Nekrich, p. 318. The Central Committee subsequently adopted a resolution setting the research parameters for the two new institutes, insisting this should be carried out in close cooperation with, among others, the Institute of Marxism–Leninism. 'V Tsentral'nom Komitet KPSS', *VI*, 1969, 4, pp. 3–4.
95. Polikarpov, p. 375.
96. Danilov, interview.
97. Polikarpov, p. 375.
98. Nekrich, p. 338.
99. Neretina, interview.
100. Gefter, interview.
101. Kagarlitsky, *Thinking Reed*, p. 200.
102. On the 'lost generation' of the intelligentsia in the 1970s see Boris Kagarlitsky, *The Disintegration of the Monolith*, trans. by Renfrey Clarke (London and New York, 1992), pp. 33–4.
103. Nekrich, p. 315.
104. Medvedev, *Lichnost' i epokha*, p. 251.
105. Nekrich, pp. 314–15.

106. *Ibid.*, pp. 317–8.
107. V. Golikov, S. Murashov, I. Chkhikvishvili, N. Shatagin, S. Shaumyan, 'Za Leninskuyu partiinost' v osveshchenii istorii KPSS', *Kst*, 1969, 3, pp. 67–82. According to Medvedev, pp. 174–5, this particular article was the 'most candid attempt ... to review the line of the Twentieth and Twenty-second Congresses' and provoked considerable *samizdat* protest. Golikov was a personal aid to Brezhnev on ideology and culture, while Chkhikvishvili was a senior official of the Department of Agitation and Propaganda.
108. Medvedev, *Lichnost' i epokha*, pp. 175–8.
109. *Ibid.*, pp. 323–7, 330–9; Gurevich, interview.
110. A. Ya. Gurevich, *Problemy genezisa feodalizma v zapadnoi evrope* (Moscow, 1970).
111. S. L. Pleshkova, 'Khronika nauchnoi zhizn'. Ob uchebnom posobii "Problemy genezisa feodalizma v zapadnoi evrope" (informatsiya o khode obsuzhdeniya knigi A. Ya. Gurevicha)', *VI*, 1970, 9, pp. 154–67. Cf. David B. Miller in 'Reviews of Books', *The American Historical Review*, 76, 1, 1971, pp. 756–7.
112. Nekrich, p. 380.
113. *Ibid.*, p. 339.
114. *Ibid.*, p. 291.
115. A letter dated 21 October 1969 to Brezhnev from D. A. Koval'chenko, then a senior researcher in the Institute of the History of the USSR, subsequently a reluctant participant in the *perestroika* ferment around historical science, confirms this. Koval'chenko objected to the attempt of Rumyantsev, in his capacity as Vice-President of the Academy of Sciences, to have Samsonov appointed institute director on the grounds that as head of 'Nauka' press he allowed Nekrich's book to be published. 'Our institute', he wrote, 'is currently in the throes of a protracted "directorial crisis" ... But it is impossible not to take into account that the appointment to the responsible post of director of the Institute of national history of a person involved in this Nekrich affair, could be construed by the majority of the communists of our collective as an indirect annulment of the C[entral] C[ommittee] resolution on the Nekrich affair and a moderating of the harsh judgement of his book. It is no secret that there are some among us who dream about achieving this.' 'General'nomu sekretariyu TsK KPSS tov. L. I. Brezhnevu', TsKhSD, f. 5, op. 61, d. 62, ll. 201–3.
116. Memorandum dated 6 April 1970. *Ibid.*, l. 206.
117. Volobuev, interview.
118. Nekrich, pp. 339–40.
119. *Ibid.*, pp. 339–41.
120. *Ibid.*, pp. 341–2.
121. Volobuev, interview.
122. I. I. Mints *et al.* (eds), *Sverzhenie samoderzhaviya: Sbornik statei* (Moscow, 1970); L. M. Ivanov *et al.* (eds), *Rossiisky proletariat: Oblik. bor'ba. gegemoniya* (Moscow, 1970). Nekrich seems to have mistakenly confused this with *The Proletariat of Russia on the Eve of the February Revolution*.
123. George M. Enteen, 'A Recent Trend on the Historical Front', *Survey*, 20, 4 (93), Autumn 1974, p. 126 and n. 19. A graduate of the State Historical

Museum in Moscow (1936), in 1937 Ivanov became a junior researcher in the Institute of History, where in 1939 he defended his *kandidat* thesis. Badly wounded in the war, in 1943 he returned to the institute. In the mid-1950s he was, among other things, head of the Group on the History of the Russian proletariat. K. N. Tarnovsky, 'Pamyati Leonida Mikhailovicha Ivanova (8 noyabrya 1909 – 10 yanvarya 1972 g.)', *IZ*, 1972, 90, pp. 355–76.
124. Ivanov *et al.*, pp. 5–16, 100–1, 108–9 and n. 41.
125. *Ibid.*, pp. 105–8.
126. Enteen, p. 122.
127. (Sekretno) 'TsK KPSS – otdel nauki i uchebnykh zavedenii', 12 June 1972, TsKhSD, f. 5, op. 64, d. 108, ll. 65, 82–3.
128. 'V Otdelenii istorii AN SSSR: Postanovlenie buro otdeleniya istorii AN SSSR ob itogakh obsuzhdeniia v institute istorii SSSR izdannykh v 1970 godu sbornikov "Rossiisky proletariat: Oblik. bor'ba. gegemoniya" i "Sverzhenie samoderzhaviya"', *VI*, 1972, 8, pp. 141–5.
129. *Ibid.*, p. 141; Ivanov, *et al.*, pp. 107–8.
130. 'V Otdelenii istorii', p. 142.
131. *Ibid.*; *Sverzhenie samoderzhaviya*, p. 55.
132. 'V Otdelenii istorii', p. 142.
133. Enteen, p. 127.
134. 'V Otdelenii istorii', p. 145.
135. Volobuev, interview.
136. V. A. Emets, V. V. Shelokhaev, 'Tvorchesky put' K. N. Tarnovskogo', *IZ*, 1990, 118, p. 214.
137. 'TsK KPSS – otdel nauki i uchebnykh zavedenii', l. 82.
138. 'VTsSPS, "O nekotorykh oshibkakh v osveshchenii istorii i roli rabochego klassa v otdelenykh rabotakh Instituta istorii AN SSSR" ', ibid., l. 66.
139. *Ibid.*; Ivanov, *et al.*, p. 6. This foreword was actually written by Yu. I. Kir'yanov.
140. 'VTsSPS', ll. 66–7; Ivanov, *et al.*, p. 55.
141. 'VTsSPS', l. 67; Ivanov, *et al.*, pp. 8–9, 132, 136.
142. 'VTsSPS', l. 68.
143. *Ibid.*
144. *Ibid*; Ivanov, *et al.*, p. 23.
145. 'VTsSPS', l. 68; Ivanov, *et al.*, p. 24.
146 'VTsSPS', ll. 68–9 (original emphasis in the report); P. V. Volobuev, 'Kharakter i osobennosti Fevral'skoi revolyutsii', in Mints, *et al.*, pp. 32–3. Enteen, p. 129 points out that a review by P. A. Golub, V. A. Laverychev, P. N. Sobolev, 'O knige, "Rossiisky proletariat: Oblik. bor'ba. gegemoniya"', *VI KPSS*, 1972, 9, p. 126 omitted the parenthetical qualification that immediately followed the quote from Volobuev: '(That is, when it would occur)'. This reversion to 'Stalinist falsification' effectively depicted Volobuev as viewing the entire revolution itself as spontaneous, not just when it erupted.
147. 'VTsSPS', ll. 68–9 (original emphasis in the report); Volobuev, 'Kharakter', p. 35.
148. 'VTsSPS', l. 69, citing Volobuev, *Proletariat i burzhuaziya Rossii v 1917 g.*, (Moscow, 1964), p. 191.

149. Volobuev, interview.
150. It was originally intended to publish 'Vopreki istoricheskoi pravde' by V. Laverychev, A. Sivolobov, P. Sobolov in the trade-union paper *Trud*, 28 April 1972. 'VTsSPS', ll. 71, 82–3. It eventually appeared under a more mundane title with a slightly different authorship, that is, P. A. Golub, *et al.*, pp. 120–32.
151. 'V Buro Otdeleniya istorii AN SSSR: Obsuzhdenie knig "Rossiisky proletariat: Oblik. bor'ba. gegemoniya" i "Sverzhenie samoderzhaviya" ', *I SSSR*, 1973, 1, p. 211. The commission was made up of Academicians Mints, B. G. Gafurov, Director of the Institute of Oriental Studies, Corresponding Members M. P. Kim and P. A. Zhilin, and Yu. A. Polyakov, editor-in-chief of *Istoriya SSSR* and a specialist in the Soviet period. Enteen, p. 127.
152. *Ibid.*, p. 213.
153. 'P. V. Volobuev ... and others assume that during the political stage of the October Revolution (the struggle for power) the proletariat entered into a bloc, an alliance with all the peasantry'. *Rossiisky proletariat*, p. 22.
154. 'V Buro', pp. 213–4 (emphasis added – RDM).
155. *Ibid.*, p. 214.
156. Golub *et al.*, pp. 126–7; Enteen, p. 129.
157. A. Kosul'nikov, A. Pedosov, 'Ovladevat' bogatym opytom leninskoi partii', *Pravda*, 13 October 1972, p. 2.
158. 'Posle kritiki: Vyvody sdelany', *Pravda*, 6 January 1973, p. 2.
159. 'Stenogramma vystuplenii chlenov Buro otdelenii na soveshchanii istorikov v Otdele nauki i uchebnykh zavedenii TsK KPSS. "O merakh po dal'neishemu razvityu obshchestvenykh nauk i povyshenii ix roli v kommunisticheskom stroitel'stve." 22 marte 1973 goda.' ARAN, f. 457, op. 1, d. 628, ll. 1–143.
160. *Ibid.*, ll. 3, 16, 18; Ivanov, *et al.*, p. 55.
161. 'Stenogramma vystuplenii', ll. 18–9.
162. *Ibid.*
163. A. Ya. Avrekh, *Tsarizm i tret'eyunskaya systema* (Moscow, 1966).
164. 'Stenogramma vystuplenii', ll. 19–20.
165. *Ibid.*, ll. 20–1. Pospelov's comments echoed those of F. M. Vanag, a consultant to Trapeznikov's Department of Science, who as a reviewer in VAK, played a crucial role in preventing confirmation and publication of Tarnovsky's doctoral dissertation awarded to him in October 1970. Emets and Shelokhaev, p. 213. What is not apparent from Pospelov's comments is the anti-Semitism that also fuelled the campaign against Avrekh. S. V. Tyutyukin, interview.
166. 'Stenogramma vystuplenii', l. 21.
167. *Ibid.*, l. 87.
168. *Ibid.*, ll. 88, 141(emphasis added – RDM).
169. *Ibid.*, A. M. Anfimov, 'Neokonchennye spory', 'P. A. Stolypin i ego agrarnaya reforma' (Unpublished manuscript, 1990), pp. 51–2, notes that three years had elapsed between the Sverdlovsk conference and the publication of its proceedings in 1972. 'And this is the surprising thing. On the eve of the conference in Sverdlovsk the theses of the papers and reports were published, where the positions of the various protagonists were defined.

The theses were ignored by those who oversaw ideology. Nobody paid any attention to the conference either ... [Moreover] during the previous decade the question of *ukladov* caused no trouble ... The explosion of imperious indignation concerning *mnogoukladnost'* ... was connected with the appearance of V. N. Yagodkin ... as secretary for ideology in the Moscow city committee of the CPSU. Judged by the political circumstances the new secretary was simply the executor of a higher authority. As an economist, it is highly unlikely that he was hunting out aberrations in historical science. But it was precisely then that the process of "putting the social sciences in order" began. The proceedings of the Sverdlovsk conference on multistructuredness served as a mere pretext for this.'

170. 'Stenogramma vystuplenii', ll. 142–3 (emphasis added – RDM).
171. 'Vazhnye zadachi istoricheskoi nauki', *VI KPSS*, 1973, 5, pp. 11–2. I. I. Mints, M. V. Nechkina, L. V. Cherepnin, 'Zadachi sovetskoi istoricheskoi nauki na sovremennom etape ee razvitiya', *I SSSR*, 1973, 5, pp. 11–2; S. Trapeznikov, 'Sovetskaya istoricheskaya nauka i perspektivy ee razvitiya', *Kst*, 1973, 11, pp. 81–3; E. M. Zhukov, 'Nekotorye voprosy teorii sotsialno-ekonomicheskikh formatsii', *Kst*, 1973, 11, pp. 87–97; K. G. Levykin, A. M. Sivolobov, G. V. Sharapov, 'O knige "Voprosy istorii kapitalisticheskoi Rossii: Problema mnogoukladnosti"', *VI KPSS*, 1973, 11, pp. 106–15; I. V. Kuznetsov, 'Ob ukladakh i mnogoukladnosti kapitalisticheskoi Rossii', *VI*, 1974, 7, pp. 20–32.
172. Report on 'The Ideological Struggle in Historical Science' presented to the Institute of History, 14 June 1973, in Robert M. Slusser, 'History and the Democratic Opposition', in Rudolf L. Tokes (ed.), *Dissent in the USSR: Politics, Ideology and People* (Baltimore and London, 1975), p. 351 (original emphasis).
173. 'Neotlozhnye zadachi istorikov', *Pravda*, 29 March 1973, p. 2.
174. Yu. A. Tikhonov, 'V Otdelenii istorii AN SSSR: Obshchee godichnoe sobranie', *VI*, 1974, 5, p. 137; Enteen, p. 131, n. 46.
175. Volobuev, interview.

7 From *zastoi* to *perestroika*

1. Kuhn, *Scientific Revolutions*, p. 150.
2. Gefter, interview.
3. *Ibid*.
4. Edward W. Said, *Representations of the Intellectual: The 1993 Reith Lectures* (London, 1994), pp. 58–62.
5. Schöpflin, p. 6.
6. Gefter, interview. Gefter in particular closely identified and associated with Tvardovsky, whom he considered 'the central figure of spiritual renewal' in the 1960s and under *perestroika*; Tvardovsky had the courage to 'accept the challenge' of renouncing Stalin and the Stalinist legacy. Gefter, '"Stalin umer vchera ..."', Afanas'ev, *Inogo ne dano*, p. 303.
7. See the appeal for radical democratic 'guarantees' against the resurrection of the 'cult of the personality', Gefter, *et al.*, 'Mir za dvadtsat' let', p. 221.
8. Bahro, pp. 189, 202.

9. Here we can concur with the observation of Feher *et al.* that opposition is a 'social factor which by its very existence indicates the legitimation crisis of the regime.' Feher *et al.*, p. 293. For the corrosive effects of the 'moral and political critique' of the 'oppositional intelligentsia' on the morale of the party-state elite see Jerome Karabel, 'Towards a theory of intellectuals and politics', *Theory and Society*, 25, 1996, pp. 220–5.
10. Zhuravlev, pp. 388, 414.
11. McNeill, pp. 13–14.
12. Anfimov, 'Neokonchennye spory', p. 48.
13. Cited in *ibid.*
14. Anfimov, pp. 49–50. Note, however, that the *Short Course* had referred to a 'socialist' socio-economic formation.
15. Medvedev, *Lichnost' i epokha*, pp. 180–3.
16. Anfimov, pp. 49–53 and n. 130.
17. *Ibid.*, pp, 49, 51, 53–4.
18. Mikhail Gorbachev, *Perestroika: New Thinking for Our Country and the Entire World* (London, 1987), pp. 18–19.
19. Richard Sakwa, *Gorbachev and His Reforms 1985–1990* (Hertfordshire, 1990), pp. 86–7.
20. Richards, p. 16.
21. Gorodetsky, interview.
22. Gefter, interview.
23. Gurevich, interview. See Gurevich, *Categories of Medieval Culture*, trans. by G. L. Campbell (London, Boston and Melbourne, 1985, first published Moscow, 1972); *Medieval Popular Culture: Problems of Belief and Perception*, trans. by Janos M. Bak and Paul A. Hollingworth (Cambridge and Paris, 1989, first published Moscow, 1981).
24. Gefter, interview. *Cf.* Kagarlitsky, *Thinking Reed*, p. 335.
25. Gefter, interview.
26. See Chapter 5.
27. Danilova, interview.
28. Volobuev, interview. Adamov died apparently in 1972, Avrekh in 1988 and Tarnovsky in 1987.
29. Bibler, interview. In fact Bibler's seminar on the philosophy and history of culture ran for 15 years, from 1966 to 1981. Tumanova participated in a Helsinki human rights group. Eventually arrested, she died shortly after being released from prison in July 1984. S. S. Neretina, 'Istoriya s metodologiei istorii', *VF*, 1990, 9, p. 155, n. 6.
30. Medvedev, *Let History Judge* (1973), pp. 509, 517–18.
31. Gefter, interview.
32. Jeff Gleisner, 'Old Bolsheviks Discuss Socialism', *Labour Focus on Eastern Europe*, 6, 1, summer 1983, pp. 3–5. Any reference to Gefter or El'konin has been expunged from the latest (1989), 'expanded' edition of Medvedev's history, an erasure possibly symptomatic of tensions between Medvedev and Gefter's circle that were apparent to Gleisner back in 1983. Gefter referred to Medvedev then as 'our privileged dissident', criticizing him for spreading illusions about the prospects for socialist democracy in the Soviet Union – quite justifiably as it turns out.
33. See the analysis of Medvedev's sources by Robert M. Slusser, 'History and the Democratic Opposition', in Rudolf L. Tokes (ed.), *Dissent in the USSR:*

Politics, Ideology and People (Baltimore and London, 1975), pp. 329–53, who concludes that overwhelmingly Medvedev did *not* draw on *samizdat* sources for his history.
34. In 1970 Danilova was explicitly accused of not only denying that the *pyatichlenka* was an integral part of historical materialism but of claiming it was obsolescent. Scanlan, *Marxism in the USSR*, p. 196.
35. In 1980 the Soviet Estonian philosopher E. N. Loone, who had participated in the sector, wrote 'I have not come across any *theoretical* arguments strong enough to support the view that the mere idea that a special "Asiatic" formation existed in the past is anti-Marxist (original emphasis).' Loone, p. 206.
36. Scanlan, p. 209.
37. Emets, p. 210. These developments are exhaustively analyzed in Pitty, 'Recent Soviet Development Debates'. Loone, p. 172, without referring to the literature of the New Direction, stated: 'All Marxists must be familiar with the concept "socio-economic structure (*uklad*)". In a number of cases it is not possible to say which formation an individual society belongs to without taking account of the multi-structured character (*mnogoukladnost'*) of, especially, its economy.'
38. Emets, pp. 215–6.
39. Yu. A. Polyakov, 'Dorozhit' kazhdym godom nashei istorii', *Literaturnaya Gazeta*, 29 July 1987, p. 10; Davies, *Soviet History in the Gorbachev Revolution*, p. 167. In March 1988 an entire conference was devoted to the relations between historians, writers and history: 'Istoriki i pisateli o literature i istorii. Materialy konferentsii', *VI*, 1988, 6, pp. 3–114.
40. V. P. Danilov, 'Nuzhen li "ukazuyushchii perst"?', *Literaturnaya Rossiya*, 22 July 1988, 29, pp. 8–9, replying to Yu. N. Afanas'ev, 'Perestroika i istoricheskoe znanie', *Literaturnaya Rossiya*, 17 July 1988, 24, pp. 2–3, 8–9; *Cf.* Davies, p. 56
41. Volobuev, interview.
42. Volobuev, *Vybor putei obshchestvennogo razvitiya: teoriya, istoriya, sovremennost'* (Moscow, 1987); *Cf.* Volobuev (ed.), *Rossia 1917 god vybor istoricheskogo puti ("krugly stol", istorikov oktyabrya, 22–3 oktyabrya 1988 g.)* (Moscow, 1989); 'Perestroika and the October Revolution in Soviet Historiography', *The Russian Review*, 51, October 1992, pp. 566–76.
43. 'Perestroika and the October Revolution', p. 571.
44. *Vybor putei*, pp. 173, 175.
45. 'Perestroika and the October Revolution', p. 571.
46. Emets, p. 218.
47. *Ibid.*, p. 219.
48. Danilov, ' "Krugly stol": istoricheskaya nauka v usloviyakh perestroiki', *VI*, 1988, 3, p. 21. In autumn 1987 Danilov was elected head of the Soviet peasantry sector in the Institute of the History of the USSR. Davies, p. 176.
49. Danilov in '"Krugly stol": Sovetsky soyuz v 20–e gody', *VI*, 1988, 9, pp. 3–13. *Cf.* Davies, pp. 16, 22, and 55 on the 'internal contradictions' of Danilov's views on collectivization.
50. Danilov, ' "Krugly stol": istoricheskaya nauka', p. 24. A year later Danilov seemed more receptive to a re-consideration of Trotsky's status as a whole: 'We are Starting to Learn about Trotsky', pp. 136–46.

51. 'Filosofiya i istoricheskaya nauka' (Materialy "kruglogo stola")', *VF*, 1988, 10, pp. 18–65.
52. Gefter, '"Stalin umer vchera ..."', pp. 310, 315 (original emphasis).
53. Volobuev, 'Perestroika and the October Revolution', p. 566; Gurevich, 'O krizise sovremennoi istoricheskoi nauki', *VI*, 1991, 2–3, pp. 21–36.
54. Volobuev, 'Perestroika and the October Revolution', p. 567.
55. Danilov, in ' "Krugly stol": istoricheskaia nauka', p. 22.
56. Thomas Sherlock, 'Politics and History Under Gorbachev', *Problems of Communism*, 37, 3–4, May–August 1988, pp. 16–42.
57. Again and again this was stressed by the Soviet participants in the joint US–Soviet round table of historians held in Moscow in January 1989. It did not go unnoticed by their US colleagues. 'Perestroika, History and Historians'.
58. Gefter, interview.
59. Debray, p. 131.
60. 'Perestroika, History and Historians, p. 787.
61. A. Ya. Gurevich, 'Istoricheskaya nauka i istoricheskaya antropologiya', *VF*, 1988, 1, pp. 56–70; 'Teoriya formatsii i real'nost' istorii', *VF*, 1990, 11, pp. 39–43; 'Sotsial'naya istoriya i istoricheskaya nauka', *VF*, 1990, 4, pp. 23–35.
62. Davies, *Soviet History in the Yeltsin Era*, p. 47.
63. *Cf.*, for example, A.A. Kara-Murza, A. K. Voskresensky (eds), *Totalitarizm kak istorichesky fenomenon* (Moscow, 1989). *Cf.*, Aleksander Yakovlev, *The Fate of Marxism in Russia*, intro. by Thomas F. Remington, foreword by Alexander Tsipko, trans. by Catherine A. Fitzpatrick (New Haven and London, 1993).
64. Danilova, interview.
65. See Graeme Gill and Roger D. Markwick, *Russia's Stillborn Democracy? From Gorbachev to Yeltsin* (London, 2000).

Bibliography

Unpublished primary sources

Interviews
Bibler, V. S. 30 April 1992.
Bovykin, V. I. 27 February 1992.
Danilov, V. P. 7 April 1992; 14, 20, 25 February 1998.
Danilova, L. V. 26 May 1992 and 10 February 1998.
Drabkin, Ya. S. 20 April 1992.
Gefter, M. Ya. 30 March and 10 May 1992.
Gorodetsky, Ye. N. 22 April 1992.
Gurevich, A. Ya. 28 February and 3 April 1992.
Ivnitsky, N. A. 25 January and 12, 17, 22 February 1998.
Kagarlitsky, B. Yu. 17 March 1992.
Moshkov, Yu. A. 23 February 1998.
Neretina, S. S. 24 March and 8 April 1992.
Pavlenko, N. I. 14 April 1992.
Shatsillo, K. N. 27 February 1992.
Tyutyukin, S. V. 17 February 1998.
Volobuev, P. V. 9 and 16 April 1992.

Archives
Archive of the Institute of Russian History.
Archive of the Russian Academy of Sciences.
Centre for the Preservation of Contemporary Documentation.

Personal Papers
Anfimov, A. M. 'Neokonchennye spory', the sixth and final chapter in 'P. A. Stolypin i ego agrarnaya reforma'. Unpublished manuscript, 1990. Edited extracts have since been published as 'Neokonchennye spory (iz arkhiva istorika)', *VI*, 5, 7, 9, 1997.
Danilov, V. P. Papers: V. P. Danilov (ed.), 'Kollektivizatsiya i kolkhoznoe stroitel'stvo v SSSR: Kollektivizatsiya sel'skogo khozyaistva v SSSR 1927–1932' (Moscow: Mysl', 1964) [*pervaya sverka*]. Unpublished proofs, first version.
Danilov, V. P. 'Kollektivizatsiya sel'skogo khozyaistva SSSR [*vtoraya sverka*].', *Sovetskaya istoricheskaya entsiklopediya* V, 7. Moscow: 'Sovetskaya entsiklopediya', 1965, pp. 484–96. Unpublished proofs, second version.
'Sovetskaya istoricheskaya nauka i zadachi partiinoi organizatsii Instituta istorii AN SSSR.' Unpublished manuscript, written principally by V. P. Danilov and K. N. Tarnovsky for the Party Committee of the Institute of History, 1965.
—— 'Stenogramma obshchego zakrytogo partiinogo sobraniya Instituta istorii Akademii nauk SSSR'. 19 fevraliya 1966 goda.
—— 'XXIII s"ezd KPSS i zadachi instituta istorii AN SSSR', 17 maya 1966 goda.

—— 'Stenogramma otkrytogo sobraniya instituta istorii AN SSSR "XXIII s"ezd KPSS i zadachi istoricheskoi nauki" ', 17 maya 1966 goda.

Ivnitsky, N. A. Papers: chapters V and VI of V. P. Danilov (ed.), 'Kollektivizatsiya i kolkhoznoe stroitel'stvo v SSSR: Kollektivizatsiya sel'skogo khozyaistva v SSSR 1927–1932' [vtoraya sverka].

Neretina, S. S, papers: A miscellaneous collection of letters, articles, reports and manuscripts, mainly from the private papers of M. Ya. Gefter.

Published primary sources

Abramov, B. A. and Kocharli, Tk. (1975) 'Ob oshibkakh v odnoi knige', *VI KPSS*, 5, pp. 134–41.

Adamov, V. V. *et al.* (eds) (1972) *Voprosy istorii kapitalisticheskoi rossii: Problema mnogoukladnosti*. Sverdlovsk: Ural'sky gosudarstvennyi universitet.

Afanas'ev, O. A. (1965) 'Obsuzhdenie v Institute istorii AN SSSR problemy "aziatskogo sposoba proizvodstva"', *Sovetskaya etnografiya*, 6, pp. 122–6.

Ambartsumov, E. A. and Erman, L. K. (1965) 'Intelligentsia', in *Sovetskaya istoricheskaya entsiklopediya*, T. 6. Moscow: 'Sovetskaya entsiklopediya', cc. 111–19.

Anfimov, A. M. (1959) 'K voprosu o kharaktere agrarnogo stroia Rossii v nachale XX veka', *IZ*, 65, pp. 119–62.

'Aron Yakovlevich Avrekh', *VI*, 1989, 3, p. 190.

Arkheografichesky ezhegodnik, 1995, pp. 324–36.

Avrekh, A. Ya. (1968) 'Russky absolyutizm i ego rol' v utverzhdenii kapitalizma v Rossii', *ISSSR*, 2, March–April, pp. 82–104.

Bovykin, V. I. (1988) 'Problemy perestroiki istoricheskoi nauki i vopros o "novom napravlenii" v izuchenii sotsial'no-ekonomicheskikh predposylok Velikoi Oktyabr'skoi Revolyutsii', *ISSSR*, 5, pp. 67–100.

—— (1990) 'Eshche raz k voprosu o "novom napravlenii"', *VI*, 6, pp. 164–84.

Bugaev, E. (1956) 'Kogda utrachivaetsia nauchnyi podkhod', *Partinaya zhizn'*, 14, pp. 62–72.

Burdzhalov, E. N. (1956) 'O taktike bol'shevikov v marte-aprele 1917 goda', *VI*, 4, pp. 38–56.

—— (1956) 'Eshche o taktike bol'shevikov v marte-aprele 1917 goda', *VI*, 8, pp. 109–114.

—— (1989) 'Doklad E. N. Burdzhalova o sostoyanii sovetskoi istoricheskoi naukii i rabote zhurnala "Voprosy istorii" (na vstreche c chitatelyami 19–20 yuniya 1956 g. v Leningradskom otedelenii instituta istorii AN SSSR)', *VI*, 9, pp. 81–96.

—— (1989) 'Doklad E. N. Burdzhalova o sostoyanii sovetskoi istoricheskoi naukii i rabote zhurnala "Voprosy istorii" (na vstreche c chitatelyami 19–20 yuniya 1956 g. v Leningradskom otedelenii instituta istorii AN SSSR)', *VI*, 11, pp. 113–38.

Danilov, A. (1969) 'K voprosu o metodologii istoricheskoi nauki', *Kst*, 5, pp. 68–81.

Danilov, V. P. (1956) 'Material'no-tekhnicheskaya baza sel'skogo khozyaistva SSSR nakanune sploshnoi kollektivizatsii', *VI*, 3, pp. 3–17.

—— (1957) *Sozdanie material'no-tekhnicheskih predposylok kollektivizatsii sel'skogo khozyaistva v SSSR*. Moscow: Akademiya Nauk SSSR.

—— (1958) 'Zemel'nyie otnosheniya v sovetskoi dokolkhoznoi derevne', *I SSSR*, 3, pp. 90–128.
—— (1960) 'K itogam izucheniya istorii sovetskogo krest'yantsva i kolkhoznogo stroitel'stva v SSSR', *VI*, 8, pp. 34–64.
—— (1965) Kollektivizatsiya sel'skogo khozyaistva SSSR', *Sovetskaya istoricheskaya entsiklopediya*, V. 7. Moscow: 'Sovetskaya entsiklopediya', cc. 484–99.
—— (1988) *Rural Russia Under the New Regime*, trans. and introduced by Orlando Figes. Bloomington and London: Indiana University Press and Hutchinson, first published in Russian 1977.
—— (1988) 'Nuzhen li "ukazuyushchy perst"?', *Literaturnaya Rossiya*, 22 July, 29, pp. 8–9.
—— (1990) 'We are Starting to Learn about Trotsky', *History Workshop Journal*, 29, pp. 136–46.
Danilova, L. V. (1965) 'Diskussiya po vazhnoi probleme', *VF*, 12, pp. 149–55.
—— et al. (eds) (1968) *Problemy istorii dokapitalisticheskikh obshchestv*, Kniga 1. Moscow: Nauka, Instituta istorii, AN SSSR.
Dokumenty sovetsko-ital'yanskoi konferentsii istorikov, 8–10 aprelya 1968 goda: Absolyutizm v Zapadnoi Evrope i Rossii; Russko-Ital'yanskie svyazi vo vtoroi polovine XIX veka. Moscow: Nauka, 1970.
Druzhinin, N. M. (ed.) (1962) *Sovetskaya istoricheskaya nauka ot XX k XXII s"ezdu KPSS*, 2 vols. Moscow: Izdatel'stvo Akademii nauk SSSR. [T. 1] *Istoriya SSSR: Sbornik statei*.
Dubrovsky, S. M. (1956) 'Protiv idealizatsii deyatel'nosti Ivana IV', *VI*, 8, pp. 121–8.
—— (1962) 'Akademik M. N. Pokrovsky i ego rol' v razvitii sovetskoi istoricheskoi nauki', *VI*, 3, pp. 3–31.
'Filosofiya i istoricheskaya nauka' (Materialy "kruglogo stola")', *VF*, 1988, 10, pp. 18–65.
Gefter, M. (1962) 'Vazhnye voprosy istorii Rossii period imperializma', *Vestnik Akademiya nauk, SSSR*, 1, pp. 138–40.
——, Drabkin, Ya. and Mal'kov, V. (1965) 'Mir za dvadtsat' let', *Novyi mir*, 6, pp. 206–30.
—— et al. (eds) (1969) *Istoricheskaya nauka i nekotorye problemy sovremennosti*. Moscow: Nauka, Instituta vseobshchei istorii, AN SSSR.
—— (1969) 'Iz istorii leninskoi mysli', *Novyi mir*, 4, pp. 135–6.
Gindin, I. F. (1963) 'Russkaya burzhuaziya v period kapitalizma, ee razvitie i osobennosti,' *I SSSR*, 2, pp. 57–80; *I SSSR*, 3, pp. 37–60.
—— (1966) 'O nekotorykh osobennostyakh ekonomicheskoi i sotsial'noi struktury rossiiskogo kapitalizma v nachale XX v.', *I SSSR*, 3, pp. 48–66.
—— (1967) 'Problemy istorii fevral'skoi revolyutsii i ee sotsial'no-ekonomicheskikh predposylok', *I SSSR*, 4, pp. 30–49.
—— and Ivanov, L. M. (1965) 'Neravnomernosti razvitiya rossiiskogo kapitalizma v nachale XX veka', *VI*, 9, pp. 125–35.
Golikov, V., Murashov, S., Chkhikvishvili, I., Shatagin, N. and Shaumyan, S. (1969) 'Za Leninskuyu partiinost' v osveshchenii istorii KPSS', *Kst*, 3, pp. 67–82.
Golub, P. A., Laverychev, V. A. and Sobolev, P. N. (1972) 'O knige, "Rossiisky proletariat: oblik. bor'ba. gegemoniya"', *VI KPSS*, 9, pp. 120–32.
Gorodetsky, Ye. N. (1989) Zhurnal '"Voprosy istorii" v seredine 50-x godov', *VI*, September, 9, pp. 69–80.

——, Yoffe, G. Z., Akopyan, G. S. and Kuznetsov, N. D. (1987) 'E. N. Burdzhalov – Istorik fevral'skoi revolyutsii 1917 goda', *ISSSR*, 6, pp. 168–73.
Grave, B. B. (1956) 'Byla li tsarskaya Rossiya polukoloniei?', *VI*, 6, pp. 63–74.
Gukovsky, A., Ugryumov, A. and Kul'bakin, V. (1968) 'Po stranitsam Sovetskoi istoricheskoi entsiklopedii: zametki istorikov', *Kst*, 4, pp. 105–14.
Gurevich, A. Ya. (1964) 'Nekotorye aspekty izucheniya sotsial'noi istorii (obshchestvenno-istoricheskaya psikhologiya)', *VI*, October, 10, pp. 51–68.
—— (1965) 'Obshchy zakon i konkretnaya zakonomernost' v istorii', *VI*, 8, pp. 14–30.
—— (1968) 'K diskussii o dokapitalisticheskikh obshchestvennykh formatsiyakh: formatsiya i uklad', *VF*, 2, pp. 118–29.
—— (1970) *Problemy genezisa feodalizma v zapadnoi evrope*. Moscow: 'Vysshaya Shkola'.
—— (1985) *Categories of Medieval Culture*, trans. by G. L. Campbell. London, Boston and Melbourne: Routledge & Kegan Paul, first published, Moscow, 1972.
—— (1989) *Medieval Popular Culture: Problems of Belief and Perception*, trans. by Janos M. Bak and Paul A. Hollingworth. Cambridge and Paris: Cambridge University Press and Editions de la Maison des Sciences de l'homme, first published, Moscow, 1981.
—— (1988) 'Istoricheskaya nauka i istoricheskaya antropologiya', *VF*, 1, pp. 56–70.
—— (1990) 'Teoriya formatsii i real'nost' istorii', *VF*, 11, pp. 39–43.
—— (1990) 'Sotsial'naya istoriya i istoricheskaya nauka', *VF*, 4, pp. 23–35.
—— (1991) 'O krizise sovremennoi istoricheskoi nauki', *VI*, 2–3, pp. 21–36.
Istochnikovedenie istorii sovetskogo obshchestva. Moscow: Nauka, 1964.
Istoriya i sotsiologiya. Moscow: Nauka, 1964.
Istoriya vsesoyuznoi kommunisticheskoi partii (bol'shevikov): kratky kurs, pod redaktsiei komissii TsK VKP (b), odobren TsK VKP (b) 1938 god. Moscow: Gosudarstvennoe izdatel'stvo politicheskoi literatury, 1952.
Istoriya Kommunisticheskoi Partii Sovetskogo Soyuza, 2nd, expanded edn. Moscow: Gosudarstvennoe izdatel'stvo politicheskoi literatury, 1963.
'Istoriki i pisateli o literature i istorii. Materialy konferentsii', *VI*, 1988, 6, pp. 3–114.
'Istoriko-partiinaya nauka: puti perestroiki i dal'neishego razvitiya', *VI KPSS*, 1987, 7, pp. 137–52.
Ivnitsky, N. A. (1962) 'O kriticheskom analize istochnikov po istorii nachal'nogo etapa kollektivizatsii (osen' 1929–vesna 1930 gg)', *Istorichesky arkhiv*, March–April 1962, 2, pp. 191–202.
—— (1962) 'O nachalnom etape sploshnoi kollektivizatsii (Osen' 1929–vesna 1930 gg)', *VI KPSS*, 4, pp. 55–71.
—— (1966) 'Opyt KPSS po pretvoreniyu v zhizn' leninskogo kooperativnogo plana', *VI KPSS*, February, 2, pp. 97–107.
—— (1972) *Klassovaya bor'ba v derevne i likvidatsiya kulachestva kak klassa (1929–1932 gg)*. Moscow, Nauka.
—— (1996) *Kollektivizatsiya i raskulachivanie: nachalo 30-x godov*. Moscow: Magistr.
'Yubilei I. F. Gindina', *I SSSR*, 1970, 5, pp. 231–2.
Ivanov, L. M., et al. (eds) (1970) *Rossiisky proletariat: oblik. bor'ba. gegemoniya*. Moscow: Nauka.

Kara-Murza, A. A. and Voskresensky, A. K. (eds) (1989) *Totalitarizm kak istoricheskyfenomenon*. Moscow: Filosofskoe obshchestvo SSSR.
'K diskussii ob absolyutizma v Rossii', *I SSSR*, 4, 1971, pp. 65–88.
Khrestomatiya po istorii KPSS, T. 2, 1925–mart 1985 g. Moscow: Izdatel'stvo politicheskoi literatury, 1989.
Khrushchev, N. S. (1976) *The 'Secret' Speech delivered to the closed session of the Twentieth Congress of the Communist Party of the Soviet Union*, intro. by Z. A. Medvedev and R. A. Medvedev. Nottingham: Spokesman Books.
Khrushchev Remembers (1971) Introduction, commentary and notes by Edward Crankshaw, trans. Strobe Talbott. London: Andre Deutsch.
Kim, M. P., *et al.* (eds) (1963) *Istoriya sovetskogo krest'yanstva i kolkhoznogo stroitel'stva v SSSR. Materialy nauchnoi sessii, sostoyavsheisya 18–21 aprelya 1961 g. v Moskve*. Moscow: Akademiya Nauk SSSR.
Kim, M. P. (ed.) (1968) *Sovetskaya intelligentsiya (Istoriya formirovaniya i rosta 1917–1965 gg)*. Moscow: Mysl'.
—— *et al.* (eds) (1971) *Problemy agrarnoi istorii sovetskogo obshchestva: Materialy nauchnoi konferentsii 9–12 yuniya 1969 g*. Moscow: Nauka.
'Konferentsiya chitatelei zhurnala "Voprosy istorii"', *VI*, 1956, 2, pp. 199–213.
'Konferentsiya chitatelei zhurnala "Voprosy istorii" v Leningrade', *VI*, 1956, 7, pp. 184–90.
Kornilov, A., Prokopenko, N. and Shirokov, A. (1970) 'Pod vidom nauchnogo poiska', *Sovetskaya Rossiya*, 28 February, 49, pp. 2–3.
Kosul'nikov, A. and Pedosov, A. (1972) 'Ovladevat' bogatym opytom leninskoi partii', *Pravda*, 13 October, p. 2.
'"Krugly stol": istoricheskaya nauka v usloviyakh perestroiki', *VI*, 1988, 3, pp. 3–57.
'"Krugly stol": Sovetsky soyuz v 20-e gody', *VI*, 1988, 9, pp. 3–58.
Kuznetsov, I. V. (1974) 'Ob ukladakh i mnogoukladnosti kapitalisticheskoi Rossii', *VI KPSS*, 6, pp. 20–32.
Lel'chuk, V. S. (ed.) (1988) *Istoriki sporyat*. Moscow: Politizdat.
Lenin, V. I. (1965) *Collected Works*, 4th edn. Moscow: Progress Publishers.
Levykin, K. G., Sivolobov, A. M. and Sharapov, G. V. (1973) 'O knige "Voprosy istorii kapitalisticheskoi Rossii: Problema mnogoukladnosti"', *VI KPSS*, 11, pp. 106–15.
Maevsky, I. V. (1957) 'K voprosu o zavisimosti Rossii v period pervoi mirovoi voiny', *VI*, 1, pp. 69–76.
Materialy XV sessii mezhrespublinskogo simpoziuma po agrarnoi istorii, vyp. 3. Vologda: Vologodsky gosudarstvenyi pedagogichesky institut, 1977.
Mints, I. I. *et al.* (eds) (1970) *Sverzhenie samoderzhaviya: Sbornik statei*. Moscow: Nauka.
——, Nechkina, M. V. and Cherepnin, L. V. (1973) 'Zadachi sovetskoi istoricheskoi nauki na sovremennom etape ee razvitiya', *I SSSR*, 5, pp. 3–16.
Mongait, A. L. (1967) 'Arkheologicheskie kul'tury i etnicheskie obshchnosti (k voprosu o metodike istoriko-arkheologicheskikh issledovanii)', *Narody Azii i Afriki*, 1, pp. 53–76.
Moshkov, Yu. A. (1966) *Zernovaya problema v gody sploshnoi kollektivizatsii sel'skogo khozyaistva (1929–1932 gg)*. Moscow: Moskovskogo Universiteta.
Nechkina, M. V. and Gorodetsky, E. N. (eds) (1985) *Ocherki po istorii istoricheskoi nauki v SSSR*, Tom V. Moscow: Nauka.
'Neotlozhnye zadachi istorikov', *Pravda*, 29 March 1973, p. 2.

'O stat'e tov. E. Bugaeva', *VI*, 1956, 7, pp. 215–22.

'Obsuzhdenie stat' S. M. Dubrovskogo "Akademik M. N. Pokrovsky i ego rol' v razvitii sovetskoi istoriskoi nauki"', *VI*, 1962, 3, pp. 31–40.

Osnovy Marksizma Leninizma: uchebnoe posobie, 2nd edn. Moscow: Gosudarstvennoe izdatel'stvo politicheskoi literatury, 1962.

Pavlenko, N. I. (ed.) (1965) *Perekhod ot feodalizma k kapitalizmu v Rossii: Materialy dlya obsuzhdeniya*. Moscow: Nauka.

—— (1991) 'Istoricheskaya nauka v proshlom i nastoyashchem (Nekotorye razmyshleniya vslukh)', *I SSSR*, 4, pp. 81– 99.

Pleshkova, S. L. (1970) 'Khronika nauchnoi zhizn'. Ob uchebnom posobii "Problemy genezisa feodalizma v zapadnoi evrope" (informatsiya o khode obsuzhdeniya knigi A. Ya. Gurevicha)' *VI*, 9, pp. 154–67.

Politichesky dnevnik,. 1964–1965. Amsterdam: The Alexander Herzen Foundation, 1972.

Polyakov, Yu. A. (1987) 'Dorozhit' kazhdym godom nashei istorii', *Literaturnaya Gazeta*, 29 July, p. 10.

'Posle kritiki: Vyvody sdelany', *Pravda*, 6 January 1973, p. 2.

Rubinshtein, N. L. (1941) *Russkaya istoriografiya*. Ogiz: Gospolitizdat.

Rumyantsev, A. (1965) 'Partiya i intelligentsiya', *Pravda*, 21 February, pp. 2–3.

Rybakov, M. B. (1971) 'O nekotorykh neopravdannykh pretenziakh', *VI KPSS*, 7, pp. 123–33.

Sakharov, A. D. (1969) *Progress and Intellectual Freedom*. Introduction, Afterword and Notes by H. E. Salisbury. Harmondsworth: Penguin.

Semenov, Yu. I. (1965) 'Problema sotsial'no-ekonomicheskogo stroiya drevnogo vostoka', *Narody Azii i Afriki*, 4, pp. 69–89.

—— (1966) 'Kategoriya "sotsial'nyi organizm" i ee znachenie dlya istoricheskoi nauki', *VI*, 8, pp. 88–106.

Shunkov, V. I. *et al.* (eds) (1969) *Perekhod Rossii ot feodalizma k kapitalizmy: Materialy Vsesoyuznoi diskussii*. Moscow: Nauka.

Shurbovany, G. P. (1971) 'Obsuzhdenie nekotorykh problem metodologii istorii', *VI*, 10, pp. 159–66.

Sidorov, A. L. (ed.) (1963) *Ob osobennostyakh imperializma v Rossii*. Moscow: Akademiya nauk.

—— (1964) 'Nekotorye razmyshleniya o trude i opyte istorika', *I SSSR*, 3, pp. 118–38.

Smirnov, A. (1972) 'Za stroguyu nauchnost', dostovernost' i istoricheskuyu pravdu', *Kst*, 16, pp. 113–24.

Stalin, J. V. (1955) *Works*. Moscow: Foreign Languages Publishing House.

—— (1972) *Marxism and Problems of Linguistics*. Peking: Foreign Languages Press, first published, *Pravda*, 20 June 1950.

—— (1952) *Economic Problems of Socialism in the USSR*. Moscow: Foreign Languages Publishing House.

Tarnovsky, K. N. (1964) 'O sotsiologicheskom izuchenii kapitalisticheskogo sposoba proizvodstva', *VI*, 1, pp. 120–32.

—— (1964) *Sovetskaya istoriografiya rossiiskogo imperializma*. Moscow: Nauka.

—— (1967) 'Put' uchenogo', *IZ*, 80, pp. 207–44.

—— (1972) 'Pamyati Leonida Mikhailovicha Ivanova (8 noyabrya 1909–10 yanvarya 1972 g)', *IZ*, 90, pp. 355–76.

—— (1990) *Sotsial'no-ekonomicheskaya istoriya rossii nachalo xx v.: sovetskaya istoriografiya serediny 50–kh–60–kh godov*, ed. with a preface by V. P. Volobuev. Moscow: Nauka.
Tikhonov, Yu. A. (1974) 'V Otdelenii istorii AN SSSR: obshchee godichnoe sobranie', *VI*, 5, pp. 137–40.
Trapeznikov, S. (1965) 'Marksizm–Leninizm – Nezyblemaya osnova razvitiya obshchestvennykh nauk', *Pravda*, 8 October, pp. 3–4.
—— S. P. (1967) *Leninizm i agrarno-krestyansky vopros*, 2 vols. Moscow: Mysl'.
—— (1973) 'Sovetskaya istoricheskaya nauka i perspektivy ee razvitiya', *Kst*, 11, pp. 68–86.
Triska, Jan F. (ed.) (1962) *Soviet Communism: Programs and Rules, Official Texts of 1919, 1952 (1956), 1961*. San Francisco: Chandler.
Trotsky, L. (1972) *The Permanent Revolution* and *Results and Prospects*, 3rd edn. New York: Pathfinder Press, 1st edn 1931.
—— (1974) *The Stalin School of Falsification*. London: New Park Publications, first published in Russian in 1932.
—— (1967) *History of the Russian Revolution*, 3 vols. London: Sphere, first published in English 1932–3. Vol. 1.
—— (1972) *The Revolution Betrayed: What is the Soviet Union and Where Is It Going?* New York: Pathfinder Press, first published 1937.
Tvardovsky, A. (1965) 'Po sluchayu yubileya', *Novyi mir*, 1, pp. 3–18.
'V Buro Otdeleniya istorii AN SSSR: Obsuzhdenie knig "Rossiisky proletariat: oblik. bor'ba. gegemoniya" i "Sverzhenie samoderzhaviya"', *ISSSR*, 1973, 1, pp. 211–18.
'V Otdelenii istorii AN SSSR: Postanovlenie buro otdeleniya istorii AN SSSR ob itogakh obsuzhdeniya v institute istorii SSSR izdannykh v 1970 godu sbornikov "Rossiisky proletariat: oblik. bor'ba. gegemoniya" i "Sverzhenie samoderzhaviya"', *VI*, 1972, 8, pp. 141–5.
'V Tsentral'nom Komitet KPSS', *VI*, 1969, 4, pp. 3–4.
Volobuev, P. V. (1958) 'Voprosy dialektiki v rabotakh V. I. Lenina o Velikoi Oktyabr'skoi sotsialisticheskoi revolyutsii', *VF*, 4, pp. 28–39.
—— (1987) *Vybor putei obshchestvennogo razvitiya: teoriya, istoriya, sovremennost'*. Moscow: politicheskoi literatury.
—— (ed.) (1989) *Rossia 1917 god vybor istoricheskogo puti ('krugly stol', istorikov oktyabrya, 22–3 oktyabrya 1988 g)*. Moscow: ANSSR.
—— (ed.) (1989) *Akademik N. I. Bukharin: Metodologiya i planirovanie nauki i tekhniki Izbrannye trudy*. Moscow: Nauka.
—— (1989) 'Takie lyudi byli vsegda!', *Sovetskaya kul'tura*, 6 May, p. 4.
—— (1990) letter, *VI*, 6, pp. 180–4.
—— (1992) 'Perestroika and the October Revolution in Soviet Historiography', *The Russian Review*, 51, October pp. 566–76.
—— (1997) Intervyu s akademikom P. V. Volobuevym', *OI*, Nov–Dec, 6, pp. 99–123.
'Vazhnye zadachi istoricheskoi nauki', *VI KPSS*, 1973, 5, pp. 7–23.
Vsesoyuznoe soveshchanie o merakh podgotovki nauchno-pedagogicheskih kadrov po istorichekskim naukam 18–21 dekabrya 1962 g. Moscow: Nauka, 1964.
Vyltsan, M. A. and Ivnitsky, N. A., Polyakov, Yu. A. (1965) 'Nekotorye problemy istorii kollektivizatsii v SSSR', *VI*, 3, pp. 3–25.

XX S"ezd Kommunisticheskoi Partii Sovetskogo Soyuza 14–25 Fevralya 1956 goda Stenographichesky otchet, Vol. I. Moscow: Gosudarstvennoe izdatel'stvo politicheskoi literatury, 1956.
'XX s"ezd KPSS i zadachi issledovaniya istorii partii', *VI*, 1956, 3, pp 3–12.
'Za leninskuyu partiinost' v istoricheskoi nauke!', *VI*, 1957, 3 , pp. 3–19.
'Za tvorcheskuyu razrabotky istorii KPSS', *Kst*, 1956, 10, pp. 14–26.
Zelenin, I. E. (1965) 'Politotdely MTS (1933–1934 gg)', *IZ*, 76, pp. 42–61.
Zhukov, Ye. M. (1973) 'Nekotorye voprosy teorii sotsialno-ekonomicheskikh formatsii', *Kst*, 11, pp. 87–97.
Zhukov, Ye. M., Trukhanovsky, V. and Shunkov, V. (1966) 'Vysokaya otvetstvennost' istorikov', *Pravda*, 30 January, p. 2.

Unpublished secondary sources

Kagarlitsky, B. (1992) 'Lecture', Moscow State University, 27 February.
Myhul, I. M. (1973) 'Politics and History in the Soviet Ukraine: A Study of Soviet Ukrainian Historiography, 1956–1970'. PhD dissertation, Columbia University.
Pitty, R. D. M. (1989) 'Recent Soviet Development Debates: the "third world" and the USSR'. PhD thesis, Australian National University.
Poggi, G. (1992) 'The State and Creative Intellectuals', Colloquium, Department of Government, University of Sydney, 11 August.
Sherter, S. R. (1968) 'The Soviet System and the Historian: E. V. Tarle (1875–1955) as a Case Study'. PhD dissertation, Wayne State University.

Published secondary sources

Afanas'ev, Yu. A. (1988) 'Perestroika i istoricheskoe znanie', *Literaturnaya Rossiya*, 17 July, 24, pp. 2–3, 8–9.
—— (ed.) (1988) *Inogo ne dano – perestroika: glasnost', demokratiya, sotsializm*. Moscow: Progress.
—— (ed.) (1996) *Sovetskaya istoriografiya*. Moscow: Rossiisky gosudarstvennyi gumanitarnyi universitet.
—— (ed.) (1996) *Sud'by rossiiskogo krest'yanstva*. Moscow: Rossiisky gosudarstvennyi gumanitarnyi universitet.
Aksyutin, Yu. (ed.) (1989) *Nikita Sergeyevich Khrushchev: Materialy k biografii*. Moscow: Politizdat.
Ali, T. (ed.) (1984) *The Stalinist Legacy: Its Impact on Twentieth-Century World Politics*. Harmondsworth: Penguin.
Al'perovich, M. S. et al. (eds) (1996) *Otreshivshiisya ot strakha. Pamyati A. M. Nekricha: Vospominiya, stat'i, dokumenty*. Moscow: Institut vseobshchei istorii RAN.
Althusser, L. (1977) *Lenin and Philosophy and Other Essays*, trans. by B. Brewster. London: NLB.
Aronowitz, S. (1998) *Science as Power: Discourse and Ideology in Modern Society*. Minneapolis: University of Minnesota Press.
Asher, H. (1972) 'The Rise, Fall, and Resurrection of M. N. Pokrovsky', *The Russian Review*, 31, 1, pp. 49–63.
Bahro, R. (1978) *The Alternative in Eastern Europe*, trans. by D. Fernbach. London: NLB.

Barber, J. (1976) 'Stalin's Letter to the Editors of *Proletarskaya Revolyutsiya*', *Soviet Studies*, xxvii, 1, January, pp. 21–41.
—— (1981) *Soviet Historians in Crisis, 1928–32*. London: The Macmillan Press in association with the Centre for Russian and East European Studies, University of Birmingham.
Baron, S. H. and Heer, N. W. (eds) (1977) *Windows on the Russian Past: Essays on Soviet Historiography since Stalin*. Columbus, Ohio: American Association for the Advancement of Slavic Studies.
Barraclough, G. (1979) *Main Trends in History*. New York and London: Holmes & Meir.
Beilharz, Peter (ed.) (1992) *Social Theory: A Guide to Central Thinkers*. Sydney: Allen & Unwin.
Bezborodov, A. B (1998) *Fenomenon akademichesgoko dissidentstva v SSSR*. Moscow: Rossiiskii gosudarstvennyi gumanitarny universitet.
Black, C. E. (1986) *Understanding Soviet Politics: The Perspective of Russian History*. Boulder, Colorado: Westview Press.
Bosworth, R. J. B. (1993) *Explaining Auschwitz and Hiroshima: History Writing and the Second World War 1945–1990*. London and New York: Routledge.
Brady, C. (ed.) (1991) *Ideology and the Historians: Historical Studies XVII*. Dublin: The Lilliput Press.
Brown, A. and Kaser, M. (eds) (1978) *The Soviet Union Since the Fall of Khrushchev*. London: Macmillan.
Burdzhalov, E. N. (1987) *Russia's Second Revolution: The February 1917 Uprising in Petrograd*, trans. and ed. by Donald J. Raleigh. Bloomington and Indianolis: Indiana University Press, first published in Russian in 1967.
Butterfield, H. (1973) *The Whig Interpretation of History*. Harmondsworth: Penguin, first published 1931.
Centre d'Etudes et de Recherches marxistes. (1978) *Sur Les Sociétés Precapitalistes: Textes choisis de Marx, Engels, Lenine*, preface de Maurice Godelier. Paris: Editions sociales.
Chesneaux, J. (1978) *Pasts and Futures or What is History For?* trans. by Schofield Coryell. London: Thames & Hudson.
Churchward, L. G. (1973) *The Soviet Intelligentsia: An essay on the social structure and roles of Soviet intellectuals during the 1960s*. London and Boston: Routledge & Kegan Paul.
—— (1987) *Soviet Socialism: Social and Political Essays*. London and New York: Routledge & Kegan Paul.
Cohen, S. F. (1977) 'Politics and the Past: the Importance of Being Historical' (review article), *Soviet Studies*, xxix, 1, January, pp. 137–45.
—— (ed.) (1982) *An End to Silence: Uncensored Opinion in the Soviet Union from Roy Medvedev's Underground Magazine, Political Diary*, trans. by George Saunders. New York and London: W. W. Norton & Co.
—— (1985) *Rethinking the Soviet Experience: Politics and History Since 1917*. New York and Oxford: Oxford University Press.
Coser, L. A. (1965) *Men of Ideas: A Sociologist's View*. New York and London: The Free Press and Collier-Macmillan.
Davies, R. W. *The Socialist Offensive: The Collectivisation of Soviet Agriculture 1929–1930*. London: The Macmillan Press, 1980.
—— (1989) *Soviet History in the Gorbachev Revolution*. Bloomington and Indianapolis: Indiana University Press.

—— (1997) *Soviet History in the Yeltsin Era*. London: Macmillan Press in association with the Centre for Russian and East European Studies, University of Birmingham.
Debray, R. (1981) *Teachers, Writers, Celebrities: The Intellectuals of Modern France*, intro. by Francis Mulhern. London: Verso, first published in French 1979.
Deutscher, I. (1966) *Ironies of History: Essays on Contemporary Communism*. London: Oxford University Press.
—— (1972) *Marxism in Our Time*. London: Jonathan Cape.
Dirlik, A. (1978) *Revolution and History: The Origins of Marxist Historiography in China, 1919–37*. Berkeley, Los Angeles and London: University of California Press.
Eley, G. (1986) 'History with the Politics Left Out – Again?', *The Russian Review*, 45, pp. 385–94.
Emets, V. A. and Shelokhaev, V. V. (1990) 'Tvorchesky put' K. N. Tarnovskogo', *IZ*, 118, pp. 202–31.
Enteen, G. M. (1974) 'A Recent Trend on the Historical Front', *Survey*, 20, 4 (93), Autumn, pp. 122–31.
—— Gorn, T. and Kern, C. (1979) *Soviet Historians and the Study of Russian Imperialism*. University Park and London: The Pennsylvania State University Press.
Feher, F., Heller, A. and Markus, G. (1983) *Dictatorship Over Needs: An Analysis of Soviet Societies*. Oxford: Basil Blackwell.
Fitzpatrick, S. (1986) 'New Perspectives on Stalinism', *The Russian Review*, 45, pp. 357–73.
—— (1992) *The Cultural Front: Power and Culture in Revolutionary Russia*. Ithaca and London: Cornell University Press.
Friedrich, C. J. and Brzezinski, Z. K. (1965) *Totalitarian Dictatorship and Autocracy*, second, revised edition. Cambridge, Mass.: Harvard University Press.
Gella, A. (ed.) (1976) *The Intelligentsia and the Intellectuals: Theory, Method and Case Study*. London and Beverly Hills, California: Sage Studies in International Sociology 5.
Gellner, E. (ed.) (1980) *Soviet and Western Anthropology*, introduction by Meyer Fortes. London: Duckworth.
—— (1988) *State and Society in Soviet Thought*. Oxford and New York: Basil Blackwell.
Gerschenkron, A. (1971) 'Soviet Marxism and Absolutism', *Slavic Review*, 30, 4, pp. 853–69.
Gleisner, J. (1983) 'Old Bolsheviks Discuss Socialism', *Labour Focus on Eastern Europe*, 6, 1, Summer pp. 3–5.
Gorbachev, M. (1987) *Perestroika: New Thinking for Our Country and the Entire World*. London: Collins.
Gouldner, A. W. (1979) *The Future of Intellectuals and the Rise of the New Class: A Frame of Reference, Theses, Conjectures, Arguments, and an Historical Perspective on the Role of Intellectuals and Intelligentsia in the International Class Contest of the Modern Era*. London: Macmillan.
Heer, N. W. (1971) *Politics and History in the Soviet Union*. Cambridge, Massachusetts and London, England: The MIT Press.
Hoare, Q. and Nowell Smith, G. (eds) (1971) *Selections from the Prison Notebooks of Antonio Gramsci*. London: Lawrence and & Wishart.

Hobsbawm, E. and Ranger, T. (eds) (1983) *The Invention of Tradition*. Cambridge: Cambridge University Press.

Hollinger, D. A. (1973) 'T. S. Kuhn's Theory of Science and Its Implications for History', *American Historical Review*, 78, pp. 370–93.

Hösler, J. (1995) *Die sowjetische Geschichtswissenschaft 1953 bis 1991 Studien zur Methodologie- und Organizationsgeschichte*. München: Verlag Otto Sagner.

Hough, J. F. (1986) *The Struggle for the Third World: Soviet Debates and American Options*. Washington, D.C: The Brookings Institute.

Iggers, G. G. and Parker, H. T. (eds) (1979) *International Handbook of Historical Studies*. Westport, Conn.: Greenwood Press.

Ito, T. (ed.) (1989) *Facing Up to the Past: Soviet Historiography Under Perestroika*. Sapporo: Slavic Research Centre, Hokkaido University.

Kagarlitsky, B. (1982) *Dialektika nadezhdy*. Paris: Slovo and La Parole, first distributed in samizdat form 1980.

—— (1988) *The Thinking Reed: Intellectuals and the Soviet State 1917 to the Present*, trans. by Brian Pearce. London: Verso.

Karabel, J. (1996) 'Towards a Theory of Intellectuals and Politics', *Theory and Society*, 25, pp. 205–33.

Keane, J. (ed.) (1988) *Civil Society and the State: New European Perspectives*. London and New York: Verso.

Keep, J. (ed.) (1964) with the assistance of Lilliana Busby. *Contemporary History in the Soviet Mirror*. London: George Allen & Unwin.

—— (1973) 'The Current Scene in Soviet Historiography', *Survey*, 19, 1 (86), Winter, pp. 3–20.

—— John L. H. (1988) *Moscow's Problems of History: A Select Critical Bibliography of the Soviet Journal Voprosy istorii, 1956–1985*. Ottawa: Institute of Soviet and East European Studies, Carleton University, 1986, corrected edition 1988.

Khorodina, T. (1994) *Istoriya otechestva i arkhivy 1917–1980–e gg.* Moscow: Rossiisky gosudarstvenyi gumanitarnyi universitet.

Konrad, G. and Szelenyi, I. (1979) *The Intellectuals on the Road to Class Power*, trans. by Andrew Arato and Richard E. Allen. Brighton, England: Harvester Press.

Kuhn, T. (1970) *The Structure of Scientific Revolutions*, second edition. Chicago and London: University of Chicago Press.

Lakatos, I. and Musgrave, A. (eds). (1970) *Criticism and the Growth of Knowledge*. London and New York: Cambridge University Press.

Lewin, M. (1975) *Political Undercurrents in Soviet Economic Debates: From Bukharin to the Modern Reformers*. London: Pluto Press.

—— (1988) *The Gorbachev Phenomenon: A Historical Interpretation*. London: Hutchinson Radius.

Loone, E. (1992) *Soviet Marxism and Analytical Philosophies of History*, trans. by Brian Pearce. Foreword by Ernest Gellner. London and New York: Interverso, first published in Russian in 1980.

MacDonald, H. M. (ed.) (1966) *The Intellectual in Politics: Symposium*. Austin, Texas: The Humanities Research Centre, The University of Texas.

Mannheim, K. (1940) *Ideology and Utopia: An Introduction to the Sociology of Knowledge*, trans. by Louis Wirth and Edward Shils. London: Kegan Paul, Trench, Trubner.

Marcuse, H. (1971) *Soviet Marxism: A Critical Analysis*. Harmondsworth: Penguin, first published 1958.
McNeill, W. H. (1986) *Mythistory and Other Essays*. Chicago and London: The University of Chicago Press.
Medvedev, R. (1973) *Let History Judge: The Origins and Consequences of Stalinism*, trans. by Colleen Taylor, edited by David Joravsky and Georges Haupt. New York: Vintage Books, first published in 1971 by Alfred A. Knopf.
—— (1989) *Let History Judge: The Origins and Consequences of Stalinism*, second, revised and expanded edition, edited and trans. by George Shriver. New York: Columbia University Press.
—— and Medvedev, Z. A. (1978) *Khrushchev: the Years in Power*, foreword by Stephen F. Cohen, trans. by Andrew R. Durkin. New York and London: Norton & Co.
—— (1991) Roi. *Lichnost' i epokha: Politichesky portret L. I. Brezhneva*, Kniga 1. Moscow: Novosti.
Miliband, R. (1977) *Marxism and Politics*. Oxford: Oxford University Press.
Miller, D. B. (1971) In 'Reviews of Books', *The American Historical Review*, 76, 1, pp. 756–7.
Miller, R. F. (ed.) (1992) *The Developments of Civil Society in Communist Systems*. Sydney: Allen & Unwin.
Nekrich, Aleksandr. (1979) *Otreshis' ot strakha: vospominaniya istorika*. London: Overseas Publications Interchange.
—— Alexander (1980) 'Rewriting history', *Index on Censorship*, 9, 4, August pp. 4–7.
—— Aleksandr M. (1989) 'Perestroika in History: The First Stage', *Survey*, 30, 4 (131), June, pp. 22–43.
Neretina, S. S. (1990) 'Istoriya s metodologiei istorii', *VF*, 9, pp. 149–63.
—— (1996) 'Mikhail Yakovlevich Gefter', *Vek XX i mir*, 3, pp. 234–7.
Novick, P. (1988) *That Noble Dream: The 'Objectivity Question' and the American Historical Profession*. Cambridge: Cambridge University Press.
O'Brien, C. C. and Vanech, W. D. (eds). (1969) *Power and Consciousness*. London and New York: University of London Press and New York University Press.
'Perestroika, History and Historians (Roundtable, Moscow, January 1989)', *Journal of Modern History*, 62, 4, 1990, pp. 782–830.
Petrov, V. (1968) *'June 22, 1941': Soviet Historians and the German Invasion*. Columbia, S.C: University of South Carolina Press.
Pipes, R. (ed.) (1961) *The Russian Intelligentsia*. New York: Columbia University Press.
Polikarpov, V. V. (1989) ' "Novoe napravlenie" – v starom prochtenii', *VI*, 1989, 3, pp. 44–61.
Rakovski, M. (1978) *Towards An East European Marxism*. London: Allison & Busby.
Raleigh, D. J. (ed.) (1989) *Soviet Historians and Perestroika: The First Phase*. New York and London: M. E. Sharpe.
Richards, H. (1988) 'Soviet Agrarian Guru Comes in from the Cold', *Times Higher Education Supplement*, 1 April, p. 16.
Rieff, P. (ed.) (1970) *On Intellectuals: Theoretical Studies, Case Studies*. Garden City, New York: Anchor Books.

Rigby, T. H. and Feher, F. (eds) (1982) *Political Legitimation in Communist States*. London and Basingstoke: The Macmillan Press in association with St Antony's College, Oxford.

Rogger, H. (1965) 'Politics, Ideology and History in the USSR: The Search for Coexistence', *Soviet Studies*, xvi, 3, January, pp. 253–75.

Rozman, G. (1985) *A Mirror for Socialism: Soviet Criticisms of China*. Princeton, New Jersey: Princeton University Press.

Said, E. W. (1994) *Representations of the Intellectuals: The 1993 Reith Lectures*. London: Vintage.

Sakwa, R. (1990) *Gorbachev and His Reforms 1985–1990*. Hertfordshire: Phillip Allan.

Sawer, M. (1977) *Marxism and the Question of the Asiatic Mode of Production*. The Hague: Martinus Nijhoff.

—— (1978–79) 'The Politics of Historiography: Russian Socialism and the Question of the Asiatic Mode of Production 1906–1931', *Critique*, 10–11, pp. 15–36.

Scanlan, J. P. (1985) *Marxism in the USSR: A Critical Survey of Current Thought*. Ithaca and London: Cornell University Press.

Schapiro, L. (1970) *Totalitarianism*. London: Pall Mall.

Schöpflin, G. (1990) 'The End of Communism in Eastern Europe', *International Affairs*, 66, 1, January, pp. 3–16.

Schumpeter, J. A. (1976) *Capitalism, Socialism and Democracy,* 5th edn with a new introduction by Tom Bottomore. London: George Allen & Unwin.

Shatz, M. S. (1980) *Soviet Dissent in Historical Perspective*. Cambridge: Cambridge University Press.

Sherlock, T. (1988) 'Politics and History Under Gorbachev', *Problems of Communism,* 37, 3–4, May–August, pp. 16–42.

Shils, E. (1972) *The Intellectuals and the Powers and Other Essays*. Chicago and London: The University of Chicago Press.

Shlapentokh, V. (1990) *Soviet Intellectuals and Political Power: The Post-Stalin Era*. Princeton, New Jersey: Princeton University Press.

Shteppa, K. F. (1962) *Russian Historians and the Soviet State*. New Brunswick, New Jersey: Rutgers University Press.

Sidorova, L. A. (1997) *Ottepel' v istoricheskoi nauke: Sovetskaya istoriografiya pervogo poslestalinskogo desyatiletiya*. Moscow: Pamyatnki istoricheskoi mysli.

Siegelbaum, L. H. (1989) 'Historical Revisionism in the USSR', *Radical Historical Review*, 44, pp. 32–61.

Slovar' sovremennogo Russkogo yazyka, T.16. Moscow and Leningrad: Nauka, 1964.

Soskin, V. L. (1974) *Iz istorii Sovetskoi intelligentsii*. Novosibirsk: Nauka.

Spechler, D. R. (1982) *Permitted Dissent in the USSR: <u>Novyi mir</u> and the Soviet Regime*. New York: Praeger.

Tokes, R. L. (ed.) (1975) *Dissent in the USSR: Politics, Ideology and People*. Baltimore and London: The Johns Hopkins University Press.

Urban, M. E. (1985) 'Conceptualizing Political Power in the USSR: Patterns of Binding and Bonding', *Studies in Comparative Communism*, xviii, 4, Winter pp. 207–26.

—— (1987) 'The Structure of Signification in the General Secretary's Address: A Semiotic Approach to Soviet Political Discourse', *Coexistence*, 24, 3, pp. 187–210.

Vladimirov, L. (1972) '*Glavlit*: How the Soviet Censor Works', *Index on Censorship*, 1, 3–4, Autumn–Winter pp. 31–43.

Watt, D. C. (ed.) (1969) *Contemporary History in Europe: Problems and Perspectives*. London: George Allen & Unwin.

Who's Who in the USSR. München: K. G. Saur, 1984.

Yakovlev, A. (1993) *The Fate of Marxism in Russia*, intro. by Thomas F. Remington, foreword by Alexander Tsipko, trans. by C. A. Fitzpatrick. New Haven and London: Yale University Press.

Yanov, A. (1984) *The Drama of the Soviet 1960s: A Lost Reform*. Berkeley: University of California, Institute of International Studies.

Zhuravlev, V. V (ed.) (1991) *XX s"ezd KPSS i ego istoricheskie real'nosti*. Moscow: Izdatelstvo politicheskoi literatury.

Zubkova, E. (1998) *Russia After the War: Hopes, Illusions, and Disappointments, 1945–1957*, trans. and ed. by Hugh Ragsdale. Armonk, N.Y. and London: M. E. Sharpe.

Index

Academic Councils (*uchenye sovety*) 69
  partkom on 206–7
Academy of Sciences 20, 28, 33, 50, 55, 56, 63, 64, 68, 69, 113, 151, 164, 200, 216
  campaign against revisionism 193
  merged with Communist Academy 62
  opposes *partkom* 208
  publishes *June 22, 1941* 210
  supports study of methodology 156
Adamov, V. V. 78, 298 n.28
  loses university post 242
  on 'multistructuredness' 97
  on Urals history 94
  Sverdlovsk anthology criticized 231, 296 n.169
Afanas'ev, Yu. A. 6, 244
  on Stalinist historiography 6, 42
aktual'nost' 159, 247
Al'perovich, M. S. 214, 218
all-Union historians' conference (1962) 69–71, 87
'alternativeness' in history (*al'ternativnost'*) 99, 101, 185, 192, 227, 243–5, 271 n.125
Anfimov, A. M. 85, 87, 98, 223, 227
  fate under Brezhnev 242
  on Russian agrarian history 85–7
  on Trapeznikov 238
  views on peasantry criticized 225
Annales 6, 264 n.201, 286 n.144
anti-Semitism 40, 217, 221
'Arakcheev regime' 17, 251 n.62
archives 49, 71, 275 n.54
  and collectivization 119, 122, 123, 126, 131, 133, 135, 136, 143, 146, 147, 152, 153
  and famine 145, 146, 278 n.158
  and *Istorichesky Arkhiv* 67, 264 n.186, 273 n.14

  increased access to 67
  party control of 68
  Sidorov on 79
Arsen'ev, A. S. 166, 191
Asiatic mode of production 44, 193
  and *pyatichlenka* 176, 182
  concept suppressed 167, 169, 176
  discussion of 166–70
Avrekh, A. Ya. 105
  biography 271 n.134, 298 n.28
  criticized 230
  fate under Brezhnev 242
  on 'political expediency' 206
  on Russian absolutism 106–9

Bahro, R. 25, 237
Bakhrushin, S. V. 40
Bakhtin, M. M. 24, 288 n.191
Barg, M. A. 166, 167
  criticized 182
Batkin, L. M. 167
Beria, L. P. 54
Bibler, V. S. 195, 242
Bogdanov, A. A. 178, 284 n.119
Bogdenko, M. L. 113, 114, 119, 141
  approach to kulaks 118
  criticizes 'Dizzy with Success' 118, 141–2
  criticizes Trapeznikov 117
  supports cooperatives 116
Bovykin, V. I. 68, 78, 81, 82, 267 n.28
  criticizes Volobuev 221, 227
  on 'multistructuredness' 98
  opposes New Direction 98, 100, 217
Brezhnev, L. I. x, 70, 137, 210, 289 n.11, 213, 216, 217
  against Twentieth Congress 90, 237, 238
  and Stalin rehabilitation 201
  and Trapeznikov 90, 200, 289 n.5
  defeats *shestidesyatniki* 242, 247

Brezhnev period
  and neo-Stalinism 156
  and revisionism x, xiii, 4, 8, 18, 76, 129, 149, 151, 152, 257 n.53
  and *zastoi* 239
  as 'Thermidor' 233
  see also 'stagnation'
Bukharin, N. I. 54, 56, 103, 125, 135, 153, 178, 255 n.15, 261 n.124, 271 n.125, 273 n.18, 275 n.46
Burdzhalov, E. N. x, 161, 235
  'affair' 51–62
  and *shestidesyatniki* 66
  and Sidorov 75, 262 n.141, 266 n.1
  and Trotskyism 54, 59
  appointed deputy editor *VI* 50
  at all-Union conference 71
  biography 259 n.88
  condemned by CC 61
  criticized by party press 58
  criticizes history 51, 54–5
  criticizes Russian chauvinism 57
  criticizes *Short Course* 56
  defends *partiinost'* 59
  dismissed from *VI* 60–1
  influenced by Kardelj 58–9
  on Bolsheviks in 1917 54, 58–9, 71
  on bureaucratization of history 55
  on party's role 59
  on readers' conferences 56
  on Russian imperialism 80
  on Trotsky 56
  publishes masterpieces 62
  sets revisionist agenda 52
  support for 58
Burlatsky, F. 240

censorship 30, 70, 134, 141, 208, 249 n.30, 265 n.202
  and Glavlit 206, 208, 210, 265, n.202, 276, n.101, 290, n.25
  'at work' 134–40
  of Danilov 134
  of Nekrich 210
  of Sector of Methodology 193
  partkom on 206
  revisionists subvert 151
  see also Glavlit
Central Committee 242, 262 n.141, 293 n.94, 291 n.38
  Academy of Social Sciences 59, 63, 126, 166, 220, 284 n.119
  and Nekrich affair, 211
  archives of 152
  campaign against Gefter 193
  discusses Danilov's *Collectivization of Agriculture* 134
  on 'cult of the personality' 57, 157, 209, 285 n.139
  promotes history 50
Cherepnin, L. V. 255 n.22,
  clash with New Direction 217
  on Russian absolutism 106, 271 n.137 and n.141
  suppresses Danilova's manuscript 194
Chesneaux, J. 193, 254 n.143
civil society x, xi, 8, 9, 31, 32, 35, 69, 237
collectivization Ch.4 *passim*
Communist Party of the Soviet Union (CPSU) 26, 38, 48, 193
  and history 36, 46, 156
  as 'collective *intellektual*' 32, 34
  see also Short Course, Twentieth Party Congress
'cult of the personality' 46, 71, 115, 123, 129, 138, 157, 285 n.139
  and collectivization 133, 142, 144
  and neo-Stalinism 205
  and *Short Course* 181
  and Stalinism 206
  distorts history 47, 48, 50, 54, 57, 155, 159, 161, 164
  downplaying of term 201, 208
  partkom on 205
'culturologists' 195

Daniel, Yu. 201, 203, 210
Danilov, V. P. x, 66, Ch. 4 *passim*, 222, 227
  and dismissal of Khrushchev 202
  and division of Institute of History 216

and 'multistructuredness' 124, 153
and Nekrich affair 213–14
and New Direction 87, 116, 124
and Medvedev 125
and R. W. Davies 136, 272 n.3
and Sector of Methodology 166
and 'State of Historical Science' 203
and Twentieth Congress 236
as 'party democrat' 200
biography 272 n.3, 299 n.48
campaign against 202
censorship of 149, 205
censured in *Kommunist* 150
clash with Selunskaya 152–3
criticizes *Short Course* 87
criticizes Stalin 115, 127, 129, 133, 147
defends October Revolution 247
dismissed as Head of Sector 150
elected to *partkom* 125, 202, 203, 214
his *Collectivization of Agriculture* banned 125–6, 149, 154, 208
his Group on Soviet peasantry 113, 114–15, 124
his supervisor 140
his use of archives 130
in Brezhnev period 152, 153, 241
knowledge of famine 146
lack of prerequisites for collectivization 112, 117
not a dissident 241
on Bukharin 128, 133, 136
on 'Bukharin alternative' 245
on 'bureaucratism' 208
on 'cult of the personality' 206
on democratic rural revolution 87
on '*figura umolchaniya*' 208, 289 n.25
on grain crisis 128
on 'human collectives' 162
on kulaks 115, 116, 127, 128, 133, 139, 153
on middle peasantry 126, 131, 132, 133, 143, 148
on Nekrich affair 213
on *partkom*'s dissolution 216

on peasant household 123
on rural evolution 87, 88
on *shestidesyatniki* 234
on socio-economic relations 115, 124, 162
on 'third wave' of revisionism 245
on Trotsky 245, 299 n.50
on village commune 114–15, 127, 153
on Yakovlev commission 131, 132
opposes full-scale collectivization, 112, 117, 126, 129, 132, 133, 148
resists neo-Stalinism 205
self-criticism 150
supports collectivization 115, 123, 124, 127, 130, 132, 142
supports cooperatives 116, 128, 130, 274 n.30
views criticized 225
Danilova, L. V. 201, 284 n.121, 288 n.192
and *perestroika* 245
and Sector of Methodology 166
and Twentieth Congress 236
criticized 178, 182
fate under Brezhnev 194, 243
her manuscript suppressed 193, 241
on Asiatic mode of production 169–70, 176
on dismissal of Khruschev 178
on feudalism 177
on geography 282 n.90
on pre-capitalist societies 175, 177
on *pyatichlenka* 176, 283 n.103, 299 n.34
on socialist societies 178
on world history 173
Davies, R. W. ix, 136
Deborin, G. A. 210, 292 n.63
'democratic' *partkom* 201–9, 289 n.15 and n.20, 289 n.21, 290 n.25 and n.37
and Nekrich affair 209, 211, 213–14
as 'invisible college' 214
as site for intelligentsia 215, 236

'democratic' *partkom* (cont'd)
  dissolution of   214, 216
  Gefter and   209, 215
  on democratization of Institute of History   207
  on *'figura umolchaniya'*   205–6
  opposes 'conjuncturalism'   212
  opposes division of Institute of History   216
  report suppressed   207
  resists neo-Stalinism   201
  supports Sector of Methodology   164, 209
Department of Science (of CC)   64, 199, 242, 286 n.147, 296 n.165
  criticized by Burdzhalov   59
  criticizes Burdzhalov   52, 53, 262 n.141
  discusses Danilov's *Collectivization of Agriculture*   125
  discusses revisionist works   223, 225
  hostility to New Direction   102
  imposes orthodoxy   239
  interrogates Volovuev   229
  invigilates history   70
  opposes 'democratic' *partkom*   208
  Trapeznikov appointed head   200
  Volobuev works in   219
  see also Trapeznikov
destalinization   6, 7, 50, 58, 60, 70, 71, 87
dialectical materialism   43, 45, 155, 158, 199, 192
dissent   *see* dissidence
dissidence   18, 19, 164, 201, 217, 238, 251 n.79, 273 n.14, 298 n.32
  and dissent   21–30, 241–3
  and 'Prague spring'   217
Drabkin, Ya. S.   242
  and Nekrich affair   213, 214
  and Sector of Methodology   166
  and Trotskyism   188, 286 n.161
  as 'party democrat'   200
  biography   259 n.78
  criticism of   188, 191
  criticizes *Short Course*   189
  elected to *partkom*   202, 209
  his publications suppressed   193
  on Lenin   188, 190
  on revisionism   48–9
  on 'social revolution'   188–9
  on Thermidor   190
Dubrovsky, S. M.   85, 86, 87
Dudintsev, V.   22

February 1917 revolution   225, 259 n.88
  conference on   96–7, 101
  Volobuev on   228–9, 231
Fedoseev, P. N.   157–8, 223
Frantsev, F. P.   157–8
frontoviki ('front-line' veterans)   113, 235
  and history   65–6, 184

Galkin, A. A.   189
Galuzo, P. G.   78, 85
  on 'multistructuredness'   95–6, 97
Gefter, M. Ya.   66, 78, 79, 180, 202, 255 n.21,
  and 'fatalistic' Marxism   180
  and Medvedev   242, 285 n.138, 298 n.32
  and *partkom*   209, 214, 216
  and party democratization   215
  and Tvardovsky   183, 297 n.6
  and Twentieth Congress   183, 236
  as dissident   241
  as head of 'Petőfi circle'   195
  as neo-Leninist   183, 195
  as 'party democrat'   200
  biography   255 n.20
  campaign against   185, 193, 194, 218, 239, 241, 288 n.189
  criticizes Burdzhalov   52, 160
  criticizes Trapeznikov   215, 285 n.139
  fate under Brezhnev   194, 243
  his Sector of Methodology   164–6, 280 n.46, 284 n.104, 286 n.147
  his theoretical seminar   195
  on 'alternativeness' in history   99, 185, 192, 245
  on 'anti-cosmopolitan' campaign   40
  on Asiatic mode of production   167

on 'cult of the personality' 155
on 'dogmatism' 165, 192
on historical consciousness 41, 256 n.27
on 'logic of research' 235
on 'multistructuredness' 99, 175
on 'new type' of historian 194
on 'Prague spring' 217
on rereading Lenin 183–7, 192
on Russian imperialism 79, 81, 83, 94
on *shestidesyatniki* 181
on *Short Course* method 180
on socio-economic formations 160, 172, 174, 181, 280 n.22
on Stalin 180
on Stalinism 245
on world history 173–4
on *zastoi* 240
on Zhukov's *Universal History* 160, 174
retrospective 196
Russia as 'second echelon' country 100
Gindin, I. F. 82, 105, 109, 158, 216, 267 n.25
and 'multistructuredness' 92, 94
biography 268 n.31, 280 n.31
on Russian imperialism 78, 81, 91
Ginzburg, Ye. 242
Glavlit 206, 208, 210, 265 n.202, 276 n.101, 290 n.25
see also censorship
Godelier, M. 167, 193
Gorbachev, M. S. ix, x, 4, 200
Gorodetsky, Ye. N. 65, 219, 234, 249 n.30, 255 n.23, 262 n.144
condemns 'public informing' 87
elected to *partkom* 209
on Burdzhalov affair 50, 259 n.85 and n.88
on Leninism 234
on *zastoi* 240
Gramsci, A. 31–2
Grekov, B. D. 40, 255 n.15, 271 n.141
Grunt, A. 78

Gulyga, A. V. vi, 164
his group on philosophy 163, 242
on 'pseudodialectics' 191
Gurevich, A. Ya. 45, 255 n.22, 257 n.53, 281 n.68
and *perestroika* 245
as 'culturologist' 195
criticized 182, 218
intellectual influences on 286 n.144
on *zastoi* 241
repudiates Marxism 246

Heer, N. W. 7–8, 9, 36
on professionalism 72
Higher Party School 41, 64, 200, 220, 259 n.88, 289 n.5
historians 34, 36, 64, 91, 118, 146, 237, 246
all-Union conference (1962) 69, 70, 156
and 'Aesopianism' 10, 70
and 'anti-cosmopolitan' campaign 40
and archives 49
and historical consciousness 41, 256 n.27
and 'historical front' 39
and International Congress of Historians 56
and Khrushchev 48, 50
and professionalism 72
and revisionism 235
and Stalinism 49, 199
and Twentieth Congress 41, 48, 49, 55
and *zastoi* 240
as intellectuals/intelligentsia 3, 13–20, 22, 29, 33, 184, 214, 235, 237
as legitimators 34–5, 37
generational conflict 87
Krasnopevtsev circle of 62
'new type' of 194
poor status of 41, 66, 67
Stalin declares war on 39
support Burdzhalov 58
see also historical science, historiography, history

historical consciousness 41, 47, 57, 100, 235
  Gefter on 246, 256 n.27
historical journals
  Burdzhalov on 55
  expansion of 67
  partkom report on 207
  role of 70
historical materialism 12, 43, 45, 90, 92, 161, 167, 179, 181, 219, 243, 284 n.119
  and pre-capitalist societies 170, 173
  and socio-economic formations 44–6, 167, 171–2, 174, 176, 178, 181–2, 239
  'crisis' in 180
  Gefter on 99
  New Direction on 104
  Volobuev on 100
  see also Short Course
historical science 8, 44, 50, 157–9, 170, 203, 204, 219, 235, 257 n.51
  and 'anti-cosmopolitanism' 40
  and comparative method 166
  and 'conjuncturalism' 206, 212
  and 'cult of personality' 50, 157, 164
  and '*figura umolchaniya*' 205
  and *partiinost'* 182, 187
  and party ideologues 182
  and *perestroika* 243, 244
  and politics 35, 206, 236
  and 'servile incompetents' 40
  and Stalin's rehabilitation 205
  and *VI* 50, 54
  as 'mendacity' 6
  Burdzhalov on 51
  degradation of 39, 51, 203, 204
  degrees in 15
  latent danger of 26, 27
  organization of 68
  partkom report on 203, 205, 206
  policing of 26
  production of 62
  re-politicization of 218
  students of (Table 2.1) 65
  'third wave' of 245

Historical Science, Sector on History of 219
Historical Sciences, XIII International Congress of 218
historiography 7, 36, 42, 43, 45, 52, 79, 80, 86, 90, 116, 159, 182, 184, 191, 210, 246, 257 n.53
  and influence of 1920s 78, 79, 92, 109, 123, 162
  and *perestroika* 6, 98, 245
  and politics 4–5, 7, 9, 22, 25–7, 35–6, 41, 42, 46, 57, 98, 101, 194, 206, 236, 247
  and Russian chauvinism 40, 52, 260 n.93
  and Twentieth Congress 4, 7, 38, 234
  as 'mythology' 5
  Burdzhalov on 54–6, 71
  defined xiv
  Eurocentrism of 94, 108, 176
  'handmaiden' to politics 5–6, 22, 25
  legacy of Sector of Methodology 243
  of Asiatic mode of production 168–9
  of feudalism suppressed 193, 241
  organization of 67–9
  professionalization of 63
  reinvigoration of 50, 75, 95
  'relative autonomy' of 41
  role of textbook 46
  Russian tradition of 41, 195, 237, 288 n.191
  Stalinist 38, 88, 101, 152, 161, 164–5, 172, 177–8, 235, 282 n.82
  Stalinist on collectivization 114, 116, 121, 123, 124
  'stultification' of 184
  supervision of 70
  see also historical science, historians, revisionism, *Short Course*
history *see* historiography
History and Sociology conference 91–2, 156, 157

History of the CPSU   46, 201, 218
  see also Short Course
Il'ichev, L. F.   156, 282
Institute of History   49, 50, 52, 63, 64, 69, 70, 71, 113, 125, 167, 201, 221, 236
  and party 'mafia'   64, 207
  and Sector of Methodology   164, 166
  democratization of   207
  divided in two   105, 150, 195, 216, 217, 293 n.93
  number of historians   64
  organization of   68
  see also 'democratic' partkom
Institute of Marxism–Leninism   33, 63, 64, 67, 166, 216, 220, 244
  and Nekrich affair   210, 211, 212
Institute of Philosophy   163, 167, 242, 281 n.54, 282 n.80
Institute of the History of Natural Science and Technology   221, 241
Institute of the History of the USSR   217, 222, 223
  Volobuev appointed Director   219
  Volobuev dismissed   76, 229, 232–3
Institute of World Economy and International Relations (IMEMO)   166, 210
Institute of World History   194, 217, 218, 241, 287 n.184, 288 n.189
intellectuals   13–37, 64, 72, 76, 105, 156, 182, 184
  defined   16–17, 235
  Gramsci on   31–2
intelligentsia   ix, x, xiv, 8–9, 13–17, 19, 20–31, 162–3, 236–7, 251 n.63 and n.79, 252 n.96, 255 n.20
  and partkom   215
  and political apparatus   25–6, 29, 36–7, 253 n.128
  and political reform   28, 30
  and 'Prague spring'   195, 216, 217, 237
  and Sector of Methodology   194
  and Stalinism   195, 200–1
  and Twentieth Congress   22–3, 37, 199
  and zastoi   241, 293 n.102, 298 n.9
  as champions of the people   ix, 23, 236
  as 'mirror' for nomenklatura   37, 237
  defeat of   233
  repression of   23, 26, 29
  see also dissidence
'invisible colleges'   13, 214, 272 n.3
Ivanov, L. M.   85, 222
  biography   294 n.123
Ivnitsky N. A.   111, 113, 114, 152
  approach to kulaks   122, 139, 140, 152
  attitude to Bukharin   135, 275 n.46
  biography   273 n.14
  censored   135–44, 151
  criticizes full-scale collectivization   121, 139, 140
  criticizes Stalin   121–2, 136, 138, 139, 140
  criticizes Trapeznikov   121, 126
  his use of archives   119–23, 136, 139, 151, 152, 278 n.54
  on famine   146, 278 n.58
  on statistics   119
  on Yakovlev commission   120–2, 139–40
  supports collectivization   134
  supports cooperatives   140

Kaganovich, L. M.   39, 42, 47, 121, 140, 147, 148, 151
Kamenev, L. B.   54, 56, 58
Kapitsa, P. L.   201
  on intellectual frustration   24–5
KGB   195, 210
Khrushchev, N. S.   ix, xiii, 4, 8, 25, 28, 30, 32, 46, 60, 62, 86, 210, 233
  and Twentieth Congress   38, 43, 47–8, 238

Khrushchev, N. S. (*cont'd*)
  dismissed as First Secretary 90, 124, 138, 178, 199, 201, 209
  historians' views of 48, 62, 240
Khvostov, V. M. 49, 150, 293 n.93
  and Nekrich affair 211
  Director of Institute of History 64, 71
  opposes *partkom* 202, 206–8, 214, 291 n.39
  opposes Sector of Methodology 164, 280 n.46
Kim, M. P. 140, 191, 296 n.151
Kir'yanov, Yu. I. 220, 222, 223, 227
Klyuchevsky, V. O. 39, 256 n.24, 288 n.191
Kommunist 53, 58, 182, 185, 218
Koval'chenko I. D. 217, 269 n.84, 294 n.115
Krasnopevtsev circle 62
Kuhn, T. ix, 6, 10, 11, 12, 13, 91, 235

Lenin, V. I. 21, 24, 38, 53, 101, 264 n.190
  on 'multistructuredness' 83, 92, 97, 104, 269 n.76
  on rural Russia 85–6
  on Russian imperialism 77, 83, 98, 100
  use of by revisionists 68, 76, 104, 151, 183–7, 192, 235, 237
Leninism 21, 56, 68, 104, 193, 205, 218, 234
  see also Marxism–Leninism
Levada, Yu. A. 242, 282 n.80
Levkovsky, A. I. 93, 243
Lisovsky, P. 205–6, 207
Loone, E. N. 245, 257 n.54, 299 n.35
Lysenko, T. D. 26, 252 n.106

Malenkov, G. M. 47
Marx, K. 43–5, 105, 153, 168, 281 n.75
  use of by revisionists 104, 169, 174, 181, 183, 189–90, 280 n.51, 284 n.121

Marxism–Leninism 25, 26, 34, 37, 42, 47, 183
  as 'holy of holies' 182
  as 'secular religion' 33
  demise of 243
  see also Institute of Marxism–Leninism, *Short Course*
Medvedev, R. A. 22, 125, 238
  Let History Judge 242, 285 n.138 and n.139, 298 n.32 and n.33
Mikoyan, A. I. 38, 128
Mints, I. I. 63, 159, 193, 296 n.151
  denounces Gefter 191
  on methodology 164, 182
Molotov, V. M. 47, 121, 122, 137, 140, 256 n.36
Mongait, A. L. 179–80
Moscow State University (MGU) 45, 53, 59, 61, 62, 113, 125, 221
Moshkov, Yu. A. xvi, 113, 119
  biography 273 n.13
  on 'grain problem' 151–2
'multistructuredness' (*mnogoukladnost'*) 75, 83, 89–97, 159, 170, 175
  and developing countries 91, 99
  and October Revolution 93
  and Trotskyism 103–4
  as new paradigm 90, 93, 97
  declared unacceptable 232
  during *zastoi* 243
  implications for *Short Course* 90
  origins of term 92
  political implications of 100
  Sverdlovsk conference on 97–9, 231, 296 n.169
  see also New Direction

Narochnitsky, A. L. 232
Nechkina, M. V. 41, 65, 219, 256 n.30
  criticizes Stalin 159, 161
  on Scientific Councils 69
Nekrich, A. M. 64, 264 n.189
  biography 291 n.53
  campaign against 210, 212, 218, 219
  elected to *partkom* 202, 211
  on *partkom* 203, 207

Index 323

on Volobuev   219, 220, 233
publishes *June 22, 1941*   209
Nekrich affair   209–19
  and neo-Stalinism   210, 212
  and *partkom*   209, 213–14
  and Samsonov   219, 294 n.115
  June 22, 1941 denounced   211–12
neo-Stalinism   61, 76, 109, 156, 199, 200, 237
  and Khrushchev's dismissal   138
  and Nekrich affair   210
  and New Direction   220
  and *partkom*   209
  and 'Prague spring'   217
  and witch hunt   218
Neretina, S. S.   195
  on '*istoriosofiya*'   288 n.199
  on 'Prague spring'   217
New Direction (*novoe napravlenie*)
  Ch. 3 *passim*, 116, 158, 216, 222, 242
  and division of Institute of History   216, 217
  and Leninism   76, 83, 104
  and 'multistructuredness'   75, 89–97, 159
  and *perestroika*   244
  and Trotskyism   102, 104, 271 n.129
  campaign against   90, 237
  contradictory views of   77, 81, 82–3, 84, 268 n.43
  criticize *Short Course*   96
  defeat of   76
  formation of   81, 267 n.25
  on October 1917   76, 77, 87–93, 99–103, 216
  on Russia   100, 104
  on Russian absolutism   75, 105–10
New Economic Policy (NEP)   114, 116, 127, 152, 190, 245, 290
Novyi mir   22, 252, 290 n.25
  and Nekrich affair   210
  and revisionism   236
  see also Tvardovsky

October Revolution   x, 12, 17, 41, 43, 68, 96, 224–5, 227–31, 235, 244–7
  see also New Direction

Pankratova A. M.   4, 49, 53, 57, 222, 255 n.15
  and Burdzhalov   61
  and Trotsky   59
  and Twentieth Congress   38, 50, 51, 60
  appointed editor of *VI*   50
  biography   259 n.85
  defends *partiinost'*   59
  premature death   60
  see also Burdzhalov affair
paradigm shift   10, 11–13, 17, 90, 156, 235
  see also Kuhn, T.
Parain, C.   193
partiinost' (party spirit)   6, 15, 158, 159
  and Burdzhalov affair   59, 61
  and Nekrich affair   212
  and revisionism   182, 187
  re-emphasis on   208
  Stalin defines   38–9
Pashuto, V. T.   194, 255 n.22
Pavlenko, N. I.   105, 106, 107, 267 n.25
Pavlovsky, G.   241
Pavlovskaya, A. I.   168–9
Pel'she, Ya. A.   212
perestroika   ix, x, xi, xiii, xv, 4, 6, 8, 9, 11, 42, 44, 46, 62, 219, 240
  and 1930s famine   146
  and alternatives in history   245
  and history of collectivization   153
  and NEP   190
  and New Direction   98
  and revisionism   247
  and *shestidesyatniki*   243, 247
Petreshuvsky, D. M.   40
Plimak Ye. G.   190, 206, 245
  elected to *partkom*   202, 209
Pokora, T.   193
Pokrovsky, M. N.   159, 185
  as 'economic materialist'   161
  demise of his school   40
  on history   38
  opposed to Trotsky   104
  partial rehabilitation   70
Polyakov, Y. A.   125, 151, 275 n.65

Ponomarev, B. N.   71, 119, 220
Porshnev, B. F.   166, 167, 288 n.192
  denounces Gefter   195
  on Asiatic mode of production
    170, 282 n.85
  suppresses Danilova's manuscript
    194
Pospelov, P. N.   223, 262 n.146
  and Nekrich affair   212
  and Stalin's rehabilitation   201
  campaigns against Volobuev   101,
    220, 221, 228, 229
  criticizes Avrekh   230, 296 n.165
  criticizes 'new direction'   230
'Prague spring'   8, 216, 237
professionalism   7, 28, 72, 235
pyatichlenka (five-membered set)
    44–5, 284 n.103
  and Asiatic mode of production
    169, 176
  as 'hollow shell'   243
  revisionist criticism of   45, 169,
    172, 174, 176, 177

Reiman, M.   216
revisionism   3, 9, 10, 57, 88, 90,
    96, 151, 158, 160, 204, 208, 222,
    226
  and Brezhnev   x, xiii, 4, 8, 76, 129,
    149, 152, 196, 222, 240
  and classical Marxism   168, 181
  and 'crisis' of social sciences   180
  and delegitimation   37, 199, 218
  and *frontoviki*   65–6, 235
  and I. I. Mints   159, 164
  and intelligentsia   13, 16, 18, 29,
    161, 205, 217, 236–7, 246
  and Leninism   24, 68, 104, 183,
    185
  and Marxism–Leninism   105, 183
  and methodology   90, 156, 241
  and Nekrich affair   209, 210
  and neo-Stalinism   109, 202
  and orthodoxy   36, 176, 179, 247
  and *perestroika*   xv, 246
  and *pyatichlenka*   45, 169, 172,
    174, 176–7
  and *shestidesyatniki*   8, 66, 181,
    236

  and Sidorov school   75, 78
  and Stalin   147, 235
  and Trapeznikov   117, 216
  and Trotskyism   170
  and Twentieth Congress   9, 22, 37,
    49, 218, 234
  and *zastoi*   239, 242
  as legal dissent   ix, 243
  as new paradigm   13
  as threat to CPSU   236, 237
  campaign against   100, 182, 193,
    217, 229, 232, 264 n.195
  defined   xiv
  influence of 1920s historiography
    on   79, 123, 162, 177–8,
    222
  versus Higher Party School   64
Rumyantsev, A. M.   101, 286 n.147,
    293 n.115
  and 'party democrats'   200
Russian absolutism   *see* New
    Direction
Russian imperialism   *see* New
    Direction
Rybakov, B. A.   150, 179, 189, 217,
    219, 229, 231, 293 n.93

Sakharov, A.   22, 26, 201
Samsonov, A. M.   210, 219, 294
    n.115
Scientific Councils (*nauchnye soviety*)
    69, 81, 82, 88
Sector of Methodology Ch. 5
    passim, 281 n.54
  and division of Institute of History
    216
  and intelligentsia   x, 194
  and *Let History Judge*   242
  and *partkom*, 202, 209
  and *perestroika*   245
  and Twentieth Congress   195
  campaign against   237
  dissolution of   193, 195
  legacy of   242–3
  see also Gefter, Ya. M.
Selunskaya V.   125, 152, 153
Semenov, Yu. I.   167, 242, 281 n.61,
    282 n.80
  on pre-class societies   175

on world history 170–2, 283 n.94, 284 n.103
Shatsillo, K. N. 78, 81
  biography 267 n.28
shestidesyatniki (people of the 1960s) ix, x, 8, 23, 24
  and *perestroika* 243, 247
  and Stalinism 181
  and Twentieth Congress 199
  as intelligentsia 196, 236
  defeat of 113, 234, 247
  defined 66, 263 n.174
  see also frontoviki
Short Course (History of the CPSU) x, 36, 41, 42–7, 52, 114, 157, 187, 189, 257 n.54, 282 n.80
  and Asiatic mode of production 169
  as 'hollow shell' 245
  as paradigm 12, 42–7, 80, 180, 235, 243
  its method 180
  on collectivization 111, 113, 119, 121, 123
  on October 1917 76
  on Russia as semi-colony 77
  on Zinoviev 54
  partkom on 204
  reissue proposed 201, 258 n.67
Shtrakhov, A. N. 211, 214
Shunkov, V. I. 201
Sidorov, A. L. 45, 82, 86, 87, 113, 290 n.25
  and 'anti-cosmopolitan' campaign 75
  and anti-Stalinism 202
  and anti-Trotskyism 103
  and Burdzhalov 52, 75, 80, 235, 262 n.141
  and New Direction 75, 78, 79, 81, 84
  biography 265 n.1
  Director of Institute of History 64, 70, 75
  his 'school' 80, 84, 92, 98
  on archives 79
  on 'cult of the personality' 158
  on methodology 88
  on Russian imperialism 78, 83, 94
  patron of Danilov 87, 113
  student of Pokrovsky 70, 79, 288 n.191
Simoniya, N. A. 243
Sinyavsky, A. D. 201, 203, 210, 242
Skazkin, S. D. 201
Snegov, A. V. 212
'social organisms' *see* Semenov, Yu. I
Society of Marxist Historians 51
socio-economic formations *see* historical materialism
Solovev, S. M. 39, 256 n.24
Solzhenitsyn, A. I. 21, 22, 49
sovietology xiv, 5, 7, 21, 28
'stagnation' period (*zastoi*) x, xi, xv, 4, 233, 247
  and intellectual life 240–1, 279 n.13
  and neo-Stalinism 137
Stalin, I. V. ix, 4, 19, 22, 24, 32, 41, 50, 51, 53, 54, 69, 81, 115, 118, 123, 177, 209, 234, 245
  and collectivization 120–2
  and 'cult of the personality' 38, 43
  and *figura umolchaniya* 205
  and historical laws 44
  and intelligentsia 17, 18
  and *Short Course* 42, 180
  campaign to rehabilitate 46, 201, 205, 210, 218
  criticism of his 'Dizzy with Success' 151
  defines *partiinost'* 38, 63
  denounced by Burdzhalov 59
  denounced by Khrushchev 38, 47
  establishes *VI* 63
  his *Economic Problems of Socialism* 78, 115
  letter to *Proletarskaya revolyutsiya* 38, 42, 77
  on linguistics 44, 161
  on Russia as semi-colony 77, 103
  partkom on 203
  war on historians 39
  wartime role reevaluated 201, 209
Stalinism x, xiii, 7, 9, 10, 23, 30, 33, 34, 42, 45, 48, 49, 59, 71, 191, 236, 244

Stalinism (cont'd)
  and alternatives in history   245
  and 'anti-cosmopolitan' campaign, 40
  and 'cult of the personality'   206
  and defeat of *shestidesyatniki*   113
  and history   6, 38
  and Nekrich affair   212
  and neo-Stalinism   201
  and revisionism   109
  and *Short Course* method   181
  in Institute of History   202
  see also Short Course, neo-Stalinism
Stuchevsky, I. A.   172
Suret-Canale, J.   167, 193
Suslov, M. A.   220

Tarle, Ye. V.   24, 40
Tarnovsky, K. N.   65, 78, 82, 85, 93, 216, 227, 289 n.15
  and Nekrich affair   214
  and New Direction   77–8, 80, 92, 267 n.25
  and *partkom*   202–3
  and *perestroika*   244
  and Twentieth Congress   236
  biography   266 n.7
  criticized   225, 230
  denounced as Trotskyite   221
  fate under Brezhnev   223, 242, 243
  on *aktual'nost'*   160
  on *frontoviki*   65
  on Lenin's thought   77, 86
  on methodology   156
  on 'multistructuredness'   83, 84, 91, 93, 98
  resists neo-Stalinism   205
  Volobuev's '*alter ego*'   220
Ter-Akopyan, N. B.   166, 168, 176
'thaw'   xiii, 8, 12, 50, 85, 86, 91, 111, 113, 236
  see also Twentieth Congress
Tokei, F.   193
totalitarianism   xiii, 5, 6, 7, 8, 9, 21, 26, 41, 247
Trapeznikov, S. P.   64, 78, 119, 150, 215, 216, 219, 222, 241, 285 n.139, 289 n.7

  and Nekrich affair   211, 214, 221
  and Stalin rehabilitation   201, 218
  biography   289 n.5, 293 n.93
  Brezhnev's *alter ego*   90
  campaign against Danilov   126, 150, 216
  campaign against Volobuev   228, 231, 232
  heads Department of Science   199–200
  imposes orthodoxy   238–9
  on collectivization   117, 118, 121, 126, 136, 138, 141
Trotsky, L. D.   43, 51, 178, 188, 195, 266 n.6, 273 n.18, 299 n.50
  demonized   56
  on *nomenklatura*   33
  'Stalin school of falsification'   54
Trotskyism   39, 191, 220, 245, 261 n.124
  and Asiatic mode of production   170
  and Burdzhalov   54, 262 n.141, 265 n.1
  and New Direction   102
Trukhanovsky, V. G.   201
Tumanova, L. B.   242
Tvardovsky, A. T.   3, 183, 200, 210, 290 n.25
  as *intelligent*   236, 237, 252 n.89
  dismissed as *Novyi mir* editor   237
  Gefter on   297 n.6
Twentieth Congress   ix, x, xiv, 4, 5, 12, 22–3, 37, Ch. 2 *passim*, 78, 79–80, 85, 86, 155, 195, 238
  and history of collectivization   113, 115, 123
  and intelligentsia   199, 217–18, 233, 235–6
  and Nekrich affair   209
  and New Direction   76
  and revisionism   183, 234, 237
  and *shestidesyatniki*   66, 199
  and *VI*   60
  Burdzhalov on   71
  partkom on   203–4
  reaction against   200, 218, 238
  see also 'thaw'

Twenty-second Congress   69, 70, 82, 85, 87, 200, 206, 209, 218
Twenty-third Congress   201, 207
Twenty-fourth Congress   222

Vaganov, F. M.   125
Vanag, N. N.   78, 79
Varga, E.   81, 82, 167
Vasil'ev, L. S.   172
Vilar, P.   166
Volin M.   209, 220
Volobuev, P. V.   x, 75, 78, 79, 103, 105, 214, 216, 219, 238
  and Avrekh   221, 227, 230
  and Burdzhalov affair   262 n.141
  and Nekrich affair   214, 220–1
  and New Direction   81, 220, 223, 231–2, 267 n.25
  and *perestroika*   244
  and Twentieth Congress   233, 236
  biography   267 n.15
  campaign against   220–32
  criticizes Bovykin   98, 102
  Director of the Institute of the History of the USSR   219–20, 233; dismissed as Director   xiii, 76, 221, 229, 232
  fate under Brezhnev   221, 241
  on 1917 Revolution   97, 224, 227
  on 'alternativeness' in history   101, 227, 244, 245, 271 n.125
  on Brezhnev 'Thermidor'   233
  on crisis in historiography   246, 257 n.51, 279 n.13
  on 'multistructuredness'   90, 98, 100
  on October Revolution   101, 102, 247
  on Russian absolutism   107–8
  on Russian imperialism   79, 81, 83, 98
  on *shestidesyatniki*   199

Voprosy istorii (*VI*)   4, 38, 63, 67, 201
  and Burdzhalov affair   50–62, 80
Voroshilov, K. E.   121
Vuzy (Higher Educational Establishments)   63, 65, 66
Vyltsan, M. A.   113, 114

writers   ix, 4, 8, 15, 18, 21, 201, 204, 237, 238, 244, 252 n.89, 299 n.39

Yagodkin, V. N.   232, 239, 296 n.169
Yakovlev, A. N.   200, 222, 228, 241
Yakubovskaya S.   208, 209, 214
Yaroslavsky, Ye. M.   185
Yevtushenko, Ye. A.   22

zakonomernosti (lawful regularities)   105, 157, 245, 286 n.144
zastoi   *see* Brezhnev period, 'stagnation'
Zelenin, I. E.   113, 114, 116–9, 143–8
  approach to kulaks   118, 143
  criticizes Stalin   143, 147
  on famine   145–6
  on MTS Political Departments   151
  opposes full-scale collectivization   148
Zhukov, Ye. M.   63, 164, 206, 221, 264 n.195
  and neo-Stalinism   201, 203, 205
  Director of Institute of World History   217
  edits *Universal History*   69, 160, 174
  hounds Gefter   241
Zinoviev, G. E.   52, 54, 56, 58, 61, 76, 128, 290 n.25